The English Cotton Industry and the World Market 1815–1896

The English Cotton Industry and the World Market
1815-1896

BY

D. A. FARNIE

Clarendon Press · Oxford
1979

Oxford University Press, Walton Street, Oxford OX2 6DP

OXFORD LONDON GLASGOW
NEW YORK TORONTO MELBOURNE WELLINGTON
IBADAN NAIROBI DAR ES SALAAM CAPE TOWN
KUALA LUMPUR SINGAPORE JAKARTA HONG KONG TOKYO
DELHI BOMBAY CALCUTTA MADRAS KARACHI

British Library Cataloguing in Publication Data
Farnie, Douglas Antony
The English cotton industry and the world market, 1815–1896
1. Cotton manufacture—England—History—19th century
I. Title
338.4′7′677210942 HD9881.5 78–40646

ISBN 0–19–822478–8

Printed in Great Britain by
Western Printing Services Ltd., Bristol

Preface

SOME EXPLANATION is necessary in order to justify the presumptuous title of this work. Its subject of study is both large and familiar since the cotton industry, as a source of perennial controversy, has been observed more continuously and closely than any other manufacture. Its time-span may appear to be too long since it has often proved necessary to expand the nominal limits of 1815–96 to cover the whole period from 1780 to 1913. Its ostensible scope may seem to be too limited since it deliberately avoids encroaching upon the pastures of other scholars and necessarily neglects several topics. The exclusion of the finishing industries is a traditional feature of almost all works on the subject and may well require no special justification. The raw cotton trade has long been a particular interest of the Liverpool school of economic historians whilst the cotton industry of Scotland has similarly become an hereditary fief of Scottish historians. The history of textile engineering, of capital investment, and of the Manchester merchants are currently the subject of study by other scholars. The exclusion of so many topics may be justified only in part by the reflection that most works on the subject have their own self-imposed limits and that only the admirable work of Ellison remains truly comprehensive. The limits adopted here have marked out an intelligible field of study which seemed large enough in its demands upon the intensive husbandry of a single cultivator.

In origin this work began as the history of a single firm: in the process of development it became a general survey of the history of the whole industry during the era of its maturity. The emphasis placed upon the impersonal influence of the market operating upon some 2,000 firms has, together with the pressure on space, necessitated the sacrifice of any detailed consideration of individual enterprises. The basic unit of industrial life appears to have been as much the mill town as the firm: the industry's most significant product may well have been neither yarn nor cloth but the factory communities of 'Cottonia'. The aim of the study has been to integrate the history of Lancashire with that of England and to relate British history to that of a wider world. It has therefore sought to assess the impact of the industry upon the outside world as well as upon the minds of men. It has tried to explore the long-term trends in its history rather than the short-term fluctuations in its fortunes, to examine the changing pattern of interests linking Lancashire to the U.S.A. and to India in the service of the world market and to make some contribution to an understanding of the history of relationships between East and West.

Certain prejudices may seem to hinder a full understanding of the history of the cotton industry. These biases no longer stem from the lure of official history so seductive to the business historian. Nor do they derive from 'the mythopoeic illusions of the patriotic imagination'[1] once congenial to the imperial historian. Rather do they arise from the intellectual legacy of the rival cosmopolitan world-views of the nineteenth century. It may be as difficult to steer a middle course between the opposed interpretations of the free-trade and Marxist schools of thought as it is to maintain a balance between the two great traditions of sociology centred respectively around the individual and the community. Most insidious of all, however, is the irrepressible present-mindedness of 'the intellectual villager who takes the fashion of his generation for the nature of mankind'.[2] The value of this particular work must indeed be limited by its teleological perspective which has however enabled the industry during the era of its maturity to be set in the framework of a longer span of time.

In essence the work provides an introductory survey of its field of study made by a single observer. It embodies one contribution to the understanding of a particular episode in history, which will undoubtedly evoke in the future as many books as it has in the past. Thus it cannot and does not aspire to any definitive or authoritative treatment of its subject. In part it rests upon the labour of others and it is hoped that it may in turn be used by others as a quarry of material and

[1] *Economic Journal*, June 1914, 277, G. Unwin in his review of J. A. Williamson, *Maritime Enterprise, 1485–1558* (1913).

[2] R. H. Tawney, 'The Study of Economic History' (L.S.E., 1932), reprinted in N. B. Harte (ed.), *The Study of Economic History. Collected Inaugural Lectures 1893–1970* (London, Cass, 1971), 96.

perhaps even of ideas. It may not redeem the workfolk of 'the much maligned region of tall chimneys and smoke'[1] from 'the enormous condescension of posterity' but it may well suggest the limits within which they led their 'drudging life of care' during their hour upon the stage of world history.

In conclusion I must thank the staff of the Central Reference Library, Manchester, for the efficiency and courtesy with which they have handled my requests over many years. I would like to express my particular appreciation of the help Mr. H. Horton of the Social Sciences Library has willingly extended upon innumerable occasions. I owe a particular debt of gratitude to Professor Ralph Davis of the University of Leicester for permitting me to make use of the statistics of 1784–6 in advance of their publication in 1978. I would like to acknowledge the help willingly extended by both Professor W. H. Chaloner and Dr. W. O. Henderson. I am also indebted to Mr. A. J. Marrison and Mr. T. Balderston for their aid in extending the limited range of my statistical techniques.

[1] Hansard, *Commons Debates*, 12 Mar. 1844, 879, Cobden.

Contents

List of Statistical Tables

List of Illustrations

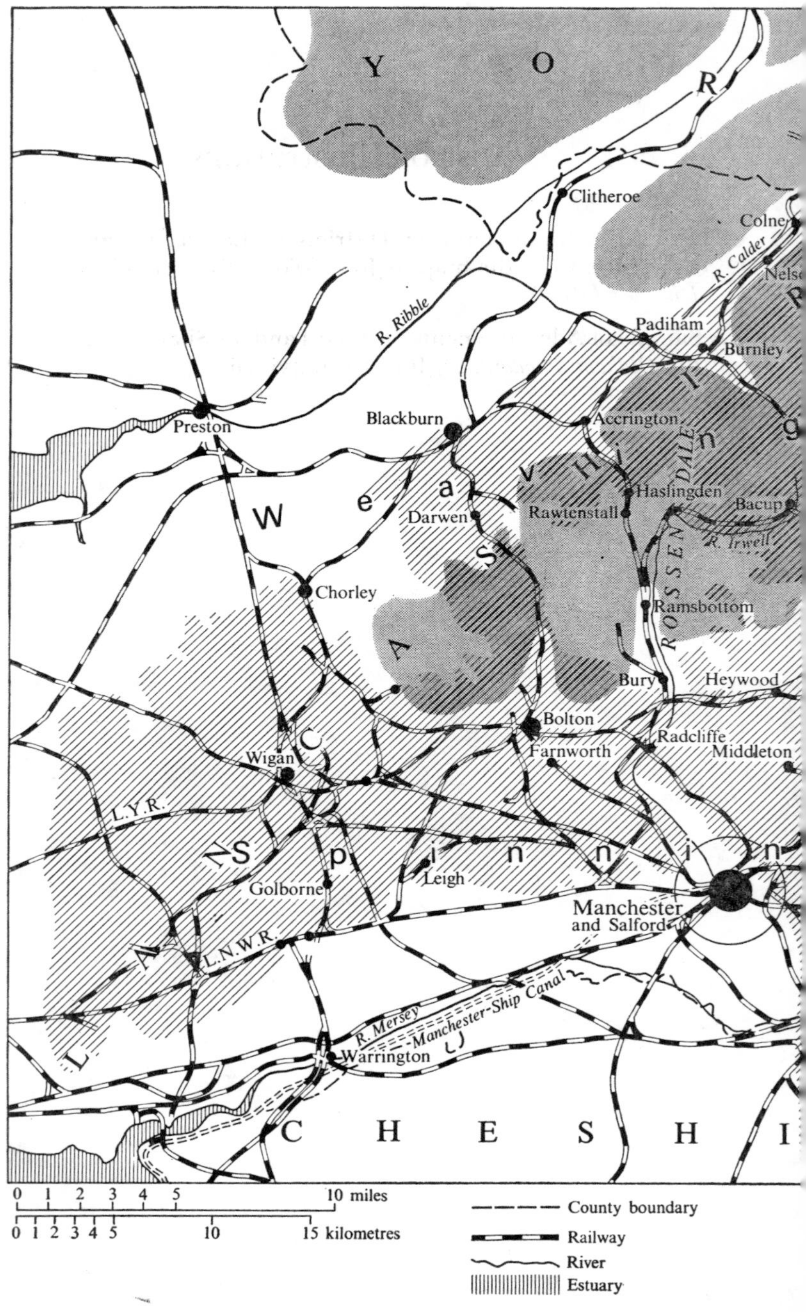

The Textile Manufacturing Districts of Lancashire and Yorksh

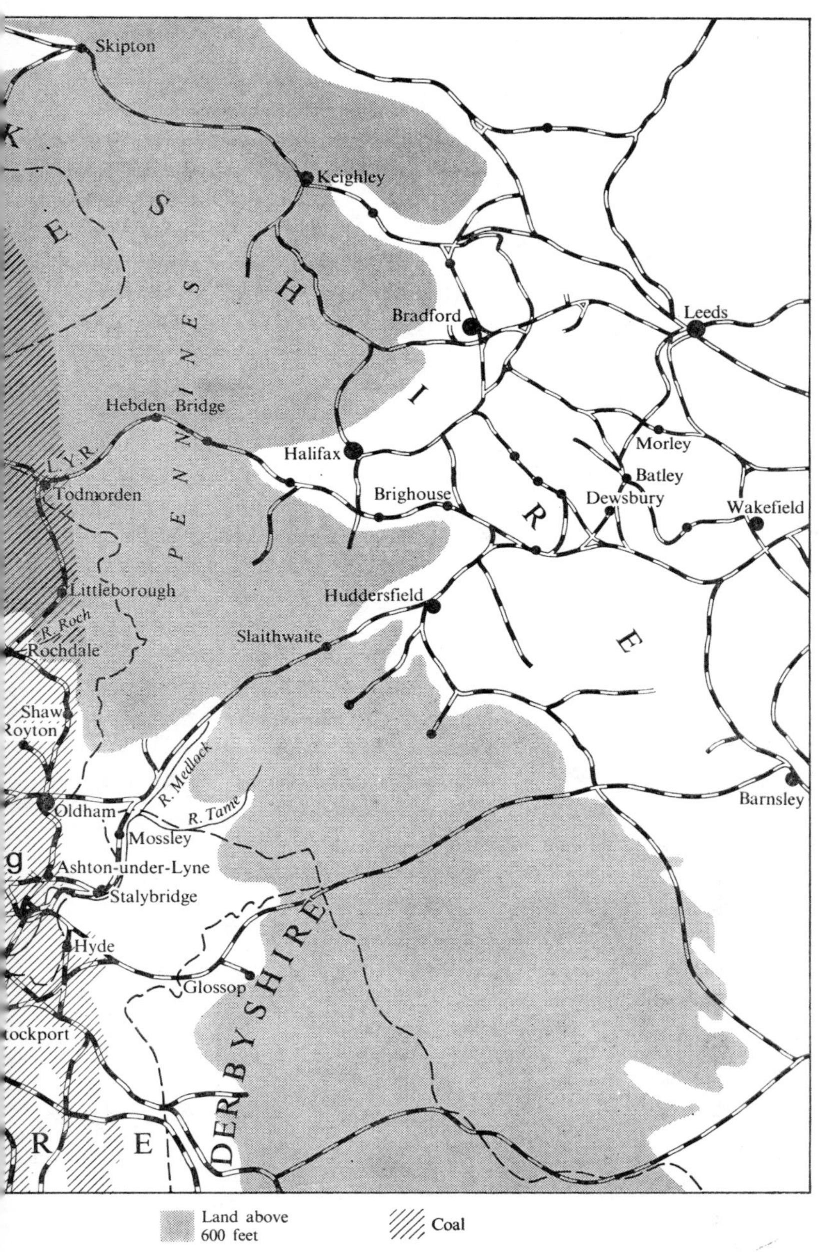

m the map in John Worrall's *Steam Users' Directory* (1888).

PART ONE

The Advent of a New Economic Order

CHAPTER 1

The Role of the Cotton Industry in Economic Development

Cotton can be no staple, because England does not produce a single ounce. . . . Can we wonder we should have a redundancy of Wool? Can we wonder our people are not employed? Can we wonder that poverty and distress should stalk among us as harbingers of desolation, which forebode the eventual fall of the British empire? Those who are lovers of invention, and fond of mechanical improvements, must admire the ingenuity of the Cotton-mills and engines lately erected in the neighbourhood of Manchester: but should those mills and engines be suffered to destroy our Woollen and Stuff manufactures, they will prove the most fatal discoveries ever made in Old England.

[Francis Moore], *The Contrast; or, a Comparison between Our Woollen, Linen, Cotton and Silk Manufactures* (London, Buckland, 1782, 52 pp.), 11, 14.

The Cotton Manufacture . . . can scarce be supposed to have made an impression equal to the importance of the object; because the progress has been rapid beyond example. —It has burst forth, as it were, upon the country, in a moment, giving a spring at the same time to the industry of the people, unexampled in the annals of the world. . . . Such at present is the nature and importance of the Cotton Manufactory—to the public at large as a source of extensive revenue and national strength —to the Landed Interest, as a means of employing the poor, and encreasing the value of the produce of the country;—and to the Commercial Interest, by the augmentation of trade, created by this astonishing combination of human and artificial labour.

Comparatively speaking, no manufacture that

> ever was introduced into any country has been so advantageous to the State. . . .
>
> It is impossible to estimate the national loss that would result from any derangement of a system which is ready to spring upon the country, fraught with advantages which no nation on earth ever enjoyed; for there is no given extent which the mind of man can conceive, to which the cotton trade in Great Britain may not go, if properly protected. . . .
>
> It is yet possible to establish in Great Britain, a pre-eminence in the Cotton Trade, which must secure it to the country, for centuries to come, *to the exclusion of all Europe.*
>
> [Patrick Colquhoun], *An Important Crisis, in the Callico and Muslin Manufactory in Great Britain, Explained* (London, 1788, 28 pp.), 1–2, 6, 21–2, 24.

BORN AND reared amidst controversy, the cotton industry has always been a mythopoeic power, first as a subject of legend in the ancient world and then as the source of a new idea-force in the nineteenth century. Its changing image has reflected the emotions it has aroused as well as the functions it has fulfilled. In origin the industry appeared as an exotic import from the East, a subverter of England's leading manufacture as well as of the traditional social order, a cause of demoralization amongst its employees, a cradle of labour combinations and a source of sporadic disturbances between 1769 and 1842. In the process of expansion it assumed increasingly the more positive guise of a creation of technical invention, a striking example of the power of man over the means of production, and a demonstration of British enterprise. It became the seed-bed of industrial capitalism and the industrial proletariat, the parent of the factory system, and a vehicle of the Industrial Revolution. It served as a stimulus to the growth of wealth as well as of population, as a seed-plot of self-made men,[1] and as the forcing-house of a new political economy. Above all, it became the source of the great divorce between

[1] I. Melada, *The Captain of Industry in English Fiction, 1821–1871* (Albuquerque, University of New Mexico Press, 1970).

the two worlds of *Past and Present* (1843), *North and South* (1855), 'Coketown' (1854), and *Cranford* (1853), and between the rival ideals of *Culture and Anarchy* (1869). With the advent of free trade the industry shed its fiscal functions, which had supplied the State with revenue from the excise on prints (1712–1831) and the import duty on cotton (1798–1845), and found a new justification for its existence in the benefits conferred upon the consuming public of the world.

To the outside world the industry presented two faces, first in 1820–60 as the basis of the Atlantic alliance between Lancashire and the Southern States of the U.S.A., and then in 1850–1900 as the exploiter of India as a market and as a source of supply of raw cotton in the service of the 'almost Anglo-Indian city' of Manchester.[1] Originally the industry had been deemed on the Continent, as well as at home, a source of weakness to Britain in so far as it undermined its inherited economic foundations and exposed its economy to the enervating influence of foreign commerce. Increasingly after 1815 it became recognized however as a source of British power at home and abroad, in peace even more than in war, and assumed the character almost of a permanent national heritage. In reaction to Marx's view of the industry as an endemic source of class conflict, it was portrayed as the basis of a prosperous and conservative society, a medium of social mobility, and a pioneer of social progress. Those successive changes in its image are faithfully reflected in the following judgements, penned respectively by a famous spinner in 1815 and by two journalists in 1852 and 1917.

It is too late to retrace our steps. Were we inclined, we cannot now return to our former state; for without the cotton trade, our increased population cannot be supported, the interest of the national debt paid, nor the expenses of our fleets and armies defrayed. Our existence as an independent power, I regret to say, depends on the continuance of this trade, because no other can be substituted in its place. True indeed it is, that the main pillar and prop of the political greatness and prosperity of our country is a manufacture which, as it is now carried on, is destructive of the

[1] L. C. Casartelli, 'Eastward Ho!', *Transactions of the Manchester Statistical Society*, 22 Mar. 1893, 78.

health, morals, and social comforts of the mass of the people engaged in it.[1]

In sixty years, this single branch of British manufactures has become of vital national importance. It is interwoven with all that relates to the employment of our population, of our capital, and of our shipping; and all that concerns our national credit, our solvency, and our domestic peace, contentment and security. Its rapid growth is wonderful; its magnitude is stupendous; and its connection with all that is precious and important in the country is so close and inseparable, that the boldest and the most far-seeing minds in the community cannot contemplate any serious vicissitude befalling it, without the utmost alarm and terror.[2]

At the zenith of its career a Mancunian journalist paid tribute to the global function of the industry, whilst recognizing its exotic nature.

It is the supreme accident of English economic history; the great departure . . . Cotton has shaped and determined the destiny of England. England has *thought* cotton . . . Like Palestine, Lancashire belongs to everybody. It is a part of human experience; the messianic corner of earth in which the new world was announced, the region in which steam and mechanism first happened to man.[3]

No other industry has so impressed the imagination of the world as has the Lancashire cotton industry. It has fulfilled that function by virtue of a unique combination of features, the rapidity of its expansion, the pioneer adoption of power-driven machinery and the factory, the world-wide extension of its commerce, its influence upon the new economic creed of free trade, its symbolic appeal to other countries as the archetype of modern industry, and its intellectual stimulus to the authors of both *The Communist Manifesto* and *A Non-Communist Manifesto*. Its massive growth fascinated the contemporary mind and

[1] Robert Owen, *Observations on the Cotton Trade, with a view to the intended Application to Parliament for a Repeal of the Duty on the Importation of Cotton Wool*, 1815, reprinted in *A Supplementary Appendix to the First Volume of the Life of Robert Owen* (London, Wilson, 1858; Cass, 1967), Vol. 1A, 16.

[2] P. L. Simmonds, 'Production and Consumption of Cotton', *Lawson's Merchant's Magazine*, Aug. 1852, 268, reprinted in *Science and Commerce. Their Influence over Manufactures* (London, Hardwicke, 1872), 196.

[3] W. H. Mills, *Sir Charles W. Macara, Bart.: a Study of Modern Lancashire* (Manchester, Sherratt, 1917), 125, 129, 130. Haslam Mills (1874–1930) was the chief reporter of the *Manchester Guardian* from 1914 until 1919.

seemed to portend the advent of a new industrial era, a new world order, and a new world outlook.

During the period 1780–1913 the average rate of growth in the industry's output, as measured in Table 1 by its main input,

TABLE 1

Consumption of Cotton and the Export of Yarn and Cloth, 1780–1913

	Average Annual Consumption of Raw Cotton (lb. m.)	Mean Annual Rate of Increase in Consumption (%)	Average Annual Volume of Exports of Yarn and Cloth (lb. m.)	Mean Annual Rate of Increase in Exports (%)
1779–81	5·708	7·4 (1780–1840)		6·7 (1801–40)
1839–41	426·3	3·3 (1840–72)	254·1	3·9 (1840–72)
1871–3	1,211	1·4 (1872–1913)	842	1·4 (1872–1913)
1912–14	2,132·3	4·6 (1780–1913)	1,444	4·0 (1801–1913)

Source: B. R. Mitchell and P. Deane, *Abstract of British Historical Statistics* (Cambridge University Press, 1962), 178–9, for consumption; R. Robson, *The Cotton Industry in Britain* (London, Macmillan, 1957), 331–3, for exports.

exceeded by almost two-thirds the mean coefficient of expansion of British industry as a whole.[1] That era of expansion comprised three distinct periods, which ended respectively in 1840, 1872, and 1913 and were characterized by successively slower rates of increase in production. During its heroic age from 1780 to 1840 the trade expanded its output at an average annual rate of 7·4 per cent, or almost six times as fast as the increase in population, as it exploited its virtual monopoly of the factory production of yarn. In the succeeding period of maturity from 1840 to 1872 the rate of expansion was more than halved as the cotton-spinning industries of Europe extended their capacity and substantially reduced the British share of the world's mill spindleage. At the same time other industries within Britain began to expand their output more rapidly than that of the

[1] W. G. Hoffmann, *British Industry 1700–1950* (Oxford, Blackwell, 1955, 1965), 29, 83.

cotton industry. During the following period of deceleration from 1873 to 1913 the industry continued to expand its output but at an average annual rate of only 1·4 per cent as the world of Asia began to regain its traditional supremacy within the sphere of textile manufacture. Not only did the industry suffer a decline in relation to its own former rate of expansion and to the rate of expansion of other trades as well as of foreign cotton industries, but also from the 1890s a decline in relation to the rate of population growth in England. Such a decrease in its rate of expansion made it much less attractive than formerly to both labour and capital and much less influential upon the economy as a whole. During the Edwardian era it enjoyed its last mill-building boom in 1904–8 and its last export boom in 1909–13, when its exports reached a level never to be equalled by any other exporter. In 1913 the industry reached its peak level of consumption, production, export, and employment. The Great War halted its expansion and ushered in a period of absolute recession by destroying its hold upon the markets of Asia and by drastically reducing its exports. Thereafter its protracted decline undoubtedly contributed to the comparative decline of the British economy as a whole during a century when textiles contributed a shrinking proportion to world trade. During the era of its world power the cotton trade had however made a notable contribution to the economic development of England by creating a new and fast-expanding source of wealth, by pioneering the establishment of a new system of industry, by transforming the foreign trade of the realm, and by revolutionizing the commercial policy of the State.

The influence of the industry upon foreign trade is more easily discernible and more readily measured than its contribution to the home trade or its influence upon the evolution of economic organization or commercial policy. The English cotton trade successfully extended its basis, as very few other cotton industries did, from the internal to the external market. The growth of production, aided by rising import duties, increasingly freed the home market from dependence upon imports of East Indian textiles. The expansion of the export trade, however, decisively liberated the industry from dependence upon the home market: it created a new growth sector wherein the industry expanded its exports faster than those of other industries, and it opened up the seductive prospect of continuing expansion in the service of extending foreign markets. In the export trade cotton manufactures rose in status from the sixth most valuable export in 1761 to the second in 1783, surpassing in value the superior textiles of silks in 1767 and linens in 1781. Only in 1803 did the exports of cotton manufactures actually surpass the value of cloth exports and so displace the woollen industry from its historic primacy in the foreign trade of the realm. The industry continued to increase its exports until they attained their peak level in 1913 and retained its primacy in the export trade until 1938, when its exports were first overtaken by those of machinery. Not until 1957 did the value of woollen exports once again exceed those of cotton manufactures, so restoring the historic supremacy of the cloth trade within the textile sector.

The cotton industry enabled England to remain a net exporter of cotton manufactures until 1958,[1] when it became a net importer for the first time since the eighteenth century. From the 1790s it notably stimulated the expansion of exports, as shown in Table 2, since it was much more export-oriented than the woollen industry. Its exports expanded in value 50 per cent faster than all other domestic exports between 1785 and 1913 and four times as fast between 1785 and 1815. Their share in domestic exports averaged 45 per cent during the years 1814–50 and rose from 34·5 per cent in 1803 to the all-time peak proportion of 51 per cent in 1830, or to thrice the share of all other textiles combined. The secular decline from 1831 in the industry's share in exports reflected the growing importance of exports of capital goods in association with the construction of railways abroad, which was itself stimulated by the needs of the cotton trade.[2] The industry's average share of exports declined from 45·4 per cent in 1831–50 to 32·7 per cent in 1851–1900 but remained remarkably stable after the Cotton Famine and did not sink below the level of 30 per cent until 1889. Its contribution to the increment in export values was

[1] *Annual Abstract of Statistics No. 98, 1961* (London, H.M.S.O., 1961), 213, 214, 220, 222, showing that the transition to net import took place in 1958 according to the quantity of goods, and in 1960 according to their value.

[2] J. Baynes, *The Cotton Trade: Two Lectures* (Blackburn, Haworth, 1857), 64.

however halved from 35 per cent in 1820–60 to 17 per cent in 1860–96 as its rate of expansion slackened.

TABLE 2

Contribution of Cotton Manufactures to the Increase in the Value of Domestic Exports from Great Britain, 1785–1913

	Average Annual Value of Exports of Cotton Manufactures (£m.)		Mean Annual Rate of Increase (%)	Contribution by Cotton Manufactures to Increment in Export Values (%)
1784–6	0·766			
		1784–6 to 1814–16	11·3	52·8
1814–16	18·733			
		1819–21 to 1859–61	2·9	35·26
1859–61	49·033			
		1872–4 to 1912–14	1·05	17·18
1872–4	77·266			
		1784–6 to 1912–14	4·0	24·79
1912–14	116·9			

Source: Professor Ralph Davis of the University of Leicester has very kindly supplied the real values for 1784–6 from his book which is to be published in 1978; F. Crouzet 'Exports and British Economic Growth, 1783–1815' (paper presented at the Economic History Society Conference, 9 Apr. 1976) also uses the real values calculated by Professor Davis; T. Ellison, *The Cotton Trade of Great Britain* (London, Wilson, 1886; Cass 1968), 60, 308, for 1820–60; R. Robson, *The Cotton Industry in Britain* (1957), 334, for 1814–1914.

The primary achievement of the industry was to expand the volume of external commerce by establishing a dynamic relationship between the import of raw cotton, the manufacture of yarn and cloth, and the export of cotton manufactures. Its expansion undoubtedly increased the role of foreign trade in the national economy. The industry became the main source of foreign exchange and earned much of the revenue necessary to finance the import trade, even if it did not create export surpluses or permit, before the 1870s, the large-scale import of commodities of substantial and general utility. It was not primarily responsible either for the immense development in the general commerce of the realm or for its vast expansion in geographical extent.[1] It nevertheless enhanced the influence of Britain in the world economy since British trade expanded upon a multilateral basis in the absence of any restrictive Anglo-American or Anglo-Indian economic symbiosis. Indeed its expansion threatened to undermine the traditional textile industries of Europe as well as of Asia and helped to provoke the successive protectionist reactions on the Continent after 1815, 1840, and 1877.

As a generator of commerce, the industry has usually been considered, especially by the representatives and heirs of the free-trade school, as an exporter. Its contribution to exports was however never systematically studied over time until the publication of the work of Robson in 1957 and has often been exaggerated. The use of figures based upon 'official' rather than upon declared values inflated the exports of the industry. Moreover, the high import-content of its exports reduced the amount of value added and assimilated it almost to an entrepôt trade, as Fay noted in 1928.[2] The value of the raw cotton embedded in the industry's gross product averaged 36 per cent between 1820 and 1900[3] and that embodied in the exports of cotton manufactures in 1850 was equivalent to half of their value. Even if the industry's exports are measured in gross rather than in net values their share of total exports never exceeded 50 per cent, save in the one exceptional year of 1830, and began to decline from 1831. Thus it may be debatable whether Britain's competitive advantages in the world market for cotton goods did in the long run inhibit the expansion of the export of capital goods and so undermine its international economic position in relation to Germany and the U.S.A. The cotton industry's position of primacy in the export trade from 1803 to 1937 was retained for less than a third of the period of the primacy of the woollen industry. In the spectrum of foreign trade as a whole the industry remained dominant for only a

[1] J. A. Mann, *The Cotton Trade of Great Britain* (London, Simpkin, 1860; Cass, 1968), 27, 31.

[2] C. R. Fay, *Great Britain from Adam Smith to the Present Day. An Economic and Social Survey* (London, Longmans, 1928), 144.

[3] P. Deane and W. A. Cole, *British Economic Growth 1688–1959. Trends and Structure* (Cambridge University Press, 1962, 1967), 187.

single generation, during the forty years from 1833 to 1873 when raw cotton provided the most valuable import and re-export while cotton manufactures supplied the most valuable export. Nor did it transform the fundamental structure of the export trade which continued until 1873 to be dominated by textiles, as it had been since the fourteenth century. The share of textiles in domestic exports increased to reach their peak proportion of 71·3 per cent in 1834 and declined thereafter, following the lead set by cotton manufactures from 1831.

The import trade in raw cotton has never attracted the attention of growth-oriented historians to the extent that the export of cotton manufactures has. The import trade was undoubtedly restructured much more slowly, much less fundamentally, and for a far shorter period than was the export trade: it was also in its nature much more limited in the transforming power which it could exert upon the economy. British consumption of cotton increased in proportion to the expansion of the new industry and to its growing concentration upon the production of cheap and coarse staples. Britain became by 1820 the largest single consumer of raw cotton in the world and remained such until 1897 when it was surpassed by the U.S.A. The consumption of cotton overtook that of wool by 1817 and amounted by 1850 to three times as much. Thus the commerce in the raw material of the country's leading industry was transferred, at the expense of British agriculture and to the benefit of British ports, from the sphere of internal to that of external trade. An import trade such as the woollen industry had never created was called into existence and grew large enough to influence the general price of imports. Imports of raw cotton rose in status from the fourth most valuable import in 1785 to the second in 1817, overtaking successively in value the imports of wine and tobacco (1785), silk (1794), tea (1809), and coffee (1817). In 1825 cotton imports first became more valuable than sugar imports and the new industry became dominant in the import as well as in the export trade. For the first time in English history a raw material rather than a luxury foodstuff or beverage held the premier position amongst the country's imports.

Cotton may have resembled in origin other colonial wares but it lent itself to a lucrative process of manufacture as they did not and thus helped to reduce the dependence of the economy upon the entrepôt trade. Raw cotton dominated the import trade from 1825 until 1873, or for only one-third of the time that cotton manufactures dominated the export trade. During those 49 years it supplied upon average one-fifth of the value of imports,[1] or only one-half of the proportion of exports supplied by cotton manufactures during the same period. The stimulus to the development of shipping and commerce was thus much less than that supplied by the export of yarn and piece-goods, especially since raw cotton was not a bulk commodity, like coal, timber, or corn, and its shipment tended to be largely a seasonal trade, confined to the autumn. Those imports nevertheless supplied the indispensable raw materials whose value was trebled in the process of manufacture. They also furnished an important index of industrial expansion which forcibly impressed itself upon the contemporary mind. They became of prime importance in the economic life of Liverpool for a century from the 1820s, furnishing its cotton brokers and merchants with their income and supplying the material basis of the developing nexus of communications along the Mersey valley.

The purchase of imports by means of exports was conducted upon unfavourable terms during two-thirds of the nineteenth century. The increasing influence of the cotton industry upon exports contributed notably to the deterioration in the terms of trade between 1803 and 1857 because production expanded even faster than demand, cotton yarn and cloth sank more rapidly in price than other exports and more steeply than imports of raw cotton, and cotton manufactures became much more important in the export trade than raw cotton did in the import trade. Thus British capacity to pay for its imports by means of its exports was reduced by the expansion of the cotton industry and by the associated depression in the general level of export prices. The primary producers however benefited from that trend in the terms of trade and expanded their imports from Britain in harmony with their growing exports. That trend was not reversed until the years 1857–73 when cotton prices experienced their steepest rise of the century. Until

[1] Averaging 21·7 per cent in 1825–53 and 18·65 per cent in 1854–73 according to the statistics in Mitchell and Deane, 282–3, 289–91, 298.

that time the long-term decline in prices had maintained the share of cotton imports in the total import trade at a fairly stable proportion, despite the massive increase in the quantity of those imports. The sharp inflation of prices during the Cotton Famine raised that share by about half to an all-time peak of 28·5 per cent in 1864, thirty-four years after cotton manufactures had attained their peak share in the export trade in 1830. The increase in the value of raw cotton imports between 1854 and 1864 amounted to 47·3 per cent of the increment in the total value of imports. As cotton prices began their long-term decline from 1864 the role of cotton in the import trade began to diminish. Imports of cotton were surpassed in value from 1874 by the imports of grain and flour and from 1898 by those of meat but nevertheless continued until 1926 to supply Liverpool with its most valuable single import. The terms of trade deteriorated anew during the depression of 1873–81 but thereafter improved between 1882 and 1900 as the price of raw cotton sank more rapidly than the price of manufactures and the decline in freight rates reduced the price of imports more than that of exports. Thus the declining rate of the industry's expansion brought with it some compensation in the enhanced purchasing-power of exports in terms of imports.

In response to the growth of British demand the U.S.A. expanded the production of cotton with unprecedented rapidity and rose to dominate the world market within the space of the single generation between 1790 and 1820. The cotton boll proved to be the most precious gift of the Old World to the New and one which far exceeded in value both the potato and tobacco because of its capacity to generate exports and to serve the needs of industry. The United States replaced tobacco by cotton as its leading export, probably in the decade of the 1800s. It displaced the West Indies in 1800 as the leading exporter of cotton and India in 1821 as the leading producer. In cotton it acquired possession of the most successful agricultural staple ever known and upon the basis of that export-oriented crop it built up the greatest plantation economy in history and re-established the old alliance between British industry and American agriculture. Thus the new republic became the largest single source of supply of imports to Britain which in turn continued to serve as the largest single foreign market for its produce. The economic links between the two peoples became so close during the upsurge of Anglo-American trade in the first half of the nineteenth century as to inspire Sydney Smith's sardonic observation in 1843: 'the great object for which the Anglo-Saxon race appears to have been created' is 'the making of calico'.[1]

That association was not without its dangers since England became dependent for the raw material essential to its leading industry upon a hostile power. Britain became more dependent upon the U.S.A. than the U.S.A. depended upon Britain because it could not obtain enough raw cotton elsewhere whereas the United States could replace its manufactured imports from other countries or through the development of home industry. Britain drew 77 per cent of its total imports of raw cotton from the U.S.A. during the forty-five years 1815–59[2] and increased the degree of its dependence until the quinquennium 1845–49, when it drew the peak proportion of 84 per cent of its cotton imports from the U.S.A. America established its control over the world price of cotton and preserved its primacy by reducing the price almost in proportion to the increase in its production. Thus it drove all competitors out of the market and triumphantly survived incessant British attempts to raise up new rivals to its Cotton States. That declining price trend was not reversed until the cotton dearth of 1857 and the Cotton Famine of 1862–4. The complete dependence of the British cotton industry upon the unpredictable annual harvest of another hemisphere also made the trade essentially speculative and exposed it to unforeseeable fluctuations in the price of its raw material. Such variations in price could not be effectively prevented by the development of alternative sources of supply, which could offer only limited and expensive insurance against excessive increases in the price of a mainly seasonal crop, largely monopolized by a single producer. No material support could be derived from the industry for such purposes since most firms, being small and specialized rather than large and integrated, remained largely uninterested in the question

[1] S. Smith, *Works* (London, Longman, 1850), 677, Letter II on American Debts, 22 Nov. 1843.

[2] J. A. Mann, 42.

of cotton supply and firmly opposed to the virtual subsidization of high-cost producers: they were content to rely upon the Liverpool market for their raw material and had no vital interest in its ultimate source so long as it arrived regularly and cheaply. They had adapted their machinery to the spinning of the American staple and thereby the economy of Lancashire to dependence upon the U.S.A. Potential rival producers required several years to reach an economic level of production and could not be tempted to enter the market by a single year of high prices such as 1850 or 1857. The industry became content to rely upon the U.S.A. for the supply of its raw material and thereby secured its needs at the lowest possible price whilst avoiding the investment of its own precious capital in the cultivation of cotton. Thus it developed a world-wide trade, importing its raw material over 4,000 miles from America and increasingly exporting its manufactures to markets 13,000 miles distant in Asia.

England was able to exploit the advantages of its intermediary position between America and Europe in order to develop a re-export trade in raw cotton as the world's source of supply shifted westwards to the U.S.A. and as the Continent began to develop the cotton industry. That trade has been studied much less than the import trade and has even been summarily dismissed as negligible, perhaps because it made no contribution to the industrial development of England. It was indeed hindered by the import duty imposed in 1798 but nevertheless supplied the country with its second most valuable re-export from 1825 and its most valuable one from 1833 when cotton displaced coffee and established the primacy which it retained until 1874. The entrepôt trade was never dominated by cotton to the extent that it formerly had been by sugar or tobacco. It handled only 17·25 per cent of the total volume of cotton imports during the 41 years of the primacy of cotton but nevertheless derived therefrom almost one-quarter of its total value.[1] Cotton established its supremacy in that trade when the importance of the entrepôt trade in the economy was declining under the influence of industrialization: it retained that status during the period after 1846 when the

[1] Reckoned to be 23·3 per cent in 1833–53, and 24·5 per cent in 1854–73, according to the statistics in Mitchell and Deane, 180–1, 282–3, 296–7, 307.

re-export trade underwent great expansion under the stimulating influence of the adoption of free-trade policies which turned the whole country into one vast free port. Re-exports of cotton expanded markedly after the repeal of the import duty in 1845, doubled their share of the total volume of imports of cotton from 7·5 per cent in 1840 to 15·5 per cent in 1850 and increased their share of the total value of re-exports from 17·6 per cent in 1831–45 to 28·4 per cent in 1846–53, before reverting to 17·6 per cent in 1854–9 with the loss of Russian demand. Thus the U.S.A. failed to assert its full economic independence of Britain as the necessary complement to the establishment of its political independence. The re-export trade was indeed an inevitable by-product of the development of the Lancashire cotton industry which had made Liverpool into the largest raw cotton market in the world. The essential efficiency of that market inhibited the establishment of independent cotton markets in the ports of the Continent, discouraged the direct shipment of American cotton to Europe, and virtually compelled American vessels to bring their cargoes to the Mersey. The re-export of cotton from the Liverpool market reduced the Continent to dependence upon the British entrepôt and replaced the traditional re-export of East Indian textiles by the re-export of the raw material as the states of Europe sought to expand their industrial potential. Not until the 1880s did Bremen develop its own cotton market and Turkestan develop the cultivation of cotton for the supply of the mills of Russia.

The re-export trade afforded financial benefits to the cotton brokers and shippers of Liverpool but was otherwise economically unproductive. It resembled the export of machinery in that it supplied the potential competitors of England with the sinews of production and tended to separate the interests of Liverpool from those of Lancashire. Re-exports usually however comprised the lower qualities of cotton while England retained the higher qualities for its own use and exported, from 1854, more Indian cotton than all other varieties together.[1] The Cotton Famine raised the trade to the peak of its importance so that it re-exported in 1862 41 per cent of the total volume of imports, supplied in 1864 40 per cent of the total value of re-exports, and handled in 1866 the record volume of

[1] J. A. Mann, 88.

389m. lb, which represented 28 per cent of total imports and 38 per cent of the value of re-exports. Thereafter those re-exports were reduced in importance by the increase in direct shipments from India to Europe after the opening of the Suez Canal and by the development of the re-export trade in the produce of Australia, the Argentine, and Asia. Re-exports of raw cotton were surpassed in value in 1874 by those of raw wool and then in 1898 by those of hides and oil-seeds, so suffering relegation to the fourth place. Raw cotton nevertheless dominated both the import and the re-export trade between 1833 and 1873, as never before or after, under the influence of the combined demand of England and Europe.

* * *

The close association between commercial and industrial expansion had been conventionally typified since the late eighteenth century by the cotton industry, regarded as the heart and focus of the process of industrialization. That relationship between the cotton industry and the Industrial Revolution was first questioned in 1962 in a reinterpretation of economic history of fundamental importance.[1] The significance of that historical revision did not lie in its origin in the traditional centres of national culture nor in its stern repudiation of the platitudes inherited from the past nor in its exposure of the reductionist fallacy involved in the exaggeration of the importance of a single factor in a complex process nor even in its implicit criticism of the Rostovian theory of the 'take-off' by a 'leading sector'. The new thesis derived its primary significance from its firm basis in economic theory and from its

[1] E. A. Wrigley, 'The Supply of Raw Materials in the Industrial Revolution', *Economic History Review*, Aug. 1962, 12–14, reprinted in R. M. Hartwell (ed.), *The Causes of the Industrial Revolution in England* (London, Methuen, 1967), 113–17; P. Deane and W. A. Cole, *British Economic Growth, 1688–1959. Trends and Structure* (Cambridge University Press, 1962, 1967), 50–5, 163, 182–92, 211–14, 293–5; H. J. Habakkuk, *American and British Technology in the Nineteenth Century* (Cambridge University Press, 1962), 181; P. Deane, *The First Industrial Revolution* (Cambridge University Press, 1965), 98–9, 114; J. Hicks, *A Theory of Economic History* (Oxford, Clarendon Press, 1969), 147–8, whose author had been Professor of Political Economy in the University of Manchester from 1938 to 1946; R. M. Hartwell, *The Industrial Revolution and Economic Growth* (London, Methuen, 1971), 185–200, 'The Industrial Revolution as an Example of Balanced Growth'.

application of aggregative analysis to the widest range of statistical data ever assembled. It was the offspring of the macro-economic theory of Marshall and Keynes: its true intellectual ancestor may well have been Sir John Clapham, whose preface to the first volume of his *Economic History of Modern Britain* (1926) had startled A. P. Wadsworth and Julia Mann. In presenting a national rather than a regional approach to economic history the thesis based itself upon quantitative rather than qualitative data and placed the cotton industry in a new statistical perspective. It interpreted economic development in terms of an evolutionary process rather than of a sudden and dramatic 'take-off into self-sustained growth', reacting especially against Hoffmann's belief in the importance of the 1780s. It emphasized the multi-sectoral nature of the process of development in opposition to the stress laid by Schumpeter and Rostow upon a 'leading sector' of the economy. Thus it diminished the autonomous role of technological change and, whilst clarifying the function of the cotton industry as the largest industrial contributor to the National Income between the 1820s and the 1840s,[1] it denied the traditional view, reaffirmed by the Lancastrian C. R. Fay in 1932, that 'cotton is the great exemplar' of the Industrial Revolution,[2] and minimized its role as the initiator of 'self-sustained growth'.

The new view was inspired by no spirit of *Schadenfreude* and eschewed any polemical approach. It made no attempt to carry revisionism to the point of paradox: it did not argue that the cotton industry had served as a positive hindrance to economic growth but simply urged that its influence had been exaggerated to the point of virtually identifying the Industrial Revolution with the development of a single industry. The new interpretation was challenged immediately in the original homeland of the cotton industry[3] but was readily accepted in Britain, even by scholars learned in the history of the industry.[4]

[1] Deane and Cole, 226.

[2] C. R. Fay, 460.

[3] M. Akhlaqur Rahman, 'Foreign Trade and the Growth of Cotton Textiles Industry in Britain', *Pakistan Economic Journal*, Sept. 1963, 1–20.

[4] M. M. Edwards, *The Growth of the British Cotton Trade 1780–1815* (Manchester University Press, 1967), 1, 236–7; D. J. Bythell, *The Handloom Weavers. A Study in the English Cotton Industry during the Industrial Revolution* (Cambridge University Press, 1969), 1–3.

A vehement reaffirmation of the traditional view was however made in defence of the Marxist idea of the industry as the progenitor of industrial capitalism. 'Whoever says Industrial Revolution says cotton.'[1] Then followed the first of a series of mild but serious demurrers. A. E. Musson elucidated the extensive spin-off effects of the industry's development, especially in revolutionizing the chemical, steam-power, and mechanical engineering industries.[2] Ralph Davis first revealed, by his pioneering calculations of the real values of foreign trade, the exact contribution made by the industry to the expansion of exports, so rehabilitating it as a prime mover in the process of export-led growth.[3] S. D. Chapman also confronted the new critics upon their own statistical ground: he concluded that they might have overstated their case and could well have underestimated both the industry's capital–output ratio and its contribution to the National Income.[4]

The Cambridge thesis did indeed suffer from certain minor limitations. It failed to explain why contemporaries allotted pride of place to the cotton industry in any discussion of economic and social change. It was to some extent anachronistic and even teleological in so far as it projected back into the past the reduced importance of that industry in the 1960s after its catastrophic decline during the 1950s. It had however fundamentally altered the parameters of debate, making it forever impossible to discuss the subject in pre-1962 terms and ensuring the acceptance of its main conclusions in the best recent study of the history of the cotton industry.[5] If a final judgement is

[1] E. J. Hobsbawm, *The Age of Revolution 1789–1848* (London, Weidenfeld, 1962), 33–7; Idem, *Industry and Empire. An Economic History of Britain since 1750* (London, Weidenfeld, 1968), 40; D. S. Landes, *The Unbound Prometheus* (Cambridge University Press, 1969), 41.

[2] A. E. Musson and E. Robinson, *Science and Technology in the Industrial Revolution* (Manchester University Press, 1969), 251–371, 393–510, reprinting revised versions of articles which appeared in the *Economic History Review*, Apr. 1959 and in the *Journal of Economic History*, June 1960; A. E. Musson, 'Industrial Motive Power in the United Kingdom, 1800–70', *Economic History Review*, Aug. 1976, 415–39.

[3] R. Davis, *The Rise of the Atlantic Economies* (London, Methuen, 1973), 311–16. See also Table 2.

[4] S. D. Chapman, *The Cotton Industry in the Industrial Revolution* (London, Macmillan, 1972), 62–72.

[5] L. G. Sandberg, *Lancashire in Decline. A Study in Entrepreneurship Technology and International Trade* (Columbus, Ohio State University Press, 1974), 1–6.

ever reached upon so contentious a topic it may perhaps seek to avoid the danger of unduly minimizing the importance of the industry in the praiseworthy attempt to eschew any undue exaggeration of its role.

The importance of the cotton industry was undoubtedly magnified during the nineteenth century by the combination of a variety of influences, by its association with the Industrial Revolution, with 'the first industrial city' and with 'the first industrial society',[1] by its pioneer application of machine-technology and its increasing use of steam-power, by the unparalleled rapidity and the sustained power of its expansion, by its close and visible association with the growth of foreign trade, by its growing concentration within Lancashire and by the extrapolation to a national scale of its transformation of the society of the industrial north. Moreover, the role of the industry tended to be exaggerated in the debates over factory reform and free trade, especially during the protectionist reaction of 1849–51. In the 1850s the claims made for the influence of the industry reached their rhetorical heights. Under the impetus of the great boom of that decade the manufacture of calico was transformed in the Victorian mind from the most prosaic of occupations into a veritable pillar of the British Empire[2] and a key link in the world-redeeming alliance between commerce and civilization. The Crimean War apparently inspired the industry's spokesmen with a new faith in the manifest destiny of their trade to spread civilization over all the surface of the earth:

THE MISSION OF THE COTTON TRADE is, to develop the resources of the nation—to multiply the springs of industry—to stimulate inventive genius—to encourage art and science—to increase profitably the employment of labour—to improve agriculture—to create large towns—to promote education—to elevate the moral and social status of the working population—to secure civil liberty—to confer political privileges—to check immorality—to encourage religion—to destroy monopolies—to give freedom to

[1] L. S. Marshall, 'The Emergence of the First Industrial City: Manchester, 1780–1850', in C. F. Ware (ed.), *The Cultural Approach to History* (New York, Columbia University Press, 1940), 140–61; C. Aspin, *Lancashire, the First Industrial Society* (Helmshore Local History Society, 1969).

[2] *The Times*, 13 Jan. 1857, 8ii, 11 Feb. 1857, 9ii, J. T. Delane; *Manchester Guardian*, 10 Apr. 1858, 5i, James Brooke, Raja of Sarawak.

all—to enkindle a spirit of loyalty—to foster probity and honour—to discountenance war—to extinguish slavery—to promote peace—and to raise Britain to be the protector of the weak, the friend of the strong, a bright example to all nations, and the grand instrument for promoting the evangelization of the world.[1]

Such an idealistic perspective reflected a firm belief that the industry was 'the most important industrial pursuit in the world' as well as 'the corner-stone of our commerce'.[2] Other publicists, moved by the alarming incidence of strikes or by the threatened dearth of cotton, were inspired in a similar exaltation of spirit to perceive the trade as 'the very life of England'[3] and as a manufacture presenting 'in its progress, rapid development, and present stupendous extent,—a phenomenon in commerce unequalled in the annals of the world'.[4] The Cotton Famine itself witnessed the maximum rhetorical magnification of the importance of the trade as 'at once the most important constituent and the most perfect type of our special industrial development',[5] 'the backbone of our national industry',[6] 'the flywheel of our national prosperity',[7] and 'the greatest manufacturing industry which ever has been established':[8] the same ordeal clearly revealed the capacity of the economy to survive the eclipse of the cotton industry. Such judgements had been paralleled by those of the 'King Cotton' theorists of Southern nationalism who were moved by the growing tension between North and South and by 'a kind of cotton insanity'[9] to exaggerate the dependence of civilization upon the supply of American cotton.

[1] J. Baynes, *The Cotton Trade* (1857), 56–7.

[2] Ibid. 1, 56, 83, 90.

[3] W. A. Jevons, 'Account of the Weavers' Strike at Padiham in 1859', National Association for the Promotion of Social Science, *Report of the Committee on Trades Societies and Strikes* (1860), 470.

[4] J. A. Mann, *The Cotton Trade* (1860), 28.

[5] T. Ellison, 'The Cotton Manufacture', *Westminster Review*, Apr. 1861, 420.

[6] J. A. Hobson, *Richard Cobden the International Man* (London, Unwin, 1918), 284, Cobden to Richard, 4 Feb. 1861.

[7] Hansard, *Commons Debates*, 24 July 1862, 752, Cobden.

[8] J. Bowring, 'Cotton', *The Exchange*, Apr. 1862, 43–4; T. Bazley, 'The Difficulties and Dangers of the Cotton Trade', ibid., Jan. 1863, 201.

[9] H. D. Woodman, *King Cotton and his Retainers. Financing and Marketing the Cotton Crop of the South, 1800–1925* (Lexington, University of Kentucky Press, 1968), 144, quoting [Carlton H. Rogers], *Incidents of Travel in the Southern States and Cuba* (New York, 1862), 234–5, written in 1856.

Capital and labor, in Europe and America, are largely employed in the manufacture of cotton. These goods, to a great extent, may be seen freighting every vessel, from Christian nations, that traverses the seas of the globe; and filling the warehouses and shelves of the merchants, over two-thirds of the world. By the industry, skill and enterprise, employed in the manufacture of cotton, mankind are better clothed; their comfort better promoted; general industry more highly stimulated; commerce more widely extended; and civilization more rapidly advanced, than in any preceding age.[1]

What would happen if no cotton was furnished for three years? I will not stop to depict what every one can imagine, but this is certain: England would topple headlong and carry the whole civilized world with her, save the South. No, you dare not make war on cotton. No power on earth dares to make war upon it. Cotton is king. Until lately the Bank of England was king, but she tried to put her screws as usual, the fall before last, upon the cotton crop, and was utterly vanquished. The last power has been conquered.[2]

Finally the propaganda of Engels and Marx and of Samuel Smiles and Schulze-Gaevernitz, though directed to opposite ends, fulfilled the same polemical function of focussing attention upon the cotton industry and implicitly exaggerating its significance.

To make possible a more just estimate of the industry's true importance one must recognize that it was not indigenous to England, like the woollen industry, but was essentially an exotic import from outside, like the silk industry. It was acclimatized with startling rapidity but sank only shallow roots in an alien soil and acquired its world-wide influence during the temporary eclipse of Asian civilization between 1830 and 1890. It attained the peak of its relative importance between 1820 and 1840 some eighty years before the peak of its absolute importance and was dethroned from its national eminence during the Cotton Famine. Thereafter it survived upon borrowed time as other societies responded to its challenge and

[1] [D. Christy], *Cotton is King: or the Culture of Cotton, and its Relation to Agriculture, Manufactures and Commerse*, by an American (Cincinnati, Moore, 1855), 37.

[2] *Appendix to the Congressional Globe*, First Session, Thirty-Fifth Congress, 70, iii, 4 Mar. 1858, Senator J. H. Hammond of South Carolina. See also *The Poems of Henry Timrod* ed. by Paul H. Hayne (New York, Hale, 1873; Arno, 1972), 125–131, 'The Cotton Boll' (1861).

developed their own cotton industries but it withered and died only in the twentieth century.

The difficulties of estimating the exact extent of the influence of the industry begin with the search for the most appropriate criteria. Each particular criterion has its own built-in limitations. The rhetoric of contemporaries quoted above suffers from an inevitable literary bias. Statistics have a quantitative and ahistorical orientation. Linkage theory has mechanistic, deterministic, and quasi-mystical overtones but may well offer

TABLE 3

The Cotton Industry as an Employer of Labour and as a Generator of Income, 1801–1901

	Number of Employees	% of Population of Lancashire	% of Labour Force of U.K.	Gross Product (£m.)	% of National Income	Value Added (£m.)	% of National Income
1801	242,000	35·96	5·04	15	6·52	11	4·78
1811	306,000	36·96	5·56	28·3	9·4	23	7·64
1821	369,000	35·04	5·95	29·4	10·10	23·2	7·97
1831	427,000	31·94	5·93	32·1	9·4	25·3	7·44
1841	374,000	22·44	4·45	46·7	10·33	34·3	7·58
1851	379,000	18·66	3·91	48·55	9·28	33·23	6·35
1861	446,000	18·36	4·13	77	11·53	47·7	7·14
1871	450,000	15·96	3·75	104·9	11·44	58	6·33
1881	520,000	15·06	3·97	94·5	8·99	62·7	5·97
1891	526,000	13·39	3·58	101·2	7·86	63·8	4·95
1901	544,000	12·44	3·26	89·2	5·43	57·2	3·48

Source: G. H. Wood, *The History of Wages in the Cotton Trade* (Manchester, Sherratt, 1910), 127–8, for the number of employees, 1806–71, the figure for 1801 being derived by extrapolation, and *Census Returns*, 1881–1901, for the number of employees, 1881–1901; B. R. Mitchell and P. Deane, *Abstract of British Historical Statistics* (1962), 20, 22, for the population of Lancashire, 1801–1911; P. Deane and W. A. Cole, *British Economic Growth 1688–1959* (1962, 1967), 143, 166, for the working population of the U.K. and for its National Income, 1801–1901; ibid., 185, 187, 212 for gross product and value added, 1801–41, 1861–1901; P. Deane, 'New Estimates of Gross National Product for the United Kingdom, 1830–1914', *Review of Income and Wealth*, 1968, 104–7, presents revised estimates which reduce the share of the industry's net product in the G.N.P. to the following proportions:

1831	5·78	1841	7·02
1851	5·92	1861	5·84
1871	5·1	1881	4·95
1891	4·36	1901	2·98

S. D. Chapman, *The Cotton Industry in the Industrial Revolution* (1972), 64; T. Bazley, 'Manchester', *Encyclopaedia Britannica* (1857, 8th edn.), xiv. 255, for a triennial estimate for 1849–51.

the best available guide to a study of the influence of a machine-based industry. An examination of several statistical series reveals the surprisingly limited role of the industry as an employer of the factors of production and as a generator of income. As an employer of labour the industry expanded its activity most rapidly in the later eighteenth century and, as shown in Table 3, reached the peak of its relative importance between 1811 and 1821 during the great age of hand-loom weaving. In 1800–30 it afforded direct employment to the equivalent of over one-third of the population of Lancashire but to less than 6 per cent of the total working population of the U.K. Its proportion of the total labour force expanded more slowly than population after 1811 in Lancashire and after 1821 in England as it became more capitalized.

A full discussion of the role of the industry as an employer of capital must wait upon the publication of the work of C. H. Feinstein and S. D. Chapman. Here it may be tentatively suggested that its importance was almost certainly exaggerated in the mid-nineteenth century since it had been the pioneer of extensive fixed investment in machinery and mills, had become more capital-intensive with the adoption of the power-loom from the 1830s, and probably employed by 1850 a larger single capital than any other manufacturing industry. It seems however to have been even less important as an employer of capital than of labour. Its fixed capital, including that invested in the finishing trades, represented at the peak of its relative importance between the 1830s and 1860s less than 3 per cent of the total stock of reproducible capital in Great Britain,[1] a share which thereafter tended to decline.

Another measure of the industry's importance may be found in the contribution of its product to the National Income, which was greatest, as shown in Table 4, between 1781 and 1821 and between 1841 and 1871. The gross product averaged over 10 per cent of the G.N.P. between 1821 and 1861 and expanded to reach its peak proportion in 1861 but never

[1] M. Blaug, 'The Productivity of Capital in the Lancashire Cotton Industry during the Nineteenth Century', *Economic History Review*, Apr. 1961, 359, 371–2; C. H. Feinstein, 'Capital Accumulation and Economic Growth in Great Britain, 1760–1860' (paper presented at the Economic History Society Conference, 10 Apr. 1976), 37, 81.

apparently exceeded the total value of all domestic exports.[1] The net product followed a slightly different pattern of development: it expanded faster than the gross product between 1782 and 1820, as it did between 1870 and 1900, and reached its peak proportion of the G.N.P. much earlier, in 1821, when

TABLE 4

Value of the Product of the Cotton Industry, 1782–1900

	Average Annual Value of Gross Product (£m.)	Mean Annual Rate of Increase (%)	Average Annual Value of Net Product (£m.)	Mean Annual Rate of Increase (%)	Contribution to the Increase of National Income (%)
1781–3	4		3		
1782–1820		5·4		5·5	12·95
1819–21	29·388		23·201		
1820–40		1·8		1·2	3·77
1839–41	41·954		29·279		
1840–70		3·3		1·9	6·22
1869–71	110·882		51·494		
1870–1900		−0·74		0·3	0·79
1899–1901	89·2		57·2		
1782–1900		4·68		2·5	3·59

Source: T. Ellison, *The Cotton Trade* (1886), 69, for 1819–21; J. A. Mann, *The Cotton Trade* (1860), 106, for 1839–41; I. Watts, 'Cotton', *Encyclopaedia Britannica* (Edinburgh, Black, 1877, 9th edn.), vi. 504, for 1869–71; P. Deane and W. A. Cole, *British Economic Growth 1688–1959* (1962, 1967), 166, 185, 188, for 1781–3 and 1899–1901 as well as for estimates of National Income.

the industry's net share of 8 per cent in the National Income was less than one-fifth of its contribution of 45 per cent to the value of domestic exports. In terms of value added to the raw material the cotton industry in virtue of its demotic function remained proportionately less productive than the woollen and worsted trade but added proportionately more to its products marketed at home than to those sold abroad. Even in the home trade the industry became a virtual cannibal, expanding at the expense of other textiles and retarding for a generation by its

[1] J. M'Queen, *General Statistics of the British Empire* (London, Fellowes, 1836), 103, for such a revised estimate, raising the gross product for 1835 above the total value of domestic exports.

successful competition the growth of the woollen, worsted, linen, and silk manufactures. Thus the net output of the main textile industries as a whole increased during the crucial decades between 1770 and 1800 at little more than the rate of population increase.[1] In so far as the home demand for cotton textiles was price-elastic and expanded with the fall in their price after 1801 the effective demand of consumers was not released for the purchase of the products of other industries by the virtual rise in their real income.

* * *

In using linkage theory to delimit the influence of the industry it will be necessary to abandon a quantitative for a qualitative and chronological approach. It will be helpful to distinguish between the two periods 1780–1830 and 1830–60 since the industry apparently achieved its maximum impact upon other trades only after 1830. The importance of the 1830s as a dividing-line is reflected in the establishment of the industry's dominant influence in all branches of foreign trade, in the spread of mechanization from spinning to weaving, in the shift of the centre of advance of mechanical engineering from London to Lancashire, in the first explicit association, by John Rae in 1834, of technical change with capital-formation,[2] and in the increasing proportion of the population of Lancashire employed in the finishing industries and the ancillary trades. Thus the quantitative increase in production between 1780 and 1830 made possible a qualitative transformation of the economy from the 1830s as the industry reached the summit of its influence as both seller and buyer.

The investment of capital in cotton spinning served not only as a creator of productive capacity and as a generator of income but also as a pace-maker for complementary capital-formation in related fields of activity. Such induced investment was determined by the strength of the linkages developed by the industry, which have been estimated to have been one-seventh

[1] Deane and Cole, 212–13, showing the net output of textiles to have risen by 31·58 per cent while population increased by 29·84 per cent.

[2] B. L. Anderson (ed.), *Capital Accumulation in the Industrial Revolution* (London, Dent, 1974), xiv, 63–82.

weaker on the Chenery–Watanabe scale than those developed by the iron and steel industry.[1] The forward linkages of the industry were those of a producer of consumer goods rather than of capital goods so that their influence was proportionately limited. The main products of the industry's spindles and looms were two, yarn and cloth. Its sole 'intermediate' product was yarn, which furnished the basic input to a number of other industries, including the hosiery and lace industries, the thread and carpet trades, and the mixed goods manufacturers of Yorkshire. The stimulus to complementary investment in those industries was limited by the survival of the proto-industrial pattern of production in lace manufacture until the 1840s and in hosiery manufacture until 1852–74. The worsted trade of Bradford had a well-established factory tradition by the 1830s, when it adopted cost-cutting cotton warps and wove them up on hand-looms as well as on power-looms. Cotton warps rejuvenated the woollen industry of Dewsbury by cheapening the cost of production of blankets. Carpet manufacturers also adopted a range of cotton warps but continued until the 1850s to use the hand-loom, especially with a Jacquard harness. In all those fields the stimulus imparted by the cotton industry to the investment of capital seems to have been limited and late. Only in the manufacture of cotton sewing-thread was a new industry developed, especially from the 1830s, upon a factory basis at the expense of the manufacturers of linen thread and became from the 1860s more capital-intensive than any other branch of the cotton industry. The export of yarn further limited the domestic influence of such forward linkages. The main outlet for yarn, however, became increasingly from the 1840s the weaving industry at home.

From the industry's looms came its main product in cloth to supply the clothing trade with its essential raw material. That forward linkage exerted a limited domestic influence through the home trade and proved of greatest service to the clothing industries of Asia. The increasing export of grey cloth until the 1880s weakened the links of the cotton industry to the domestic finishing industries and in effect exported abroad the

[1] A. O. Hirschman, *The Strategy of Economic Development* (New Haven, Yale University Press, 1958), 106–7, for the ratio of 72:62 between the iron and steel industry and the textile industry.

earnings of the dyers, bleachers, and printers. At home the clothing industry drew most of its material from the woollen industries and was revitalized by the advent of ready-made clothing. The entrenched interest of Lancashire in the fustian industry undoubtedly discouraged the local development of the new trade, fostered its expansion in Leeds and undermined Manchester's monopoly of textile distribution both at home and abroad.[1] The clothing industry long remained a preserve of the small master and an employer of labour even more than of capital, being forced to pay for the new sewing machine a monopoly-price, based upon patents.[2] Factory production nevertheless developed in the manufacture of rainwear in Manchester and Salford, which thus attracted the rubber industry.

The cotton industry did not produce a range of by-products, like the coal industry. Almost its sole by-product was the cotton waste made in increasing quantities as production expanded. The Cotton Famine raised the waste trade to new importance, especially in 1862 as the consumption of Surat increased, but compelled the industry to reduce the proportion of its waste as the price of cotton rose. The industry reduced that proportion by almost one-third between 1862 and 1871[3] and so manufactured proportionately more yarn and cloth from every bale of cotton. In the 1870s it still discarded some 12 per cent of its consumption of cotton in the form of waste and so supplied an immense mass of material to the cotton waste industry.[4] That industry developed in south-east Lancashire and Rossendale in the closest association with the spinning of coarse yarns which created more waste than fine yarns. Its firms conformed to the classic type of satellite industry and operated on a much smaller scale than the firms of the parent industry. They manufactured upon specialized machinery a wide range of cheap and useful textiles: they produced coarse sheeting in competition with the linen industry and encroached on the preserves of the woollen

[1] *Manchester City News*, 8 Dec. 1888, 4iv, 'A Review of the Home Trade Question'; *Textile Mercury*, 25 Mar. 1893, 219, 'Is the Woollen Trade Leaving Manchester?'

[2] *Meliora*, Apr. 1861, 132, 'Labour and Machinery'.

[3] I. Watts, 'Cotton', *Encyclopaedia Britannica* (1877, 9th edn.), vi. 504.

[4] P. L. Simmonds, *Waste Products and Undeveloped Substances* (London, Hardwicke, 1873), 8, 263.

trade by making flannelette and even blankets.[1] The domestic economies created by the increased use of waste were however limited by the export first of waste twills, to supply French manufacturers with the foundation material for beautiful furnishing fabrics,[2] and then of the cotton waste itself, especially from Oldham from the 1880s.[3]

The backward linkages of the industry were far more important than its forward linkages because they developed earlier and more strongly to stimulate the output of all the dependent trades supplying it with inputs. The industry drew its main input in raw cotton wholly from abroad and thus developed in sharp contrast to the woollen industry in so far as it imparted no direct stimulus to British agriculture or to the associated home trade. The woollen industry secured its raw material until the 1830s mainly from British sheep grazed upon British soil and was thus secured against any threat to its source of supply caused by an interruption to foreign commerce. That industry catered mainly for the home trade[4] and increased the value of its raw material proportionately much more than the cotton industry. Thus it was much more closely linked to the traditional interests of the nation and especially to the agricultural interest. In response to the cost-cutting competition of the cotton industry it successfully extended its supply of raw material by the increasing use of 'reborn wool' which from the 1840s became the basis of the shoddy industry of the Dewsbury district.[5]

The expansion of the cotton industry certainly imparted a great stimulus to the production of cotton in America, inspired the agrarian colonization of the South and linked together in mutual dependence the economies of Lancashire and the U.S.A. Cotton cultivation became a staple industry in the Southern States probably to a greater extent than cotton manufacture became a staple industry of Lancashire, although even in the South the influence of the cotton crop has been exaggerated at the expense of the role of the subsistence crop of maize. The

[1] Simmonds, op. cit., 264–5.

[2] *Textile Manufacturer*, Jan. 1882, 2.

[3] T. Thornley, *Cotton Waste, its Production, Manipulation and Uses* (London, Scott, 1912), 180–1.

[4] M'Queen, *General Statistics* (1836), 110.

[5] Simmonds, op. cit., 26–7, 106–7.

commercial policy of England until 1846 favoured the import of cotton rather than of corn, the labour of slaves rather than of the free farmers of the American West, and thus indirectly the expansion of the Slave Power in the U.S.A. The British demand for cotton stimulated the export of capital to the U.S.A. and the expansion of primary production throughout the 'Cotton States' (1858) of the 'Cotton Kingdom' (1861) during the booms of the 1830s and 1850s.[1] Whether the industrial expansion of the South was in fact retarded by the concentration of its resources upon agricultural production and by the influence of the slave plantation may continue to be debated. The Southern market for cotton manufactures was however increasingly captured from Lancashire, especially after 1820, by the mills of New England. Nor did British shipowners benefit as much as Americans, until the Civil War, from the stimulus imparted to the transatlantic carrying trade by the rise of the cotton economy outside the protection of the Navigation Laws. The economic services rendered by the North may well have made the South more of an Anglo-American condominium than an exclusive province of 'the informal empire of Britain'.[2]

Apart from raw cotton, the industry required mills, machinery, power, light, and mill stores, so creating an expanding domestic demand for the products of a widening range of trades. Mill building became a specialized activity in Lancashire as the cotton industry quickly expanded beyond the stage of using converted buildings. Even before the construction of mills was revolutionized by Fairbairn from the 1830s, it required the production of bricks, slate, timber, glass, and iron, stimulated the import of timber from the Baltic and America, and created employment for architects, contractors, joiners, builders, brick manufacturers, and timber merchants. The demand for machinery was undoubtedly limited by the low and stable capital–output ratio of the cotton industry, which contrasted with that of the iron and steel industry, but nevertheless generated the most important of all backward linkages. The

[1] J. G. Williamson, *American Growth and the Balance of Payments 1820–1913. A Study of the Long Swing* (Chapel Hill, University of North Carolina Press, 1964) 42, 105.

[2] E. J. Hobsbawm, *The Age of Capital, 1848–1875* (London, Weidenfeld, 1975), 78.

adoption of iron machinery stimulated both iron-founding and engineering. Investment in power-looms was discouraged before the 1830s, partly by the competition of the hand-loom. The demand for such machines became important as the decline of the hand-weavers deprived manufacturers of any reserve supply of labour and compelled them to invest capital in power-looms. During the decade 1835–45 the initial demand and the replacement demand for spinning and weaving machines absorbed only 3·8 per cent of the total production of wrought iron but may well have accounted for 37 per cent of the increment in its production, a share which might be increased to 50 per cent by including the demand for preparatory machinery, steam-engines, boilers, bleaching kiers, and cylinder-printing machines.[1] The expansion of iron-founding was accompanied by that of brass-founding, copper- and tin-plate working, and wire-drawing, which in turn stimulated the mining of the ores of lead, tin, copper, and iron.

The provision of machinery was undertaken by the engineering industry which manufactured first spinning machinery and then, with the adoption of the power-loom, weaving machinery. The spread of the power-loom was encouraged by the continued investment in spinning machinery, so that the rise of the power-weaving industry of Burnley became a complement to the spinning trade of Oldham. The development of spinning in Oldham nevertheless depreciated from the 1870s the value of the capital invested in the spinning mills of north Lancashire. The development of weaving in the Burnley area fulfilled a similar function of creative destruction by retarding the expansion of weaving in the Preston–Blackburn area. The stimulus to the production of textile machinery was however substantial and sustained. The specialized sector of light engineering was supplemented by the development of heavy engineering as the demand for steam-engines and boilers increased at the expense of the water-wheel. Engineering became another seed-bed of mechanical invention, especially under Richard Roberts, and proved even more important in fostering innovation than the cotton industry proper. It derived a great stimulus from the advent of the railway in the

[1] P. Bairoch, *Révolution industrielle et sous-développement* (Paris, Mouton, 1963, 4th edn., 1974), 90–1, 106, 249.

1840s when the engineers of Manchester, Oldham, Bolton, and Blackburn embarked upon a wave of sustained expansion. That industry remained closely dependent upon the demand of the cotton industry and provides the clearest example of a new trade called into existence by the revolution in spinning technology, as it was not by the development of cotton spinning in India, China, or Japan. The demand for power to drive the industry's machines was met first by the use of water-wheels and then by the use of the steam-engine, the demand for which emanated largely from the cotton industry, especially in the towns of the Lancashire plain.[1] The consumption of coal as fuel increased with the spread of the steam-engine until the industry was using by 1870 about one-third of the coal mined in Lancashire. The demand for light was met first by the use of tallow candles and then by that of coal-gas, ranking Lancashire second only to London during the nineteenth century in its production of gas.

The demand for mill-stores created, especially from the 1830s, a range of satellite industries which supplied the industry with minor inputs, including oil, sizing material, chemicals, bobbins, and belting. The demand for lubricating oil increased in proportion to the expansion of the industry, to its use of machinery, and to the loss of power through friction. That demand revived the whale fisheries from the 1790s and increased markedly from the 1830s as machines were used more intensively in response to the statutory restriction of the length of the working day. The supply of such a minor item in the costs of a mill proved immensely profitable to the oil-refining industry, which resembled the thread industry in its capacity to maintain high margins on the sale of an instrumental commodity vital to its customers. The demand for sizing materials stimulated the quarrying of china clay in Cornwall and was also met by the import of farina and tallow, the manufacture of soap, and the use of flour, the sole input of the industry derived directly from British agriculture. The demand of the finishing trades for chemicals, especially acids and alkalis such as bleaching powder, together with that for soap and glass, created from the 1790s the heavy chemical industry of the

[1] A. E. Musson, 'Industrial Motive Power in the United Kingdom, 1800–70', *Economic History Review*, Aug. 1976, 434.

lower Mersey, with its own demands for inputs of coal, salt, lime, and sulphur. From the 1780s the demand for dyestuffs revived the indigo trade, which provided India with its chief export until the 1830s. The development of coal-tar dyes from the 1850s created a new organic branch of the chemical industry and further extended the use of the by-products of coal mining but benefited Germany much more than Britain, which became dependent upon the new German dyestuffs industry. The application of chemical technology to the cotton industry proper began only in 1895 with the adoption of the mercerization process, which used caustic soda to endow cotton cloth with a permanent silk-like lustre.[1]

The manufacture of bobbins, shuttles, baskets, skips, and packing cases became specialized industries, increased the demand for timber, and extended at first the sphere of domestic production in the wooded regions of the Lake District and Ireland. Such industries were usually conducted on a much smaller scale than the cotton industry. The manufacture of bobbins, however, developed to meet an immense demand and became the speciality of a single firm: Wilson Brothers of Todmorden expanded markedly from the establishment of their mill in 1835 and secured a world monopoly, based upon twelve successive patents and upon extreme division of labour.[2] For the needs of the preparatory machinery in spinning mills, Rochdale supplied roller cloths and Wrexham supplied roller leathers to cover the drawing rollers while the West Riding furnished card-clothing made from iron wire, set first in leather and then in rubber. Other trades supplied the belting, strapping, and ropes used for the transmission of power. All such suppliers became dependent upon the host industry and those that became most dependent acquired a vested interest in maintaining its rate of expansion.

The cotton industry may well have fulfilled a very limited national function as an income-generator and as an employer of the production factors, providing on average in 1821–61 only 7·3 per cent of the G.N.P., employing only 4·7 per cent of

[1] D. A. Clibbens, *Chemistry and Clothing* (London, Royal Institute of Chemistry, First Dalton Memorial Lecture, 1945), 9.

[2] *Textile Manufacturer*, Jan. 1883, 35, July 1890, 359, Nov. 1896, 415–16; *The Century's Progress: Lancashire* (London Printing & Engraving Co., 1892), 199.

the labour force of the U.K. together with an even lower proportion of its fixed capital,[1] and never rivalling the woollen cloth industry at its peak as an employer of labour. That industry nevertheless became the pre-eminent occupation of the Lancashire region, employing at least as many hands in its associated manufactures as in the production process proper. The concentration of that trade may have discouraged imitative development elsewhere after the 1850s but it also encouraged a high degree of regional specialization in economic activity. Thus it created an 'industrial atmosphere' favourable to innovation and inspired the formulation in 1891 of Marshall's idea of the 'external economies' generated by a vast array of ancillary trades, numbering 154 by 1870.[2] Until the 1840s Lancashire remained unique in England as an industrial society. The expenditure of its dependent population, and especially of its mill-girls, increased with the decline of the hand-loom weavers and was directed mainly to the consumer-goods industries, so stimulating the development of retail trade, the food, drink, and patent-medicine industries, the building trade, the clothing industry, and the manufacture of clogs, shawls, wallpaper, oil-cloth, furniture, and clocks. The presence of the cotton industry attracted the paper industry to Lancashire from the 1820s, to tap an expanding market as well as a growing source of supply of cotton rags. Agriculture outside the cotton districts benefited from the growing demand for food, first in west Lancashire and Cheshire, next in Ireland, and then from the 1870s in America. Facilities of transportation developed to carry the massive volume of internal trade generated by the needs of that expanding population of avid consumers. Canals achieved their greatest importance between 1770 and 1850 less in the direct service of the cotton industry than in that of its dependent population.

The industry extended its influence within the economy by providing a striking example of the success of new methods of production. Cotton spinning was essentially process-centred rather than product-centred, and therefore became a pioneer of machine-technology, a seed-bed of indigenous invention, and

[1] See Table 3.

[2] John Murray, *Handbook for Shropshire, Lancashire and Cheshire* (London, Murray, 1870), xl–xli.

a school of machine-making.[1] Its technical innovations may have been largely inapplicable outside the sphere of textiles but nevertheless helped to revolutionize the largest complex of industries in Europe. Its example stimulated the adoption of machine spinning by the worsted, woollen, and flax industries while its power-loom supplied the model for the power-looms developed for weaving linen, jute, and silk and its cylinder-printing machine was applied to the production of newspapers and wallpaper. Foreign demand for the new machines developed to such an extent as to strain to the very limits the machinery of enforcement of the acts prohibiting the export of machinery.[2]

* * *

The emergence of a new complex of economic activity in a thitherto backward and peripheral region created a deep gulf of mutual incomprehension between the two worlds of 'North and South'. The new industry could not, like the cloth industry, be easily absorbed into the traditional agrarian structure of society: it differed profoundly from the older manufactures in its demotic origins and function, serving as it did the poor of the world and enhancing the wealth of nations rather than of classes. The divorce between the two cultures of England became apparent in the campaign for freedom of trade and in the birth of a new school of radical politico-economic thought which drew its strongest material support from the cotton industry. That school exalted the role of commerce and industry as the true pioneers of civilization and as the great benefactors of mankind in its hope to secure the abolition of all harmful restraints upon economic activity. It even boldly reinterpreted history in a bid to wrest the custody of the national tradition from the representatives of the aristocratic and military society of the south.[3] 'To Arkwright and Watt, England is far more indebted for her triumphs than to Nelson

[1] Hirschman, 147–8.

[2] D. J. Jeremy, 'Damming the Flood: British Government Efforts to Check the Outflow of Technicians and Machinery, 1780–1843', *Business History Review*, Spring 1977, 1–34.

[3] J. R. McCulloch, *The Principles of Political Economy* (London, Longman, 2nd edn., 1830), 120–1.

and Wellington.'[1] 'It is to the spinning-jenny and the steam-engine that we must look as having been the true moving powers of our fleets and armies, and the chief support also of a long-continued agricultural prosperity.'[2] That new quasi-religious gospel was preached in the interest of the producer as well as of the consumer. The restriction of governmental functions to an absolute minimum was advocated from distrust of a landlord-dominated government and from fear of an inevitable administrative bias against the distant north. International peace was regarded as essential in order to prevent any interruption in the supply of raw material to, or in the shipment of manufactures by, the industry which had, in the view of List,[3] been the greatest beneficiary of the French Wars but which had become more dependent than others upon the fortunes of foreign commerce. Trade with the whole world rather than with the colonies was favoured because the colonies were negligible as suppliers of raw cotton, offered only a limited market for cotton goods,[4] and even from 1853 imposed retaliatory tariffs upon imported textiles.[5] Manchester may also have deplored London's taste for luxury textiles.[6] The cleavage between the two worlds was deepened by particular as well as by general influences. The growth of foreign production was reflected in the decline in the British share of U.S. cotton exports from the peak proportion of 77·8 per cent in 1830–1, in the increase in the exports of yarn to Europe down to the 1840s, and in the stabilization of the quantity of piece-goods shipped thereto. The pressure of falling prices was reflected not

[1] E. Baines, *History of the Cotton Manufacture in Great Britain* (London, Fisher, 1835), 503–4; A. Ure, *The Philosophy of Manufactures* (London, Knight, 1835; Cass, 1967), 107–8.

[2] G. R. Porter, *The Progress of the Nation* (London, Knight, 1836), i. 188.

[3] F. List, *The National System of Political Economy* (London, Longmans, 1885, trans. from the 1st edn. of 1841), 55.

[4] According to J. A. Mann, *The Cotton Trade* (1860), 43, 90, and the *Annual Statement of Trade for 1859* the colonies and dependencies (excluding Hong Kong which has been regarded as an entrepôt for the Chinese market) supplied during the forty years 1820–59 14·9 per cent of the volume of cotton imported into Britain and imported 24·5 per cent of the value of British exports of cotton manufactures: India alone supplied 13·8 per cent of the raw cotton and imported 13·6 per cent of the cotton manufactures.

[5] R. Burn, *A Sequel to the Darkening Cloud, or England's Commercial Decline* (Liverpool, Liverpool Courier, 1857), 17.

[6] M'Queen, *General Statistics* (1836), 221.

only in the continuing adverse movement of the terms of trade but also in the much slower rate of increase in the value of the industry's net product between 1820 and 1840, so reinforcing the pressures for the abolition of restrictions upon commerce.

The slow-changing language of the land reflected the birth of a new way of life in the formerly backward north. The traditional values of English society seemed to be threatened by the new industry's total dependence upon foreign sources of supply of raw material as well as upon foreign shipping, its dedication to the pursuit of gain, its addiction to speculation, its crass and increasingly cosmopolitan materialism, and the diffusion amongst its dependents of 'cotton mill morality'. Under the influence of 'industrialism' (1829) and 'romanticism' (1831) the south of England tended to view with disdain the 'nouveaux riches' (1828) of the 'moneyocracy' (1834), the 'cotton lords' (1823) of the 'cottonocracy' (1843), the 'millocrats' (1839) of the 'millocracy' (1843) and the 'cottoneers' (1843) or 'cottonians' (1846) of 'Cottonia' (1864).[1] For its part the north chafed beneath the restraints imposed upon its enterprise by the 'feudalism' (1839) or 'landlordism' (1844) of the 'landocracy' (1846) of the south.

The campaign for the establishment of freedom of trade marked the unprecedented irruption into national politics of a traditionally non-political community. The successive measures of the 1840s dealt major blows to the historic vested interests of English society. The abolition of the import duty upon raw cotton in 1845 severed the last fiscal link between the State and an industry which, unlike the woollen industry, had never been an efficient revenue-raising machine since its exports had never been taxed and its employers had doggedly refused, ever since 1785, to permit their trade to be turned into the traditional type

[1] All attributions on this page and on page 40–1 may be verified in the *O.E.D.*, except for 'cottonocracy', from J. Easby, *Manchester and the Manchester People* (Manchester, Literary Agency Office, 1843), 17, 'landocracy', from the *Manchester Guardian*, 21 Jan. 1846, 6iii, Mr. Birchwood, and 'Cottonia', from *The Times*, 19 Aug. 1864, 8iv. As the intermediary between the Continent and England, Carlyle was responsible for enriching the English language with a range of phrases including 'environment' in 1827; 'cosmopolitanism' in 1828; 'industrialism' in 1829; 'philistinism' and 'romanticism' in 1831; 'Chartism' and 'the condition of England question' in 1839; 'Mammonism', 'shopkeeperism', 'millocracy', 'merchant-prince', 'captains of industry', and 'cash-nexus' in 1843; 'calico millenium' in 1850; and 'promoterism' in 1872.

of milch-cow. The loss to the State was great since the industry's gross product surpassed in value from 1852 to 1893 the public revenue itself. The repeal of the Corn Laws deprived the country's greatest and most fundamental interest of protection and implicitly recognized the cotton industry as the nation's leading industry in place of agriculture: it promised to usher in a new moral world wherein calico would be exchanged for corn and the interests of primary and secondary producers would be knit together in a peaceful and prosperous equilibrium. The repeal of the Navigation Laws fostered the expansion of American shipping at the expense of British vessels in the carrying trade.

The influence of the free trade school has undoubtedly been exaggerated by its intellectual heirs, as much as has the influence of the cotton industry itself upon the course of the Industrial Revolution. That school never achieved the eminence nor accomplished the ends desired by its most vocal and radical representatives. It failed to become a dominant influence in England or abroad, to elevate the commercial idea to the position of the supreme governing power within the State or to convert the outside world to belief in its ideals. It may have helped to check any further formal extension of the British Empire between 1844 and 1874 but it probably encouraged the spread of informal empire based upon economic influence. In Britain it remained simply a school of thought, originated only a single organization in the Anti-Corn Law League and was never formed into a party.[1] Its influence upon the evolution of the Liberal party and of Liberal policy was far less than that of the Whig grandees or the Nonconformist conscience. It never possessed recognized leaders and never produced a general programme which could have commanded the assent of all the diverse sections of its supporters. The mercantile community of Manchester has been inappropriately identified with the creed of the Manchester radicals. Apparently it remained true to its pragmatic and conservative traditions, supporting the agitation for free trade from motives of expediency rather

[1] Goldwin Smith, 'The Manchester School', *Contemporary Review*, Mar. 1895, 377–89, reprinted in *Reminiscences* (New York, Macmillan, 1910), 215–37; N. McCord, 'Cobden and Bright in Politics, 1846–1857', in R. Robson (ed.), *Ideas and Institutions of Victorian Britain. Essays in honour of George Kitson Clark*. (London Bell, 1967), 87–114.

than of principle. The abolition in 1843 of the restrictions upon the export of machinery was indeed opposed by traditionalist cotton spinners.[1] The capture of the Manchester Chamber of Commerce by free-trade fanatics provoked the secession of the conservative mercantile élite and their organization of the separate Manchester Commercial Association (1845–58).[2] The campaign against the Corn Laws may well have exhausted the political energies of Manchester, which ceased thereafter to speak with a united voice and never again succeeded in imposing its policies upon the nation. The middle class of Lancashire gave no support to the various successor-campaigns which were launched by the Manchester radicals against the aristocratic and military society of southern England and which sought to secure such ends as the establishment of free trade in land, the disestablishment of the Church of England, the introduction of a national non-sectarian system of education, the extension of parliamentary and financial reform, the abolition of the East India Company as the 'landlord of India', and the establishment of international peace as the necessary basis of a 'calico millenium'.[3]

The new gospel of what Disraeli called in 1846 'the Manchester school' failed to win the allegiance of the aristocracy, of London society, of the world of literature, art, and culture, or even of the leading political economists. Indeed it generated a profound revulsion throughout society which was reflected in the spread of the Oxford Movement, in the birth of 'Young Englandism' (1848), 'Christian Socialism' (1850), and 'Pre-Raphaelitism' (1851) as well as in the bitter diatribes of Carlyle against the 'Dismal Science' (1849) of political economy and the 'pig philosophy' (1850) of *laissez-faire*.[4] The growth of

[1] A. E. Musson, The 'Manchester School' and Exportation of Machinery, *Business History*, Jan. 1972, 17–30.

[2] *Manchester Guardian*, 16 Apr. 1845, 4iv, 21 Jan. 1846, 6i–iii, 11 Feb. 6ii–vi, 14 Feb., 7i–iii; A. W. Silver, *Manchester Men and Indian Cotton, 1847–72* (Manchester University Press, 1966), 15–16, 99.

[3] T. W. Reid, *The Life, Letters and Friendships of Richard Monckton Milnes, First Lord Houghton* (London, Cassell, 1890), i. 436, quoting Carlyle in 1850; C. Gibbon, *The Life of George Combe, Author of 'The Constitution of Man'* (London, Macmillan 1878), ii. 309, 4 June 1852.

[4] Carlyle, 'Occasional Discourses on the Negro Question', *Fraser's Magazine*, Dec. 1849, 672; Idem, *Latter Day Pamphlets* (London, Chapman, 1850), 379, 'Jesuitism'.

industry and commerce was deplored by sensitive minds as an agent for the spread of 'philistinism' (1831) and 'provincialism' (1836) throughout the cultural life of the realm in place of Arnold's Hellenic ideals of 'sweetness and light'. Thus a hostile reaction developed towards such venal tendencies as individualistic 'atomism' (1836), 'Mammonism' (1843), 'money-grubbing' (1849), 'quill-driving commercialism' (1849), 'millocratism' (1849), and 'hedonism' (1856). Manchester became a standing rock of offence to poets, literati, and aesthetes and the new civilization inspired Carlyle to preach an impassioned sermon upon the need of a mercenary age, captivated by a 'mechanical philosophy', for the creative leadership of a working aristocracy of 'Steamengine Captains of Industry'.[1] In so adverse an intellectual climate the creed of free trade failed to attract the working classes, whose members either emigrated to the lands of high protection overseas or built up at home trade unions upon an essentially defensive and protectionist basis.

The long-term influence of the adoption of free trade must be carefully distinguished from its short-term repercussions. In the long run the new policy benefited the cotton industry by facilitating the import of raw materials and foodstuffs, the expansion of exports and of world trade, the spread of a market economy, and the extension of British power and influence. It also provided the economic élite of industrial Britain with an intelligible world-view, based upon an idea-force of unparalleled inspiring power. In the short term, however, it ushered in a period of bitter debate which raged from 1846 until 1853 and ended only with the emasculation of the original gospel of free trade. The repeal of the Corn Laws did not set an acceptable example to Europe or inspire the speedy and general adoption of policies of free trade. Europe and America preferred to follow the teaching of List and Carey rather than that of Ricardo and Mill. England's unilateral adoption of a policy of free trade was a momentous gamble. That act assumed that the superiority of the states of Europe to Britain in almost all walks of life did not extend to economics, that their historic policies of protection were the product of blind ignorance or

[1] Idem, *On Heroes, Hero-Worship, and the Heroic in History. Six Lectures* (London, Fraser, 1841); idem, *Past and Present* (London, Chapman, 1843), 288, 361, 363.

vested interest, that all civilized peoples were really inspired by a burning enthusiasm for free imports, that England's example would exert an irresistible moral force upon her neighbours and induce them to follow her lead, and that the effects of the resulting general reciprocity would more than compensate for the loss of protection. It pre-supposed that England could usurp the role of France as the leader of Europe and could benefit even if her example were not followed. It assumed that England could abandon her traditional policy of 'commercial treaties, supported by arms' whereby she had risen from the fifth rank of states to the first and avoid relegation to her former position,[1] and that she could open her ports without restriction to foreign imports, deprive herself of any power of retaliation against hostile tariffs, compete successfully against a hundred countries with closed ports, and still remain the focus of imperial trade without any preferential tariff.

England's new policy defied the general tendency towards increased levels of tariff protection apparent during the 1840s and may even have encouraged reactive protectionist tendencies in Europe, especially in Prussia. The repeal of the Corn Laws did not create an economic symbiosis between the industrial power of Britain and the great producers of grain because British exports did not increase markedly to the grain-growing states. The trade of Lancashire in particular had been shifting away from the wheat-producing societies of the western hemisphere to the millet- and rice-growing societies of Asia. The repeal of the Corn Laws undoubtedly stimulated the export of grain from the U.S.A. and Russia but it did not convert the great exporters of corn into the largest markets for British manufactures. The implicit sacrifice of the best of all markets for British industry in the home trade in exchange for the most poverty-stricken markets in all Europe in the corn-producing lands of the Ukraine and Poland proved to be a very poor bargain for the textile industry and for the country as a whole.[2] The increase in the export of cotton manufactures

[1] A. Alison, 'The Ministerial Measures', *Blackwood's Edinburgh Magazine*, Apr 1850, 387, quoting 'Major-General Sir William Napier's Opinion of Free Trade Generally. Extract from a Letter to Mr. Lloyd Caldecot', 2 Feb. 1850.

[2] A. Alison, 'The Crowning of the Column, and Crushing of the Pedestal', *Blackwood's Edinburgh Magazine*, July 1849, 125, reprinted in *Essays, Political, Historical and Miscellaneous* (Edinburgh, Blackwood, 1850), i. 531.

to the Levant in return for the import of grain, especially in 1855, was a product not of the natural growth of legitimate commerce but of the artificial forcing-house of war. The balance of American exports to Britain did not shift from slave-grown cotton to 'free wheat' until the depression of the Cotton Famine in 1862–4 and the change only became permanent from 1874. The continuing expansion of the Slave Power in the U.S.A. cruelly mocked the libertarian rhetoric of the free-trade school and threatened to place Britain in the dilemma of an enforced choice between national honour and national prosperity.[1]

The policy of free trade stimulated the re-export trade much more than the export of domestic manufactures and thus facilitated the import of raw materials by the industrial competitors of Britain. The opening of the British market to foreign wheat did not prevent either Russia or the U.S.A. from further developing their own cotton industries. The growth of the American cotton industry reduced the degree of British dependence upon the American crop after it had drawn in 1845 the peak proportion of 87 per cent of its imports from the U.S.A. The American example was imitated in the 1850s by Canada, Mexico, Brazil, and India and cotton prices rose as demand increased from 1854 to outdistance supply, especially in the dearth of 1857. Nor did Lancashire free itself from dependence upon imperial markets: the share of foreign countries in its exports had risen during the 1840s but declined during the 1850s with the growth of exports to Australia and India.

The repeal of the Corn Laws did not give an immediate and unprecedented impetus to the cotton trade. It did not check the decline in the long-term rate of its expansion which had set in during the depression of 1837–42. Nor did it inhibit the associated tendency towards the restriction of competition in such sections of the trade as bleaching and calico printing. Instead of an era of prosperity repeal ushered in the commercial crisis of 1847 when foreign exporters of corn perversely demanded sovereigns or bullion in preference to cotton goods.[2] The

[1] T. Ellison, 'The Cotton Manufacture', *Westminster Review*, Apr. 1861, 440.

[2] A. Alison, 'The Crowning of the Column', op. cit., 128–9, reprinted in *Essays* (1850), i. 535–6; idem, 'Free Trade at its Zenith', ibid., Dec. 1849, 760, 763, reprinted in *Essays* (1850), i. 625, 628.

export of cotton manufactures sank in value by 13·2 per cent in the ensuing commercial depression of 1846–9. Unemployment rose to unprecedented heights and the institution of the workhouse was generalized throughout a county where *per capita* poor rates had ranked amongst the lowest in the kingdom. Wages were sharply reduced by 10 per cent in 1847 and did not regain their pre-crisis level until the wartime boom of 1853–5. The commercial depression inspired the protectionist reaction of 1849–51, which in turn provoked the counter-campaign of publicity for the free-trade cause centring around the Great Exhibition of 1851.

The great debate inaugurated in 1846 was ended by the Crimean War which accelerated the transformation in the world outlook of the economic élite of Lancashire begun in 1850 by Palmerston's Don Pacifico speech. The first international conflict of the free-trade era generated economic prosperity rather than depression and dispelled the dream of perpetual peace cherished since 1851. The war infected all classes in Lancashire with the military spirit and encouraged Manchester's gravitation towards the Church of England.[1] It rallied Mancunian opinion to the support of Palmerston and paved the way for the decisive rejection of the representatives of the Manchester School in the post-war general election of 1857[2] when the importance of state action in the extension of the China market and of the informal empire of Britain was clearly recognized by the electorate. As the economy of the market failed to achieve full independence from the State the ethic of free trade became an end in itself rather than a means to a higher end and was transformed from a sovereign method of social regeneration into a mere mechanical interchange of commodities.

[1] [R. Lamb], 'Manchester', *Fraser's Magazine*, June 1853, 623.

[2] *Manchester Examiner*, 30 Mar. 1857, 2iii; A. W. Silver, *Manchester Men and Indian Cotton* (1966), 82–4.

CHAPTER 2

The Localization of the Industry in Lancashire

> Everywhere in Europe the hand-weaving districts have become seats of the modern textile industry. Gerhart von Schulze-Gaevernitz, *The Cotton Trade in England and on the Continent* (London, Simpkin, 1895), 123.

THE COTTON industry became more highly localized than any other contemporary manufacture in so far as it concentrated itself progressively within a third of a single county. That trend virtually identified Lancashire with a single trade and has often been interpreted in teleological terms which have largely deprived the cotton industries outside Lancashire of any historical significance and have relegated them to oblivion as ventures doomed from their very beginnings. During the heroic age of the industry it became dependent upon the water-wheel, the water-frame, and the hand-loom and became widely dispersed in quest of cheap power, extending itself over a larger area than ever before or afterwards. In the age of the steam-engine, the mule, and the power-loom it became increasingly concentrated in location. From the 1790s the industry expanded more rapidly in Lancashire than elsewhere as the mule began to assume technological leadership from the water-frame. The spread of the power-loom, the construction of a railway network, and the growth of a whole complex of dependent industries from the 1830s reinforced that centripetal trend. Within Lancashire the cotton industry developed at the expense of other textile industries and so acquired a relative immunity from competition for the factors of production. Outside Lancashire the industry suffered, especially after 1840, from the competition of other trades, such as the linen industry in Ulster, the hosiery industry in the east midlands, the woollen cloth industry in Yorkshire, and commerce, engineering, and shipbuilding in Glasgow. As the general rate of expansion of the industry slackened after the depression of 1837–42 the establishment of mills outside the Lancashire region became much less frequent and ceased altogether after 1861. The Cotton Famine exerted a decisive influence in hastening the geographical concentration of the industry, which was reinforced by the upsurge of yarn production by the mills of Oldham in the 1870s and by the shrinking profit margins in spinning after 1875. Under those pressures the decline of the industry outside Lancashire became manifest first in a relative stagnation and then in an absolute deterioration which, once begun, proved irreversible.

The influences which brought about that high degree of localization may be classified as original and acquired advantages. The original advantages of Lancashire comprised its poverty, its climate, its water supply, its textile tradition, and its mechanical inventions. The acquired advantages included its supply of coal, machinery, and labour, its access to the markets of Liverpool and Manchester, its low transport costs, and its auxiliary industries. The foundation of the industrial development of Lancashire lay in the comparative poverty of its natural resources which was accentuated by its relative isolation. Until the eighteenth century the society between Ribble and Mersey had maintained a largely self-contained existence upon the fringe of civilization. Cut off from the rest of England by barriers of mountain and marshland, it lay far distant from the great centres of economic activity and from the main channels of commerce. The poverty of a barren frontier region was manifest in the small population, in the limited supplies of stone and timber for building, and in the staple diet of oatmeal and offal: it also provided the great spur to the development of manufactures and the institutional framework for such development since it maintained the freedom of its communities from control by gild, corporation, or lord of the manor.

The clay soil of east Lancashire above the infertile millstone grit was unsuitable for arable cultivation and unrewarding to the farmer, being heavy, cold, and damp and lacking the lime needed to neutralize its acidity. Its poor quality contrasted sharply with the fertility of the soil in west Lancashire and created a broad division of function between the pastoral farming of the east and the arable farming of the west. The comparative sterility of the land in the east cheapened its price and facilitated its colonization from the sixteenth century by numerous smallholders who developed pastoral farming upon a basis of small-scale enterprise, satisfied their other needs through the sale of produce, and were thus drawn early within the sphere of influence of a money economy. Those farmers enjoyed all the freedom of frontiersmen and developed the habits of self-reliance essential to survival in so inhospitable a region, supplementing their income from the proceeds of a domestic textile industry. They developed the manufacture of coarse woollens under the influence of Yorkshire as west Lancashire developed the manufacture of linen under the influence of Ireland. The geographical division between the woollen and linen regions of the country broadly reflected that between the pastoral and arable economies and that between the prosperous society of the plain and the impoverished society of the eastern moorland frontier. Under the influence of mercantile capitalists, those two industries produced for sale rather than for subsistence and became the hosts upon which in the eighteenth century the cotton industry was grafted. The textile tradition of Lancashire was thus indigenous in origin and was not a product of the chance settlement of foreign immigrants in the fourteenth century, as maintained in the legend created by Thomas Fuller in his *Church History of Britain* (1655).[1] That myth nevertheless harmonized with the tradition of hospitality to the foreigner cherished in Manchester and was thereafter readily accepted, being perpetuated in the work of the founding fathers of economic history, Cunningham, Ashley, and Lipson.[2]

The high natural humidity of the region proved a valuable asset as the cotton industry expanded at the expense of the cloth industry because humidity remained essential in the manufacture of cotton and linen as it was not in that of wool. That humidity was maintained by the prevailing westerly winds which became saturated with moisture as they flowed unchecked

[1] T. Fuller, *The Church History of Britain* (London, Williams, 1655), Book IV, 111–12, XIV. Cent., A.D. 1336.

[2] A. P. Wadsworth, 'The Myth of the Flemish Weavers', *Transactions of the Rochdale Literary and Scientific Society*, xxl. 27 Nov. 1942, 52–60.

across the warm waters of the Atlantic and were forced to shed their moisture only when they reached the windward slopes of the Pennines. The mountainous backbone of northern England served a dual function: it kept back to leeward the harmful dry easterly winds and it attracted to its western slopes the rain-bearing westerlies, whose prevalence raised the moisture-content of the air almost to saturation-point and gave the region a rainfall higher than the national average. The Rossendale outcrop fulfilled a similar function to that of the Pennines and markedly extended to the west the area characterized by heavy rainfall and high humidity. The great clay bed of south Lancashire ensured the retention of the maximum amount of water and thus maintained the atmosphere in a state of natural moistness. Such a high degree of natural humidity was exceeded in England and Wales only on Dartmoor and supplied the most effective and economical means of conditioning cotton, even after the invention of artificial humidifiers.

Humidity was essential to an industry using cotton fibres which, being hygroscopic, became more pliable, less brittle, and easier to process as their moisture-content increased towards its optimum level. A high degree of humidity notably reduced the resistance to drawing and spinning which a dry and 'harsh' fibre would otherwise have offered. Thus it facilitated the preparatory processes of production, reduced the incidence of breaks in the yarn, and minimized the arduous and time-consuming labour of piecing together broken ends. It also neutralized the tendency of static electricity to make yarn fuzzy and difficult to handle. The yarn so spun proved superior in both quantity and quality to that spun under less favourable conditions because less waste was created and the thread was more uniform in consistency. The influence of humidity made possible the localization of coarse spinning in Oldham and of fine spinning in Bolton since those two localities received the highest rainfall in Lancashire. In weaving the influence of humidity was much more important than in spinning because it reduced the incidence of faults in the web, facilitated the production of a better and heavier cloth, and made possible the development of fine weaving. Hand-loom weavers humidified their warps by dressing the threads with size, by working in a cellar rather than in a ground-floor dwelling, and by using a damp earthen floor beneath their loom, supplemented by a bowl of water when the wind was dry. Power-loom manufacturers secured similar benefits by seeking out valley-floor sites, by using a single-storey shed built close to or sunk into the earth, and by placing porous flags beneath their looms. The influence of humidity became even more important in facilitating the manufacture of the best quality of cloth from the worst quality of yarn as the quality of raw cotton deteriorated. The introduction of the practice of 'steaming', or artificial humidification, was necessitated by the enforced use of Surat cotton during the Cotton Famine and testified to the technical and commercial value of a favourable micro-climate. The importance of humidity was recognized by all observers and disputed by none.[1] Its true value was proved by the harmful influence of a dry east wind, which reduced the humidity in the atmosphere to such an extent that threads broke faster than piecers could mend them and the spinning of very high counts became almost impossible. Such a wind reduced the quantity of cloth woven and the amount of wages earned by weavers by nearly one-tenth and worsened even more the quality of both yarn and cloth. Thus the influence of Lancashire's natural humidity could be estimated as the economic equivalent of a protective tariff of 10 per cent.[2]

Humidity was not the sole or even the predominant cause of the concentration of the cotton industry in east Lancashire but was invariably recognized until 1927 as an important contributory influence. In that year the geographer H. W. Ogden first depreciated the importance of humidity in a reaction against the exaggerated claims made by climatic determinists.[3] He suggested that rainfall and the peculiarly soft water it produced had exerted a more powerful influence than humidity

[1] W. Hoyle, *An Inquiry into the Causes of the Present Long-Continued Depression in the Cotton Trade* (London, Simpkin, 1869), 16; B. A. Dobson, *Humidity in Cotton Spinning* (Manchester, Heywood, 1897), 9, 15; C. H. Lander, *Ventilation and Humidity in Textile Mills and Factories* (London, Longmans, 1914), 9–10, 13–15, 42–4.

[2] Albert D. Shaw, *Extracts from a Special Report on the Cotton Goods Trade of Lancashire* (Manchester, Ireland, 1883), 28–33.

[3] H. W. Ogden, 'The Geographical Basis of the Lancashire Cotton Industry', *Journal of the Manchester Geographical Society*, 1927, 8–30, published in a special issue devoted to authoritative papers on the north-west of England designed for the International Geographical Congress at Cambridge in 1928, and reprinted in the *Journal of the Textile Institute*, 18, 1927, T573–94.

in the localization of the industry. He recognized that east Lancashire enjoyed a much higher rainfall than west Lancashire but distinguished between humidity and rainfall in order to depreciate the importance of humidity in itself. He reasoned that humidity could not have been the sole localizing influence since west Lancashire was, in his estimation, just as humid as east Lancashire. He thought that the soft lime-free water of the Carboniferous region of the east was far superior for industrial purposes to the hard water of the Triassic region of the west and was far more important than humidity as a localizing influence. Apparently he was inspired to champion the cause of soft water as a determining influence in industrial location by the work of a chemical engineer,[1] who had studied the influence of water only in terms of its chemical composition and only in relation to the ancillary processes of dyeing and bleaching. Thus Ogden exaggerated the role of the finishing industries in determining the location of the cotton manufacture and paid no attention to the central processes of spinning and weaving.

The Ogden thesis embodied a major revision of historical tradition in the iconoclastic vein fashionable during the 1920s. What appears truly remarkable in retrospect about such a provocative concept is not that it was rapidly accepted by historians, especially by those outside Lancashire, in the revisionist climate of the 1930s but that Ogden himself should ever have formulated such an idea in flat contradiction to his own long experience beneath the implacable grey skies of Manchester. The original thesis has been simplified and even distorted in the process of its diffusion so that it has been assumed that Ogden wholly denied the influence of humidity and minimized that of rainfall upon the location of the industry. The argument has never been accepted by Lancastrian scholars and remains to the informed observer fundamentally unbalanced, superfluous, and untenable. It lacks the corroboration of any contemporary evidence and is based upon statistics of 1893–1922, unsupported by any awareness of historical variation in degrees of water-hardness, in the regional incidence of rainfall, or in the fineness of counts spun. Apparently Ogden believed that fine spinning had developed in the later nineteenth century rather than in the later eighteenth century and he certainly exagger-

[1] A. A. Pollitt, *The Technology of Water* (London, Benn, 1924), 62–6.

ated, as Wilfred Smith noted in 1948,[1] the hardness of the water in west Lancashire in contrast to the softness of that in east Lancashire, thereby creating a fictitious difference between the two areas. Above all, he wholly neglected to consider the comparative advantages in soil and climate of west Lancashire for agricultural pursuits and those of east Lancashire for industrial avocations. The survival of so ambitious an historical revision mildly embarrassed later geographers and necessitated its emphatic refutation in 1960 by H. B. Rodgers.[2] No longer should it be necessary for historians to support a thesis abandoned by geographers or boldly to reject for no valid reason the inherited tradition of the locality, the accumulated wisdom of the past, and the unanimous opinion of all contemporary experts.

The most important natural resource of east Lancashire lay in its water supply. The rivers of the region were non-navigable and served primarily as sources of water, being fed regularly throughout the year by streams from the great natural reservoirs formed by the peat bogs of the uplands. The millstone grit beneath the peat served as a perfect natural filter to remove any impurities. The clay soil of the vales prevented excessive leakage through the earth as the rivers made their way to the plain and the sea. The blanket of humid air prevented excessive evaporation into the atmosphere. Such an abundant supply of water was essential to the industries whose demands absorbed up to half of the water used in Manchester and Oldham. The finishing industries consumed enormous quantities of water and required a soft lime-free water which would neither waste soap nor resist dye and which remained tenfold as important to them as it was to the spinning and weaving industries. The bleaching, dyeing, and printing industries exerted a strong attractive force upon their supplier-industries and enabled Lancashire to centralize all the processes of the manufacture of calico within the bounds of the region of lime-free water, to the south of the limestone beyond the Ribble, and to the north-west of the limestone of the Derbyshire Peaks.

* * *

[1] W. Smith, *An Economic Geography of Great Britain* (London, Methuen, 1949), 466–8.

[2] H. B. Rodgers, 'The Lancashire Cotton Industry in 1840', *Transactions of the Institute of British Geographers*, 1960, 142.

The acquired advantages of Lancashire reinforced its original advantages and provided its industry with an increasingly valuable range of cost-cutting facilities, which developed in proportion as the industry increased in size and in the degree of its local concentration. They comprised the auxiliary industries of the cotton region, its steam-engineering industry, its textile engineering industry, its reserves of coal and iron, its great markets, and its pioneer railway system. The increasing use of steam-power in place of water-power undoubtedly gave Lancashire a growing advantage over other regions in its possession of the cheapest coals, the softest water, and the most efficient heavy engineering industry. In the age of the water-wheel the narrow rocky valleys or cloughs of Rossendale had been dammed with relative ease and a minimum of expense in order to build up the head of water necessary for the supply of power. The rivers of east Lancashire had exerted a magnetic attraction upon industry, drawing mills to their banks in such numbers as to become the hardest-worked watercourses in the world. The use of water-power had however developed throughout the whole area of the Pennine uplands and had undoubtedly operated as a decentralizing force, encouraging the dispersion of industry rather than its concentration. That trend was reversed after the perfection of the steam-engine, which first became a competitive prime mover with the invention of the governor in 1788 and was applied to drive the mule partially in the 1790s and fully from 1830 with the development of the self-actor. Steam-power was even applied by 1815 to the roller-spinning frame which when so driven became the throstle-frame and the ancestor of the ring-frame. The steam-engine had one minor advantage over the water-wheel in that its boiler could supply heat through steam-pipes as well as power. Its main advantage in the elimination of any natural restrictions upon the production of power increased when factory legislation from 1819 limited the 'making up' of time lost during summer droughts.

The adoption of the steam-engine gave a new impetus to the cotton industry, especially in the towns of the Lancashire plain where water-power was lacking or limited in amount. Its capacity for driving more machines from a single source of power required more efficient transmission-systems, facilitated an eventual increase in the size of the individual mill, and enhanced the competitive capacity of Lancashire factories in relation to water-powered country mills. Its application to the 'steam-loom' from the 1820s opened up a whole field of manufacture thitherto closed to the water-wheel and gave a new intensity to the spread of steam-power in Lancashire between 1820 and 1850. Water-power apparently provided the cotton industry with more power than steam-engines did until the mid-1820s and was still ranked by Baines in 1835 as one of the primary advantages of Lancashire for the successful prosecution of manufactures.[1] Its great economic advantage was that it was free where steam-power was not. Thus it continued in use, especially for throstle-spinning, in the vales of Yorkshire, Cheshire, and above all, of Derbyshire where the water-wheel had first been successfully applied to the spinning of cotton and where it continued until the early 1850s to furnish more power to the industry than did the steam-engine. In 1850 water-wheels still supplied 30 per cent of the power used by the English cotton industry outside Lancashire but only 6·7 per cent of the power used by the industry within Lancashire.

Lancashire acquired a growing advantage over other regions through the development of steam-engine manufacture and through its possession of cheap supplies of coal, which also supplied gas from 1803 for lighting mills. The cotton industry became increasingly concentrated upon the south Lancashire coalfield, where all the cotton towns save Preston were located, because low-grade boiler fuel, unlike expensive domestic coal, could not bear high transport costs. The importance of cheap fuel costs as a localizing influence has been emphasized by H. B. Rodgers to such a degree that he has almost seemed to favour a geological determinism in place of the hydrological determinism of Ogden. Fuel costs were not however of primary importance to the industry in an age of high profit margins. The beam-engine coupled with the Lancashire boiler developed by Fairbairn in 1844 and improved by the insertion of the Galloway tubes invented in 1849 served as a comparatively

[1] E. Baines, *History of the Cotton Manufacture* (1835), 85; A. J. Taylor, 'Concentration and Localisation of the British Cotton Industry' (M.A. thesis, University of Manchester, 1947), 104; S. D. Chapman, 'The Cost of Power in the Industrial Revolution in Britain: the Case of the Textile Industry', *Midland History*, 1976, 1–23.

economical prime mover. Coal remained cheap in Lancashire, which ranked until 1883 as the largest producer after Durham, and consumed most of its own production until the opening of the Manchester Ship Canal. The very abundance of coal discouraged any economy in its use until prices rose sharply during the coal famine of 1871–3,[1] when the feed-water heater invented in 1845 began to win general acceptance as a fuel-economizer and so paved the way for the spread from the 1890s of the super-heater. Fuel costs were much less than either the cost of raw material or the cost of labour. They were most important in the coarse trade and least important in the fine trade, where they were easily absorbed by the high price of the product. The decline in transport costs between the 1830s and the 1860s cheapened the cost of coal to local mills. Country mills beyond the limits of the coalfield undoubtedly faced a challenge to their position from the adoption of the steam-engine in the plains but compensated for their distance from a colliery by such other factors as cheapness of land, of plant, or of labour. Even within Lancashire the steam-engine does not seem to have exerted a major determining influence upon the location of the industry since it neither reduced the attractive power of the rivers and canals nor attracted mills away from the waterside towards the coalfields. The colliery towns undoubtedly acquired a well-balanced mill-and-pit economy but did not become major centres of the cotton industry. The great centres of coal production grew up around Wigan in south-central Lancashire and remained separate from the main cotton towns of east Lancashire, where the steam-engine gave the mill its typical chimneyed profile and the factory-town its distinctive horizon of massed mill chimneys.

The textile engineering industry supplied the cotton trade of Lancashire with an invaluable support which had no parallel elsewhere in Britain or in the world. That industry developed two main branches in light engineering, which supplied first spindles and then power-looms, and in heavy engineering, which supplied prime movers. Native and immigrant talent established the trade upon a firm basis during the eighteenth

[1] *Manchester Guardian*, 27 August 1872, 4iii, 20 Feb. 1873, 8iii, 26 Feb. 5vi, 15 March, 9v, 24 Mar., 3iv; A. Hildebrandt, 'Economy of Fuel in Mills', *Journal of the Society for the Promotion of Scientific Industry*, Oct. 1874, 35–8.

century. Thereafter its further development was stimulated by the rapid expansion of the local market, by the close association between engineers and spinners, by the exacting requirements of the fine spinners, by the restrictive practices favoured by the aristocratic mule spinners, and by the pressure exerted by machine-spinning upon the unmechanized process of hand-weaving. The market for textile machinery became large enough to permit the separation of the industry both from the cotton industry and from general engineering. That vital auxiliary trade concentrated closely upon the task of supplying the local staple industry, did not diversify into new fields, and provided no seed-bed of engineers for other industries. In the east midlands frame-smiths remained oriented to the demands of the hosiery industry while in Glasgow mechanical talent was diverted from the 1830s into marine engineering. In Lancashire engineering became specialized in the service of the cotton textile industry. The massive expansion of the local market reduced the industry's costs by providing full employment for highly skilled and specialized workers and enabled it to supply machinery of the highest quality at the lowest price and in the shortest time. Even the most specialized of cotton firms were freed from the need to maintain their own expensive repair-shops and reserve-stocks of machinery and spares, which remained indispensable to isolated or foreign mills and raised their costs in proportion.

Textile machine-makers remained less specialized than firms in the cotton industry. To some extent they limited their own market by the manufacture of machines which were solid, heavy, and intended to last rather than to be speedily replaced. They sought to expand their market by aiding the continued expansion of the cotton industry, by encouraging the more rapid depreciation and replacement of machinery, by undertaking the perpetual improvement of their products and the constant refinement of the industrial arts, and by educating their clients in their own view of technology as a progressive rather than a static instrument of production. Competition within their ranks encouraged a long-term reduction in the price of machinery since engineers were too jealous of their compeers ever to consider united action, least of all in the maintenance of prices. Machine-makers helped to finance the purchase of machinery by their customers, whether large or small. They extended loans to reliable customers amongst the large employers to permit them to improve and extend their plant. They encouraged the renting of room and power by small masters in both the spinning and weaving industries, so giving Lancashire a source of new employers lacking elsewhere. Their influence powerfully stimulated the progress of mechanization and accentuated the pressure of competition by placing a premium upon innovation. In an industry traditionally hostile to exclusive rights few barriers to effective competion were raised by monopolistic patents save in the case of the self-acting mule and the combing machine.

Textile engineering found security from the recurrent depressions which afflicted it, especially in 1826 and 1841, in the supply of foreign markets. The repeal in 1843 of the Act of 1786 forbidding the export of machinery gave legal sanction to what had become a customary practice in defiance or in evasion of the law. That triumph for freedom of trade helped to make Lancashire the textile workshop of the world and the home of the skilled artisan: it enabled Manchester to replace London as the metropolis of engineering, with a separate 'Engineering Exchange' close to the Royal Exchange. In turn the machine-making industry achieved such a degree of general technical superiority as to establish British supremacy within every other branch of modern industry.[1] The export of spinning machinery proved of more immediate benefit to Russia than to any other country and imparted a distinct impetus to what S. G. Strumilin in 1944 termed its 'industrial revolution' of 1830–60.[2] That trade was rightly deemed to be contrary to the long-term interests of Lancashire but could not be curtailed because the engineering industry had effectively established its own functional autonomy. The cotton industry of Lancashire suffered little harm since textile engineering began for the first time to profit from the economies of large-scale production, transmitted to Lancashire the benefits of the experience acquired in the service of the world market, and notably improved the foreign

[1] J. R. M'Culloch, *The Principles of Political Economy* (Edinburgh, Black, 1849, 4th edn.), 107.

[2] W. L. Blackwell, *The Beginnings of Russian Industrialization* (Princeton University Press, 1968), 42–7, 402–3; M. E. Falkus, *The Industrialization of Russia 1700–1914* (London, Macmillan, 1972), 31–40.

inventions such as the ring spindle which it absorbed. The importance of the export of machinery must not however be exaggerated since it included the export of second-hand machines, especially from Oldham after the Great Exhibition of 1851, and comprised spinning rather than weaving machinery: it developed only gradually in scale, became significant only after the depression of 1877–9, and was deemed worthy of separate record in the trade statistics only from 1893.[1] In the long run the engineering industry undoubtedly facilitated the world-wide dispersion of the cotton industry and then became its residual heir in Lancashire: in the short run its influence served powerfully to reinforce its increasing concentration within the Lancashire region.

* * *

The expansion of the markets of Liverpool and Manchester provided Lancashire with a great and growing advantage over other regions in the development of the cotton industry. The services of Liverpool were indispensable to a manufacture wholly dependent upon imported raw material but have been inappropriately minimized in the past by an exaggeration of the role of the export market of Manchester. Liverpool grew more rapidly in population and wealth than Manchester during the first half of the eighteenth century and became by 1800 the second city of the kingdom as well as the premier city of the county, the seat of its mercantile élite, and the summit of the social gradient extending from the Pennines to the sea. It was originally and remained primarily a port of import rather than of export for the cotton industry. The expansion of its import trade in raw cotton was facilitated by its transatlantic connections and by the supersession of the West Indies by the U.S.A. as the major source of supply. Liverpool had replaced London as the main port for the import of cotton from 1795 as the U.S.A. expanded its production after the invention of the saw-gin. From 1800 onwards it imported more cotton from the U.S.A. than from the West Indies, whose exports declined from 1804 under the impact of American competition. Its share of the number of bales imported first

[1] *Textile Mercury*, Jan. 1894, 22–3, May 1895, 365.

exceeded 50 per cent in 1803 and first surpassed 75 per cent in 1807.[1] The new staple trade afforded effective compensation to the port for the loss of the slave trade, whose abolition effectively doomed the cultivation of cotton in the West Indies. The imports of cotton increased from a negligible proportion of its general trade until they became its largest single import, probably in the 1820s when the 'cotton triangle' was established between the ports of New Orleans, New York, and Liverpool. A large-scale export trade in cotton goods also developed after its merchant-shipowners entered the trade to India in 1814 and that to China in 1834. That export trade in the manufactures of its industrial hinterland developed markedly in the 1820s when Liverpool's share in the exports of the kingdom apparently first exceeded that of London. It furnished much more profitable freight than did raw cotton and supplied the outward cargoes lacking to the Continental rivals of Liverpool such as Le Havre. Thus by 1850 the port attracted, especially from the U.S.A., up to tenfold the tonnage of shipping registered in Liverpool itself and was thereby able to enjoy the advantage of lower freight rates than its competitors. It became the first and greatest harbour of England and the world, clearing until 1884 more tonnage than London and conferring upon its industrial hinterland a large advantage over the midlands. As America became the leading source of supply of raw cotton, Liverpool became the great market for cotton and attracted to its wharves the cotton of Bombay and Alexandria. Thus it became the universal depot and market for the cotton crops of the world and made available to spinners a wider range of choice than that possessed by lands confined to the use of home-grown cotton.

Liverpool beat down the competition for the cotton trade of all rival ports such as Bristol, Glasgow, and Hull and prevented the emergence of any new competitors such as Birkenhead or Fleetwood. The growth of its cotton market contributed to the decline of the cotton market of Manchester after 1814 since two such markets could no longer coexist within a range of forty miles. With its hinterland the port developed close ties and maintained its historic role as the great agent in the

[1] M. M. Edwards, *The Growth of the British Cotton Trade 1780–1815* (1967), 111, 250–1.

improvement of communications within Lancashire, becoming the primary and essential intermediary between the outside world and the cotton industry located deep in the interior. It financed the construction of the Liverpool–Manchester railway between the county's two great markets and along its main commercial axis. The influence of that railway decisively centralized the raw cotton market in Liverpool, especially at the expense of Glasgow, separated it physically from the market for manufactured cotton in Manchester, and made the direct purchase of cotton in the U.S.A., even by large spinners, increasingly uneconomic. It made possible the weekly visit by Lancashire spinners to buy cotton in a market where they enjoyed the widest possible range of choice, the services of highly skilled brokers, and the facilities for rapid shipment to the mill of the cotton railways, especially after the rate wars of 1849–51.[1] Those spinners derived from such regular and close contact a great advantage over spinners in other regions, especially since the brokers were linked by origin and function more closely to the cotton districts than to other parts: they could reduce their stocks to a minimum supply of 3–4 weeks and replenish them as necessary from Liverpool. Continental spinners followed the example of Lancashire spinners and used the services of commission agents but paid 2 per cent more than English customers and had to carry large reserve stocks in extensive warehouses, so requiring a correspondingly larger capital.

The Liverpool cotton market became the most highly specialized of markets. The sale of raw cotton invited speculation more than any other commodity because it satisfied a demand which was inelastic in the short term. Fluctuations in its price were greater than in that of any other raw material but were less acute in Liverpool than in Le Havre. The market was very difficult to corner because of the vast quantity imported, the small proportion handled by even the largest of importers, and the capacity of raw cotton to survive storage for years without suffering the deterioration which affected most other agricultural produce. The combination of skill, audacity, will-power, and capital necessary to accomplish such a manœuvre was very rarely mustered with success. Spinners

[1] F. C. Mather, *After the Canal Duke* (Oxford, Clarendon Press, 1970), 195–225.

nevertheless thrice in 14 years, in 1833, 1838, and 1847, adopted the most unusual tactic of working short-time in order to force down prices. They did not need to repeat that combined action until the four successful corners of 1879, 1881, 1883, and 1888. Liverpool became increasingly devoted to commerce as its industries declined after 1815 and increased its population more rapidly than Manchester between 1821 and 1871, when 'the largest purely mercantile community on this side of the Atlantic'[1] enjoyed its golden age as a cotton market. Thereafter its monopolistic position was undermined by a combination of influences, the direct import of raw cotton from India by Continental ports after the opening of the Suez Canal, the organization in 1870 of the New York cotton market for future trading, and the relaying of the Atlantic cable in 1872 and the resultant extension of the commercial influence of New York. Liverpool however developed its own futures market in raw cotton and triumphantly survived the opening of the Manchester Ship Canal, preserving its standards until 1923 as the basis of all European transactions in cotton.

The great market for cotton manufactures remained in Manchester, which displayed a prodigious and terrible momentum in the rapidity of its expansion from the status of the seventh largest town in the country in 1775 to that of the third largest in 1801. Between 1790 and 1820 the town experienced a great industrial boom: thereafter its trade developed even more rapidly than its manufactures and its commercial hegemony within the cotton industry became virtually unassailable, so enabling Lancashire to profit from the early development of a mercantile metropolis. The bases of its pre-eminence were laid and strengthened neither by Nature nor by the State but by the hand of man. Manchester enjoyed few advantages of site or location since it did not lie upon the main route to the north and lacked the great advantage possessed by Glasgow in its estuary and port. Nor did it enjoy the protection conferred by a fort, by walls, or by a military barracks. Lastly, it was denied the prestige derived from the exercise within its limits of political, administrative, legal, or ecclesiastical functions, remaining dependent upon the Lancaster assizes until 1835 and

[1] J. Bryce, 'General Report on the County of Lancaster', *Schools Inquiry Commission* (London, Eyre, 1868), ix. 733.

upon the see of Chester until 1853. Those disadvantages were not redressed by any aid from the State. The supreme advantage of such an unhistoric city lay in its freedom from control by borough, guild, or mercantile monopoly and in its lack, until 1838, of a corporation. That freedom from the traditions of the past was reinforced by the dynamic influence of a young, immigrant, and cosmopolitan population and by the absence of any sense of the Greek idea of the city. The lack of any communal spirit nurtured an unrestrained and hyperintelligent individualism which contrasted sharply with the corporate tradition of Liverpool and made the city a standing rock of offence to the aesthetic sensibility of the southerner.

The merchants of Manchester had been merchant–manufacturers in the eighteenth century: they became pure merchants in the early nineteenth century, conducting the home trade from their warehouses and the export trade through the Exchange. They remained the central figures within the industry, standing between producer and ultimate consumer. They supplied the capital and the managerial ability necessary for the effective organization of the labour of industrial Lancashire: they reduced the working capital necessary to the manufacturer by bearing all the costs of reaching the distant consumer. Their capital, their specialized knowledge, and their mercantile connections made them the virtual employers of the bulk of the operatives within the industry, as the shipowners of Liverpool became the effective employers of the port's dockworkers. 'They are the generals and rulers of human toil.'[1] They used the Chamber of Commerce to enhance their opportunities to profit by the operation of a market economy with the very minimum of legal or conventional restraints. Their influence was reinforced by that of specialized yarn and cloth agents and by that of foreign merchants, who became far more important in Manchester than they were in Liverpool or even in London.

Manchester became a great centre for the generation of capital as the weekly turnover in its trade decupled from £1m. in the 1850s to £10m. in the 1880s:[2] it concentrated within its

[1] H. Taine, *Notes sur l'Angleterre* (Paris, Hachette, 1872), 295.

[2] *The Times*, 11 Feb. 1857, 5v, T. Bazley; *Manchester Guardian*, 11 Mar. 1882, 12iv, T. B. Moxon.

limits a much higher proportion of the wealth of the shire than of its population and reinvested much capital in the improvement of the communications essential to its function. As the great citadel of private enterprise it remained notably inhospitable to joint-stock companies. Such a climate of opinion proved equally unfavourable to the development of such working-class institutions as trade unions and co-operative societies, to the toleration of parliaments of labour, and to the reception of the labour theory of value. Unrest erupted at Peterloo and in what Carlyle called 'the Manchester Insurrection' of 1842 but remained sporadic rather than endemic, partly because of the high level of wages. The town became a great forcing-house of commercial enterprise through the influence of competition and the financial discipline of short terms or cash payment. That new school of business training became a Mecca for aspirant merchants and the true metropolis of the middle class.[1] Therein money became 'the universal leverage of society' and commerce the predominant means of pecuniary accumulation and of social mobility. Economic activity became almost the sole channel of social ascent, fulfilling the function performed by education in the twentieth century. The self-made man became the archetypical Manchester man and remained infused by an abiding scorn for unearned hereditary wealth. Inevitably the brisk pace of life, the fiercely competitive atmosphere, and the unrelenting stress upon monetary values engendered a high degree of status-anxiety amongst the socially mobile and thereby made the town a dynamic centre of economic growth.

One distinct advantage of Manchester lay in its ancient textile tradition and its wide range of manufacturing industries, especially its finishing trades. Those industries enabled merchants to control the finishing processes of cloth and so to preserve their position as merchant-converters. They were extended by the development from the 1790s of fine spinning, based upon the mule and the high degree of local humidity. During the wars of 1793–1815 the town also acquired a silk industry which flourished beneath the protection from French competition conferred by the war and so confirmed the tendency for the most valuable branches of the textile trade to settle in Man-

[1] M. Arnold, 'My Countrymen', *Cornhill Magazine*, Feb. 1866, 153.

chester. The development of engineering made the city from the 1820s a centre of technical innovation, especially in spinning technology. The extension of communications was undoubtedly the most important single determinant of the expansion of its commercial influence. The town served as the focus of the river and road system of east Lancashire, being sited at the junction of three rivers and of five Roman roads and lying conveniently for communication with Yorkshire just to the west of the narrowest section of the Pennines. The extension of turnpike roads and canals compensated for its natural disadvantages, enhanced its influence within the surrounding region, and prevented the rise of any competitive market by providing the adjacent towns with easier links with itself than with each other and by establishing itself as the essential intermediary between the cotton district and the rest of the country. The town became the centre of an increasingly dense cobweb of communications, transportation, and commerce which made it the focus of the industry of all Lancashire and a vast reservoir for the production of 280 villages and towns. Thus it became identified, as 'Cottonborough' (1851) or as 'Cottonopolis' (1854)[1], with the avid pursuit of a single trade.

Manchester benefited from the expansion of population and wealth throughout the north, the growing concentration of the cotton industry within the orbit of its influence, the increasing diversification of its products, the growing dependence of the industry upon distant markets, the great boom in the exports of yarn, and the expansion of the trade of Liverpool. Ready access to the world's greatest market for cotton manufactures conferred upon Lancashire a unique advantage lacked by the industry elsewhere, whether in Britain or abroad. The improvement in communications facilitated the extension of Manchester's financial influence through the development of its banking and insurance facilities and through the successive establishment of the first provincial branch of the Bank of England in 1826 and of the first provincial banking clearing house in 1872. During the great crisis of the Cotton Famine the influence of the Manchester market became paramount

[1] W. H. Ainsworth, *Mervyn Clitheroe* (London, Routledge, 1858, first published in parts in 1851–2), 4, 60; [J. Lowe], 'A Manchester Warehouse', *Household Words*, 6 May 1854, 269.

throughout the trade as turnpikes were abolished on the main roads leading from the city, the cotton railways issued contract-tickets to country manufacturers, and Manchester banks established branches in the cotton towns. The completion of a world-wide network of cables in 1870–2, under the guidance of the Manchester merchant John Pender,[1] decisively centralized the world market in cotton goods in Manchester. The advent of the telephone in the early 1880s reinforced the hegemony of the city as a centre of communications.

'Cottonborough' became the aggressive central force within a decentralized trade and 'the heart of the industry of the United Kingdom'.[2] Its function was not political, social, religious, or cultural but essentially economic and primarily commercial. It was not a capital of industry so much as an emporium of commerce: its mills were heavily concentrated in the ghetto of Ancoats and its artisans lacked the support of any ancient craft traditions or any sense of corporate unity. Manchester never became the sole commercial capital of Lancashire but was forced to concede to Liverpool superiority in population, commerce, and wealth. Within east Lancashire, however, its power remained invincible since the industry could afford only one great entrepôt and intercivic jealousy was almost as great as in Italy. Thus the attempts by Blackburn in 1865 and by Rochdale in 1884 to establish their own independent exchanges failed for lack of support. The primary function of Manchester was the gathering of commercial intelligence, its secondary function the exchange of goods at the most profitable prices in the light of such intelligence. The impersonal force of the market operating through merchants and manufacturers found there its most congenial base of operations. The real heart of the city became the Exchange, 'the parliament house of the lords of cotton',[3] rather than the church or the town hall and its supreme function remained that of a pure entrepôt, a Shanghai of the north.

The Manchester market became the main unifying bond

[1] *The Times*, 8 July 1896, 10i–ii, *Manchester Weekly Times*, 10 July 1896, 3vi, 4ii.

[2] F. Engels, *The Condition of the Working Class in England* (Oxford, Blackwell, 1958, 1971), 50.

[3] W. C. Taylor, *Notes of a Tour in the Manufacturing Districts of Lancashire* (London, Duncan, 1842), 10.

within an increasingly differentiated industry: it mobilized the energies of society, co-ordinated the activities of a myriad small firms and united their productive efforts under the auspices of 'the metropolis of the manufacturing world',[1] so intensifying the links between commerce and industry to the highest degree. It became the principal agent in the transformation of the way of life of Lancashire and in the diffusion from 'the Utopia of Bentham'[2] of the gospel of economic rationality. Manchester differed profoundly from the factory towns of Lancashire in its functions as a metropolis, as a nodal centre of communications, and as a monopolist of the most profitable sectors of the cotton trade, being dedicated to commercial and financial pursuits and especially to the export trade. Its manufactures included a highly diversified cotton industry as well as substantial engineering and publishing industries. It also differed from the cotton towns in the size and rate of growth of its population, in the diversity of its occupations, and in the size and wealth of its middle classes as well as in the high wages earned by its working classes. Its cosmopolitan population included foreign and Irish colonies and contained many more specialized trades and professions than the factory towns could afford. It is therefore misleading to describe those towns as 'all of them little Manchesters'[3] 'dependent upon the great central mart, as colonies are dependent upon the mother country'.[4] They remained as proud of their independence as the cities of medieval Italy or Flanders and as jealous of Manchester as that city was of London. They were even spurred on by its massive expansion to assert the more their own individuality. Thus Manchester exerted neither political nor cultural influence within the shire. The centralization of economic life around such a metropolis nevertheless seriously unbalanced the life of the towns of Lancashire as they lost their commercial functions and were forced to specialize purely in industrial activity.

[1] P. Gaskell, *The Manufacturing Population of England* (London, Baldwin, 1833), 229.

[2] L. Faucher, *Études sur l'Angleterre* (Paris, Guillaumin, 1845), i. 323.

[3] *Morning Chronicle, Supplement*, 21 Dec. 1849, IV, 'The Manufacturing Districts. Manchester'.

[4] D. Buxton, 'On the Rise of the Manufacturing Towns of Lancashire and Cheshire', *Transactions of the Historic Society of Lancashire and Cheshire*, 8 May 1856, 199–200.

'Cottonopolis' itself paid a certain social price for its economic pre-eminence. It became a centre for the manufacture of rents as its population expanded, the density of settlement increased to a level surpassed only in Liverpool, and land values rose. Space was increasingly put to the most profitable use by means of overbuilding, overcrowding, and the creation of cellar-warehouses. As commerce expanded at the expense of industry population began to decline from the 1850s in the central township and the wealthier classes of 'the most aristocratic town in England' segregated themselves from the poorer.[1] As a town without a founder, hero, or symbol Manchester for long remained a city in search of a myth which would elevate its citizens above the prosaic level of their daily working life. That myth it ultimately found in the creed of free trade and in the identification of commerce with civilization, thereby supplying Lancashire with a moral leadership largely lacking in other regions. In the climactic decade of the 1840s Manchester reached the peak of its importance in both Lancashire and England and its mercantile community helped to revolutionize the commercial policy of the State. Thereafter it proudly ranked itself as the second city of the Empire, '*the heart of the kingdom*',[2] the primary source of its power, and 'the very symbol of civilization, foremost in the march of improvement, a grand incarnation of progress'.[3]

* * *

The progressive development of transport facilities proved particularly important to Lancashire which had remained isolated from the rest of the country until the eighteenth century. Such facilities transformed what had been one of the most backward regions into one of the most advanced, endowing the shire with an increasingly dense network of inland communications and giving it a growing advantage over other older regions. They linked it to the rest of England and gave it a vested interest in

[1] R. Parkinson, *On the Present Condition of the Labouring Poor in Manchester; with Hints for Improving It* (London, Simpkin, 1841, 23pp.), 12; C. Shaw, *Manufacturing Districts. Replies of Sir Charles Shaw to Lord Ashley, M.P. regarding the Education, and Moral and Physical Condition of the Labouring Classes* (London, Ollivier, 1843), 9–10.

[2] *Manchester Guardian*, 13 Dec. 1845, 2v, Prospectus of the *Manchester Examiner*.

[3] *Chamber's Edinburgh Journal*, 17 Apr. 1858, 251, 'The City of Men'.

their further improvement, especially in times of declining prices. Being closely oriented to the service of the developing staple trade, those facilities were particularly necessary because of the industry's dependence upon the import of raw cotton and its increasing dependence upon the export of cotton manufactures. They proved especially valuable in the carriage of cheap, bulk commodities, and, above all, of the cotton and coal which became in the age of steam the main supplies used by the industry. They notably extended the influence of the markets of Liverpool and Manchester and that of a market economy in general. They enlarged the catchment area for the supply of Lancashire and made it less dependent upon local raw materials and foodstuffs by facilitating their carriage from much further afield. Thus they enabled its population to expand far beyond the limit imposed by its own natural resources. They undoubtedly captured the imagination of contemporaries, especially when railways enhanced the stability of society and brought to an end the era of sporadic riots which had erupted between 1769 and 1842. Inevitably the importance of such facilities tended to be exaggerated by contemporaries in contrast to the influence of such prosaic factors as power costs.

Canals did not play the same central role in the cotton districts which they did in the economic development of Liverpool, the midlands, or of South Wales. Their construction coincided with the great age of the water-wheel and of the geographical dispersion of the industry. Lancashire acquired ten canals, of which five served the cotton districts, especially those to the north and south of Rossendale. Those waterways offered the great advantage of cheap transport and exerted an attractive force upon mills comparable to that of the rivers whose water they consumed and whose influence they extended. The hilly heartland of east Lancashire in Rossendale presented however a barrier to canal construction and remained deprived of the benefits of cheap water transport since its rivers were unnavigable and its terrain was skirted rather than penetrated by canals. At least as important as the building of canals was the construction of roads, which served as the chief means for the communication of intelligence in the pre-telegraph age and as the main vehicles of a market economy. They linked Liverpool to Manchester and to the factory towns: they radiated from

Manchester as canals did not and made it the Rome of the empire of 'Cottonia', which they also connected with the rest of England.

Railways fulfilled national, regional, and local functions. On a national level they counteracted the subversive anti-metropolitan influence of the canals and enabled London to reassert its influence upon the life of the nation. They built their first regional system in Lancashire under the influence of the cotton lords[1] and thereby centred the early railway system upon Manchester as the canal system focussed upon Birmingham, so largely enhancing the economic advantages enjoyed by the industries of Lancashire. They endowed the county with a modern system of transport which competed with the existing system, brought to an end the construction of new roads between the 1840s and the 1860s, and shattered the monopoly of the Bridgewater and Mersey Navigation. They linked Lancashire to Yorkshire by three trans-Pennine lines between 1841 and 1847 and then between 1846 and 1852 they penetrated Rossendale, so extending their influence more widely than that of the canals.

The railways fulfilled additional functions to the transport of goods. The railway companies provided storage facilities in their warehouses and so reduced the need of local spinners for outbuildings and storerooms. They also transmitted market intelligence by telegraph and furnished the market economy with a highly effective vehicle. They linked the factory towns of the shire to the markets of Liverpool and Manchester before they linked them to one another. They helped to extend the influence of Manchester throughout industrial Lancashire, though they did little to reduce the vitality of local particularism. In their most important function in the transport of goods, especially the cheap bulk commodities of cotton and coals, they nevertheless found it difficult to compete with the canal companies since their routes followed the same general direction of the natural watershed. They therefore established control over their rivals between 1846 and 1854 and diverted from them the traffic in raw cotton so that by 1850 they were

[1] S. A. Broadbridge, 'The Early Capital Market: the Lancashire and Yorkshire Railway', *Economic History Review*, Dec. 1955, 200–12; idem, *Studies in Railway Expansion and the Capital Market in England 1825–1873* (London, Cass, 1970), 160–5.

carrying more cotton inland from Liverpool than the canals. The Bridgewater and Mersey Navigation succeeded in preserving its independence of the railways until 1872 and so delayed for two decades the establishment of a new monopoly in place of the old. The influence of the railways extended the markets of the local coal industry but also increased the degree of competition for those markets by enabling new collieries to be opened. The railways became such an integral part of the cotton economy that their blockage by heavy snowfalls in the winter of 1854 brought commerce and industry to a virtual standstill.[1]

Their influence facilitated the process of regional concentration within the industry. By stimulating the expansion of market gardening and dairy farming they secured to the factory operative the advantage of the cheap food thitherto enjoyed by the agricultural labourer. Their attractive influence became greatest in the engineering industry and in the coarse cotton trade, remaining least in the fine trade. In general they did not divert the construction of new mills from the side of rivers and canals before the 1870s, even in the newly developing districts. They did not attract new mills to their side because of their relative proximity in the cotton towns, the highly developed haulage industry, and the low cost of transport of cotton goods.

The railways benefited some centres of production more than others. Inevitably they favoured the towns through which they passed at the expense of those they bypassed. They proved most useful to towns rather than to villages, to large towns rather than to smaller ones, and to junctions rather than to through-line towns. Their influence undermined the advantages conferred upon Liverpool by the great canals and contributed to its relative commercial decline after 1850. Although their construction consolidated the nodal position of Preston they could not prevent its relative industrial decline after 1854 and they even furthered that decline by facilitating the expansion of textile engineering in Bolton and Oldham at its expense. They did however virtually create the cotton manufacture of many villages which had lacked the advantage of canal transport. Their advent ushered in the era of rapid expansion in Rossendale and Blackburn from the 1840s and thus promoted the

[1] *Manchester Guardian*, 7 Jan. 1854, 8i.

geographical separation of weaving from spinning. Their influence extended along the trans-Pennine routes to draw within the commercial orbit of Manchester such outlying townships as Glossop in Derbyshire and Brighouse and Skipton in the West Riding. Thus they furthered the process of centralization within the industry.

* * *

Under the combined influence of such factors the cotton trade became increasingly a Lancashire industry, steam-powered, mechanized, and urbanized. East Lancashire became the home of the greatest concentration of manufacturing industry that the world had ever known and progressively enhanced its competitive advantages for the pursuit of modern industry: it converted the penury of Nature into comparative abundance, transformed one of the poorest counties into the second richest in the country, and raised the value of its barren lands to unprecedented heights. The interpretation of that remarkable example of industrial localization has often been excessively deterministic and materialistic. Sometimes it has relied upon the reductionist fallacy implicit in the invocation of a single dominant factor such as the presence of soft water, cheap fuel, cheap transport, or cheap machinery. Such explanations need to be subsumed within a wider perspective which takes into account the interaction of a variety of factors and their constant refraction through the moral resources of the local population. The progressive concentration of the industry gave it access to an abundant local supply of the factors of production and especially to the labour of a population increasing under its powerful and prolonged stimulus. Lancashire increased its population faster than the rest of the country throughout the eighteenth and nineteenth centuries and rose in status from the fifth most populous county of the realm in 1701 to the second in 1801, having surpassed the West Riding in the 1780s and 1790s. It increased its population apparently in direct proportion to the increase in the consumption of cotton by a labour-intensive industry, adding thereto two persons for every additional bale used between 1781 and 1811 and one person for every extra bale used between 1811 and 1891. The growth of population was a rural as well as an urban phenomenon and the growth of large cities took place in two distinct phases. During the first phase the two towns of Liverpool and Manchester increased their joint share of the population of the county from 5·7 per cent in 1700 to 34 per cent in 1850. In the second phase the share of those two cities was reduced as five other towns reached the level of 100,000 inhabitants, Salford during the 1850s, Blackburn, Bolton, and Oldham during the 1870s, and Preston in the 1880s. The influence of Manchester was thus challenged after 1850 upon two fronts, by the growth of the other conurbations of the British Isles and by the growth of the urban population of industrial Lancashire. Thus its proportion of the population of the shire was reduced from 15·6 per cent in 1851 to 12·5 per cent in 1871 and its proportion of the rateable value of the shire from almost 20 per cent in 1850 to 9·5 per cent in 1896.

The manufacturing population of the shire remained under the influence of folkways inherited from the rural past even in the largest towns, which were simply overgrown villages. That rustic tradition explains their utilitarian attitude towards the land, their preference for investment in property, especially cottages, their irreverent disposition towards constituted authority, their loyalty to family, kin, and locality, and their preference for personal to impersonal relationships between the members of 'a race of people strange, shrewd, ignorant; but above all, full of character and strong human feeling'.[1] Their bluntness and reserve served as essential defence mechanisms within the closely woven web of local society and proved keys to success in business since they worked always to their own advantage. Their contempt for culture other than music was reinforced by a respect for money and by a quasi-peasant cunning, shrewdness, and tenacity which proved an effective substitute in daily life for book-learning.

Their comparative immobility stemmed from their rural roots and made the cotton industry highly immobile once it had been domesticated within the shire. Lancashire retained more of its native population than any other county, received little long-distance immigration, and swamped its immigrants

[1] *Household Words*, 27 Jan. 1855, 563, E. Gaskell, 'North and South'.

through a high indigenous birth-rate.[1] The deep-rooted conservatism of that population was in part the heritage of a long cultural isolation and contrasted sharply with the liberalism of Manchester. That distinctive trait fostered a non-political consciousness and effectively limited the process of economic change to the purely technical sphere, so making possible its local acceptance in towns which became 'industrial but not modern'.[2] The conservative disposition of the semi-rural factory population was reinforced by the Saxon myth which seems to have gained wide currency during the nineteenth century, aided by an aversion to the Norman aristocratic tradition of the south as well as to the Celtic tradition of the Irish immigrants. That myth represented the inhabitants of east Lancashire as an indigenous Saxon stock and the mill workers as largely Saxon in origin.[3] The distinction between ethnic Lancashire and cosmopolitan Manchester was reflected in the gulf dividing the large villages or small towns of the Rossendale region from the larger towns upon its periphery, a difference which gave rise to completely opposed views on the condition of the factory workers.[4]

The greatest acquired advantage of the industry derived from the skill of workfolk reared in 'the cradle of enterprise and the home of inventions'.[5] Its labour force was dominated by female labour to a far greater degree than that of the woollen industry: the female population of Lancashire responded to the demands made from the 1830s upon its capacities and increased until 1901 more rapidly than the male population. The local economy offered full employment to women in the cotton industry and to men in coal-mining and engineering, so creating a socio-economic balance between the demands of mill, pit, and workshop. The employment of mill-girls reinforced the con-

[1] J. T. Danson and T. A. Welton, 'On the Population of Lancashire and Cheshire . . . 1801–51', *Transactions of the Historic Society of Lancashire and Cheshire*, 13 Jan. 1859, 40–2; 9 Feb. 1860, 52.

[2] E. A. Wrigley, 'The Industrial Revolution and Modernization', *Journal of Inter-disciplinary History*, Autumn 1972, 258.

[3] W. A. Abram, 'Social Condition and Political Prospects of the Lancashire Workmen', *Fortnightly Review*, 1 Oct. 1868, 427.

[4] L. Faucher, *Études sur l'Angleterre* (1845), i. 377–441, 'La Manufacture rurale'; H. J. F. Schulze, *Nationalöconomische Bilder aus Englands Volksleben* (Jena, Mauke, 1853), 291–2.

[5] J. Watts, *The Facts of the Cotton Famine* (London, Simpkin, 1866), 39.

servatism of the population, especially since the rearing of the young was entrusted during mill-hours to the elderly, and made the factory-hands seem more of 'a set of spiritless milksops' than a revolutionary class-conscious proletariat.[1] The skills of that hereditary caste were unrivalled elsewhere in the textile world outside India and furnished the industry with one of its greatest local advantages.

The increasing concentration of the cotton industry within Lancashire took place at the expense of the industry of the Celtic lands and of the country mills upon the immediate borders of the shire. The cotton industry of Ireland declined from 1825 after its loss of protective duties, and that of North Wales in the 1860s. In Scotland the increasing concentration of resources upon thread manufacture was reflected in the successive decline of the number of its employees after 1861, of its spinning spindles after 1874, of its power-looms after 1885, and of its doubling spindles after 1890. The country mills dated from the heroic age of the industry and the era of its greatest dispersion. Invariably small in size, they usually relied upon water-wheels for the supply of power and spun low counts of yarn upon antiquated machinery, usually throstle-frames. Those mills displayed remarkable powers of survival and enjoyed the great advantages of cheap land, cheap machinery, and cheap labour together with relative immunity from the administration of the Factory Acts. They were not reduced to bankruptcy by the pace of constant technical innovation and even adopted auxiliary steam-engines from the 1830s to service their water-wheels. They nevertheless began to decline in importance as the mills of Lancashire began from the 1830s to speed up their pace of production. Their facilities for communication with the distant markets of Liverpool and Manchester became increasingly inadequate with the spread of the railway, the telegraph, and the telephone. The Cotton Famine caused many such mills to close down permanently. The survivors then faced from the 1870s the blighting competition of the Oldham mills, which also contributed to the decline of the spinning industry of Scotland after 1874. Their cheap labour proved less efficient than the dear labour of the factory towns of Lancashire,

[1] A. B. Reach, *Manchester and the Textile Districts in 1849* (Helmshore Loca History Society, 1972), 37.

especially after the hours of labour were shortened by one-tenth in 1875. Efforts to revive such isolated mills by joint-stock companies never succeeded where private enterprise had failed.

The sheer mass of industry concentrated within Lancashire permitted the division of labour and specialization of function to be carried to a degree unknown elsewhere. The local growth of ancillary industries such as the finishing trades, the cotton waste industry, the mill-building industry, and the chemical industry created a wide range of external economies which further reinforced the superiority of Lancashire over other regions. Such economies even became to some extent a substitute for the internal economies of large-scale production and enabled the industry to survive and flourish upon a basis of small-scale enterprise.

Great as the advantages of Lancashire became, they did not bring within its boundaries all branches of the industry in the same degree, certain sections remaining more widely dispersed than others and usually developing along lines which did not compete with the staple products of Lancashire. Thus spinning and weaving became much more concentrated in Lancashire than the finishing industries which remained further afield in order to secure the ample supplies of soft water essential to their processes. Steam-powered mills were inevitably more localized than those dependent upon water-power because the influence of the steam-engine was centripetal as that of the water-wheel was centrifugal. Hand-loom weaving was much more widely dispersed than power-loom weaving because of its traditional association with subsistence agriculture and because of the close dependence of power-weaving upon both the yarn and cloth markets of Manchester. Waste spinning became more highly localized than spinning proper because of its total dependence upon the supply of cotton waste. In contrast doubling was much less concentrated within Lancashire than spinning because of the existence of many markets for doubled yarn: in 1867 far more doubling spindles were recorded outside than inside Lancashire and they were especially concentrated in the West Riding, in order to supply fine warps for the Bradford trade in mixed goods. Similarly mule-spinning became more concentrated in Lancashire than either throstle-spinning or ring-spinning. The manufacture of thread as a luxury trade could afford a lower degree of localization than the staple trade of the county and thrived upon the fringe of ethnic Lancashire, in the West Riding, in Derbyshire, and, above all, in Paisley in Renfrewshire. Specialized weaving firms became more localized in the Lancashire region than combined firms which in turn were more localized than specialized spinning firms, catering for the yarn markets of Nottingham, Leicester, Bradford, and Glasgow as well as of Manchester. Private employers were proportionately more important in the trade of Lancashire than joint-stock companies, which supplied an acceptable means of raising capital in outlying areas. Capitalist enterprises found the commercial climate of Lancashire far more congenial than did co-operative associations of producers. In Lancashire spinning and weaving firms were larger on average than their compeers outside since they profited by the internal and external economies available to specialized firms located near to their market. Combined firms tended on the other hand to be larger outside Lancashire than their fellows within the county, which included many small waste-manufacturing firms. Industrial plant was proportionately more concentrated in Lancashire than were firms, because of the number of small employers outside its borders. Capital was thus more localized than enterprise and labour more so than capital. Similarly male labour was more concentrated within Lancashire than female labour and adult labour more so than child labour because trade unions were stronger within the heartland of the industry while country mills remained more dependent upon cheap labour.

Lancashire did not become wholly dependent upon a single staple industry. It remained a complex of three major economic regions oriented respectively towards the pursuit of agriculture, commerce, and industry and centring respectively around the cities of Preston, Liverpool, and Manchester. Within Lancashire, the cotton kingdom was broadly contained between the Ribble, the Mersey, and the Pennines to the east of a line between Preston and Warrington. The very high degree of its local concentration masked considerable complexity of structure and organization beneath a deceptive appearance of unity. The distinctive regional character of the industry reached its highest degree in the climactic year of 1913. The proportion of the county's population directly dependent upon the cotton industry reached two successive peaks during the nineteenth century, first in the 1820s when hand-loom weaving expanded to its maximum extent, and then in the 1850s when the machine-based industry reached the summit of its relative importance. Nowhere did the industry employ directly more than one-third of the population of a cotton town. Indirectly it gave employment to most of the population of the cotton districts, even though it failed signally to enlist their deepest loyalties.

The industry of Lancashire was based upon the mill village as well as the factory town and upon the workshop as well as upon the mill. The workshops of the county employed more hands in 1891 than those of any other region outside London. Even domestic industry expanded side by side with factory industry until the 1830s and experienced a renaissance with the spread of the sewing-machine in the 1860s and of the knitting-machine in the 1880s. The county retained other textile industries and so developed them, especially under the stimulus of the Cotton Famine, that by 1891 it ranked second to Yorkshire in the number of hands employed in the woollen industry, second to Cheshire in the hatting industry, third after Nottinghamshire and Leicestershire in the manufacture of hosiery, third after Worcestershire and the West Riding in carpet-manufacture, and fourth in the manufacture of silk after Cheshire, the West Riding, and Warwickshire.[1] It established the ready-made clothing industry during the 1860s but did not develop it upon a scale similar to that of London, Leeds, or Glasgow and clung with filial piety to the old-established fustian manufacture, the true parent of its greatest trade. Nor did Lancashire become a purely textile county: it employed a large proportion of its total population in such labour-intensive pursuits as engineering, mining, commerce, and transportation and led the country in the number of its transport workers. Thus the large-scale expansion of the cotton industry did not reduce the inhabitants to total dependence, either economic or moral, upon a single dominant trade. The process of geo-

[1] *Manchester Guardian*, 15 Nov. 1864, 8i–ii, 22 Nov., 6ii–iii, 29 Nov., 6ii–iii, 'The Industrial Life of Lancashire'; J. Niven, 'On the Statistics of Some Lancashire Industries', *Transactions of the Manchester Statistical Society*, 12 Apr. 1899, 107–54.

graphical concentration was never completed since the comparative advantages of Lancashire were never great enough to secure it a permanent world monopoly: its acquisition of the industry became in the long run simply one stage in the process of its dispersion throughout the world.

PART TWO

The Main Trends in Production and Trade

CHAPTER 3

The Growth of the World Market

> On India we rely, and if we lose India, Lancashire is practically ruined.
> *Second Report of the Royal Commission on the Depression of Trade and Industry*, 1886, Q.4958, Thomas Stuttard of Burnley, 11 February 1886.

THE COTTON industry may have been a by-product of 'Mercantilist' policy but became in the process of development the great vehicle of a market economy. Its products were intended for sale rather than for use by the producers: increasingly they were designed for consumption in the widest of markets and were manufactured to satisfy a constantly renewed demand amongst the poorer populations of the world. Those goods were not indeed destined for immediate sale to the consumer since they were not fully processed: they did however furnish the essential material to the clothing industries of the world, which in turn supplied one of the three primary needs of man as a consumer.

The industry had been created in order to supply the markets of Europe with an alternative to Indian calico, to replace England's imports by an indigenous product, and thereby to transform the re-export trade into an export trade in domestic manufactures. In the process of development the industry became increasingly geared to the supply of foreign markets and acquired an export bias which remained without parallel in any other industry, either at home or abroad, and generated an intense export-led boom in the economy. From the 1780s it supplied the main stimulus to the increase in value of exports and enlarged its contribution to exports for fifty years until 1830, to the astonishment of the most enlightened of contemporary observers. England surpassed India as the largest exporter of calico and so established, probably in the 1790s, the primacy in the world market which it lost only in 1933, to

Japan. Its development of the cotton industry differentiated it profoundly from all other states, making it not only the first manufacturing country in the world but also the source of the largest and most important trade in the world. 'No nation ever had a more universal commerce than this.'[1] Its successful specialization in the supply of foreign markets stemmed from a unique combination of factors which reduced the costs of production of the new industry, made it progressively more competitive with other textile industries, inhibited the establishment of competitors elsewhere, and maintained its superiority to such rivals as did emerge.

The greatest single advantage enjoyed by the industry after 1801 undoubtedly lay in its access to an ample supply of cheap raw material. The pioneer mechanization of spinning between 1770 and 1800 had reduced the cost of production of yarn but had increased the demand for raw cotton so much as to treble its price in the New York market during the 1790s. Moreover, the rise in weaving rates until 1792 prevented the price of cloth from falling as rapidly as that of yarn. Thus the price of cotton manufactures did not begin to decline until a vast new source of supply of cotton was opened up in America and freed the industry from dependence upon the inelastic supply of Sea Island cotton and upon the restricted export capacity of the West Indies, Brazil, or the East Indies.

The invention of the saw-gin in 1793 effectively opened the interior of the southern states of the U.S.A. to the new crop by virtue of its peculiar suitability for handling short-stapled Upland cotton.[2] Cheap cotton was the product of the capital and enterprise of the planters, employing slave-labour upon cheap, abundant, and fertile soil and extending the frontier of cultivation in Georgia and South Carolina. The expanding 'Cotton Zone' derived 'increasing returns' from the cropping of new soils and supplied Atlantic commerce with a new staple of dynamic potential. The centralization of the European cotton market in Liverpool conferred upon Lancashire spinners a substantial cost-advantage over their Continental rivals.[3]

[1] E. Baines, *History of the Cotton Manufacture* (1835), 531.

[2] S. Bruchey, *Cotton and the Growth of the American Economy: 1790–1860* (New York, Harcourt, 1967), 43–75.

[3] R. Jannasch, *Die Europäische Baumwollen-Industrie* (Berlin, Allgemeine Verlags-Agentur, 1882), 57–79.

The long-term decline in the price of raw cotton from the maximum level reached in 1799–1801 lasted until 1898 and was interrupted only by the sharp rise caused by the war of 1812 and by the decade of inflation of 1855–64. That decline in the price of the industry's raw material proved of pre-eminent importance in reducing its costs of production because the cost of raw cotton formed the largest single element therein.

Cheap cotton gave the industry an incomparable advantage over all other textiles and enabled it to reduce the price of its products 'at a speed which has no precedent in the history of manufacturing industry'.[1] The declining price of raw material proved especially important in opening to manufacturers the widest of markets since it reduced the price of coarse, stout, and serviceable fabrics much more than that of finer fabrics, with their greater labour content. Thus the productivity of American agriculture proved of unprecedented and unparalleled importance in reducing the costs of British industry. The decline in cotton prices made a far larger contribution throughout the whole of the nineteenth century to the reduction in the price of manufactures than either cost-cutting technological innovations or improvements in labour productivity.[2] That contribution proved particularly important as the mechanization of the manufacturing process reached its limits.

Weaving costs proved less easily reducible than spinning costs but reflected the decline in weaving rates made possible by the vast expansion in the number of hand-loom weavers. Then the spread of the power-loom in the 1830s, and its improvement in the 1840s, ushered in a new wave of cost-cutting mechanization and notably enhanced the industry's competitive power in relation to the hand-loom industries of the world. In both spinning and weaving entrepreneurs made their own distinctively demonic contribution to the cutting of costs since they were denied any opportunity of profit from connections with the State and therefore had to seek their profit purely in the market, thereby securing the income which served as the primary source of status in their society. Their contribution was

[1] P. Deane, *The First Industrial Revolution* (1965), 89.

[2] J. Pope Hennessy, 'On the Causes of the Fall in the Price of Manufactured Cottons', *Proceedings of the British Association*, 1858, Miscellaneous Proceedings, 178–9; H. B. Heylin, *Buyers and Sellers in the Cotton Trade* (London, Griffin, 1913), 11–12, 'Statistical History of the Cotton Trade 1815–1911'.

supplemented by the external economies generated from the 1830s by the growth of ancillary industries throughout east Lancashire.

The expansion of demand concurrently with that of supply laid the basis of the industry's world-wide dominion. In the extension of its outlets it made the great transition from seeking a vent for the surplus production created by the mechanization of spinning to developing its comparative advantages in the systematic exploitation of the world market as it became increasingly export-oriented. Foreign demand expanded markedly after 1815 in reaction to the unbalanced extension of the industry's spinning power beyond the immediate absorptive capacity of the internal market and under the pressure of five successive sharp slumps in the home trade, in 1819–20, 1826–32, 1837–42, 1847–50, and 1855.[1] Those recessions may have reflected not only the impact of cyclical depression but also the associated reduction in purchasing-power amongst the extensive community of hand-loom weavers. Their influence was manifest in a sharp reduction in export prices and in a substantial increase in the volume of exports.

The industry benefited from the vast growth of world trade in association with the spread of Western civilization, British power, and a market economy, especially from the 1830s when cash-crop production began a long-term process of expansion in Asia and the export of piece-goods from Lancashire to the East entered upon a phase of long-term growth. Manchester shippers became the indispensable intermediaries between the industry and its overseas markets: they were recruited increasingly from the ranks of foreigners and, with the support of British shipowners, extended the outlets for Lancashire calico throughout much of the world. Cotton provided an ideal clothing for wear within the expanding subtropical empire of Britain and proved much more suitable for carriage over long distances than other commodities designed to meet primary needs because it was less perishable than corn and more valuable than building materials. Like food and shelter however, clothes satisfied non-economic aspirations as well as utilitarian needs, even when made from unpretentious calico. They

[1] A. H. Imlah, *Economic Elements in the Pax Britannica: Studies in British Foreign Trade in the Nineteenth Century* (Cambridge, Harvard University Press, 1958), 125.

served as a symbol of civilization and conferred status upon their wearers by associating them with the representatives of the greatest imperial power of the century and by opening to them doors which would otherwise have remained closed. Clothing also served as a token of acceptance of the Christian faith and as a quasi-sacramental manifestation of the inward and spiritual grace distinguishing one's brethren in Christ from mere 'naked savages'. The wearing of clothes was encouraged by the fervent religiosity of the Victorian mind and was especially favoured by the missionary apostles of the cult of 'Christianity and calico' who thus strengthened the alliance forged between the forces of 'commerce and civilization'. For whatever purpose clothing was worn, it brought its wearers within the sphere of influence of a money economy by encouraging them to earn the means to buy it.

Within the broad spectrum of textiles demand shifted away from traditional fabrics towards the new cotton cloth in the production and sale of which England for a time enjoyed unique competitive advantages. The demand for calico proved much more elastic than that for woollen cloth and experienced a long-term process of expansion as the population of the world increased faster than ever before and found it necessary to renew cotton garments more frequently than those made from hardier material. As new and larger levels of demand were successively tapped a revolutionary and irreversible process was set in motion, immeasurably improving the quality of clothing of the poor, creating an unprecedented visible equality in material attire, democratizing a taste for consumption, and accelerating the spread of the progress-ethic.[1] As the industry extended its markets to a world-wide scale, it became increasingly subject to different influences in the prospering civilized markets of the West from those operative in the populous traditional markets of the East: demand was determined by the expansion of purchasing-power in both East and West in so far as it was much more income-elastic than price-elastic[2] but in the Orient it was governed by the reduced incidence of

[1] J. Michelet, *Le Peuple* (Paris, Hachette, 1846; Didier, 1946), 57–8, on the revolutionary influence of the decline in the price of printed calico in 1842.

[2] G. Wright, 'An Econometric Study of Cotton Production and Trade, 1830–1860', *Review of Economics and Statistics*, May 1971, 119, reprinted in P. Temin (ed.), *New Economic History. Selected Readings* (Harmondsworth, Penguin, 1973), 79.

dearth as much as by the growth of population and production for the market. In the short term demand remained liable to fluctuate, like that for shelter but unlike that for food, since the renewal of clothing was not a vital necessity and could be postponed in the event of a harvest failure, a consequent rise in food prices and the diversion of purchasing-power from textiles to cereals. In the long run however the industry's markets expanded in harmony with the world-wide extension of the influence of British shipping, the erosion of the protective influence of high transport costs, the decline of subsistence economies, the increased penetration of a market economy, and the growth of a large-scale trade in food as well as in raw materials. The adoption of free-trade policies reinforced that trend by opening the British market to the output of primary producers and by arousing millenial hopes of the birth of a new, cosmopolitan, and 'indivisible republic of merchants'.[1] The export trade proved buoyant beyond all precedent and expanded in volume between 1834 and 1873 three times as fast as the home trade,[2] setting in motion the largest flow of textile exports ever known in the history of the world. The expansion of the Indian market served as the prime mover behind that trend, powerfully reinforcing the export bias of the industry.

The increase in exports helped to undermine subsistence economies and the subsistence-ethic wherever they came within the expanding sphere of influence of commerce, so generating a long-term expansion in world trade and fostering a tendency to identify a subsistence economy with poverty and a market economy with wealth, created by the gains from trade. The survival power of the subsistence economies nevertheless remained considerable, prevented the British cotton industry from establishing a monopoly of world production, and restricted it, at the peak of its relative importance in 1853, to the supply of only 45 per cent of the world's total consumption of cotton cloth.[3] The capacity to command an expanding share of the world market firmly identified the industry with the cause of a market economy and enabled Manchester from the

[1] F. List, *The National System of Political Economy* (London, Longmans, 1885, trans. from the 1st edn. of 1841), 259.

[2] Mann, 106; Ellison, 306–7.

[3] T. Bazley, 'Cotton Manufacture', *Encyclopaedia Britannica* (Edinburgh, Black, 1854, 8th edn.), viii. 455–6.

1840s to reassert its imperial influence over Lancashire. The demands of market production exerted a dual influence upon the manufacturing population. On the one hand they encouraged the assimilation of labour to a marketable commodity, compelled the few producers' co-operatives founded within the industry to conform to the expectations of the market, and prevented the 'working-class limiteds' of Oldham from creating any new pattern of industrial relations. The separation of production and consumption also compelled the operatives to share the burden of successive and regular short-term fluctuations in demand. The dictates of the market imposed a permanent pressure upon wages, which was felt most keenly in time of cyclical depression and would have been absent from an industry oriented to the home trade. On the other hand the secular expansion of demand compensated abundantly for such short-term fluctuations and allied the interests of the operatives with those of the export trade as well as of the empire, strongly reinforcing their conservative disposition. The coincidence of the long-term expansion of output and sales seemed to demonstrate the broad truth of Say's law of markets whereby supply created its own demand. The industry thus remained until the 1870s less concerned with the markets for its calico than with its annual supply of raw cotton.

The employers derived from their service of the market not only their profits and prestige but also their unique sense of mission as the standard-bearers of the first industry ever to claim the world market as its own. Both masters and men elaborated the doctrine of free trade into a quasi-religion and dutifully accepted the Sisyphean task of social regeneration through the medium of commerce, hoping apparently to succeed where the Christian Church for two millenia had failed. The inspiring myth of the industry's destiny as the pioneer and handmaiden of civilization harnessed the energies of the inhabitants of Lancashire during an era of dynamic expansion to the creative task of clothing the naked of the world, thereby fulfilling a function of undisputable importance. The quest for commercial supremacy necessitated the ethical exaltation of activity over contemplation and entailed some social and cultural sacrifice. 'If we must choose between a Titian and a Lancashire cotton-mill, then, in the name of manhood and morality, give us the cotton-mill.'[1] The seductive lure of the export market also engendered an exaggerated and short-sighted faith in the world-wide function of the British cotton industry, in the permanence of its competitive advantages, and in it capacity to escape the curse of mortality foredooming all commercial empires.[2] From such a viewpoint the supply of the world market came to seem the manifest destiny of Lancashire, foreign competition appeared as an unnatural and impious flouting of the decrees of Providence as well as of political economy, and the loss of one market merely fostered the search for another as an effective substitute. So profound an export bias undermined the balance of the cotton trade and of the whole economy. It diverted interest from the development of other industries and of the home trade to the service of markets which remained less intensely developed, less wealthy, and less profitable. In the short term such a bias exposed the economy, until the 1860s, to the recurrent impact of cyclical fluctuations in demand. In the long run it fostered the development of an overspecialized and inflexible structure of production which proved unable to adapt to the loss of those foreign markets upon which the industry had become overdependent. The relentless pursuit of short-term gains was however an inevitable product of the short-term perspective enforced upon the businessman by the impersonal discipline of the market.

* * *

The links between the cotton trade and manufacture may be demonstrated by an examination firstly of the industry's two chief products and then of its main markets, especially in Asia. In the export trade yarn served as the pacemaker until 1843 and thereafter yielded its function to cloth. The export of yarn attracted far more attention at the time than later because it undermined the monopoly of the hand-loom weavers, divorcing the spindle from the service of the domestic shuttle and diverting its product to supply foreign weavers. Unlike the export of cloth, the export of unprocessed yarn provoked in the years

[1] *Spectator*, 6 Aug. 1870, 953, [R. H. Hutton], 'Mr. Ruskin's Philosophy of Art'.

[2] W. B. Adams, 'English Cotton Trades, Indigenous or Exotic?', *Journal of the Society of Arts*, 27 Jan. 1854, 168.

1800–20 a debate about its morality since it separated the interests of Manchester from those of its dependent hinterland of weavers.[1] In that debate the interests of the market emerged victorious: the interests of Manchester and Lancashire were reunited only from the 1840s as power-weaving spread and realized the full employment-creating potential of the industry.

Exports of cotton yarn freed England from dependence upon Germany by replacing the imports of linen yarn, which reached their peak value in 1805 and declined sharply after 1825. Those exports flowed to Germany, which had been the main source of supply of linen yarn to Manchester and became the largest buyer of cotton yarn from the beginning of the trade in 1792. The new trade undermined the domestic manufacture of linen in Germany and created, in the German exporters, the nucleus of the foreign mercantile interest in Manchester, 'the last and greatest of the Hanseatic towns'.[2] It also institutionalized the specialized spinning mill and so laid the basis of the horizontal pattern of organization which characterized the industry from the 1880s. During the twenty-four years 1819–42 exports of yarn represented 28·5 per cent of the total quantity spun and 24·2 per cent of the total value of the exports of cotton manufactures. The sharp contrast between the increase in yarn exports and the comparative stability in the value of cloth exports in the 1820s and 1830s reinforced the hostility of Manchester to the Corn Laws. The trade attained three successive peaks between 1842 and 1884, the peak of its comparative importance in 1842 in its share of the total quantity spun as well as of the total value of exports, its maximum value in 1872, and its maximum volume in 1884.

Exports of cloth had grown more slowly than the consumption of cotton between 1815 and 1842 but assumed the lead from yarn exports and increased faster from 1843 than both the consumption of cotton and the exports of yarn. Those exports increased between 1843 and 1896 more than thrice as fast as yarn exports and half again as fast as cotton consumption, as hand-woven goods were replaced by machine-woven goods. Exports of hand-woven cloth may perhaps have been under-

[1] W. Radcliffe, *Origin of the New System of Manufacture commonly called Power-Loom Weaving* (Stockport, Lomax, 1828; Clifton, Kelley, 1974).

[2] A. J. P. Taylor, 'Manchester', *Encounter*, Mar. 1957, 3.

recorded in official statistics but apparently reached their peak level in 1830,[1] a notable achievement in a textile world still based upon the hand-loom. Thereafter they were increasingly displaced by power-woven cloth, manufactured at falling prices. The exports of cloth extended over a wide spectrum of products whose value increased in proportion to their degree of finish and to the amount of skilled labour they incorporated, from the cheapest unbleached calico or 'grey cloth' through bleached and printed piece-goods to the most expensive yarn-dyed, or piece-dyed cloth. The product-mix of exports was transformed by the eastward shift of the industry's markets as exports of grey cloth to Asia increased rapidly from the 1820s, printed and dyed goods became relatively less important from the 1820s until the 1880s, and the average quality of cloth exports, as measured by Sandberg, underwent until 1890 a long-term decline.[2] Exports of cloth experienced their most rapid growth in volume in the three decades between 1830 and 1860, rising above the level attained in the previous year in three out of every four years and doubling their quantity every six years in response to the expansion of foreign demand.

The civilized markets of Europe and the U.S.A. became the first to develop their own cotton industries and reached the peak of their relative importance as markets in the later eighteenth century, Europe in 1781–2 and the U.S.A. in 1795,[3] while the other regions of the world achieved the peak of their relative importance as markets for piece-goods much later, Latin America in 1840, the Levant in 1870, and Asia in 1888.[4] As the markets of Asia expanded their consumption Europe and the U.S.A. together sharply reduced their share of the total volume of piece-goods exported from 68 per cent in 1820 and 42 per cent in 1830 to 27 per cent in 1850 and 8 per cent in

[1] R. Burn, *Statistics of the Cotton Trade* (London, Simpkin, 1847), Tables 6 and 9.

[2] L. G. Sandberg, 'Movements in the Quality of British Cotton Textile Exports, 1815–1913', *Journal of Economic History*, Mar. 1968, 8–12.

[3] M. M. Edwards, *The Growth of the British Cotton Trade 1780–1815* (1967), 243.

[4] The 1870 peak for the Levant may be an illusion created by the trade statistics. The recorded export of piece-goods to 'Egypt' included goods which were shipped by the overland route to India and China but were entered in the trade returns down to and including 1873 as if they were destined for Egypt. They rose sharply between 1866 and 1869, reached a peak of 377 m. yards in 1870 and declined by 42 per cent during 1874 when their destination was reclassified to exclude Egypt. See *Manchester Courier*, 14 July 1875, 4v.

TABLE 5

Relative Shares of the Main Markets of the World in the Exports of the British Cotton Industry, 1820–1896

	Volume of Exports of Piece-Goods (in millions of yards)			Proportion (%)		
	1820	1850	1896	1820	1850	1896
Europe	144·619	266·98	375·094	58·23	19·66	7·19
America	79·831	464·878	901·827	32·14	34·23	17·28
U.S.A.	23·802	104·23	55·301	9·58	7·67	1·06
Latin America	52·951	325·156	818·88	21·28	23·94	15·69
Levant	7·888	155·692	421·154	3·18	11·46	8·07
Asia	14·191	426·366	3,014·793	5·71	31·39	57·77
India		314·453	2,038·034		23·15	39·06
China		73·209	542·815		5·39	10·4
Africa	1·665	29·587	259	0·67	2·18	4·96
Total	248·36	1,358·183	5,218·249	99·73	98·92	95·27

	Value of Exports of Cotton Manufactures (£m.)			Proportion (%)		
	1820	1850	1896	1820	1850	1896
Europe	10·825	9·681	13·12	65·54	34·26	18·92
America	4·316	8·222	12·794	26·13	29·1	18·45
U.S.A.	1·195	2·504	2·455	7·23	8·86	3·56
Latin America	2·944	5·074	10·332	17·82	17·96	14·9
Levant	0·414	2·601	5·492	2·51	9·2	7·92
Asia	0·851	6·887	30·112	5·15	24·37	43·42
India		5·221	18·434		18·48	26·58
China		1·021	5·882		3·61	8·48
Africa	0·097	0·489	3·443	0·59	1·73	5·31
Total	16·517	28·257	69·355	99·92	98·66	94·01

Note: Europe includes Malta, Greece, Wallachia, and Moldavia; Latin America includes the West Indies; the Levant comprises Turkey, Syria, and Egypt, with Tripoli, Barbary, and Morocco for 1820 only; Africa includes Madagascar but excludes Egypt and the African islands of Portugal and Spain; India excludes Ceylon and the Straits Settlements; China includes Hong Kong.

Source: *Tables of the Revenue, Population, Commerce &c. of the United Kingdom and its Dependencies, Part I. From 1820 to 1831* (London, Knight, 1833; Parliamentary Papers, 1833, vol. 41), 65, where the total yardage of 'printed or dyed cottons' exported in 1820 is misprinted as '13,469,117' instead of as '134, 687, 144'; *Tables of the Revenue, Population, Commerce &c. of the United Kingdom, Part XX. 1850* (London,

H.M.S.O., 1852, 1466), 127; *Annual Statement of the Trade of the United Kingdom for 1896*, 162–6; J. A. Mann, *The Cotton Trade of Great Britain* (London, Simpkin, 1860; Cass, 1968), 124–5, Table No. 25, furnishes a full table of the value of exports to every country between 1820 and 1858 but does not give quantities and does not separate yarn from cloth; T. Ellison, *The Cotton Trade of Great Britain* (London, Wilson, 1866; Cass, 1968), 63–4, supplies two valuable tables of the volume of exports of yarn and cloth to the six main area-markets of the world for eight bench-mark years between 1820 and 1882. In respect of Europe my own calculations differ from those of Ellison, whose figures relate to volume and not to value.

1896. Europe had reached the summit of its relative importance as a market first in the 1780s and again in 1800–20. Thereafter it became much less important as its imports expanded less rapidly than those of other continents and comprised from 1823 more yarn than cloth. Its share of the volume of piece-goods exports declined from 58 per cent in 1820 to 31 per cent in 1830 and it was surpassed as a market for piece-goods first by America in the 1820s and then by Asia in the 1840s. Exports of piece-goods to Europe continued to expand and reached their peak volume in 1887, with maximum exports to Germany in 1872, to France in 1874, to Russia in 1882, and to Italy in 1887. Lancashire adjusted to the relative decline in demand from the Continent and the U.S.A. and found compensation in the expanding markets of South America, Asia, and Africa. Exports to Latin America reached their absolute peak in 1895, those to China and Japan in 1905, and those to India and the Levant in 1913. Such less wealthy markets differed profoundly from those of Europe and the U.S.A. in that they remained more important for the volume than for the value of their imports.

In America the U.S.A. remained England's most valuable trading partner but usually imported more woollen than cotton manufactures, except during the 1820s and 1850s, and was more important as a market to Yorkshire than to Lancashire. In the peak year of 1795 it had absorbed, with Canada, 54 per cent of the industry's exports. In the nineteenth century it reached the summit of its importance as a market in 1815–16 after the conclusion of the war of 1812. By 1821–5 its imports had declined to 12 per cent of the value of the exports of cotton manufactures but comprised 32 per cent of the value of British exports to the U.S.A. and 11 per cent of the value of U.S.

merchandise imports.[1] The U.S.A. progressively displaced its imports by its own manufactures as it developed its own cotton industry, expanded its spindleage more than sixfold during the 1820s, and pioneered the protection of the new industry by tariffs, especially from 1816. The cotton industry of New England surpassed in aggregate production the volume of imports in 1823 and possibly surpassed their value during the next decade.[2] Its products effectively excluded Lancashire from the market for coarse cloth, especially in the slave-holding South. The U.S.A. nevertheless remained from the 1830s the main market for cotton manufactures of high quality, for mixed stuffs, and for sewing cotton as well as for the superior products of the hand-loom. In the boom of the 1850s the imports of cotton manufactures from Britain into the U.S.A. surpassed in value its imports of woollen manufactures for the first time since 1826–30 and absorbed 10 per cent of the exports of the cotton industry.[3] The traditional supremacy of woollens was restored from 1861 on the outbreak of the Civil War and the inauguration of a regime of high protection. American imports of cotton manufactures declined from their all-time peak level of 1860 but still ranked the U.S.A. as the largest single market of Lancashire in the Americas until 1884. The U.S.A. was surpassed in the value of its imports by Brazil in 1884 and then by Argentina in 1891, so declining in status to the third largest market in the Americas. The British cotton industry suffered a great loss through its progressive exclusion from a market where nature and climate dictated the wearing of cotton cloth and where population and purchasing-power were expanding more rapidly than anywhere else in the world. As in the trade with India, England failed to establish a full symbiosis with the U.S.A. based on the exchange of calico for raw cotton.

Latin America became the most important of all neutral markets to Lancashire because of the comparative poverty of

[1] J. Potter, 'Atlantic Economy, 1815–60: the U.S.A. and the Industrial Revolution in Britain', in L. S. Pressnell (ed.), *Studies in the Industrial Revolution presented to T. S. Ashton* (London, Athlone Press, 1960), 258–9, reprinted in A. W. Coats and R. M. Robertson (eds.), *Essays in American Economic History* (London, Arnold, 1969), 31–2.

[2] R. B. Zevin, 'The Growth of Cotton Textile Production after 1815', in R. W. Fogel and S. L. Engerman (eds.), *The Reinterpretation of American Economic History* (New York, Harper, 1971), 123; L. G. Sandberg, *Lancashire in Decline* (1974), 254.

[3] Potter, 259–61.

the bulk of its population, the limited size of its domestic textile industry, the absence of any factory industry outside Mexico and Brazil, and the predominant orientation of its hand-looms to the production of woollen cloth. It had become an important market first in 1808 as a result of its emancipation from Iberian rule and had surpassed the U.S.A. as a market by 1820, increasing even more in importance after the final establishment of the independence of the Spanish colonies in 1821–5. It did not become a market for yarn before the 1890s but remained one essentially for cloth and especially for the cheaper varieties. By 1829 Latin America was importing more piece-goods than Europe and by 1840 it had reached the peak of its relative importance as a market, importing 32·2 per cent of the volume of piece-goods exported and 17·5 per cent of the value of the industry's exports and buying per head of population more than sevenfold as much cloth as the average inhabitant of the world. In terms of value it continued to increase its absorptive capacity and reached the peak of its relative importance in 1864 when it imported 20·6 per cent of the value of piece-goods exported. Within the subcontinent Brazil and Argentina always remained pre-eminent as markets. Brazil retained until 1903 its primacy as the most valuable single market of Lancashire by virtue of its size, its tropical climate, its large population, the concentration of settlement upon its coastal fringe, the export-orientation of its economy, and the absence of competition from Portuguese textiles. Its imports of cotton manufactures were also facilitated by its Anglophile tradition, by the favourable tariff granted under the Treaty of Commerce of 1810,[1] and by the shipping links developed with Liverpool. Those imports expanded in harmony with its increased exports of primary produce and responded particularly to the growing demand for its raw cotton. As a source of cotton supply it replaced the West Indies during the war of 1812 and ranked second to the U.S.A. until 1832 and third after the U.S.A. and India until 1852. It responded also to the expansion of the slave trade in the 1830s and 1840s and to the abolition of the colonial prefer-

[1] A. K. Manchester, *British Preëminence in Brazil. Its Rise and Decline. A Study in European Expansion* (Chapel Hill, University of North Carolina Press, 1933; Chicago, Octagon, 1964), 69–109.

ences on cotton in 1845, on coffee in 1851, and on sugar in 1854, which gave its producers full access to the British market. For sixty years Brazil became the largest market for prints from 1834, when it surpassed the U.S.A., until 1894 when it was surpassed by Turkey. Increasingly its own cotton industry supplied the domestic market, especially from the 1880s.[1] It also favoured the cotton goods of the U.S.A. under the reciprocity treaty of 1891 and reduced its imports of Lancashire goods from their maximum level of 1892.

From the 1870s Argentina expanded its imports in harmony with the growth of its metropolitan population, the construction of its railways by British enterprise, the opening of the pampa to the cultivation of grain, the extensive investment of British capital, and the increased export of wheat, maize, and frozen meat. It transformed its trading deficit with Britain into a surplus from 1894 and so set the pattern followed by Latin America as a whole from 1898. The value of its imports of cotton manufactures surpassed those of Chile in 1877, those of the U.S.A. in 1891, and those of Brazil in 1903, when it became the largest single market in the Americas. Argentina reached the peak level of its imports of piece-goods in 1912 and so compensated Lancashire for the decline of its exports to Mexico after 1882, to Brazil after 1892, and to Chile after 1907. It provided a most effective complement to the British economy. Its imports were representative of those of the subcontinent as a whole, which became increasingly from the 1880s a market for cheap dyed goods and especially for coloured cottons carefully designed through the heavy use of size to appear attractive and to sell cheaply.[2] The share of printed and dyed goods in the total value of exports of piece-goods had declined from 54 per cent in 1820 to 39 per cent in 1880 but recovered thereafter to 43 per cent in 1896. The share of dyed goods alone rose from 11·7 per cent in 1889 to 14·3 per cent in 1896 while their share in the exports of cloth to Latin America increased from 15 per cent to 19·5 per cent. Thus Lancashire survived the

[1] S. J. Stein, *The Brazilian Cotton Manufacture: textile enterprise in an underdeveloped area 1850–1950* (Cambridge, Harvard University Press, 1957), 191.

[2] A. J. Marrison, 'Great Britain and her rivals in the Latin American cotton piece-goods market, 1880–1914', in B. M. Ratcliffe (ed.), *Great Britain and her world, 1750–1914. Essays in honour of W. O. Henderson* (Manchester University Press, 1975), 309–48.

growth of competition with its yarn and grey cloth in the markets of Asia by the more intense exploitation of the markets of South America.

* * *

The growth of exports to India transformed the pattern of Anglo-Indian trade and provided the British Empire with a new economic basis. India had been the birthplace of the cotton industry and had become the greatest producer, consumer, and exporter of calico in the world, supplying the markets of Asia as well as those of Europe. English traffic with India had begun originally as an import trade and had become a tribute trade after Plassey but could develop no complementary export trade while England's main exports were woollens designed for temperate markets rather than for tropical climes. The cotton industry however supplied a product ideally suited to the Indian climate and made possible an astonishing reversal of roles, enabling Britain to become a large-scale exporter to India such as it had never been during the great age of the East India Company and of the woollen cloth industry. The commercial conquest of the subcontinent was however no mere response to the reduction of comparative costs or to the expansion of market opportunities: it was a product of the transformation of the political structure of trade and it was buttressed by the maintenance of a political balance of power in favour of British industry.

The essential preliminary step to the tapping of the vast domestic market of India was the exclusion of Indian textiles from their markets in Europe and Britain, where their competition had aroused bitter complaints during the commercial crisis of 1788. To attain that end the import duties on East Indian piece goods were increased thrice in 1797, 1798, and 1799 and nine times more between 1802 and 1819, being reduced only in 1826.[1] Those imports reached their peak value

[1] *An Account of the Specific Rates of Duty Chargeable in England on all Articles the Produce of the East Indies, Appendix No. 5 to the Report from the Select Committee on the Affairs of the East India Company* (735–ii of 1832, 1831–2 x. Part 2), 594–5; E. Baines, op. cit. 325; A. Tripathi, *Trade and Finance in the Bengal Presidency (1793–1833)* (Calcutta, Orient Longmans, 1956), 84, 102, 134.

in 1800 and their peak quantity in 1802,[1] under the stimulus of the Warehousing Act of 1799. Thereafter they declined sharply under the influence of the continuing expansion of muslin manufacture in Lancashire and Scotland, the decline in the price of American cotton after 1801, the steep rise in the import duty in 1799 and 1803, and the renewal of the war in Europe, where markets were further restricted by the Continental Blockade. Thus the East India Company lost what had seemed since the seventeenth century as solid a staple traffic as the spice trade was to the Dutch.

The export of cotton goods to India had been undertaken first in the 1780s in a gesture of supreme presumption[2] and had begun to increase from 1804; but it developed on a large scale only after the London-based East India Company lost its monopoly of the India trade in the Charter Act of 1813, in a concession designed apparently to extend employment and to preserve the tranquillity of the manufacturing population after the first appearance of 'luddism' in 1812. As soon as the trade was opened to the outports the export of piece-goods began from Liverpool in 1814 and increased to an unprecedented and unanticipated extent,[3] inaugurating a century of expansion lasting until 1913. The development of the Indian market during that period took place in three distinct phases:

1. Between 1814 and 1843 the absolute superiority of the Indian market to all others was established.
2. Between 1844 and 1886 that market expanded to the peak of its relative importance.
3. Between 1887 and 1913 that market continued to expand, at a declining rate, to the peak of its absolute importance.

The stimulus to commerce given by the opening of the new market proved immediate, substantial, and sustained since exports to India, as shown in Table 6, consistently expanded faster than to any other market. Exports of cotton goods surpassed in value from 1817 the exports of British woollens to

[1] *Considerations on the Danger and Impolicy of Laying Open the Trade with India and China* (London, Longman, 1812), 116.

[2] H. R. C. Wright, *East Indian Economic Problems of the Age of Cornwallis and Raffles* (London, Luzac, 1961), 192–243, 'Cotton Piece Goods'.

[3] *An Account of Manufactured Cotton Goods, Printed and Plain, which have been Exported from Great Britain to ports and places to the eastward of the Cape of Good Hope from 1st January 1813 to 1st January 1822* (457 of 1822, xxi. 307).

India. Those exports raised the value of private exports from 1814 above that of Company exports and responded markedly to the further erosion of the privileges of the Company in

TABLE 6

Comparative Rate of Expansion of the Indian Market, 1820–1913 (%)

	1820–55	1856–86	1887–1913
Mean Annual Rate of Increase in the Volume of Piece-Goods Exported:			
to India	10·2	5·5	2·1
to the rest of the world	5·4	2·9	1·4
Incremental Share of India	24·33	60·23	57·36
Mean Annual Rate of Increase in the Value of Piece-Goods Exported:			
to India	5·3	4·2	2·8
to the rest of the world	1·6	0·8	2·4
Incremental Share of India	31·16	66·2	39·66
Mean Annual Rate of Increase in the Total Value of Cotton Manufactures Exported:			
to India	5·8	4·3	2·6
to the rest of the world	1·7	1·5	2·2
Incremental Share of India	27·46	46·42	32·42

Source: *Annual Statements of Trade* for 1855, 1856,1886, 1887, 1913; T. Ellison, *The Cotton Trade of Great Britain* (1886), Table No. 2; L. G. Sandberg, *Lancashire in Decline* (1974), 142, 165–8, 258–62.

1823 and to their total abolition in 1833.[1] Exports of cotton manufactures increased their share of British exports to India from 6 per cent in 1814 to 20 per cent in 1818, supplied over 50 per cent by 1828, and continued to increase their share to the all-time peak proportion of 73 per cent in 1871. The development of the new market radically altered the distribution of exports: it furnished abundant compensation for the absolute decline from 1821 in the value of exports to the West Indies, it halved Europe's share of the total volume of piece-goods exports between 1820 and 1830 and it supplied the industry with an imperial function.

The traditional balance of the textile trade between East and

[1] K. N. Chaudhuri, 'India's Foreign Trade and the Cessation of the East India Company's Trading Activities, 1828–40', *Economic History Review*, Aug. 1966, 345–63.

West was decisively and apparently permanently overturned in favour of Europe. India had been surpassed first by Britain as an exporter of calico, probably in the 1790s, and then by the U.S.A. as a producer of raw cotton in 1821: in the 1820s she became a net importer of cotton goods instead of a net exporter. The exact influence of that commercial revolution upon her native crafts remains a highly contentious issue in the absence of adequate contemporary evidence. In Bengal the hand-loom weavers apparently suffered less from the threat of alien competition than from the exclusion of their products from the markets of Europe. The crisis in their trade seems to have been most acute in the muslin manufacture of Dacca, where the East India Company closed down its factory in 1818.[1] The loss by India of her sole manufactured export transformed her foreign remittances thereafter into raw materials and allegedly effected 'a commercial revolution, productive of so much suffering to numerous classes in India and hardly to be paralleled in the history of commerce'.[2] The plight of the hand-loom weavers seems however to have been exaggerated by the defenders of the Company in the debate preceding the renewal of its charter in 1833.[3] Their condition seems to have been mistakenly assimilated to that of the declining hand-weavers of Lancashire. The crisis of their trade seems to have been only local and temporary and to have been followed by a renaissance as they responded to the challenge of alien competition.

The transformation of Anglo-Indian commerce exerted a

[1] H. J. Ghosal, 'Cotton Industry in Bengal, Bihar and Orissa during the Early Nineteenth Century', *Journal of Indian History*, Aug. 1939, 195–214; idem, *Economic Transition in the Bengal Presidency (1793–1833)* (Calcutta, Mukhopadhyay, 1950, 1966), 20–39, 282–5.

[2] *Report from the Select Committee on the Affairs of the East India Company: General Appendix to Report* (734 of 1832), 275, Minute of Lord William Bentinck, Governor-General, 30 May 1829; R. D. Mangles, 'Wrongs and Claims of Indian Commerce', *Edinburgh Review*, Jan. 1841, 357–62.

[3] R. M. Martin, *The Political, Commercial and Financial Condition of the Anglo-Eastern Empire, in 1832* (London, Parbury, 1832), 124–9; J. Crawfurd, *A Sketch of the Commercial Resources and Monetary and Mercantile System of British India* (1837), reprinted in K. N. Chaudhuri (ed.), *The Economic Development of India under the East India Company 1814–58. A Selection of Contemporary Writings* (Cambridge University Press, 1971), 240–1; K. N. Chaudhuri, 'India's International Economy in the Nineteenth Century: an Historical Survey', *Modern Asian Studies*, Jan. 1968, 33–8.

profound influence upon the British cotton industry: it made possible the movement towards free trade and the ultimate removal of protective import duties in 1846, secured Lancashire against any threat of Indian competition in the markets of Europe, and created the possibility of the export of raw cotton by India and the consequent emergence of a true Ricardian harmony of interests in place of a tributary relationship.[1] The failure to evolve any such interchange may help to explain why Mill perfected the theory of international trade in the context of commerce with Europe and not with India. That subtropical realm had been opened to the products of Lancashire only by the abrogation, in the interests of competition, of the commercial privileges of a chartered monopoly. It proved a far superior market to that of the colonies of settlement, expanded its merchandise imports between 1814 and 1854 almost sixfold as fast as its exports, and thus financed British imports of tea from China as well as its imports of cotton from the U.S.A.[2] India not only remained the exclusive preserve of English and Scottish merchants, virtually free from any threat of foreign competition. It also served as the fulcrum of Oriental commerce and as the inspiration of hopes for the expansion of Lancashire's trade throughout the whole littoral of Asia and the archipelago of the East Indies. In the event the increase in the export of cotton goods to India was not accompanied by any immediate large-scale expansion of exports to Java or to China. The export of opium from India however provided the key to trade with China, where Lancashire hoped after the Charter Act of 1833 to find another market comparable to India.

The industry's markets were so extensive that a full thirty years from 1814 to 1843 were required to establish the superiority of the Indian market to all others. In 1820 India had imported slightly more in value of cotton manufactures than the Gibraltar entrepôt and had ranked as the eighth largest overseas market of the cotton industry. Thereafter she surpassed the West Indies as an export market in 1822 and rose in status from the fifth largest market in 1821 to the third in 1827 and

[1] W. J. Barber, *British Economic Thought and India 1600–1858. A Study in the History of Development Economics* (Oxford, Clarendon Press, 1975), 122–3.

[2] Chaudhuri, *Economic Development of India* (1971), 25, 37–8.

to the second in 1836, when she surpassed both the U.S.A. and Brazil. The establishment of the primacy of the Indian market, first in volume in 1839 and then in value in 1843, was almost wholly unexpected in England and marked a most important turning-point in the history of the Lancashire cotton trade. That industry adapted itself to the new vent for its calico, continued to increase its exports to India faster than to any other market, and acquired therein a vested interest lacked by any other staple industry of the realm. In the expansion of its exports to India it found compensation for the stabilization of its exports of piece-goods to Europe in the 1840s and 1850s. It secured a new lease of life and increased, until 1881, its export bias as Asia became from the 1840s a more extensive market than Europe for piece-goods and from the 1860s a more valuable one. Britain remained the largest foreign supplier of the Indian market until it was surpassed by Japan in 1935–6. India remained from 1843 until 1939 the most valuable export market of the British cotton industry.

India became more important as a market for cloth than for yarn, for unfinished than for fully finished cloth, and for cheap than for expensive goods. Her distinctive imports became the grey goods which were white or plain unbleached calicoes shipped in the loom state and used for the manufacture of shirting. England supplied those unfinished grey goods because it could not print designs or colours acceptable to the refined taste of Indian consumers who had been accustomed for millenia to appreciate the pure and simple in design and the subdued harmonies of colour appropriate to the brilliant sunlight of their homeland.[1] Britain could not in fact compete with the dyeing and printing industry of the East and produced only one type of dyed goods palatable to Oriental taste in Turkey red cloth and yarn. Thus it found in India a market for the very cheapest of its products. Its exports of plain calico to India first surpassed those of muslins, in length in 1818 and in value in 1823, and then exceeded those of dyed or printed calico, in length in 1824 and in value in 1827.[2] India and

[1] A. Wynter, *Curiosities of Toil* (London, Chapman, 1870), i. 155, 160, 'Indian Textile Fabrics'.

[2] M. Desai, 'Demand for Cotton Textiles in Nineteenth-Century India', *Indian Economic and Social History Review* ,1971, 346–7.

China goods became by 1835 the cheapest of all the export products of the industry and remained such throughout the century.[1] The pervading influence of the Indian market transformed the structure of the whole export trade in cotton goods and depressed their general level of quality as the total exports of grey and bleached goods exceeded those of printed and dyed goods first in quantity from 1826 and then in value from 1842. Thus the export trade in piece-goods became dominated by plain unfinished cloth and so established the pattern which it retained for eighty years until 1923. Blackburn perfected in 1841 the plain calico power-loom and so made possible the extensive manufacture of cheap goods for Indian consumption. It became the largest centre of production of India goods and the main importer of yarn. Oldham became the leading source of supply of the Blackburn yarn market. Both towns derived a considerable stimulus from the expansion of the Indian trade and both became in large measure dependent on it, unlike the centres of the home trade. From 1843 England expanded its exports of piece-goods more rapidly than those of yarn and its exports of cheap cloth more rapidly than its exports of fine cloth. India became the greatest single beneficiary from the long-term decline in the price of cotton and cotton manufactures, since the price of raw cotton formed a far higher proportion of the total price of grey goods than of that of finer goods. That decline in price enabled Lancashire to tap more extensively the immense market of the subcontinent since demand proved to be price-elastic and expanded with the decline in price.

For a variety of reasons the British cotton industry succeeded in penetrating the Indian market to a far greater extent than it tapped the Chinese market. The demand for Lancashire goods was satisfied at the expense of the indigenous industry and developed in harmony with the reorientation of the economic structure of Indian society, with the increasing transformation of the country from an exporter of manufactures into an exporter of agricultural produce, with the increasing monetization of taxation, with the increasing demand in Britain for the raw materials of India as well as in China for its opium, and

[1] Sandberg, 'British Cotton Textile Exports' (1968), 14.

with the equalization in 1828–36 of the import duties on East Indian produce with those on West Indian. That process of development did not transform India's export surplus into an import surplus and may well have enabled English exports to generate more Indian exports, so reinforcing the pressure exerted by the transfer payments to England. India remained the ideal market for the cotton industry. Unlike Europe or China she used cotton for the entire clothing of her people because its light and absorbent fabric was perfectly adapted to her tropical climate and to the limited resources of her agricultural society. The growth of the indigenous population progressively extended the market for Lancashire goods and created an immense aggregate demand, based upon a limited consumption per head by a vast and expanding number of people and further extended by a probable increase in both income per head and consumption per head of cotton cloth.

The extension of British power within the subcontinent differentiated India fundamentally from China and encouraged her to accept England as her clothier as well as her ruler. The educated orders of society adopted British goods as a symbol of superior status and as a means of association with the British Raj. The supply price of those goods was reduced by the erosion of the monopoly of the East India Company, by the increase in freedom of trade, by the abolition in 1844–8 of internal transit dues in an achievement never imitated in China, by the extension of transport facilities within India, by the expansion of shipping, and by the development of communications between England and India. British trade with India expanded most rapidly when it was conducted by the long sea route around the Cape: the more expensive overland route through Egypt did not apparently succeed in attracting shipments of piece-goods before the 1860s. Such an achievement by sail-based traffic was the more notable because of the competitive attraction of Atlantic commerce: it furnished Liverpool with a much more valuable trade in the export of piece-goods than the import of raw cotton. The growth of trade with India increased the dependence of Lancashire first upon the East India Company and then upon the Government of India for the extension of transport facilities, for the maintenance of minimal barriers to its exports, and for the avoidance of any protectionist measures in the interests of indigenous manufacturers.

The size of the potential market in India, however, remained limited not only by the material poverty of the population but also by the recurrence of poor harvests, by the religious inhibitions upon marriage during the inauspicious twelfth year of the Hindu calendar, by the limited extent of cash-crop cultivation, by the autarchic character of the village community and by the massive resilience of the indigenous cotton industry. The village communities preserved the subsistence basis of their economy, especially in Agra and Oudh, and were not undermined by the influx of Lancashire cottons, as was thought by Marx in 1853 and by Cunningham in 1882. Their primary reliance upon agriculture enabled the extensive manufacturing population of the countryside to find in spinning and weaving an ideal occupation for the hot dry season of the agricultural year. The hand-loom weavers were further sustained by the strength and inelasticity of feminine demand, particularly for fine and fully finished fabrics. They designed their products to meet the exact needs of their customers in the most conservative of markets and profited by the sheer incapacity of Britain to rival in quality the muslins of Bengal. They ceased to decline in number, apparently after the crisis of the 1820s, and may well have swelled their ranks, though probably not in proportion to the growth of population.[1] They adapted their industry to the new conditions of trade and imported from England cheap mill-spun yarn in increasing amounts to supply their looms. Those imports of yarn began in 1817 and were first recorded in the trade statistics of India from 1824. They breached the monopoly of the indigenous spinner and may thus have produced a sympathetic decline in the price of domestic yarn, to the benefit of local weavers. The export of yarn to those weavers was deplored in Lancashire in 1823 as an ill-omen for the future prosperity of the English cotton industry since it might enable them to survive the competition of Lancashire cloth, to drive the steam-looms of England out of existence,

[1] M. D. Morris, 'Towards a Reinterpretation of Nineteenth-Century Indian Economic History', *Journal of Economic History*, Dec. 1963, 612–13, reprinted in the *Indian Economic and Social History Review*, Mar. 1968, 8–10; idem, 'Trends and Tendencies in Indian Economic History', *Indian Economic and Social History Review*, Dec. 1968, 377–84.

and to become 'weavers for the whole world'.[1] Such apocalyptic fears were exaggerated and remained unrealized in their original form. The Indian weavers demonstrated the extent of the growing demand for mill-spun yarn and provided the new spinning mills of Bombay from the 1860s with their main market but also presented a great obstacle to their adoption of the power-loom.

Such constraints limited Lancashire at first to the markets of the three Presidency towns and prevented it before the 1850s from tapping the markets of the rural interior. For fifteen years from 1843 India thus remained the main overseas market of the cotton industry but merely as the first amongst equals. Only the post-Mutiny boom exposed her to the full impact of the revolution in power-weaving, sharply increased the consumption per head of imported cloth, raised her share of the industry's exports markedly from 15·5 per cent in 1856–7 to 25·8 per cent in 1858–9, and established her dominant influence in the export trade. India also supplied an entrepôt from which Lancashire yarn and calico were re-exported to markets within the traditional sphere of her country trade around the littoral of the Indian Ocean. The astounding growth of trade with India compelled the cotton industry to reject the anti-imperialism of Cobden and to support the expensive military budget of India as well as the opium trade with China. It powerfully reinforced the conservative disposition of the cotton world and encouraged it to support governmental policies intended to serve its interests.

The Indian market proved remarkably buoyant, expanding its imports from Lancashire much faster than any other market. It increased its imports of piece-goods almost twice as fast as the rest of the world between 1820 and 1886 and 50 per cent faster between 1887 and 1913. Exports to India invariably expanded during a general boom in trade and very often increased in years of widespread economic depression,[2] so that Indian demand became an important counter-cyclical influence. Thus the Indian market cushioned the cotton industry against the full effects of the depression of 1837–42, became

[1] R. Guest, *A Compendious History of the Cotton Manufacture* (Manchester, Thomson, 1823; London, Cass, 1968), 48–50; criticized by Baines, 527.

[2] As in 1826, 1839, 1854, 1857, 1861, 1866, and 1877.

therein the pre-eminent outlet for cheap cloth, and so encouraged the spread of specialized power-weaving firms for the supply of a market absorbing more than half of the increment in the exports of cotton cloth. The same counter-cyclical function was fulfilled during 1854 and helped to rescue the industry from the depression induced by the outbreak of the Crimean War. A shrinkage in Indian demand was primarily responsible for only two major depressions suffered by the industry, in 1847–8 and 1891–3,[1] but also proved an ancillary influence in ten recessions experienced between 1829 and 1897.[2] The nature of such fluctuations in demand was fully understood by Larpent in 1840 as well as by Baird Smith in 1861, and was clearly explained in 1870 by Ollerenshaw, who first related them to the variations of the harvest and thereby to the comparative incidence of the rain-bearing monsoon. 'In proportion that grain is cheap and plentiful or scarce and dear in India, will our trade in Lancashire be flourishing or depressed.'[3] His theory deepened the local understanding of the nature of the Indian market and demonstrated the close dependence of the cotton industry upon the fortunes of Indian agriculture. It was quickly accepted because it explained the depression of the 1870s as a product of the five successive years of poor harvests in Asia from 1874 to 1878.[4] Ollerenshaw paved the way not only for the bold formulation in 1875 of the sunspot theory of an eleven-year trade cycle[5] but also for the establish-

[1] The reduction in Indian demand accounted for 67 per cent of the decline in the volume of piece-goods exports in 1847 and for 32 per cent of the loss of export values by the industry in 1847–8. It was also responsible for 105 per cent of the decline in the volume of piece-goods exports in 1891 but only for 30·5 per cent of the loss of export values in 1891–3.

[2] In 1829, 1831, 1837, 1841–2, 1845, 1860, 1869, 1878–9, 1884–5, and 1897.

[3] J. E. Ollerenshaw, 'Our Export Trade in Cotton Goods to India', *Transactions of the Manchester Statistical Society*, 13 Apr. 1870, 114.

[4] *Manchester Guardian*, 15 Aug. 1879, 4iv, 'The Manchester Market and the Eastern Trade'.

[5] W. S. Jevons, *Investigations in Currency and Finance*, ed. H. S. Foxwell (London, Macmillan, 1884), 194–205, 'The Solar Period and the Price of Corn', a paper read to the British Association in 1875; W. T. Hesketh, 'The Influence of Sun-Spots on Prices. Professor Jevons' Theories Explained', *Transactions of the Manchester Statistical Society*, 9 Dec. 1914, 16; R. D. Collison Black, 'W. S. Jevons and the Economists of his Time', *Manchester School*, Sept. 1962, 216–20.

The cyclical incidence of sunspots had first been announced in 1843 by H. S. Schwabe (1789–1875) of Dessau, on the basis of observations extending over seventeen years.

ment in 1877 of the first Indian Famine Fund in Lancashire.[1]

The establishment of such famine funds may be assumed to have been intended to maintain Indian demand for Lancashire goods. The theory of the ultimate dependence of that demand upon the incidence of the monsoon may however be debatable. The poorest members of Indian society undoubtedly lay outside the market for Lancashire goods throughout the century and thus remained uninfluenced by harvest-induced variations in purchasing-power. Bumper harvests in a limited local market might also reduce the monetary returns reaped by ryots and thereby their effective demand. On the other hand, high agricultural prices, such as were experienced during the Cotton Famine, diffused prosperity amongst the sellers of primary produce. Even high grain prices expanded purchasing-power amongst a numerous class of grain dealers. Whether the enlarged demand of those dealers concentrated upon calico or extended to more luxurious textiles and whether, if it did enhance the demand for imported cloth, it was sufficient to counterbalance the depressed demand amongst the ryots, remains contentious. Informed contemporaries however regarded the social penetration of Lancashire cloth as much more extensive in India than in China and accepted the conclusion elaborated by Ollerenshaw on the basis of his examination of the trade statistics during the twelve years 1858–69. Increases in the retail price of seven food grains over the 38 years 1861–98[2] seem to have harmonized with reductions in the import of Lancashire goods in the wake of at least three of the four great famines of the period, i.e. in 1860, 1877–8, and 1897–8. The influence of the Orissa famine was apparently reflected not in any absolute reduction in such imports during 1866 but in a much smaller increase in the volume of imports to Calcutta than in that of imports to Bombay or Madras.

The expansion of Anglo-Indian trade in textiles encouraged efforts to develop a symbiosis between the two countries on the basis of the exchange of raw cotton for calico. Such schemes invariably exaggerated the potential capacity of India for the

[1] *Manchester Guardian*, 22 Aug. 1877, 5i–ii, 6ii–iii.

[2] *Select Committee appointed to Inquire into the Indian Currency, Index and Appendices* (C.39376 of 1899), 163–71, Appendices 30–8.

production of cotton.[1] They also minimized the difficulties involved in converting Lancashire from dependence upon the medium-stapled cotton of America to the use of short-stapled Surat as well as those inherent in replacing a multilateral by a bilateral pattern of trade. India did indeed supply England during the forty years 1820–59 with 13·8 per cent of the total weight of its imports of raw cotton[2] and remained important until 1891 as an auxiliary source of supply but never furnished more cotton than the U.S.A. except in 1818 and again in 1862–6, under the stimulus of the unprecedented price inflation of the Cotton Famine. Indian cotton remained burdened for thirty years until 1828 by a discriminatory import preference in favour of West Indian cotton and could not hope to secure, in the era of free trade, either an export bounty or an import preference.[3] Thus India did not regularly supply England with more cotton than Brazil until 1832 and did not regularly ship more cotton to England than to China until 1849. She could not compete upon equal terms with America and tended to increase her exports of cotton only in response to a short crop in the U.S.A. and to the high prices attendant thereon so that her export-response lagged by a year behind any reduction in American exports. The pressure of Lancashire interests in years of high prices upon the sole imperial source of cotton supply saddled the Indian taxpayer with the heavy cost of several 'cotton roads' and 'cotton railways'.[4] Manchester failed however to convert the 'official mind' of India to a commercial view of its great fief, which remained much less important as a supplier of raw cotton than as an outlet for Lancashire calico.

* * *

England did not support its textile exports by the export of capital but by the maintenance of full freedom of access to its

[1] J. Briggs, *The Cotton Trade of India* (London, Parker, 1840), 2; T. Ellison, *A Hand-Book of the Cotton Trade* (London, Longman, 1858), 73.

[2] J. A. Mann, *The Cotton Trade of Great Britain* (1860), 60.

[3] G. R. Porter, 'Examination of the Recent Statistics of the Cotton Trade in Great Britain', *Journal of the Statistical Society*, Dec. 1850, 307.

[4] W. J. MacPherson, 'Investment in Indian Railways, 1845–1875', *Economic History Review*, Dec. 1955, 177–86; R. J. Moore, 'Imperialism and "Free Trade" Policy in India, 1853–4', ibid., Aug. 1964, 135–45; C. W. Grant, *Bombay Cotton and Indian Railways* (London, Longman, 1850), 7, 9–41.

'natural and legitimate' market in India. That freedom was threatened first by the import tariff of India and then by the expansion of the cotton mills of Bombay. On three separate occasions between 1860 and 1895 Lancashire interests succeeded in securing a modification of the import duty in order to enhance their competitive position, to discourage the unwelcome side-effects of a revenue tariff, to curb the irrepressible urge of the Indian community to erect tariff dykes in self-defence, and to bestow upon the vast British dependency in the East the benefits of free trade. The first campaign against the import duty imposed for fiscal purposes after the Mutiny was waged under the pressure of a growing depression in the cotton industry caused by the overstocked condition of its markets and especially by the decline in exports to India in 1860 and 1861. Those efforts required two years in order to secure by April 1862 a revision of the customs valuations and a halving of the obnoxious duty by the reinvigorated Government of India which had replaced that of the East India Company.[1] The campaign supplied a precedent for the two later agitations of 1874–9 and 1894–5. Immediately its success facilitated the sale during 1863 of the industry's accumulated stocks and made possible a revival of productive activity in Lancashire from May 1863, despite the continued rise in price of the industry's raw material caused by the American Civil War. The great cotton boom of 1861–5 induced in Bombay by the war gave less stimulus to the import of piece-goods than to the efflux of silver from Britain to India. Indian imports of Lancashire cloth expanded markedly only in 1865–8 when prices resumed their long-term decline and the peak volume of imports attained in 1859 was surpassed in 1867. Thereafter consumption was further extended by the opening of the Suez Canal, which helped to raise during 1871 the share of cotton manufactures to their all-time peak proportions of 73 per cent of the total value of British exports to India and 57 per cent of the total value of India's merchandise imports.

The second campaign waged by Lancashire began in 1874 under the stimulus of a new commercial depression and the

[1] P. Harnetty, *Imperialism and Free Trade: Lancashire and India in the mid-nineteenth century* (University of British Columbia Press, Manchester University Press, 1972), 7–30.

beginning of the long decline in silver prices, which lasted from 1873 until 1902. That agitation was directed against the competition of the new mills of Bombay which enjoyed in 1873–4 a boom comparable to that in contemporary Oldham. Those mills employed Parsi capital and cheap Maratha labour upon English machinery and cheap cotton to produce the cheapest coarse counts in the world for the largest of all markets. They spun yarn in order to supply not power-looms but hand-loom weavers in India and in China, whose market was tapped from 1873 under the stimulus of the decline in the rupee exchange. Their competition was regarded in England first with incredulity, then with alarm, and finally with horror.[1] Their yarn increasingly replaced Lancashire yarn in the export trade of India, whose re-export of foreign yarn declined from the peak value recorded in 1877–8. The agitation by Lancashire against what it regarded as a protective import duty evoked prolonged opposition from the British administration in India and from the Bombay Millowners' Association established in self-defence in 1875. Thus it required five years in order to secure in 1879 the eventual remission of the duty on all grey cloth made from yarn up to counts of 30, so as to preserve the surviving heavy trade and prevent any loss of the medium or shirting class of goods by Britain. That concession was apparently made in the vain hope of rallying support in Lancashire to the Disraeli ministry in the anticipated general election. Its effect was to produce an immediate and rapid substitution in the export trade of duty-free shirtings made from 30s for the dutiable finer fabrics made from 30s–50s, to make retention of the duties pointless, and to reinforce the stimulus to exports supplied by the good harvest of 1879. The value of the piece-goods shipped to India rose during 1880 by a massive 43 per cent and the share of imports in the total consumption of cotton cloth first rose to more than half.

The complete abolition of the cotton duties in 1882 inaugurated a brief period of free trade between the two countries and fostered the hope that India might supply England with wheat as well as cotton and thus with both a shield and a

[1] J. A. Mann, *The Cotton Trade of Great Britain* (1860), 73–8; R. A. Arnold, *The History of the Cotton Famine* (London, Saunders, 1864, 1865; Cass, 1966), 17.

weapon against American protectionism.[1] England remained unhampered by foreign competition in its main market and profited by the marked increase in population during the 1880s,[2] raising her exports to India to new heights. In 1886 they reached the all-time peak proportion of 43·7 per cent of her total exports of piece-goods. Lancashire failed however to regain the trade in coarse goods which it had lost to its native competitors. The natural advantages of India for the manufacture of coarse yarn and goods remained unimpaired, even after the passage of the first Indian Factory Act in 1881. Her cotton mills did not decline in number, as had been expected,[3] but expanded anew from 1882 and at a faster rate than ever before, doubling their spindleage during the next decade. They adopted ring-spinning from 1883 and spun coarse counts which became increasingly competitive in the markets of Asia, reducing English exports of yarn to China from their maximum volume of 1880 and those to Japan from their peak level of 1881. India increased the proportion of her yarn exported by one-third from 1882–3: she first became a net exporter of yarn from 1882 and first shipped in 1883 more yarn to China than did Britain, tapping therein an enormous market closed to the mills of Lancashire.[4] She exported a much higher proportion of her yarn than Britain had ever done and supplied by 1893–4 36·54 per cent of the world's exports of yarn, having reduced the British share to 51·22 per cent.[5] The growth of her industrial capacity began to remould the pattern of her foreign trade and carried further the transformation begun during the 1870s: it increased the share of manufactures in her exports, decreased their share in her imports and reduced the British share in both her exports and imports from their peak proportion of 1870–6.[6] The mills of Bombay became much more

[1] *Manchester Examiner and Times*, 12 Dec. 1882, 4v, 'The Prospects of Growth in Our Cotton Trade. Our Customers—India'.

[2] K. Davis, *The Population of India and Pakistan* (Princeton University Press, 1951), 26–7.

[3] *Manchester Examiner*, 28 Nov. 1882, 4iv, J. C. Fielden.

[4] *Manchester Guardian*, 22 Dec. 1888, 4vi, A. Galbraith, 'Lancashire and Bombay'.

[5] F. Merttens, 'The Hours and Cost of Labour in the Cotton Industry', *Transactions of the Manchester Statistical Society*, 18 Apr. 1894, 174.

[6] *Statistical Abstract Relating to British India from 1865 to 1874* (London, Eyre, 1875 C-1350), 35; *Statistical Abstract Relating to British India from 1872/3 to 1881/2. Seventeenth Number* (London, Eyre, 1883 C-3775), 90–1, which together show the

dangerous competitors of Lancashire than the mills of either the U.S.A. or of Europe.[1] They expanded their production more rapidly than imports increased from Britain, enhanced their competitive capacity during the era of free trade, and so extended the cultural renaissance of India to the economic field. Thus they began to shift the cotton industry back towards its traditional home in Asia where India enjoyed the advantage of a central location in relation to the world's largest markets for cotton yarn and cloth.

The interests of Lancashire in the Eastern trade had been recognized in 1884 by the inclusion of a Manchester merchant amongst the seven non-official British directors appointed to the board of the Suez Canal Company, on which he became the first and last representative of the cotton trade.[2] The threat to those interests implicit in any transfer of industrial power from Europe to Asia inspired the Manchester Chamber of Commerce in 1887 to set on foot its own inquiry into the competition of Bombay.[3] The danger became more prominent during the acute depression of 1891–3, which afflicted Blackburn in particular and generated an Asiatic scare in the economic world almost comparable to that of 1690–1720. Lancashire interests were able to secure a succession of measures intended to curb the competitive power of their Indian rivals, including an Indian Merchandise Marks Act in 1889 and a second Indian Factory Act in 1891. The closing in 1893 of the Indian mints to the coinage of silver introduced a gold-exchange standard,[4] reduced the advantage of the Bombay

U.K. share of Indian exports to have reached a secondary peak of 55·75 per cent in 1870–1 after that of 1864–5 and its share of imports to have reached a peak of 80·2 per cent in 1876–7.

[1] Ellison, 317–24.

[2] John Slagg (1841–89) was the godson of Cobden and the author of the valuable report, *The Cotton Trade of Lancashire and the Anglo-French Commercial Treaty of 1860, being a Report of the English Evidence at the French Commercial Enquiry of 1870* (London, Longmans, 1870, 126pp.). He served as president of the Manchester Chamber of Commerce in 1881 and, in succession to Bazley, as the senior M.P. for the undivided constituency of Manchester during the five years from 1880 to 1885. For his obituary see the *Manchester Guardian*, 8 May 1889, 5ii, viii.

[3] Manchester Chamber of Commerce, *Bombay and Lancashire Cotton Spinning Inquiry. Minutes of Evidence and Reports* (Manchester, Ireland, 1888, 397pp.).

[4] O. Heyn, *Die Indische Währungsreform* (Berlin, Guttentag, 1903), 121–4, 128–32, 150–8; *The Bimetallist*, Nov. 1900, 125–8, Dec. 1900, 139–43, 'Currency Legislation and the Bombay Mills'.

mills in the China market by 16 per cent and ushered in a recession in India's exports of yarn, which only surpassed their volume of 1892–3 four years later.[1] The subsequent increase in imports from Europe made tariff reform an almost inevitable result of the monetary reform. The intellectual foundations of the free-trade regime were undermined by the introduction of the idea of protection into Indian economic thought by the Maratha Brahman, Mahadev Govind Ranade, in 1890–2, with the sanction of the anti-British school of historical economics.

The restoration in 1894 of the Indian import duty brought to an abrupt end the period of free trade inaugurated in 1882 but was presented as a purely fiscal necessity. That measure produced a wave of anticipatory shipments of cloth, increased the export of piece-goods to India by 22 per cent during 1894, and raised the proportion of piece-goods taken by the Indian market to 42·8 per cent in 1894. During 1895 the volume of exported piece-goods shrank by 24 per cent in the steepest fall of the whole fifty years between 1848 and 1898, under the influence of famine as well as of the new tariff. Lancashire manifested its intense hostility to the new duty in the general election of 1895[2] and secured from February 1896 a reduction in the duty on cotton piece-goods from 5 per cent to 3½ per cent,[3] effected, as in 1879, by the fiat of the Viceroy against the opposition of his own Council. The subsequent increase in its exports of piece-goods to India by 16·5 per cent during 1896 restored the belief in its natural monopoly of the markets of Asia and weakened any incentive to develop alternative outlets. Even its exports of yarn enjoyed a brief spurt, to China in 1895–8 and to India in 1896–7. Its exports of piece-goods were undoubtedly restrained by the Malthusian checks imposed upon the growth of India's population during the 1890s. Those exports did not surpass their record volume of 1894 until 1905 but soared during the great Edwardian boom in Indian exports, which made Britain more dependent upon

[1] Heyn, 213.

[2] H. Pelling, *Social Geography of British Elections 1885–1910* (London, Macmillan, 1967), 243, 247, 253, 260.

[3] P. Harnetty, 'The Indian Cotton Duties Controversy, 1894–1896', *English Historical Review*, Oct. 1962, 684–702.

the export surplus of its Eastern fief in order to finance its trading deficits with the rest of the world. Britain was relying increasingly on India for the continued expansion of its exports of calico at a time when the rate of increase in those exports to India had been since 1887 on a long-term downward trend.[1] That growing dependence was based in part upon unilateral fiscal concessions which Britain could never have secured from any independent state.

The short-term economic gains of Lancashire were the fruit of political concessions made by a Conservative ministry in 1895, as in 1879, in the apparent pursuit of electoral advantage and were purchased at a high long-term price. A countervailing excise buttressed the reduced import duty of 1896 and was maintained until 1917 at the same level as the import duty in order to neutralize any benefit to the Indian mill-owners. From 1896 until 1925 it remained in the consciousness of Indian intellectuals and nationalist politicians as a symbol of arbitrary dominion and alien exploitation because it was levied upon the coarse fabrics which never had, and never could have, competed with the products of Lancashire.[2] The excise also benefited the indigenous hand-loom weavers,[3] whose tax-exempt production increased side by side with that of the power-looms to reach its peak in 1938. The Swadeshi ('own country') movement provided, especially from 1905, an invisible but effective substitute for a higher tariff and even in an acapitalistic culture helped to transform the cotton mill into a new national institution. Between the wholly diverse cultures of India and Lancashire any true rapprochement was virtually impossible. Both Lancashire and Manchester were united in their attitude towards India by the common force of religious conviction and economic interest. The establishment of a local Asiatic Society in Manchester, such as was imaginatively proposed in 1893,[4] could hardly have served to bridge

[1] L. G. Sandberg, *Lancashire in Decline* (1974), 143.

[2] R. C. Dutt, *India in the Victorian Age. An Economic History of the People* (London, Paul, 1904), 543.

[3] G. Watt, *The Commercial Products of India* (London, Murray, 1908), 616, 618, 'The Cotton Plant'.

[4] L. C. Casartelli, 'Eastward Ho! or, Some Considerations on our Responsibilities in the East', *Transactions of the Manchester Statistical Society*, 22 Mar. 1893, 77–100.

the widening gap between the two worlds. The Anglo-Indian relationship lost the moral basis bequeathed by Ripon in 1884 and tended to become exploitative rather than co-operative. Even a purely economic symbiosis was precluded by India's failure to compete with the U.S.A. as a supplier of wheat and by the drastic decline between 1890 and 1892 in England's imports of Indian cotton, which left Lancashire almost wholly dependent upon America. The moral foundations of British economic power in India had been irretrievably weakened by the triumph of a purely manipulative policy.

The importance of India to the British cotton industry needs to be quantified, as in Table 7, in order that it may be neither exaggerated nor minimized. The export of piece-goods may appear to have been much more important in the trade of India than in that of Britain but was in fact more important to Britain because of its greater dependence upon foreign trade. The Indian market undoubtedly proved to be an ideal market since its unexpectedly large imports comprised not yarn but cloth. Its influence raised the Lancashire cotton industry to the status of a world industry, averted a catastrophic decline in its rate of growth after the depression of 1837–42, and extended its life-span for fifty years after it had reached the peak of its importance in the British economy. It became far more important to the cotton industry than to any other British industry and gave Manchester an interest therein lacked by Bradford or Birmingham since cotton manufactures represented 64 per cent of Britain's total merchandise exports to India between 1856 and 1886. It stimulated the development of many small power-weaving firms while the great combined firms remained firmly based in their extensive home trade. It never became as important to Manchester, Bolton, or Preston as to the towns on the frontier of industrial Lancashire such as Oldham and Burnley. It provided the largest single source of employment in north-east Lancashire and enlisted local interests in conservative opposition to Ripon's reforms. 'The loss of India through ambitious new schemes, through mal-administration or misgovernment, would be indeed a terrible calamity to north-east Lancashire.'[1]

[1] *Manchester Examiner and Times*, 27 Feb. 1883, 4iv, [J. C. Fielden], 'The Cotton Trade of North-East Lancashire'.

TABLE 7

Expansion of the Indian Market for British Cotton Manufactures, 1820–1896

(%)

	Proportion of the Total Volume of Exports of Piece-Goods	Proportion of the Total Value of Exports of Cotton Manufactures	Proportion of the Total Value of Merchandise Exports to India	Proportion of the Total Value of Merchandise Imports into India
1820	5·7	5·15	28·44	
1821	7·39	6·98	32·21	
1822	6·86	6·66	38·14	
1823	5·26	5·16	25·94	
1824	5·72	4·79	27·61	
1820–4 Average	6·06	5·75	30·47	
1825	5·52	4·67	28·66	
1826	8·61	7·44	31·36	
1827	9·9	9·81	47·6	
1828	10·34	10·6	52·68	
1829	9·87	8·59	49·65	
1825–9 Average	8·85	8·22	41·99	
1830	11·74	9·76	56·75	
1831	10·3	9·65	58·88	
1832	11·24	9·39	54·99	
1833	9·22	8·1	52·29	
1834	7·01	6·21	49·48	
1830–4 Average	9·9	8·62	54·48	
1835	9·29	8·14	56·43	
1836	11·65	10·48	60·25	
1837	12·08	10·49	59·81	
1838	11·61	10·13	63·09	
1839	13·8	12·24	63·3	
1835–9 Average	11·69	10·3	60·58	
1840	18·35	15·7	64·3	
1841	19·42	14·6	61·26	
1842	21·18	14·12	59·2	
1843	23·5	16·79	61·48	
1844	22·88	18·57	62·28	
1840–4 Average	21·07	15·96	61·7	

Table 7 (contd.)

1845	21	16·12	62·8	
1846	21·75	16·96	67·48	
1847	15·85	13·62	58·11	
1848	16·9	13·39	59·83	37·52
1849	20·17	14·86	58·47	43·72
1845–9 Average	19·13	14·99	61·34	40·62
1850	20·95	16·66	58·69	40·5
1851	20·99	16·77	64·64	50·34
1852	20·5	15·75	64·02	47·64
1853	20·16	15·52	62·04	51·6
1854	28·28	20·66	65·43	52·4
1850–4 Average	22·18	17·07	62·96	48·5
1855	21·91	16·8	53·47	45·63
1856	20·8	15·32	49·61	43·21
1857	21·18	15·57	46·51	37·48
1858	31·35	24·03	56·53	45·12
1859	34·6	27·63	67·1	48·21
1855–9 Average	25·97	19·87	54·64	43·93
1860	26·04	20·71	63·51	47·07
1861	28·69	22·57	64·47	45·9
1862	27·57	23·39	58·8	42·55
1863	29·7	27·62	65·71	44·01
1864	25·07	22·9	62·98	46·99
1860–4 Average	27·41	23·44	63·09	45·3
1865	25·01	19·87	62·31	46·66
1866	21·18	17·28	64·44	52·03
1867	22·81	17·67	57·42	49·62
1868	28·33	20·53	65·39	52·47
1869	21·86	16·16	61·79	49·49
1865–9 Average	23·84	18·3	62·27	50·05
1870	24·1	17·97	66·49	56·27
1871	27·1	17·99	72·57	56·74
1872	24·48	16·32	70·81	56·55
1873	28·56	19·43	70·34	56·2
1874	31·2	21·85	67·35	56·05
1870–4 Average	27·09	18·71	69·51	56·36
1875	31·42	21·89	64·75	51·86
1876	31·89	22·08	66·66	52·95
1877	34·13	24·11	65·88	51·3
1878	32·97	22·88	64·78	46·24
1879	32·49	22·53	67·44	49·47
1875–9 Average	32·58	22·7	65·9	50·36

Table 7 (contd.)

	Proportion of the Total Volume of Exports of Piece-Goods	Proportion of the Total Value of Exports of Cotton Manufactures	Proportion of the Total Value of Merchandise Exports to India	Proportion of the Total Value of Merchandise Imports into India
1880	37·33	27·92	69·29	52·89
1881	34·54	25·5	68·97	51·06
1882	35·31	25·76	67·18	49·62
1883	36·6	26·53	63·63	47·64
1884	37·19	26·4	62·78	46·21
1880–4 Average	36·19	26·42	66·37	49·48
1885	38·05	26·89	61·52	46·87
1886	43·69	30·77	67·64	49·72
1887	36·95	27·1	62·91	44·09
1888	40·39	29·5	65·28	47·34
1889	40·01	28·27	64·38	44·88
1885–9 Average	39·82	28·51	64·35	46·58
1890	39·44	29·89	66·11	44·92
1891	37·38	27·33	62·58	43·09
1892	37·98	26·33	62·21	40·93
1893	40·58	28	62	43·78
1894	42·85	29·86	67·78	46·57
1895	34·14	22·77	58·58	37·16
1896	39·04	26·56	61·25	41·37
1890–6 Average	38·77	27·25	62·93	42·55

Source: The statistics of exports to India are available in the *Tables of the Revenue, Population, Commerce &c. of the United Kingdom . . . From 1820 to 1831* (1833), in the *Tables Showing the Trade of the United Kingdom with different Foreign Countries and British Possessions . . . from 1831 to 1840* (1842), in J. A. Mann (1860), 117–18, Tables 18 and 19 for 1827–59, and in the *Annual Statement of Trade* for 1860–96. The absolute figures for 1815–1913 for both volume and value may be found in Sandberg (1974), 258–62.

The percentages in column 4 have been calculated from the figures in the *Statistical Abstract relating to British India*, 1840–96.

The merchandise exports to India in column 3 relate to exports of British goods only and exclude foreign produce. The merchandise imports into India in column 4 include imports from foreign countries and relate to the official year ending on 31 March, i.e. the figures for 1896 refer to the year ending on 31 March 1897.

Exports to India nevertheless remained more important in volume than in value and represented a smaller proportion of the value of the exports of all cotton manufactures than of piece-goods alone, a smaller share of the gross product of the industry, and an even smaller proportion of the value added by the industry. Lancashire never supplied more than a fraction of the coarse cloth consumed in India[1] and narrowed the basis of its market as it improved the average quality of both its yarn and cloth exports to India from the 1870s.[2] The renaissance of Indian industry took place first in the sphere of machine-spinning, checked the growing dependence of India upon Lancashire yarn, and reduced the share of cotton manufactures in the merchandise imports of India from their peak proportion of 57 per cent in 1871. The share of cotton manufactures in British exports to India also declined from their maximum share of 1871 but to a slighter degree so that British trade with India failed to become diversified. Cloth exports to India continued to expand to reach their absolute peak only in 1913, whereas yarn exports had reached their maximum in 1888 and exports of unbleached grey goods had reached their highest level in 1890. The competitive power of Lancashire remained strong enough to secure for it more than half of the total Indian market for cloth between 1880 and 1915.[3] India had however become relatively less important as a market since the 1880s. Yarn exports to India had reached their peak proportion of the industry's exports by volume in 1880 and piece-goods their peak proportion therein in 1886. At the summit of its comparative importance the Indian market only equalled in *per capita* consumption that of the whole outside world: in 1886 it imported only 30·8 per cent of the total value of the exports of cotton manufactures and only 22·2 per cent of the gross product of the cotton industry. The year 1886 was however, like 1894 and 1913, not really typical of the whole period. During the forty-seven years 1850–96 India absorbed only 22·7 per cent of the total value of the industry's exports. Thus any overemphasis upon its role as the key to the expansion of industrial capitalism in Britain would be only slightly less misleading than any stress upon the West Indies as the main source of capital for the Industrial Revolution of the eighteenth century.

* * *

[1] W. W. Hunter, *The Imperial Gazeteer of India* (London, Trübner, 1886, 2nd edn.), vi. 600.

[2] Sandberg, 'British Cotton Textile Exports' (1968), 18.

[3] F. Utley, *Lancashire and the Far East* (London, Allen, 1931), 286.

China was separated from Britain by an even wider cultural abyss than India and was at first regarded by British manufacturers as a more easterly extension of the Indian market. In fact it remained profoundly different from India in many important respects, in its colder climate, its much larger population, its greater self-sufficiency, its more resilient culture, its formal independence of foreign powers, its intense repugnance to the admission of foreign trade and traders, and its greater capacity to resist the adoption of innovations from the West. Its inhabitants were less dependent than those of India upon cotton clothing since they also wore fur and silk. China maintained its own cotton industry[1] and had developed the export of 'nankeens' to England but faced a similar challenge to India from the expanding industrial and commercial power of Lancashire. Its exports of nankeens reached their peak quantity in 1819.[2] Its imports of British cotton manufactures were diverted from the overland route via the Russian entrepôt to the cheaper sea route via the Cape. Lancashire piece-goods failed however to penetrate the Chinese market as fast as the Indian and were not sold at a profit in Canton until 1827.[3] Thereafter British purchases of nankeens reached their peak volume in 1828 and were surpassed in 1831 by British exports of cotton manufactures to China. Those exports first exceeded in value the exports of woollen and worsted manufactures to China in 1837, after the East India Company had lost its monopoly of the Canton trade in 1833, but did not expand markedly or immediately after the Opium War of 1840–2, as had been expected.[4] They certainly did not enter into competition with the products of the local hand-loom: even less did they begin to drive them from the market. They were unsuitable in design, being too light in weight and too expensive

[1] M. Elvin, *The Pattern of the Chinese Past* (London, Eyre, 1973), 268–84, 'Rural Markets and Rural Industries'.

[2] H. D. Fong, *Cotton Industry and Trade in China* (Tientsin, Nankai University, 1932), 273.

[3] Ibid. 244.

[4] G. R. Porter, *The Progress of the Nation* (London, Knight, 1836), iii. 114–15; J. A. Hobson, *Richard Cobden* (1918), 197–8, Cobden to Henry Richard, 14 Jan. 1857; G. W. Cooke, *China* (London, Routledge, 1858), 185–209; E. LeFevour, *Western Enterprise in Late Ch'ing China. A Selective Survey of Jardine, Matheson and Company's Operations, 1842–1895* (Cambridge, Harvard University Press, 1968), 35–7, 167.

for a peasant community. Thus British imports of tea and silk continued to be financed from India's export surplus rather than from the proceeds of British exports to China.

The attractions of the vast untapped market of Cathay, embracing an estimated 37 per cent of the world's population in 1850, were probably influential in reconciling Manchester to dependence upon the Palmerstonian State. As the trade of Hong Kong and Shanghai expanded during the Tai-Ping Rebellion (1853–64) and the value of exports to China recovered after the depression of 1853–5 support grew in Manchester for the empire-building activity of Bowring in Hong Kong and of Brooke in Sarawak on the flank of the route to the China seas and the land of four hundred million potential customers. In the general election of 1857 precipitated by the 'Arrow War' the representatives of the Manchester School were decisively defeated by the supporters of Palmerston.[1] The manufacture of China goods had shifted during the strike of 1853–4 from Preston to Blackburn, the home of the Indian trade, but remained much less valuable than the export trade to India. The population of China suffered heavy losses of over 10 per cent during the Tai-Ping Rebellion and thereafter, for almost a century, grew much more slowly than the population of the rest of Asia. India with only half the population of China consumed sixfold as much imported cloth per head.[2]

In the post-Mutiny boom China nevertheless rose in status from the seventh largest foreign market of the cotton industry in 1858 to the third in 1859–60, after India and the U.S.A., and to the second in 1861. Not until 1868 did China establish a firm position as Lancashire's second largest customer after India. In that year the export of cotton manufactures to China, especially to the markets of the Yangtze valley, entered upon three years of rapid expansion as the disruptive effects of the Tai-Ping Rebellion subsided and the shipments of tea and silk from Shanghai expanded by the new short route opened via the Suez Canal. Lancashire calico first became competitive in price with the product of the native hand-loom as American cotton after the Civil War sank more rapidly in price than Chinese cotton and the practice of heavy sizing was extended in

[1] A. W. Silver, *Manchester Men and Indian Cotton 1847–72* (1966), 82–5.

[2] Ellison, 152.

order to meet the demand for cheap though inferior cloth. The export of T-cloths, which closely resembled Chinese-woven cloth, expanded as their manufacture was extended to Burnley from 1868.

China responded to the alien encroachment upon its indigenous domestic industry by capitalizing upon the decline in yarn prices, by increasing its imports of yarn between 1870 and 1900 at a rate twentifold greater than its imports of cloth, by reducing its domestic spinning industry, and by reorganizing its hand-loom weaving upon the basis of large-scale production for the market.[1] Exports of yarn to China and Japan supplied no less than 86 per cent of the increment in the exports of yarn during the decade of the 1870s. Exports of cloth to China slackened their rate of growth during the 1870s, as British imports of China tea declined from their maximum level of 1877, but were supplemented by increased exports to South-East Asia, especially to Java, from which Dutch tariffs had effectively excluded them for fifty years from 1824 until 1873. Exports to China expanded anew during the 1880s but suffered a reduction in their rate of increase after 1890 in harmony with the declining importance of its imports of opium and of its exports of tea and silk. The quality of exports improved thereafter as they grew less rapidly in amount.[2] Those shipments served Lancashire as a stabilizing influence since they tended to increase when exports to India declined[3] and to shrink when exports to India increased.[4] The persistent lack of information in the West about the condition of trade and agriculture in China shrouded in mystery the factors governing local demand.[5] Manchester belatedly recognized the influence of the devastating floods of 1873, 1876, and 1882 as well as of the severe droughts of 1877–8 and 1892–4 in reducing the demand for its goods but hoped to extend its sales by a variety of mechanical means and especially by the extension of communications on

[1] R. H. Myers, 'Cotton Textile Handicraft and the Development of the Cotton Textile Industry in Modern China', *Economic History Review*, Dec. 1965, 617–19, where the total imports of yarn include those from India and Japan as well as Britain.

[2] Sandberg, 168–9.

[3] In 1845, 1852, 1860, 1864–5, 1879, 1881, 1885, 1887, and 1895.

[4] In 1839–40, 1846, 1850, 1854, 1873, 1877, 1883, 1886, and 1892–3.

[5] *Manchester Guardian*, 1 Jan. 1875, 4vi.

the Indian model. Thus it gave a favourable reception to several ambitious schemes mooted between 1886 and 1894 for an Indo-Burmese railway and a Burmo-Chinese railway,[1] which would have been even less economic ventures than a Euphrates valley railway.

The Chinese empire remained a fundamentally hostile and conservative market which Britain had vainly sought to 'open up' by seven successive treaties between 1842 and 1895. Its vast size restricted Western contacts to the treaty ports along its coasts and enabled its diverse regions to maintain a virtual self-sufficiency. Its autarchic economy produced no bulk exports to pay for imports and delayed until 1888 the conversion of its export surplus into an import surplus. Its subsistence agriculture, harvesting two crops of grain and cotton every year, supplied the raw material for the hard-wearing cloth which was woven on a domestic basis at no expense and was worn by the bulk of the population. The imports of plain cloth and coarse yarn from Lancashire made their greatest headway in the markets of the southern provinces but did not penetrate far into the interior. They were used not by the rural peasant masses but by the hong clerks, bookkeepers, shopkeepers, merchants, and craftsmen of the large coastal cities in order to clothe themselves in traditional Chinese style. The ineradicable Chinese preference for Chinese cloth was maintained by the absence of roads and railways and was reinforced by the internal tax-barriers, which had been generalized from 1861 during the Tai-Ping Rebellion and fulfilled the function of the prohibitive tariff dismantled by foreign intervention. An increase in the *per capita* consumption of Lancashire cloth even to the Japanese level of 1883 would have trebled the aggregate

[1] A. R. Colquhoun, *Across Chryse, being the Narrative of a Journey of Exploration through the South China Border Lands from Canton to Mandalay* (London, Low, 1883), ii. 189–241; idem, *Amongst the Shans* (London, Field, 1885), 300–23, 373–86; idem, *Dan to Beersheba. Work and Travel in Four Continents* (London, Heinemann, 1908), 194–208; H. S. Hallett, *Eastern Markets for Lancashire: treating with India and Burmah* (London, King, 1889, 24pp.); idem, *Eastern Markets for Lancashire: treating with Southern China and Indo-China* (London, King, 1889, 12pp.); idem, *A Thousand Miles on an Elephant in the Shan States* (Edinburgh, Blackwood, 1890), 414–34, 464–73; idem, 'The Remedy for Lancashire. A Burma–China Railway', *Blackwood's Edinburgh Magazine*, Sept. 1892, 348–63; H. F. Hibbert, 'Railway Extension in India and Burmah', *Transactions of the Burnley Literary and Scientific Club*, 6 Nov. 1894, 58–60.

value of the Chinese market while an increase to the Indian standard would have quintupled its value, making it the largest single overseas market of the cotton industry.[1] Such pipe-dreams remained unrealized and cotton manufactures failed to establish the same preponderance in the import trade of China as in that of India, supplying during the thirty years 1867–96 49 per cent of the imports of India but only 33 per cent of the imports of China.[2] Only in 1890 did they surpass opium as its most valuable import.

The indigenous hand-loom industry had developed to an enormous extent after 1870 and had extended from the cotton-growing provinces of the south into central and western China, where it enjoyed the advantages of cheap labour, cheap silver, cheap foreign yarn, and, above all, the official encouragement manifest in the differential taxation of foreign piece-goods.[3] Its supplies of foreign yarn extended from British to Indian yarn from 1873 and then to Japanese yarn from 1894. That vast industry was immeasurably more important than the hand-loom industry of India.[4] Its products were well suited to serve the needs of the vast expanding market of indigenous China and suffered no displacement by foreign competition. They outweighed the quantity of cotton cloth imported in 1891 over sevenfold and supplied fully 70 per cent of the teeming population of the interior with cheap, warm, and durable clothing, unadulterated by oversizing.[5] Their competition restricted the extensive penetration of Lancashire calico, which was in consequence much higher in quality than that exported to India and remained of service only to the secondary and peripheral market of the treaty-port economy. The limited degree of 'development' of the Chinese market undoubtedly deprived Lancashire of potential short-term profit but proved in the long run a blessing in disguise since it averted any increased dependence upon the markets of Asia and thereby

[1] Ellison, 154.

[2] See Table 7 and Fong, 248.

[3] Kang Chao, 'The Growth of a Modern Cotton Textile Industry and the Competition with Handicrafts' in D. H. Perkins (ed.), *China's Modern Economy in Historical Perspective* (Stanford University Press, 1975), 167–201, 320–4.

[4] A. Feuerwerker, 'Handicraft and Manufactured Cotton Textiles in China, 1871–1910', *Journal of Economic History*, June 1970, 338–78.

[5] *Report of the Mission to China of the Blackburn Chamber of Commerce 1896–7* (Blackburn, North-East Lancashire Press Co., 1898), 216–17.

an even more catastrophic collapse of its prosperity than in the event it actually suffered.

From 1890 China began slowly to follow the example set by Japan as well as India and established its own factory industry.[1] Those new spinning mills were mainly financed by the capital of the merchant importers of Shanghai. The yarn they spun in increasing quantities for the hand-looms of the interior prevented the imports of foreign yarn from rising beyond the peak volume attained in 1899 and condemned them to share after 1918 the decline experienced by the imports of British yarn since 1880. China's imports of British piece-goods reached their peak level in 1905, the year of the beginning of the cultural resurgence of Asia. Its total imports of piece-goods included an increasing proportion from Japan and continued to expand until 1920, declining markedly after it regained in 1928 the tariff autonomy lost in 1842.

Japan never supplied a market for piece-goods comparable to that of India or China but consistently imported from 1869 more yarn than cloth on the pattern typical of Europe since 1823. Its imports of yarn from England trebled during the 1870s, reached their peak in 1881 and were thereafter increasingly displaced by imports from India, which first equalled them in 1885. The Japanese market reached the peak of its relative importance for Lancashire in 1879, earlier than any other country in Asia. The explosive growth of cotton spinning in the 1880s, especially in Osaka, was based on the spinning on ring-frames of even coarser counts than those of Indian mills.[2] The rapid growth of that industry should not have surprised the cotton spinners of the West as much as it did, since the Japanese had very quickly mastered its technology and had speedily become independent of English workmen. They had successfully overcome their one great disadvantage in the comparative lack of indigenous cotton of suitable staple by importing their raw material first from China and then from

[1] R. S. Gundry, *China Past and Present* (London, Wilson, 1895), 129; *Manchester City News*, 30 Nov. 1895, 4iii, Duke Alcock, 'China versus Japan in Cotton Spinning'; J. Hesford, 'The Cotton Trade in China and Japan—Present and Prospective', *Lectures and Papers, Bolton and District Managers' and Overlookers' Association*, 1896, 135.

[2] H. Dyer, *Dai Nippon. The Britain of the East. A Study in National Evolution* (London, Blackie, 1904), 171, for statistics of 1888–1901.

India. They enjoyed the advantages of an old tradition of textile manufacture and a supply of young female hands who lived cheaply on rice and fish and worked the double shifts intolerable to Lancashire workers, so enabling mills to run night and day for seven days a week and to spread their fixed costs over the maximum possible amount of production.

Under such stimuli the domestic production of cotton yarn displaced imports from India from 1888, surpassed the total volume of imports from 1891 and replaced the silk industry by 1894 as the country's leading industry. In that year an import duty was imposed upon yarn at the same rate as upon cloth, creating a tariff unique in the world in its refusal to tax yarn less than cloth. In 1894 Japan also began the large-scale export of yarn to China, in competition with the yarn of Bombay, and then developed power-loom weaving to supply the military demand for uniforms generated by the Sino-Japanese War. It began to export yarn to the market opened up by that war in Korea and became successively a net exporter of yarn in 1897 and one of cloth in 1909. It continued to increase its imports of piece-goods from Britain until they reached their all-time peak level in 1905 under the stimulus of the Russo-Japanese War. The rise of that new industry threatened to relegate India to the status of a supplier of raw cotton to the mills of Japan, which replaced Germany from 1896 as the largest export market for Indian cotton, and, unlike Britain, made raw cotton much more important in its import trade than cotton manufactures were in its export trade. Bombay felt more threatened by Japan than did Lancashire, whose textile engineering industry benefited from the opening of a great new market additional to that of India.[1]

The Japanese challenge was made first in the China market through the successful capture of the incremental trade in yarn. Japan's exports of yarn to China reduced those of India to that market from their peak volume of 1906 and exceeded in succession those of Britain in 1910 and those of India in 1914. Japan developed primarily as an exporter of yarn rather than of cloth until 1916 and surpassed India in the value of its exports of yarn in 1913 and in the volume of its production of yarn in 1915. It achieved self-sufficiency earlier than India,

1 *Textile Recorder*, Sept. 1896, 129–30, 'Japanese Ambitions'.

despite its later start and assumed from 1913 second place to Britain as an exporter of yarn. Thus it laid a sound foundation for the great forward leap during the inter-war years when it surpassed Lancashire as a supplier of piece-goods to China in 1925 and to India in 1935.

Asia responded to the industrial challenge of the West by developing first its imports of yarn, then its own mill industry, and finally but slowly the power-weaving from the 1890s of grey cloth. The reinvigoration of hand-loom weaving paved the way for the successful establishment of spinning mills and for the entry of the Orient on to the modern industrial scene. The export of yarn from Lancashire to those weavers stimulated the development of machine-spinning in Asia in proportion to the size of the trade by creating demand and paving the way for indigenous enterprise. In that process of development the export of yarn served as the crucial catalyst, as Hirschman has argued, and the export of machinery merely marked the final stage. Thus the cotton industry became through its shipment of yarn abroad a suicidal trade, committed to the creation of foreign competitors. The new coarse spinning industries of India and Japan benefited from their proximity to the local market since transport costs formed a larger proportion of the cost of yarn than of cloth and a larger proportion of the cost of coarse counts than of fine counts. In the yarn trade Lancashire experienced its first great defeat in the world market, self-inflicted though it was, and began to suffer a secular contraction in its overseas markets as the exports of yarn to Asia declined from their peak volume of 1884 and shrank most sharply in the Far East. Thus the primary producers of the Orient rejected Lancashire's claim to monopolize their markets and declined to accept any unilateral extension of the division of labour to an international scale which would have assigned them in perpetuity to a subordinate role in the world economy. In response to the development of foreign spinning industries Lancashire shifted the balance of its trade away from the new economic battleground of eastern Asia. Thus exports of yarn to Asia reached their peak proportion of total yarn exports in 1880 and exports of piece-goods to Asia reached their peak proportion of the total exports of cotton cloth in 1888. That trend was however masked by the continuing expansion in the export of piece-goods to Asia, and especially to India, up to the peak level achieved in 1913. Lancashire also improved the quality of its production and its exports, so raising them above the competitive range of its new rivals: thus it improved the quality of its yarn exports from 1881 and of its cloth exports from 1890. Finally, from 1881 it began to pay increasing attention to the home market.

* * *

By virtue of its size, extent, longevity, imperial associations, and high statistical profile, the export trade has inevitably overshadowed the home trade, which has been neglected by all believers in the world-wide mission of the cotton industry and especially by the intellectual heirs of the Manchester School. The domestic trade nevertheless provided the industry with its original, primary, and natural market and continued to serve as the nearest, richest, and most profitable vent. The size of the home market was undoubtedly limited by the coldness of the English climate and by the filthy atmosphere of the large cities. Under such conditions cotton clothing was suitable for wear only during the summer and when worn tended to become quickly soiled by smoke and smut. The market was further restricted by the competition of both foreign and British textiles and by the influence of fashion which favoured the more luxurious fabrics of silk and worsted rather than the essentially functional cotton cloth. Those obstacles were largely overcome by the ability of the industry's employers to secure protective duties which progressively excluded East Indian textiles from the home market and by their ingenuity in exploiting the distinctive commercial properties of the cotton fibre. Cotton would combine readily with almost all other textile fibres and therefore formed an ideal constituent of mixed fabrics. It proved more suitable than any other fibre to mechanical spinning. It could be dyed in all colours, bleached as thoroughly as linen, and printed more effectively than silk. It could be made into a wide range of incredibly diverse fabrics covering the whole spectrum of textiles. The cotton industry therefore competed with other textile industries by imitating their products, borrowing their names, and marketing its imitations at a lower price. The traditional fustian ceased to be from the 1780s a hard-wearing mixture of linen and cotton and became an all-cotton product which supplied the original staple of the Manchester trade and replaced the lower quality of woollen cloths worn by the labouring orders, dividing male society between the wearers of broadcloth and the wearers of fustian. The cotton industry extended its competition with the linen trade by producing imitations of staple linen-shirting fabrics and selling them under such traditional names as cambrics and drills. It encroached upon the other main pillar of the domestic trade by producing sheeting, made first from 1823 from linen wefts and cotton warps and then in the 1850s from both cotton wefts and cotton warps, so completing the elimination of linen sheeting from the market which had begun in the 1830s.

The cotton industry competed with the silk industry by the successive manufacture of cotton velvets and velveteens from the 1740s, of muslins from the 1780s, of bandanna handkerchiefs and Paisley shawls from 1802, of poplin shirting from the 1820s, and of sateens for linings and dress goods from the 1830s. Above all, cotton prints revolutionized feminine dress and captured a fashion-conscious market amongst working-class women,[1] who thereby secured the luxury of silk at the price of cotton and became the major beneficiaries of the marked expansion in their production after the abolition of the excise in 1831. The cotton industry benefited by the long peace of the nineteenth century which deprived the woollen industry of military orders. From the 1830s it competed with that ancestral trade by producing cloth so superbly finished as to resemble either West Country broadcloth or Yorkshire tweed. The cheapness of cotton extended remorselessly the penetrative power of the new fibre and made it the most generally useful and the most widely used of all textiles. In so far as demand was both price-elastic and income-elastic the home trade expanded with the fall in the price of cotton goods and with the rise in income of the working classes. The utility of cotton clothing was extended by the institution of washing, a ritual which enjoyed quasi-religious sanction, especially under the influence of

[1] P. Gaskell, *The Manufacturing Population of England* (1833), 143.

Wesley, and tied the women of the lower orders to the wash-tub. Thus the domestic market experienced until the 1860s a long-term process of expansion as the working classes and the middle classes increased in numbers and wealth, a succession of good harvests effectively liberated their purchasing-power, and the cotton industry zealously extended its range of products to appropriate the markets of its rivals and to suit the taste and pocket of its new customers. Its influence in clothing the poor was so highly esteemed that it was even deemed to have contributed to the growth of population by inhibiting mortality.[1]

The home trade was increasingly captured by Manchester from London as the population of the northern counties expanded during the 1830s to exceed in numbers the inhabitants of the southern counties, as railway facilities were energetically extended under Lancashire auspices, and as Manchester extended its trade after 1836 from heavy calico into fancy goods. The home trade firms of Cottonborough conducted that trade not through the Exchange but from their warehouses and served as intermediaries between the country manufacturers of Lancashire and the country drapers of the whole of the British Isles. Those merchant houses fitted their trade into the pattern established for the service of the linen-draper and extended their commerce throughout the whole range of textiles, enabling their clients to secure all their needs through a single account and making 'Manchester goods' a synonym for textiles in general. From the 1830s they abandoned any interest in retail trade in order to concentrate upon their wholesale trade and to avoid competing with their own clients. They harnessed the energies of the country manufacturers to their service and abstained from manufacture on their own account to avoid competing with their suppliers. They profited by the increasing adoption of the new power-loom which proved particularly suitable for the weaving of plain goods for the needs of their trade.

Between 1830 and 1860 with the aid of the railways, the support of the banks, the services of an expanding army of commercial travellers, and the extensive facilities of their warehouses they established the supremacy of Manchester

[1] J. A. Mann, *The Cotton Trade of Great Britain* (1860), 32.

over Cheapside in what was the second largest distributive trade in the kingdom after that in food. Their warehouses gradually extended into the residential area of the town and were built from 1839 in the style of the palaces of Renaissance Italy, especially of Venice: their construction endowed the city with its most representative buildings and helped to make Manchester for a generation the centre of the country's most progressive architecture[1] as well as 'the inland metropolis of the North—the Florence, if I may so describe it, of the nineteenth century'.[2] Those firms preserved their monopoly of distribution by preventing provincial wholesalers from buying direct from the manufacturer and by establishing in 1841 their own Home Trade Association, an organization which the more competitive shipping merchants never imitated.

The home trade was put at grievous risk by the repeal of the Corn Laws and sank twice as much as exports in the depression of 1847. During the decade of the 1850s however the climate improved after the close of the 'little ice age' of 1590–1850 and produced a crop of the fine summers essential to a flourishing home trade. Effective demand for dress goods was extended, especially amongst mill-girls, by the rise in real wages and by the statutory establishment from 1850 of the Saturday half-holiday and the English week-end. In that decade the home trade in cotton goods enjoyed a boom: it survived without embarrassment the removal in 1846 of the last protective duties on imports, first surpassed in value the home trade of the woollen industry, and attained in 1860 what Hoffmann[3] regarded as its peak level of the nineteenth century, a level exceeded only in 1925.

During the Cotton Famine and especially in 1862 the industry, which had sold at home 39·5 per cent of the gross value of its product between 1834 and 1860, suffered large losses to its older rivals. Men replaced their fustians by broadcloth or shoddy suits and their cotton shirts by flannel ones

[1] C. Stewart, *The Stones of Manchester* (London, Arnold, 1956), 36.

[2] *Manchester Courier*, 3 Jan. 1876, 5iii, Thomas Worthington, 'Architectural Progress in Manchester', a presidential address to the Manchester Society of Architects founded in 1837.

[3] W. G. Hoffmann, *British Industry 1700–1950* (1955, 1965), 88, apparently in error since he identified the consumption of raw cotton per head of population with the home trade.

while women replaced their cotton prints by the cheap half-woollen dress goods of Bradford. Increased expenditure upon drink at the expense of clothing by an intemperate population was blamed for the subsequent depression of 1866–9 by a Methodist temperance crusader.[1] In the boom of 1871–3, however, expenditure upon drink increased simultaneously with that upon clothing and the industry recaptured its lost markets with the aid of cheap American cotton, especially when wool rose in price by 50 per cent during 1871. The home trade surpassed the record volume of 1860 in 1871 and exceeded in 1872 the record value of 1860 by 21 per cent. Undoubtedly it expanded less rapidly in aggregate value and much less rapidly in volume than the export trade between 1820 and 1881 so that its share of the industry's gross product sank from 44·5 per cent in 1819–21 to 34·3 per cent in 1881. It nevertheless remained proportionately more valuable than the industry's foreign trade because it catered for a wealthier market, profited by the non-economic element in the demand for fashionable goods, and increased the comparative unit-value of its goods while export goods sank in unit-value. Thus in 1850 the home trade consumed goods which embodied a unit-value one-third greater than that of export goods and incorporated only one-third of the raw material used by the industry but represented 50·5 per cent of its net product. In 1881 it consumed goods representing a unit-value almost double that of export goods and incorporating only one-seventh of the raw material used but embodying one-third of the net product.

The trade expanded under the secular influence of the growth of population, the increase in its purchasing-power, and the extension of a market economy. It freed itself from dependence upon the home harvest as the nation's food supply was extended to draw upon the harvests of the world, suffering its last depression of the traditional type under the influence of the short harvests of 1866–7. It still remained subject to seasonal boom in spring and autumn but passed increasingly under the influence of the fashion-cycle with the transition from a rural to an urban civilization and from a society of

[1] W. Hoyle, *An Inquiry into the Causes of the Present Long-Continued Depression in the Cotton Trade with Suggestions for its Improvement, By a Cotton Manufacturer* (London, Simpkin, 1869, 17pp.).

status-orders to one of classes. Fashion became more influential as ready-made clothing replaced fustian and as mill-girls freely indulged their taste for conspicuous consumption, to the concern of traditionalist minds.[1] The trade could even extend sales by raising rather than by lowering prices since a rise in price implied that goods were fashionable and scarce and so diverted demand from other textiles to cotton goods.[2]

The merchant houses of Manchester lost their monopoly of the home trade in the 1880s to the C.W.S. and to their rivals in London, Leeds, and Glasgow as the West Riding regained full control of the cloth trade and Glasgow secured compensation for the decline of its cotton industry.[3] The home trade in general became subject to certain restricting influences through the decline in the rate of population-growth, Parnell's boycott of English goods, the competition of the drink trade, the superior attraction of high-status textiles, the occurrence of such poor summers as that of 1888, and the impact of cyclical depression, which thrice afflicted the home trade more than the export trade, in 1873–9, in 1884–5, and in 1891–3. The industry's internal markets were nevertheless maintained and extended by the rise in real wages caused by the fall in food prices, the competitive extension of credit terms to drapers, the calico-parties of 1882–3,[4] the increase in neo-protectionist sentiments, reinforced by the Merchandise Marks Act of 1887, the propaganda of the arts and crafts movement, and the more extensive use of soap. Manufacturers were encouraged to pay increasing attention to the home trade by the decline in the rate of expansion of exports, the depression in the Bradford dress-goods trade and the calico-printing industry, the decline in demand for plain goods with the advent of the bicycle, and the

[1] *Manchester Examiner and Times*, 16 Nov. 1878, 6vi, 21 Nov., 6vi, 'Mill Hands and Dress'; *Manchester City News*, 3 Nov. 1894, 4vi, 'Our Female Workers: Dress and Unthrift'.

[2] *Textile Manufacturer*, Aug. 1894, 338.

[3] *Manchester City News*, 13 Oct. 1888, 5iv, 'The Manchester Home Trade. Present Position and Future Prospects' by 'Forty Years', 20 Oct., 6v–vi, 'Why is the Manchester Home Trade Bad?', 27 Oct., 4iii–iv, 5ii–iv, 3 Nov., 5i–iii, 10 Nov., 5i–iii; 17 Nov. 5i, B. Armitage, 'The Collection of Accounts', 24 Nov., 4v–vi, 'A Review of the Home Trade Question', the first of three weekly articles, 1 Dec., 4vi–5i, 8 Dec. 4iv–v; R. Spencer, *The Home Trade of Manchester* (London, Simpkin, 1890, 278pp.).

[4] *Manchester Guardian*, 26 June 1882, 8iii–vi, 25 June 1883, 8iv–vi.

increase in foreign imports. Thus they adapted themselves to the rise of the ready-made clothing trade and the shoddy industry and developed extensively the manufacture of fancy goods on Jacquard and dobby looms in competition with Continental manufacturers as well as with domestic calico printers. They also competed for the status-oriented market by devising products similar to those of other textile industries. Thus they resumed the historic cannibal function of their trade and made 'flannelette' (1876) to compete with the flannel industry, cheap Bradford-style goods to compete with the worsted trade, 'linenette' (1894) to compete with the linen trade, and schreinered or mercerized goods such as 'silkette' or 'silcot' (1894) to compete with the silk trade. Those products testified to their continuing adaptability to changes in market demand but remained peripheral to the great staple trade in 'domestics', i.e. shirting and sheeting. The home trade expanded markedly after the record exports to India in 1880 and raised its proportion of the industry's gross product from 26·8 per cent in 1861–81 to 28·2 per cent in 1882–96.[1] From 1882, when its volume surpassed the record level of 1871, until 1900 it expanded at a rate twice as fast as the export trade. By 1900 it had reattained the peak *per capita* consumption of 1860 and its aggregate consumption had reached a level double that of 1850. Thus Manchester survived the scare of 1888 and secured ample indirect compensation for the loss of its monopoly of textile distribution.

[1] There is no continuous series of statistics for the home trade comparable to that available for the export trade. Of the statistical surveys cited in the bibliography, Bazley (1857), 255, supplies figures of value and volume for 1847–56, Mann (1860), 106, for 1834–59, Forwood (1870), 382, for 1860–8, Watts (1877), 504, for 1867–76, and Ellison (1886), 308–9, for 1871–85. The quinquennial averages for 1876–1904 presented by W. A. S. Hewins in the *Report of the Tariff Commission* Vol. 2 (The Textile Trades), 1139, Table 29, wrongly assume that the average price of home manufactures was identical to that of exports. Of modern studies, R. C. O. Matthews, *A Study in Trade-Cycle History, 1833–1842* (Cambridge University Press, 1954), 151, presents estimates of value for 1825–42 and Blaug (1961), 376, estimates of both value and volume for the whole period 1827–90, which differ however from those of the accepted authority, Ellison.

CHAPTER 4

The Cotton Famine and the Loss of National Pre-eminence

> The Cotton Famine is an event that has burnt itself into the history of Lancashire.
> *London Quarterly Review*, January 1865, 313.

THE DEPRESSION of production during the Cotton Famine proved to be the most severe in the whole history of the industry and took it almost unawares, since it followed upon a decade of expansion almost as intense as that of the heroic age of 1780–1840. The industry had revealed its traditional phoenix-like capacity for recuperation after the successive crises of the 1840s and had experienced during the 1850s, to the surprise of Tory Protectionists, a great wave of credit-based expansion. The boom of the 1850s was stimulated by the growth of demand in the U.S.A. and Australia as well as in Asia and the Levant, by the rise in prices and in mill margins, by the improvement in technology, by the increased supplies of labour and capital, and by the enhanced specialization of function both between Liverpool and Manchester and between spinning and weaving firms, especially in the most rapidly developing centres of industry. The factory system acquired a firm social foundation as the inspiring ethos of free trade spread more widely, factory legislation extended a protective shield over mill-girls and children, wages began their long-term rise as Irish migration was diverted from Lancashire to the U.S.A., and the power-loom secured general acceptance by the 'sons and daughters of the loom', so reducing the number of hand-weavers as rapidly as it had during the 1830s. As power-weaving expanded upon the basis of Indian demand and small-scale enterprise the industry increased its employees by 24 per cent but its factories by as much as 62 per cent, and weavers' wages rose twice as fast in north-East Lancashire as in south Lancashire. The perfection of the carding-engine, the mule, and the loom stabilized the technology of the industry and ended an era of three successive generations of inventive workers, depriving operatives of any intellectual interest in their labour and canalizing their energies into demands for higher wages.

During the 1850s the industry increased its consumption of cotton by 66 per cent but doubled the quantity and value of its piece-goods exports. Those exports increased twice as fast as yarn exports, which were depressed between 1847 and 1853 by competition from Russia and Prussia in their respective domestic markets. The industry's home trade rose in value to exceed for the first time that of the woollen trade and the expansion of cotton weaving advanced the frontier of 'Cottonia' at the expense of the woollen industry in those districts of north-east Lancashire bordering upon Yorkshire. The boom culminated in the unprecedented imports and exports of 1858–61, in a vast extension of productive capacity and in the industry's first joint-stock boom in 1860–1. In the climactic year of 1860 the cotton trade attained a new peak of importance in the national economy: raw cotton supplied 17 per cent of the value of imports and 18·9 per cent of that of re-exports while cotton manufactures accounted for 38·3 per cent of the value of domestic exports. The value added by the industry amounted to 7·1 per cent of the gross National Income and the continued growth of population in Lancashire concentrated 12 per cent of the inhabitants of England and Wales into 3 per cent of the kingdom's area and into a highly vulnerable salient of the national economy.

The industry had become increasingly dependent upon foreign sources of supply and foreign markets, and appeared more than ever an exotic pursuit as its export trade expanded even faster than its home trade. It had however always been more concerned with the supply of raw cotton than with the market for its finished goods. The supply of raw material remained the weakest point in its armour, proving obstinately inelastic and failing to respond immediately to the increasing demands made upon it in both Europe and America. The U.S.A. slightly reduced its share of the world's production of cotton from the peak proportion of 1850 and the share of cotton in its exports from the peak proportion of 1851 because the extension of cultivation was limited by the shortage of capital and labour consequent upon the marked rise in slave prices. As the rising tide of Northern hostility to the South threatened the whole security of a slave-produced supply of cotton,[1] Dalhousie in India pursued a cotton-oriented policy of annexation and railway construction[2] but failed to impose through the influence of the Indian crop any restraint upon American prices.

Stocks of cotton in England declined from the all-time peak level of 1845 by over two-thirds by the close of 1856, and prices doubled between 1848 and 1857 under the influence of the short crops of 1849, 1850, and 1857. That sharp inflation brought to an end the long decline in prices experienced since the 1800s and affected England much more than the states of the Continent, whose cotton industries were protected from competition by tariffs. Rising prices became a danger rather than a stimulus. Increasingly from 1854 they diverted profits from the spinner to the planter, threatened the industry with the possibility of a much more severe dearth of cotton than that feared in 1846 or 1850, and especially afflicted producers for the Indian market because of their heavy consumption of raw material. The prospective dearth inspired the foundation of the Cotton Supply Association (1857–72)[3] as a 'Cotton League' on the model of the Anti-Corn Law League in an effort to develop India as a source of supply and so to reduce the industry's dependence upon the slave power of England's great foe. The U.S.A. had been the main source of raw cotton since 1803 and had defeated successive attempts by Britain to raise up rival producers, driving all competitors out of the world market by its overwhelming ability to export the best and cheapest cotton. England had reduced its share of the American crop from the all-time peak proportion attained in 1833–4 and its share of American cotton exports from their all-time peak proportion of 77·8 per cent in 1830–1 to 70·7 per cent in 1859–60. The U.S.A. nevertheless supplied 77·5 per cent of the total quantity of cotton imported into Britain during the

[1] J. T. Danson, 'On the Connexion between Slavery in the United States of America and the Cotton Manufacture in the United Kingdom', *Journal of the Statistical Society*, Mar. 1857, 1–21; T. Ellison, *A Hand-Book of the Cotton Trade* (1858), 110–20.

[2] A. W. Silver, *Manchester Men and Indian Cotton 1847–72* (1966), 53, 74.

[3] *Manchester Guardian*, 22 Apr. 1857, 3v–vi.

decade 1851–60 and 80 per cent in the exceptional year 1860, when it produced two-thirds of the world's cotton and supplied more than three-quarters of all the cotton entering into world trade.[1]

The cotton industry was far less dependent upon a single market than upon a single source of supply but nevertheless exported 64·5 per cent of the total value of its products. Increasingly its exports flowed to Asia, and especially to India, which in defiance of all expectation had become in 1843 the industry's most valuable single overseas market. In the boom which followed the suppression of the Indian Mutiny India and China raised the value of their imports in 1858–60 to double the level of 1855–7. In 1860 43 per cent of the value of the industry's exports was taken by four markets, 20·7 per cent by India, 8·7 per cent by the U.S.A., 6·8 per cent by Turkey, and 6·5 per cent by China. In that year a crisis of over-production began to afflict the industry in both Britain and Europe and blighted the cherished expectations of continued expansion.

* * *

The unprecedented prosperity of the four years 1858–61 brought about an inevitable reaction, since productive capacity had grown by one-fifth since 1856 and had surpassed the absorptive capacity of the industry's markets, arousing grave concern among informed observers.[2] The home trade in fancy goods and muslins was 'almost annihilated' during 1860 by a cold summer and a deficient harvest.[3] Exports to India also shrank in 1860, and those to the Levant as well as to the U.S.A. in 1861. The export of piece-goods to India declined from their peak level of 1859 by 18·5 per cent in quantity and by 15·25 per cent in value during 1860, sharply reducing that market's share in the total volume exported from 34·6 to 26 per cent: the average time of turnover of consignments rose sharply, and prices in Calcutta began in March 1860 to recede towards their level of 1856. During the summer India houses

[1] G. McHenry, *The Cotton Trade: its Bearing upon the Prosperity of Great Britain and Commerce of the American Republics* (London, Saunders, 1863), 59–61.

[2] A. Redgrave, 'On the Progress of Textile Manufactures in Great Britain', *Journal of the Society of Arts*, 8 Mar. 1861, 259, T. Bazley.

[3] *Manchester Examiner*, 1 Jan. 1861, 7iii.

began to fail as their expected returns failed to materialize, under the depressing influence of the doubling in 1859 of the import duties on cotton goods, of the 'enormous enhancement' in the customs valuations in 1860,[1] and of the diversion of expenditure from clothing to food after the failure of the monsoon rains. From September the first of a series of six bad harvests attracted the capital of merchants in India from the textile trade into the grain trade in quest of the profits from the famine which was expected to occur during 1861. That succession of bad crops destroyed the prosperity of Lancashire's largest foreign market at a time when the close association between the Indian harvest and the consumption of Manchester goods was not fully understood. The price of such characteristic export products as T-cloths reached a low point during February 1861, at a level 7½ per cent below that of twelve months earlier, while shirtings reached their nadir between February and June at a price level 15 per cent lower than that of a year earlier.

During 1861 the decline in the export of piece-goods to Madras was offset by the expansion of exports to the much larger markets of Bombay and Calcutta. Exports of cotton manufactures to the industry's fourth largest foreign market, Turkey, declined however by 22 per cent in quantity and by 32 per cent in value after the Levant crisis of 1860, a loss which was only half offset by the expansion of exports to Naples and Sicily which followed in the wake of the expedition of the Thousand. The export of cotton manufactures to the U.S.A. sank by 64·5 per cent in quantity and by 67 per cent in value after the outbreak of war, representing 30 per cent of the total loss in exports by the industry during 1861. Little compensation was provided for the loss of the industry's second largest foreign market in the expansion of its exports to France by £336,000, which amounted to only one-ninth of the decline in exports to the U.S.A. The crisis of over-production was indeed accentuated by the optimistic expectations entertained of the potential capacity of the French market, which was opened only from 1 October 1861 after the expiry of twenty-one months' grace from the signature of the Anglo-French Treaty of Commerce. Similar delusive hopes were entertained of

[1] ibid.

'that huge market of four hundred millions'[1] opened by treaty in 1860 in China, exports to which in fact declined during 1861 by 2 per cent from their 1860 peak before plunging by a further 55 per cent during 1862. The reduction in the value of the exports of cotton manufactures by £6,140,000 accounted for 57 per cent of the total reduction in British exports during 1861.

The saturation of the markets for cotton goods led to a decline in the number of orders placed with the industry and to an increase in manufacture for stock. Such stocks had built up rapidly towards the end of 1860, when their value amounted to over £20m., the equivalent of 23·5 per cent of the industry's annual product. During 1861 their volume increased by a further 21·4 per cent from 242m. to 293m. lb. of goods[2] worth over £25m., the equivalent of 33·6 per cent of the industry's annual product. That progressive accumulation of stocks reflected a growing excess of supply over demand and the sheer incapacity of supply to create its own demand, so ushering the industry from a phase of prosperity into one of depression. Mill margins, the most sensitive index of profitability, had averaged 68 per cent upon the price of raw cotton during the decade 1850–9 and had reached 81 per cent in 1860 but were halved in 1861 to a meagre 40 per cent. That shrinkage in margins exerted a growing pressure upon costs as producers began reluctantly to reconcile themselves to a future of lower prices. Efforts made during February 1861 to reduce wages by 5 per cent proved successful, and strikes in opposition failed in Bolton, Ashton-under-Lyne, and Blackburn, since employers could afford to work short time in a falling market. In May the weavers of Colne finally capitulated after a strike unprecedented in its duration of fifty weeks, so shattering the power of the first Weavers' Amalgamation, which had been established in 1858. In April, May, and June many Manchester shippers were compelled to suspend payment,[3] while others were brought to the verge of bankruptcy, since they could not dispose of their

[1] S. Osborn, *The Past and Future of British Relations in China* (Edinburgh, Blackwood, 1860), 10.

[2] W. B. Forwood, 'On the Influence of Price upon the Cultivation and Consumption of Cotton during the Past Ten Years', *Journal of the Statistical Society*, Sept. 1870, 382.

[3] McHenry, 54.

shipments except at a ruinous sacrifice of 40–50 per cent of their value. The influence of the Civil War nevertheless served to avert the impending threat of ruin: it brought a shower of riches in place of the anticipated hard times and opened up a prospect of unparalleled rewards to the fortunate holders of stocks.

* * *

The war of 1861–5 not only reduced the export of cotton manufactures to the U.S.A. but also imperilled the security of the supply of raw cotton to the mills of Lancashire. The cotton industry had, however, accumulated very large stocks of raw material and had already begun to suffer from a market crisis, so that no shortage of cotton existed even when distress became most acute during 1862. The cotton harvest of 1859 had been the largest in the history of the U.S.A., being twice as abundant as the short crop of 1850 and reducing the price of the raw material to its lowest level of $5\frac{7}{8}$*d.* per lb. in July 1860. The good harvest of 1860 and its accelerated shipment in anticipation of the eventuality of war, especially after the election of Lincoln, permitted the heaping up of stocks in England. End-of-year stocks had declined from their peak level of 1845, sufficing in 1850–4 for twenty-one weeks' supply and in 1855–9 for thirteen weeks' supply, but rose to sixteen weeks' supply at the close of 1860. Thus the price of cotton remained low for six months after the bombardment of Fort Sumter on 12 April. The belief in a war of ninety days' duration checked the advance in price which alone could have called forth increased supplies from outside the U.S.A.: that belief was not dispelled until the Confederacy secured its first military victory at Bull Run on 21 July.

The declaration on 19 April of a blockade of the Southern ports by the North remained a symbolic act, since effective enforcement along 3,500 miles of coastline proved impossible for over a year. That act nevertheless raised freight rates, insurance premiums, and cotton prices:[1] it encouraged from July a recourse to short-time working, a transfer from coarse to fine spinning, and a renewal of efforts to replace the U.S.A. by

[1] *The Economist*, 13 July 1861, 758–60, 'Threatened Famine of Cotton'.

India as a source of supply. The invincible faith of *The Economist* in the commanding power of a market economy to call forth the necessary supplies remained, however, unshaken. 'We share to a considerable extent the instinctive conviction of the Lancashire merchants and manufacturers, that an article grown by an eager seller and consumed by an eager buyer will find its way from the one to the other, in spite of all hostile barriers and prohibitions.'[1] The initial rise in prices attracted a swarm of speculative buyers into the Liverpool market during July in search of profit from gambling on the continued absence of American stocks from the markets of Europe. Even American buyers were attracted into that market at the end of August by the prospect of buying cotton either for speculation or for reshipment to New York. During August margins began to shrink as yarn and cloth prices failed to respond to the rise in price of the raw material. During September cotton prices first surpassed the famine level reached in 1857. From October mills resorted increasingly to short-time or to half-time working or even closed down, especially in the coarse spinning trade, which used much more raw cotton than the fine trade and was most affected by the saturation of its markets.

The influence of the market crisis was both compounded and concealed by the influence of the war. Supplies of American cotton were raised in price by the risks of blockade-running but continued to flow across the Atlantic and furnished in 1861 71 per cent of the cotton imported by Europe and 65 per cent of that imported by Britain. Total imports into England remained at a very high level throughout the year and proved to be only 12 per cent below the level of 1860, since India increased its contribution by a massive 75 per cent. By the end of the year aggregate stocks had risen to a peak quantity of 789,300 bales,[2] or to the equivalent of seventeen weeks' supply, the highest level since 1854. Those stocks were nevertheless less useful to Lancashire than they appeared to be, since half comprised short-stapled Surat, which was no substitute for the medium-stapled American most favoured for wefts. Speculators had moreover raised their purchases to an all-time

[1] *The Economist*, 10 Aug. 1861, 870, 'Cotton and the Civil War'.

[2] John Pender & Co., *Statistics of the Trade of the United Kingdom with Foreign Countries from 1840* (London, Simpkin, 1869), 6, 9.

peak level, buying 5 per cent more than the total volume of imports and securing control of all the stocks held in the ports. Those stocks must be clearly distinguished from those held at the mills because of the immense socio-economic distance between Liverpool and Lancashire, which was increased by the growing diversion of enterprise from industry into commerce and especially into speculative commerce. Stocks at the mills had declined during 1861 by 55 per cent from four weeks' supply to two weeks' supply, while those held in the ports had increased by 17·6 per cent from twelve weeks' supply to fifteen weeks' supply.

Any further ruinous depression of prices was checked by the outbreak of war and by the locking up of the 1861 crop by the blockade. It also became possible for the industry's spokesmen to represent the crisis as one of supply rather than of demand and to blame the war for the industrial depression, since short-time working began only after the start of hostilities. Such an interpretation harmonized with the fashionable political economy in its concern with scarcity rather than with abundance as the central problem of economic life. The cotton lords inevitably preferred to accept and to diffuse an explanation of the depression which conformed to their own world outlook. Their interpretation served an important social function since it effectively concealed the congested nature of the industry's markets and the notable imperfections of a market-oriented system of production, so encouraging the spread of a stupefying misconception in both Lancashire and England. In their view Lancashire had fallen victim to an act of God, and the operatives were therefore called upon to display heroic fortitude under suffering which was no fault of their own or of their employers.

Du Fay & Co., the authors of the most authoritative cotton circular of the day, first revealed to the public the disturbing truth of the industry's overstocked markets in Asia[1] and were roundly rebuked by the Manchester merchant Samuel Mendel (1814–84) in the assured tones of the pander-publicist presenting as accepted fact the most debatable of propositions. 'However tedious and wearisome may be the reiteration of the fact, still it must be admitted that the course of our market is

[1] *Manchester Guardian*, 3 Aug. 1861, 4ii.

more seriously influenced by the war in America than by any other cause or causes.'[1] Mendel was the leading shipper from Manchester to Asia and, having raised his declared profits to £250,000–£300,000 per annum in the post-Mutiny boom, knew better than any other merchant in Manchester the truth of Du Fay's assertions. He nevertheless deliberately misrepresented the influence of the war and so misled all who accepted his asseverations at their face value instead of treating them as controversial contributions made to a debate by an interested party.

The oppressive influence of overstocked markets was forgotten after the 1860s and was submerged for two generations thereafter beneath the general consensus of later opinion, which attributed the great economic crisis of the decade to a shortage of cotton which had not in fact existed. Thus the free-trade interpretation was diffused amongst an uncritical posterity without either rebuttal or demurrer and was finally enshrined in 1947 in a very popular novel.[2] It was first undermined by Owsley in 1931 and by Henderson in 1932,[3] a generation before it was finally demolished by Fohlen in 1956 and by Brady in 1963.[4] Brady undertook a drastic revision of the conventional interpretation of the crisis. He showed convincingly that the Civil War was not responsible for the industrial depression in Lancashire, did not seriously deplete the stocks of raw cotton held in Britain, and was important only in so far as it induced expectations of a future shortage of supplies. He blamed the depression almost wholly upon the preceding period of production which had expanded far in excess of any existing demand. His thesis has not yet been challenged: even less has it been refuted in its interpretation of the crucial years 1861 and 1862, since it explains so much that would otherwise remain inexplicable. Thus the saturated

[1] *Manchester Guardian*, 4 Sept. 1861, 2ii.

[2] Thomas Armstrong, *King Cotton* (London, Collins, 1947).

[3] F. L. Owsley, *King Cotton Diplomacy. Foreign Relations of the Confederate States of America* (University of Chicago Press, 1931, 1959), 549–50; W. O. Henderson, 'The Cotton Famine in Lancashire', *Transactions of the Historic Society of Lancashire and Cheshire,* 3 Mar. 1932, 38–9; idem, *The Lancashire Cotton Famine 1861–1865* (Manchester University Press, 1934, 1969), 11–12.

[4] C. Fohlen, *L'Industrie textile au temps du Second Empire* (Paris, Plon, 1956), 253–4, 285, 314; E. A. Brady, 'A Reconsideration of the Lancashire "Cotton Famine" ', *Agricultural History,* July 1963, 156–62.

markets of the cotton industry remained largely unresponsive for eighteen months after the close of 1860 until the autumn of 1862. In such a situation producers remained more concerned with their markets than with their supply of raw material. Lancashire therefore launched a campaign against the Indian import duty, under whose apparent protection the number of cotton mills in Bombay had trebled in number to nine during 1860. The campaign succeeded in securing in three successive stages between November 1860 and April 1862 a revision of the customs valuations and a halving of the obnoxious duty,[1] so setting a precedent for the similar campaigns of 1874–9 and 1894–5. The immediate effects were to facilitate the sale of existing stocks rather than to reduce the incidence of unemployment, since margins remained unprofitable. Cotton spinners therefore showed little or no interest in the efforts of the Cotton Supply Association to develop alternative sources of supply.

* * *

Consumption and employment had been reduced by one-third by December 1861 when news of the *Trent* affair provoked an outburst of war fever in England, especially in Liverpool. The new-born hope that the Royal Navy might break the blockade reduced the price of cotton by 17 per cent in a precautionary anticipation of the advent of the American crop. Such expectations vanished by the end of December when prices resumed their rise and wholly eliminated the margin of spinners during January 1862, the price of raw cotton even exceeding that of coarse yarn. By May consumption had been reduced by half and employment in only slightly less degree. Then cotton prices doubled during the next three months, rising by an astounding 50 per cent in the three weeks after 15 August in the greatest single fluctuation of the war, precipitated by the series of reverses suffered by the North.

The Union Navy completed its blockade of the four main

[1] P. Harnetty, 'The Imperialism of Free Trade: Lancashire and the Indian Cotton Duties, 1859–1862', *Economic History Review*, Aug. 1965, 177–86; idem, *Imperialism and Free Trade: Lancashire and India in the Mid-Nineteenth Century* (1972), 7–30.

cotton ports by the capture of New Orleans on 29 April, but the Union army was repelled in its first bid to capture Richmond at the second battle of Bull Run on 29–30 August in Lee's most brilliant campaign. Thereafter the great military aristocracy of the planter states threatened to enthrone itself in permanence upon the American continent from the Potomac to Panama. All hopes of a speedy end to the war receded and expectations of future cotton supply were fundamentally transformed in harmony with the interlinked assumptions of a continuation of hostilities, the exclusion of American cotton from the world market, and the consequent perpetuation of rising prices. Stocks in Liverpool were markedly depleted by the consequent sudden increase in demand. They had been thought sufficient in July for six months' consumption but were deemed adequate in September for only three weeks' consumption,[1] as the demand for export raised prices sharply and excluded Lancashire spinners from the market in favour of speculators, thereby markedly reducing employment.[2] The average number of days of work available per operative had sunk from the customary six per week to four in December 1861 and to three and a half in April 1862, but shrank to two and a third in November 1862. The trades dependent upon the cotton industry began to suffer a sympathetic depression in their prosperity. Unemployment reached its peak in December when cotton was at thrice its pre-war price and one-fifth of the total population of Lancashire was drawing relief.

During 1862 the volume of the imports of cotton plummeted by 58 per cent. The U.S.A. furnished a smaller quantity than in any year since 1804 and supplied only 3·2 per cent of the total volume. Egypt became an additional source of supply, especially of long-stapled cotton, and increased the volume of its exports to England by 50 per cent. India increased the volume of her exports to England by only 8·6 per cent after their great upward leap during 1861 but provided more cotton than the U.S.A. for the first time since 1819 and furnished 74 per cent of the total imports. In that worst of years for production and

[1] *The Economist*, 5 July 1862, 730, 'The Cotton Market', 6 Sept. 1862, 981, 'The State of the Cotton Market'.

[2] John Mills, *Vox Humana. Poems* (London, Unwin, 1897), 40–4, 'No Cotton! Autumn, 1862'.

employment the consumption of cotton fell, however, by 55 per cent to the lowest level since 1849 and to 42 per cent of the peak consumption of the exceptionally prosperous year 1860. In the year of scantiest supply the expanded spindleage of the industry was thus restricted to half its peak pre-war consumption. Stocks held at the mills declined by 80 per cent during the year, or much more rapidly than in 1861, and were sufficient at its close for only two and a third weeks at the current level of reduced consumption. Stocks held in the ports, however, declined only half as much, by 38 per cent, and represented the equivalent of over twenty weeks' supply.

Mill margins reached their lowest point during 1862, averaging only 18 per cent upon the price of raw cotton. The gross value of the industry's product sank by 42·5 per cent. The quantity of goods consumed in the home market declined by 41 per cent and the quantity exported by 39 per cent, shipments of piece-goods to China falling by 67 per cent and those to India by 31·6 per cent. Exports of yarn declined much more than exports of cloth, sinking in volume by 48 per cent to the level of 1836 while exports of piece-goods fell by 34·4 per cent to the level of 1854. The increase in prices half offset the decline in the volume of trade, exports of yarn and piece-goods shrinking in volume by 37·8 per cent but in value by only 21·6 per cent. The decline in shipments to India and China represented 38·6 per cent of the total loss in value of exports. That slump brought to a temporary halt the immense flow of cotton textile exports and proved to be, in its severity rather than in its duration, the greatest depression in the whole course of the industry's history. Exports did not recede again to the low level of 1862 until 1938 in respect of piece-goods, until 1940 in respect of yarn, or until 1943 in respect of the value of exports of cotton manufactures. Cotton manufactures nevertheless retained their primacy in the export trade, reducing their share from 38·3 per cent in 1860 to 29·6 per cent in 1862. The terms of trade were unfavourably affected as the price of imports rose more than that of exports. The doubling of cotton prices raised import prices in general by 12·5 per cent during 1862 in one of the steepest increases in British economic history. In that year the gross barter terms of trade sank by one-third below their level of 1859. The balance of payments was not plunged into deficit, but the surplus on current account declined in 1861 and 1862 to half the average annual level of 1856–60.[1] The sharp rise in import prices produced no sympathetic wage inflation because food prices remained low and unemployment was increasing in the newly christened 'labour market' (1861).

* * *

During 1862 Liverpool's shipping tonnage declined by only 7 per cent and the receipts of the Mersey Docks and Harbour Board shrank by only 12 per cent, despite the reduction in the volume of cotton imports by nearly three-fifths. The port found compensation in the transfer of American vessels to Liverpool registry, in the organization of blockade-running ventures, in the expansion of the jute and grain trades, and in the development of trade with India and with the Mediterranean. Above all, cotton broking enjoyed a golden age, despite the reduced volume of imports. The number of brokers nearly doubled under the influence of the rise in prices, the increase in the number of transactions, and the boom in re-exports. The Cotton Brokers' Association projected in 1862 the construction of a new Exchange, which was completed in 1867; it also found it necessary for the first time since its establishment in 1842 to establish its own rules and committee in 1863 and to issue its own circular in 1864.

The port had been in 1861 the main centre of opposition to the blockade but developed from 1862 a vested interest in its maintenance as rising prices brought in their wake an influx of unearned wealth to the holders of stocks and re-exports expanded from 22 per cent of total imports in 1861 to the all-time peak proportion of 41 per cent in 1862. It established its full autonomy in the service of the world market and became the main repository of stocks, which outweighed those held at the mills threefold at the close of 1860 but ninefold at the close of 1862. Those stocks, together with its contraband trade, gave Liverpool an overwhelming advantage in the entrepôt trade over Glasgow and Le Havre and enabled it to

[1] A. H. Imlah, *Economic Elements in the Pax Britannica: Studies in British Foreign Trade in the Nineteenth Century* (1958), 72, 96.

reap monopoly profits as prices rose. Sales to speculators for the rise required the investment of large capitals and quintupled from 16·5 per cent of total imports in 1860 to the peak proportion of 88 per cent in 1862,[1] effectively excluding Lancashire spinners from the market.

The average annual exports of raw cotton almost doubled, from 131,670,000 lb. in 1850–9 to 256,150,000 lb. in 1860–5, and increased their proportion of total imports from 14·3 per cent to 29 per cent. If those exports had not doubled, then the consumption of cotton by the mills of Lancashire might have been maintained in 1862–5 at an average level of 683,680,000 lb., or only one-seventh less than in 1850–9. Thus Liverpool exalted the interests of the re-export trade over those of secondary industry and divorced its function from that of its manufacturing hinterland, even attracting cotton back from the mills to its market and re-exporting it to New York. Such re-exports helped, together with the expansion in the carrying trade for foreigners, to pay for the vast increase in the price of cotton imports. The stocks of raw cotton in the port were, however, increasingly composed of Surat and were not in demand in Lancashire to the extent that they were on the Continent. France was much more dependent even than England on American cotton but adapted the machinery of its spinning mills to the consumption of Surat more extensively than did England. Thus it replaced Russia as the main foreign customer of Liverpool from 1862 until 1866 and made Britain the main source of its supply in place of the U.S.A., since it could secure the substitute Indian cotton in no other market. That increase in the demand for exports maintained domestic prices at a high level and prevented them from declining as imports increased after 1862.

*　　*　　*

The severity of the shortage of cotton has undoubtedly been exaggerated by the habitual representation of the exceptional consumption of 1860 as typical. The annual average consumption had been 796,240,000 lb. in the decade 1850–9, rising by 31·3 per cent in 1860–1 to 1,045,500,000 lb., the

[1] Ellison, *The Cotton Trade of Great Britain* (1886), Table No. 1.

largest consumption thitherto ever attained. It sank in 1862–5 to 559,200,000 lb., which was 55·5 per cent of the level reached in the years 1860–1 but only 22·7 per cent below the average level of 1850–9. To describe such a reduction in consumption as a dearth would be sheer hyperbole unless the phrase were intended to divert attention from the real cause of economic distress. 'If a man surfeited himself with food daily, and circumstances should arise that restricted him to half supplies, we would not say that individual was suffering from famine. This was precisely the case as to manufactures.'[1]

There was no real shortage of cotton in Lancashire even during 1862, when distress was most acute, though the stocks were located in Liverpool rather than at the mills. As the war continued stocks began to be depleted and the essential inelasticity of cotton supply was strikingly revealed. Lancashire had developed what was essentially 'a forced exotic trade',[2] ineluctably dependent upon the Cotton Kingdom of the South for its supply of medium-stapled cotton. No potential competitor could respond in less than a year to the stimulus of high prices, and most required five years in order to reach their maximum productive capacity. No other country would, however, try to fill the void left by the U.S.A. for fear of the immense stocks locked up in the South by the blockade and of the threat of overpowering competition from America in the future. The most effective guarantee to other producers would have been a differential import duty on slave-grown cotton, which could not, however, be imposed because of the deep entrenchment of the policy of free trade in England and the massive inertia of the vast commercial complex focused on the U.S.A. Thus Brazil continued to exploit its comparative advantages for the production of coffee, West Africa remained devoted to the production of palm oil, Natal and Queensland developed the cultivation of sugar rather than of cotton, while Burma expanded its cultivation of rice at the expense of cotton. No substantial or sustained material support was given in Lancashire, least of all in Liverpool, to the propaganda of the

[1] M. J. McHaffiie, '*Was It a Cotton Famine?*' *Being Twelve Letters from The* '*Times*' *Money Article* (London, Wilson, 1865, 24pp.), iii.

[2] *Spectator*, 27 Dec. 1862, 1433–4, 1444–5, W. B. Adams, 'The Political Economy of the Cotton Manufactures'.

Cotton Supply Association or to the covey of cotton companies which sought to supplement its activities.

Egypt expanded its production of high quality cotton and replaced wheat by cotton as its staple export but did so without the benefit of direct foreign investment, technology, or enterprise and surprised Lancashire as much as India disappointed it,[1] achieving recognition for the first time as '*par excellence* a cotton-growing country, the finest perhaps in the world'.[2] India had become in 1861 the main focus of the aspirations of all who hoped to end Britain's slavish dependence upon the U.S.A. She ranked second to the U.S.A. as a grower of cotton in 1860 but produced only 18 per cent of the world's total supply, in contrast to the 66 per cent produced by the U.S.A., and supplied only 15 per cent of Britain's imports. In 1862–5 she furnished, on average, 55 per cent of those imports. She would nevertheless have needed to increase her production threefold and her exports ninefold in order fully to replace the U.S.A. as a source of supply, to shift back from west to east the centre of gravity of the cotton trade, and permanently to displace New Orleans by Bombay as the largest cotton-exporting port in the world.[3] Thus she revealed for the first time the limited size of her cotton crop[4] and so dispelled the dream of an Anglo-Indian economic symbiosis based upon the exchange of cotton for calico.[5] The increase in her exports to England was achieved by diverting cotton from the China market as well as from home consumption, by planting cotton in preference to cereals, and finally by extending the area under cultivation.[6] Indian cotton was short in staple, weak and

[1] E. R. J. Owen, *Cotton and the Egyptian Economy 1820–1914* (Oxford, Clarendon Press, 1969), 89–121; D. S. Landes, *Bankers and Pashas* (London, Heinemann, 1958), 69–101, 'Klondike on the Nile'; E. M. Earle, 'Egyptian Cotton and the American Civil War', *Political Science Quarterly*, Dec. 1926, 520–45; T. Crawford, 'On the Cotton Supply', *Journal of the Society of Arts*, 19 Apr. 1861, 404, 410–11; J. Ninet, 'La Culture du coton en Égypte et aux Indes', *Revue des deux mondes*, 15 Juillet 1866, 352–5.

[2] I. Watts, *The Cotton Supply Association: its Origin and Progress* (Manchester, Tubbs, 1871), 67, 71.

[3] W. R. Cassels, *Cotton: an Account of its Culture in the Bombay Presidency* (Bombay Education Society, 1862), 345–7.

[4] Samuel Smith, *The Cotton Trade of India, being a Series of Letters written from Bombay in the Spring of 1863* (London, Wilson, 1863), 50.

[5] J. Ninet, 'La Culture du coton en Égypte et aux Indes', op. cit., 359–67.

[6] P. Harnetty, 'Cotton Exports and Indian Agriculture 1861–1870', *Economic*

coarse in fibre, and defective in colour: it could not compete in price or quality with American and could not overcome the persistent partiality of Lancashire for Middling Orleans. Thus it became a great staple of the re-export trade of Liverpool rather than a staple of consumption in the mills of Lancashire. The increase in the import of Indian cotton raised the volume of intra-imperial trade to new heights but precipitated a great drain of bullion from 1863, when the value of cotton imports first exceeded the value of the exports of cotton manufactures, and so paved the way for the financial crisis of 1864. Fortunately the exporters of raw cotton increased their imports of piece-goods, which expanded notably to Colombia, Egypt, and Bombay during 1863, and to Brazil during 1864, and so prevented any further deterioration in Britain's terms of trade.

The shortage of American cotton compelled employers to re-equip their mills in order to spin Surat, and especially to improve their preparatory processes, so exerting a similar influence to the cotton dearth of 1857. Spinners speedily discovered to their astonishment the real capacity of Surat and raised by 1862 the highest counts spun from pure Surat from 24s to 50s[1] but did not succeed in permanently reducing their deep-rooted distaste for Indian cotton. The process of opening the tightly packed raw material became wholly automatic

History Review, Aug. 1971, 414–29; idem, *Imperialism and Free Trade: Lancashire and India in the Mid-Nineteenth Century* (1972), 132–3, which lists the eight articles published by the author between 1962 and 1971; F. A. Logan, 'India—Britain's Substitute for American Cotton, 1861–1865', *Journal of Southern History*, Nov. 1958, 472–80; idem, 'India's Loss of the British Cotton Market after 1865', *Journal of Southern History*, Feb. 1965, 40–50; A. W. Silver, *Manchester Men and Indian Cotton 1847–72* (1966), 158–291; D. Tripathi, 'Opportunism of Free Trade: Lancashire Cotton Famine and Indian Cotton Cultivation', *Indian Economic and Social History Review*, Sept. 1967, 255–63.

[1] D. K. Clark, *The Exhibited Machinery of 1862: a Cyclopaedia of the Machinery Represented at the International Exhibition* (London, Day, 1862), 44.

The degree of fineness of yarn was measured from the eighteenth century by the number of hanks per pound weight and was expressed in the 'count' of hanks required to weigh one pound. Since the hank remained constant in length at 840 yards the number of hanks per pound increased as the yarn became finer. Counts were divided into four main categories: coarse (16–40), medium (50–90), fine (80–150), and superfine (150–300). Districts and firms specialized in the spinning of particular counts from distinctive types of cotton. Rossendale counts were 20s, Blackburn counts 30s, Oldham counts 32s, Preston counts 50s, Bolton counts 60s, and Manchester counts ranged above 100. See D. J. Jeremy, 'British and American Yarn Count Systems: an Historical Analysis', *Business History Review*, Autumn 1971, 336–68.

through the use of the Crighton Opener, invented in 1861, as did the subsequent process of scutching through the application of the ingenious piano-feed regulator developed in 1862. The rollers of the drawing frame were readjusted to handle the short-stapled Surat.[1] In the process of weaving heavy sizing became customary on warps of Surat and waste yarn in order to give them the tenacity of twist essential for good weaving and to permit the increased use of China clay or 'Lancashire cotton' as the most economical substitute for cotton yarn, carrying further a trend which was to reach its height during the 1870s. Steam jets were also used from 1862 to humidify weaving sheds using Surat yarn so as to reduce the number of breakages of warp and weft. Both techniques of oversizing and of steaming were accepted as necessities in the 1860s but became the object of hostile agitation by the operative weavers in the 1870s and 1880s. The reorganization of the preparatory processes entailed such an extensive investment of capital that it amounted almost to the creation of a new industry. Those processes were so greatly improved that the self-acting mule could be used in place of the hand mule in the spinning of coarse and medium counts up to 60s where the previous limit had been 50s.[2] The labour-saving effects of such innovations were counterbalanced by the need for increased labour in the manufacture of Surat, so that the employment of labour did not decline to the same extent as the consumption of cotton. Those innovations gave a great stimulus to the textile engineering industry and consolidated the technical supremacy of the Lancashire cotton industry in the world.

* * *

In the field of business organization the crisis benefited private employers at the expense of companies, large firms at the expense of small ones, spinners at the expense of manufacturers, and merchants at the expense of producers. The surviving

[1] W. Weild, 'On the Construction of Drawing Rollers for Spinning Machinery', *Proceedings of the Institution of Mechanical Engineers*, 7 May 1863, 66, 73.

[2] K. Neste, *The Mule Spinning Process, and the Machinery Employed In It* (Manchester, Heywood, 1865), 62; J. Platt, 'On Machinery for the Preparing and Spinning of Cotton', *Proceedings of the Institution of Mechanical Engineers*, 1 Aug. 1866, 232, 242.

hand-loom weavers were adversely affected by the reduction in the supply of yarn, by the cutting off of the sole surviving demand for hand-woven muslins—that from the western U.S.A. and Canada—by the increase in the competitive capacity of the power-loom in the fancy trade and by its application in 1864 to the weaving of woollens, which closed off a large field of alternative employment. The depression also abruptly ended the first era of company formation in the cotton industry. The new co-operative manufacturing companies were wholly unprepared for such an eventuality, and their prospects for profit-sharing were blighted before they had made any profits to divide. The use of loan capital proved a fair-weather technique of industrial finance since the increased burden of interest payments devoured the capital of share-holders. Working men found that their shares had lost all market value but had to be mortgaged as an essential pre-condition to drawing relief. Over half of the ninety-two companies registered in the industry in 1860–1 disappeared within ten years, their mills reverting to the possession of private employers and often into the hands of those who had been the original vendors. The surviving companies tended to become less co-operative in spirit and more considerate of the rights of capital, so conforming to the dominant ethos of the trade. The aspirations of the working class to economic in-dependence were not, however, extinguished but diverted into the sphere of consumers' co-operation. The thirty co-operative stores in the cotton districts survived the crisis without a single failure and succeeded in 1863 in establishing the C.W.S.

Specialized manufacturers of cloth had expanded more than any other group of employers during the 1850s and had trebled in number but occupied the lowliest position in the industry's hierarchy of status, operating with a low proportion of floating capital and working virtually from hand to mouth. Such small masters could not exploit the opportunities open to wealthier employers. They carried no stocks on which to make a profit since they did not unite the business of spinner or of exporter to that of manufacturer. They had no funds for speculation, and found that much more capital was necessary than formerly in order merely to carry on their business in a time of rapidly rising prices. Their profit margins were reduced to the minimum during 1863 as those of spinners expanded from their low point of 1862. Their ranks provided the bulk of the casualties after prices began to decline in 1864.

The depression encouraged the withdrawal from the cotton industry of its leading employers, led by Thomas Bazley (1797–1885),[1] and reinforced the geographical concentration of the British cotton industry within the Lancashire region, where society displayed the greatest resilience under pressure. Country mills on the fringes of the shire, from Flintshire to Lonsdale and Carlisle, were so adversely affected that they closed down. In Lancaster the cotton mills completed the process of adaptation to the manufacture of oil-cloth, while two new mills established in Warwickshire in 1860 after the Cobden–Chevalier Treaty were converted to the manufacture of worsted. The industry became stabilized in Derbyshire as well as in Cheshire and underwent further expansion after the 1860s only in the West Riding, particularly in the Pennine valleys linking it to Lancashire. The textile industry of Ulster underwent a large-scale conversion from the use of cotton to the use of flax and that of Scotland from the manufacture of muslin to that of sewing thread,[2] using the automatic spooling machine invented in 1858 and the highly productive ring-doubling frame from 1867. The production of thread, being undertaken for a world market, proved far less susceptible to cyclical depression than muslin manufacture as well as the most profitable branch of the whole cotton trade.[3]

The crisis ended the great age of the small firm in cotton spinning, since such concerns lacked the necessary capital to maintain their purchases of cotton and to adapt their machinery to handle Surat. Its other effects within the field of business organization are more debatable. It does not seem to have encouraged the rise of separate spinning and weaving firms and certainly did not deprive the combined spinning and weaving

[1] *Great Industries of Great Britain* (London, Cassell, 1879) i. 8, R. Smiles, 'Sir Thomas Bazley, Bart., M.P.'; *Manchester Examiner*, 20 Mar. 1885, 5ii–iii, 8ii–vi; *Manchester Faces and Places*, iii, 10 Dec. 1891, 43–5.

[2] A. J. Robertson, 'The Decline of the Scottish Cotton Industry', *Business History*, July 1970, 116–28.

[3] W. D. Rubinstein, 'British Millionaires, 1809–1949', *Bulletin of the Institute of Historical Research*, Nov. 1974, 202–23, shows in an invaluable table that of 24 millionaires from the cotton industry, dying between 1830 and 1942, 16 (including 11 from the Coats family) were thread manufacturers.

firm of its dominant position within the industry, since vertical integration served to cushion the impact of depression, and the combined firms continued to increase their spindleage until 1870 and their loomage until 1880. Nor did it precipitate the decline of the spinning industry in north-east Lancashire, since that industry expanded to a peak in the 1870s. The weaving trade became the main sphere in which new small firms were established, control of the industry as a whole being thereafter concentrated in the hands of the large firms.

* * *

The cotton operatives of Lancashire were far more numerous and far more concentrated than any comparable group on the Continent and were much more dependent upon the export market. They had benefited by the long-term rise in their money-wages which had begun in the 1850s. They had earned praise as perfect models of self-improvement[1] and as 'the industrial defence of the country and conquerors of the world—the true army and navy, the source of our wealth, the payers of our taxes, and the maintainers of our glory'.[2] Their invincible immobility and excessive specialization had, however, made them 'mere animate machines, with one function and no more'[3] and compelled them to bear an increasing burden of unemployment.

The extent of the distress in Lancashire seems, however, to have been exaggerated by outside observers in order either to make political capital in the Conservative interest or to facilitate the raising of relief funds. The cotton industry was less important than in 1830, when it had supplied 51 per cent of the country's total exports and had been less concentrated in its location. It was not the sole industry of Lancashire and had never dominated the life of the shire to the extent that cotton cultivation had dominated the Cotton States. The operatives had never made the mill a centre of their life and preserved intact their friendly societies, co-operative societies, trade unions, and family structures. Thus they retained ample

[1] F. Harrison, 'Lancashire', *Westminster Review*, July 1863, 217.
[2] *The Times*, 25 Aug. 1862, 8iii.
[3] Ibid. 14 Aug. 1862, 8iv–v.

reserves of moral strength in addition to their accumulated savings. 'The mill operatives of Lancashire are the proudest people in the county, and the people of Lancashire are the proudest of Her Majesty's subjects.'[1]

The health of the operatives does not seem to have suffered, although the evidence for a balanced judgement is difficult to secure because of the general lack of information about the condition of the labouring classes, the prompt publication of patent apologias,[2] the undeveloped nature of public health administration, and the traditional technique of the organs of public opinion of minimizing the significance of national disasters. No shortage of food or harvest crisis coincided with the industrial crisis because the American West shipped its surplus grain to England instead of to the South. Emigration reduced the industry's labour force during 1862 by 50,000 hands, or by 13 per cent, and so diminished the pressure of demand upon existing supplies. Food prices thus remained low and prevented any recurrence of the mortality associated with the Irish Famine. No general rise in the death-rate occurred comparable to the fall in the marriage-rate and birth-rate. The reduction in the employment of women strengthened family structures and improved the health of their children, as the reduction in the consumption of drink improved the health of adults.

It is incredible how little harm has been done by the cotton famine. Even the public houses go on as usual. The truth is the operatives living on two-thirds of their former wages are better off than the average English labourers; and what cotton has lost, wool and flax have gained. Still even these explanations do not account for the facts. All one can say is the facts are so.[3]

The unemployed bore their affliction with the phlegm of the Saxon and the stoicism of the peasant and earned lavish praise from their social superiors for their pacific and law-abiding disposition. They remained in imaginative bondage to the most popular of American novels in *Uncle Tom's Cabin* (1852)

[1] T. Ellison, 'Distress in Lancashire', *The Exchange*, June 1862, 153–4.

[2] D. Noble, 'Fluctuations in the Death Rate', *Transactions of the Manchester Statistical Society*, 26 Oct. 1863, 1–18; J. Whitehead, *Notes on the Rate of Mortality in Manchester* (Manchester, Ireland, 1863, 38pp.).

[3] W. D. Jones, 'British Conservatives and the American Civil War', *American Historical Review*, Apr. 1953, 540, quoting Lord Stanley to Disraeli, 31 Oct. 1863.

and they therefore endured their ordeal in the belief, held rightly or wrongly, that it served the realization of the noblest of causes.[1] They suffered far less in physical health than in the loss of their treasured independence, finding that the soup they supped lacked savour and the bread they broke was bitter:

To thrust to sum'dy else for bread,
An' by th' relief keep torin' on,
Maks honest folk to hang their yead,
An' crushes th' heart o' th' preawdest mon.
We know'n it's not eawr bread we ate,
We know'n they're not eawr clooas we wear,
We want agen eawr former state,
Eawr former dhrudgin' life o' care.[2]

The poor law authorities were forced during the autumn of 1862 to moderate their doctrinaire enthusiasm for the labour test and to replace that humiliating device by sewing classes and adult schools. Those schools helped to bridge the gulf between the middle class and the working class: they first educated the womenfolk of the cotton towns in their domestic duties and the menfolk in their letters, extending the market for thread as well as for printed literature. The tardy acceptance of public works on the French model produced a permanent improvement in the public health of those communities.

Unemployment was least in those towns with a diversified economy and greatest in those most dependent on the cotton industry, on the supply of American cotton, and on the spinning of coarse counts and the weaving of plain cloth.[3] The demand for relief was nevertheless not directly related to the intensity of distress:[4] it was apparently greatest where the Irish were most numerous, where public houses flourished most, where

[1] In a radically revisionist study, *Support for Secession. Lancashire and the American Civil War* (University of Chicago, 1972), Dr. Mary Ellison has forcefully argued that support for the cause of the South, though not for slavery, was general in the factory towns. This pioneer reinterpretation supplies a welcome corrective to the conventional view embodied in Stanley Broadbridge, 'The Lancashire Cotton Famine, 1861–1865', *Our History*, Winter 1961, 20pp., reprinted in Lionel M. Munby (ed.), *The Luddites and Other Essays* (London, Katanka, 1971), 143–60.

[2] Joseph Ramsbottom, *Phases of Distress: Lancashire Rhymes* (Manchester, Heywood, 1864), 88, 'Gooin' t' Schoo' '.

[3] [R. Lamb], 'Our Manufacturing Districts', *Fraser's Magazine*, Sept. 1862, 366.

[4] [W. Harrison], 'The Distress in Lancashire', *Macmillans Magazine*, Dec. 1862, 153–5.

co-operation was weakest, and where wealthy residents were fewest. Many towns successfully adapted their industry to the changed conditions of trade. Blackburn had profited more than any other town by the expansion of the Eastern trade during the 1850s and had become more dependent than any other upon the cotton industry, which together with engineering provided subsistence for 89 per cent of its population.[1] Thus it was the worst afflicted by the Indian famines, by the shrinkage in margins, and by the reduction in the supply of American cotton. In response its employers introduced in 1862–3 the manufacture of bordered dhotis, using the Blackburn dobby developed in 1858. They increased their spindleage by a massive 50 per cent and their loomage by 33 per cent,[2] raising their share of the power-looms in the British cotton industry from one-sixth to a quarter. The Blackburn Exchange was built between 1863 and 1865 as the centre for a weekly yarn market serving all of east Lancashire and as a potential rival to the Manchester Exchange.

Oldham depended wholly upon American cotton and was the most pro-Southern town in the whole shire but carried on a coarse trade wherein Surat could effectively replace the customary staple. The local textile engineers Hibbert and Platt successfully adapted their machines to the spinning of Surat and so gave their district a great competitive advantage over other towns.[3] They transformed the self-acting mule for medium counts into a machine unequalled elsewhere in its productive capacity and so enabled whole mills to be built thenceforward on a self-actor basis. Local spinners made large profits by speculating in cotton, which was held in the large stocks necessary to their coarse trade. Between 1860 and 1863 they profited by the low prices for machinery, undertook the construction of new mills, and extended their spindleage by one-fifth at a time when other towns were suffering deep distress. Finding that Surat could be used to spin far finer counts than had thitherto been thought possible, they greatly reduced their production of very coarse yarns and increasingly

[1] W. Gourlay, *History of the Distress in Blackburn, 1861–5* (Blackburn, Haworth, 1865), 15–16.

[2] Ibid., 177.

[3] *Manchester City News*, 1 Apr. 1865, 3i–ii, 8 Apr. 3ii–iii, 15 Apr., 3ii–iv, 'Platt Bros. & Co., of Oldham'.

left that trade to Rossendale. Their large new mills contained longer mules and more spindles than those of any other town in the district and served as models for the limited mills launched in 1874–5. They spun Oldham counts of 32s which required little twist and could therefore be spun at progressively faster speeds, to the benefit of the operative spinners earning piece-rates. Hibbert & Platt doubled the number of their hands, from 3,500 in 1859 to 7,000 in 1871, became the largest firm in the whole engineering industry, and supplied the borough with both of its M.P.s from 1865 until 1872, their expansion being one of the major by-products of the Cotton Famine. Oldham also became a main centre of the trade in cotton waste, which experienced an unprecedented boom as the demand for waste grew faster than the supply. The proportion of waste in spinning rose sharply from 10.5 per cent in 1860 to 17 per cent in 1862, while the demand for waste, as an economical substitute for cotton, increased vastly. Oldham opened its Exchange for that trade in 1864, five years before Manchester followed its example.[1] The expansion in the number of waste dealers provided a large reservoir of commercial ability and capital for investment in the joint-stock companies of 1873–5.

During the decade of 1861–71 Oldham increased its population by 20 per cent, Blackburn by 31 per cent, Bolton by 32 per cent, Burnley by 42 per cent, and Rochdale by 66 per cent. Some diversification of industry took place with the development of the building of iron ships in Preston between 1857 and 1867, of the hatting industry in Stockport and Hyde, and of the woollen manufacture, especially the felt trade, in Rossendale. The number of hands employed in Lancashire in the woollen industry increased by 87 per cent from 9,227 in 1861 to 17,180 in 1870 as cotton looms undertook the manufacture of mixed fabrics, for which Egyptian cotton proved particularly suitable. Rochdale benefited by that boom and its flannel manufacturers accumulated capital which was to be reinvested in the Rochdale limiteds of the 1880s. Burnley developed the manufacture of light printing cloths in the place of T-cloths, installed new narrow and fast-running looms, and expanded even faster than Oldham, which increasingly supplied it with yarn. Bolton suffered least of all the cotton towns, being one of the last to

[1] *Manchester Guardian*, 30 Jan. 1864, 5v, 21 Apr. 1869, 5i.

establish a relief committee and earning no mention by Arnold in his *History of the Cotton Famine* (1864). The local economy was superbly balanced and diversified, with bleachworks and engineering shops which were largely independent of the cotton industry. As a centre of medium-fine spinning Bolton consumed far less cotton than Blackburn and did not depend so much upon American cotton. Its trade benefited by the increased supply of Egyptian long-stapled cotton and by the new French demand for fine yarns and mixed fabrics. Its population increased at twice the average rate for Lancashire as a whole. Its operative spinners were successfully unionized from 1861 and set the example followed in 1865 by its weavers in one of the oldest centres of the craft.

Manchester benefited as much as Bolton by the Anglo-French Treaty of Commerce and at the peak of distress in December 1862 had fewer recipients of relief than Ashton, which had less than one-tenth of its population. That great market of the industry possessed a multiplicity of trades and had a smaller proportion of factory operatives in its population than the mill towns of Lancashire. It also profited by the growth of the home trade in textiles other than cotton and expanded its commerce at the expense of its industry, increasing the number of its merchants by half during the 1860s. Residences in its central township were replaced by commercial offices, while house building continued unchecked in the other townships. Mancunian influence was further extended within the cotton district as market prices became increasingly important to producers. Manchester banks established branches in the cotton towns from 1862, as stocks of cloth were sold off at much higher prices than had been expected. The Royal Exchange was rebuilt from 1867 for the third time since its foundation in 1809. 'Cottonborough' was also fortunate in having many wealthy residents, many local relief committees, and a poor law administered with humanity.

* * *

The rise in prices continued for eighteen months after unemployment had begun to decline from its peak in December 1862 as speculation persisted under the influence of the attraction exerted by the cotton market upon the surplus capital of the manufacturing sector and of the competition for business by the new banking and financial companies. Margins remained low, however, for only twelve months from July 1862 to June 1863. During 1863 yarn exports reached their lowest point but the total value of exports rose by 26 per cent, and shipments to the East, especially to Bombay and Madras, cleared away the stocks accumulated since 1860. Fears of a speedy settlement of the war receded after the invading forces of the North were repulsed, at Chancellorsville on 2–4 May 1863, for the fifth time in twenty-one months. In August–October an immense demand for goods for all foreign markets sprang up in Manchester, and the price of cotton rose by 31 per cent as stocks were finally exhausted and sank to their lowest level since 1839. During 1863 the average weekly consumption of cotton rose by one-sixth above the level of 1862 and its average price, which in 1860 had been one-third that of wool, first exceeded that of its old rival. The threat of a true cotton famine emerged for the first time into the realm of possibilities and led to a marked increase in the number of speculative transactions in cotton 'to arrive' (i.e. in maritime sales), especially in Indian and Egyptian cotton. The inflation of prices raised the share of imported cotton in the total value of imports from 17 per cent in 1860 to the all-time peak of 28·5 per cent in 1864: it also doubled the share of re-exports of cotton in the total value of re-exports so that it formed 40 per cent thereof in 1864.

A self-perpetuating cycle of expectations had been generated since 1862, based upon the assumption of a continuation of the war and its associated rising prices. Those prices reached their peak in Liverpool in the week ending 23 July 1864, when Fair Uplands touched 32¼*d.* per lb., or fourfold its price in 1860 and almost as much as the peak price of 1814, so measuring the true dependence of Lancashire upon the medium-stapled cotton of America. As the tide of war turned finally and decisively against the South and Sherman occupied in Atlanta the base of the Confederate Army a long-term decline in prices inevitably followed. That decline preceded by a decade the onset of the Great Depression in the economy as a whole and took place in four cyclical slumps, interrupted by four booms, reaching its nadir in 1898. It reduced the wealth of all merchants holding large stocks but benefited mill-owners holding small stocks. It permitted the progressive recapture of the industry's export markets and opened up new opportunities to such firms as those of Rylands, Tootal, Haworth, and Armitage. Such entrepreneurs with strong capital backing and a secure basis in the home trade could acquire or build mills cheaply and install machinery at a much lower cost as well as in a more durable manner than they could in seasons of busy trade. Their example was imitated by merchants in Manchester and by engineers in Bolton and Blackburn. Those firms rapidly expanded their operations and supplied the industry with a new generation of leaders. Rylands & Sons in particular became during the 1860s 'the recognized and undisputed head and leader of the cotton trade', 'the monarchs of the cotton industry of England'.[1]

The deflation of prices took place in a series of embarrassing fluctuations and agonized spasms.[2] The price of raw cotton fell much more than that of yarn and the price of yarn more than that of cloth, so anticipating in 1864–9 the pattern of 1873–96. That decline was bitterly resented by businessmen in the absence of any system of 'hedging' capable of reducing the impact of such unforeseen fluctuations, and produced successive waves of business failures which inspired Marx's meditations on the mutability of capital. In September–October 1864 the price of cotton sank by 30 per cent, its average weekly consumption shrank by 67 per cent, and 120–30 manufacturers were reduced to bankruptcy as margins reached their lowest point. Between January and March 1865 the price of cotton plunged by 43·5 per cent as the Confederacy finally disintegrated, and another hundred manufacturers became insolvent. The revival of trade thereafter restored full employment to the industry, with cotton selling at virtually the same price as in the season of deepest distress in November 1862, i.e. an inflated level treble that of 1860. The financial

[1] *Manchester of Today* (London, Historical Publishing Company, 1888), 79; *Bulletin of the John Rylands Library of the University of Manchester*, Autumn 1973, 93–129, 'John Rylands of Manchester'.

[2] J. Kelly, 'The End of the Famine: the Manchester Cotton Trade, 1864–67—a Merchant's Eye View', in N. B. Harte and K. G. Ponting (eds.), *Textile History and Economic History: Essays in Honour of Miss Julia de Lacy Mann* (Manchester University Press, 1973), 354–86.

crisis of October 1865 then reduced cotton prices by 20 per cent and caused a third wave of failures among manufacturers.

The crisis of 1866 ushered in three years of depression which proved gloomier than the years of the Cotton Famine itself and served as a harbinger of the Great Depression of 1873–96 in so far as they saw a depression of prices rather than of production.[1] That depression was centred primarily in the home trade, whose value was halved between 1866 and 1869 under the influence of the poor harvests of 1866–7 while the value of exports sank by only 10 per cent. The re-entry of the U.S.A. into the cotton market during 1866 was reflected in the record volume of imports of cotton, which first exceeded those of the *annus mirabilis* 1860. The marked expansion in the export to the U.S.A. of cotton manufactures, the value of which doubled in 1865 and 1866, also helped to re-establish Anglo-American commerce on its pre-war basis and to frustrate official hopes to maintain India as a source of supply of raw material. During 1867 the imports of cotton from the U.S.A. exceeded those from India for the first time since 1861 and the value of the exports of cotton manufactures exceeded the value of the imports of raw cotton for the first time since 1862. The rate of expansion of production and exports was not permanently affected by the Cotton Famine but returned in 1867 to pre-crisis levels. The export of piece-goods responded to the stimulus of abundant harvests in India and first exceeded in 1867 their record level of 1860, so following the example set by the exports of thread in 1866. Exports of yarn proved the slowest of all to recover from the depression and did not surpass their level of 1860 until 1872 but improved their quality notably between 1862 and 1868, in sharp contrast to cloth exports.[2] The expansion of production and of exports was nevertheless accompanied by a drastic shrinkage in margins which declined during 1869 almost to the low level of 1863

[1] A Manchester Man [R. Burn], *The Present and Long-Continued Stagnation oj Trade: Its Causes, Effects and Cure* (Manchester, Heywood, 1869, 39pp.); W. Hoyle, 'The Depressed Condition of the Cotton Trade', *Preston Guardian*, 16 Oct. 1869, 2iv–v; idem, *Our National Resources; and How They Are Wasted. An Omitted Chapter in Political Economy* (London, Simpkin, 1871, 157pp.); *Manchester City News*, 28 Aug. 1869, 2v, 4 Sept., 2v, 11 Sept., 2iv–v, 'Trade in Manchester', reprinted as *Trade in Lancashire, By a Merchant* (Manchester, 1869, 16pp.).

[2] Sandberg, 'British Cotton Textile Exports' (1968), 10.

as the price of cloth fell even more rapidly than that of cotton. The average annual number of liquidations reached between 1865 and 1869 a peak level of 101, which was never to be approached during the remainder of the century. The number of compositions far exceeded that of formal bankruptcies. Between 1867 and 1869 two-thirds of the manufacturers in east Lancashire failed to meet their financial engagements, compounded with their creditors, or retired from the trade, while the property of surviving firms was reduced in value by as much as 60 per cent. Prophecies of ruin abounded on the Manchester Exchange in 1869, as they had in 1826 and 1842, and disappeared only on the revival of trade in 1870–3.

The traumatic experiences of the 1860s had important repercussions on the development of economic thought, especially in relation to commercial fluctuations. The basic pattern of the trade cycle was elucidated by the Manchester banker John Mills.[1] The foundations of demand theory were laid by Hoyle in relation to the home trade[2] and by Ollerenshaw in relation to the export trade.[3] Hoyle located the basic cause of the industrial depression in the increased expenditure on drink by an intemperate population. 'Here is the great secret of our present bad trade; people cannot pour money down their throats and put it on their backs at the same time; and so long as we spend seventeen times as much on drink as we do on cotton goods, we can never, long together, have anything but stagnation in trade,'[4] Ollerenshaw emphasized the close dependence of the export trade upon the fortunes of the Indian harvest. Jevons was inspired by his research to formulate in 1875 the bold and imaginative theory linking the credit crises of industrial Britain to the harvest failures apparently associated with periods of minimal sunspot activity. He applied that theory in 1878 to Anglo-Indian trade and thus replaced

[1] J. Mills, 'On Credit Cycles, and the Origin of Commercial Panics', *Transactions of the Manchester Statistical Society*, 11 Dec. 1867, 5–40, idem, 'On the Post-Panic Period 1866–70', ibid. 8 Mar. 1871, 81–104.

[2] W. Hoyle, *An Inquiry into the Causes of the Present Long-Continued Depression in the Cotton Trade with Suggestions for its Improvement, By a Cotton Manufacturer* (London, Simpkin, 1869, 17pp.).

[3] J. E. Ollerenshaw, 'Our Export Trade in Cotton Goods to India', *Transactions of the Manchester Statistical Society*, 13 Apr. 1870, 109–24.

[4] Hoyle, 11.

Mills's psychological interpretation of crises by a materialistic explanation. In 1865 Jevons had assumed the material basis of British power to lie in coal and iron rather than in textiles, thus formally depriving the cotton industry of its primacy within the British economy. Applying Malthus's principle of population to the supply of coal, he gloomily foretold an eventual coal famine on the model of the Cotton Famine and a tragic end to the brief span of British greatness.[1] For his part Marx seems to have been largely unconcerned with the crisis of overproduction but deduced in 1865 from the convulsive expansion and contraction in the sources of cotton supply that a capitalist system of industry was fundamentally irreconcilable with rational patterns of production in agriculture.[2] Froude concluded from the boom in imperial commerce, and from the increase in the British share of India's exports from 39 per cent in 1859–60 to the all-time maximum of 67·5 per cent in 1864–5, that 'trade follows the flag',[3] and became one of the leading apostles of the new gospel of empire. Nairoji deduced his anti-imperialist drain theory in part from the post-war decline in the exports of silver to India.[4] Thus both industry and empire were revalued in comprehensible materialist terms in place of the idealistic interpretation characteristic of the 1850s, when 'commerce and civilization' had seemed to march hand in hand.

The effects of the crisis continued to be felt throughout the 1860s and 1870s. The imports of Indian cotton increased sharply once more in 1869 in response to the rise in prices during 1868 and 1869, and consumption thereof exceeded that of American cotton. They were surpassed by the imports of cotton from the U.S.A. in 1870, despite the opening of the Suez Canal, but rose again in 1872, though for re-export rather than for consumption by the mills of Lancashire. Not until 1872 was the Cotton Supply Association dissolved and not until 1873 did the Government of India reluctantly recognize Indian incapacity to compete in the world market with

[1] W. S. Jevons, *The Coal Question; an Inquiry Concerning the Progress of the Nation, and the Probable Exhaustion of our Coal-Mines* (London, Macmillan, 1865, 349pp.).

[2] K. Marx, *Capital* (Chicago, Kerr, 1909), iii. 141–4, 152–62.

[3] J. A. Froude, 'England and her Colonies', *Fraser's Magazine*, Jan. 1870, 4.

[4] D. Nairoji, 'The Commerce of India', *Journal of the Society of Arts*, 17 Feb. 1871, 239–48, 301–7.

American cotton. Thus Lancashire increased its dependence upon the supply of American cotton and upon the markets of Asia for piece-goods, so reverting to the pre-war pattern of its trade. In those fields of central importance to the industry the Cotton Famine represented only a temporary aberration from the norm and ushered in no new trend. The consumption of raw cotton in England, the production of yarn, and the profits of cotton spinning regained the level of 1860 in 1871, under the influence of the enormous crop of 1870, but the price of cotton did not return to the average level of 1860 until 1876, when the U.S.A. decisively re-established its supremacy as the world's leading producer and exporter.

* * *

The true significance of the Cotton Famine has been obscured by the conventional interpretation of history in the evolutionary perspective favoured by the Victorian and Edwardian age. The crisis of the 1860s was no transient episode: it had political as well as economic repercussions, making it a fundamental turning-point in the history of Lancashire, as it was not in that of Scotland or of the Continent.[1] Its influence undermined the predominance of the Manchester School in national affairs, dethroned cotton from its pride of place in the national economy and shattered its hypnotic hold on the national imagination. 'We have reckoned on this manufacture as the pride of our country, and the best security against the possibility of war. . . . That which had been our pride has become our humiliation and our punishment. (Cheers).'[2] Paradoxically that reversal of fortune occurred at the very time that the Manchester School appeared at its noblest in the defence of the cause of non-intervention against the prevailing current of pro-Southern sentiment[3] and at the same time that the cotton industry was liberated against its will from its guilt-laden association with the Slave Power in America. Furthermore, the distribution of

[1] H. Galle, *La 'Famine du Coton,' 1861–1865. Effets de la guerre de Sécession sur l'industrie cotonnière gantoise* (Université Libre de Bruxelles, 1967), 138–9.

[2] *Manchester Guardian*, 3 Dec. 1862, 3iv, Lord Derby.

[3] *Spectator*, 15 Feb. 1862, 179, 'The Manchester School at its Best'.

relief to the unemployed vindicated the Manchesterian principle of individualism, since it was effected without any recourse to intervention by the State and without the benefit of a grant from the Exchequer, a national rate-in-aid or even parochial loans.

The Cotton Famine inflicted a spectacular humiliation upon the great industry of Lancashire but did not create any distress outside that one region. Indeed, it served to divert capital from the cotton trade into banking and finance, encouraged the reinvestment of cotton profits in the iron industry, and made Manchester the main centre of share-dealing in iron and steel companies. Thereby it fostered the spirit of speculation characteristic of the boom of the 1860s which culminated in the crises of 1864 and 1866. The decline of 8 per cent in the total value of British exports during 1861 reflected the dependence of the economy upon the cotton industry: the decline of only 2 per cent therein during the black year of 1862 measured the country's ability to reduce that dependence. England as a whole was not plunged into a depression and even enjoyed extraordinary prosperity. The gross national product grew faster than ever before as capital was diverted into more productive channels. Government revenues persistently exceeded expenditure, and the deficits of 1860–1 and 1861–2 did not recur until 1868–9. 'An industry which we conceived to be essential to our commercial greatness has been utterly prostrated, without affecting that greatness in any perceptible degree.'[1]

The cotton lords became the object of a new attack by the Conservative press of the metropolis and were reproved for their 'brutal indifference', their 'monstrous stinginess and ingratitude', and their shameful neglect of 'their enormous obligations to Cotton labour'.[2] 'They sit as still as their own machinery, and as cold as their own boilers; or they are gone off nobody knows where . . . The great Cotton Lords have disappeared with their own cotton.'[3] Secure in the support of a sycophantic local press, the cotton magnates remained unmoved by the public reproaches of the Prime Minister,[4] Charles

[1] *The Times*, 7 Jan. 1864, 8vi.
[2] Ibid. 27 Aug. 1862, 10iii, 12 Nov. 1862, 8v–vi.
[3] Ibid. 2 Sept. 1862, 8iii.
[4] Hansard, *Commons Debates*, 30 July 1862, 1027, Palmerston.

Kingsley,[1] the Positivist Dr. Bridges,[2] and *The Times*[3] but thereby widened the gulf of incomprehension between the two worlds of 'North and South'. National charity filled the gap left by the inadequacy of local subscriptions for the relief of distress and enabled Lancashire to survive with its staple industry working at only half capacity. The cotton trade was reduced in status from a national to a regional interest and never regained the image of a world-regenerating power which it had proudly borne during the 1850s. It became more specialized and therefore more fragmented: it lacked any national spokesman of the stature of Bazley until the advent of Macara in the 1890s, since John Rylands remained the most unassuming of captains of industry.

In the first of the two standard histories of the episode the radical Arthur Arnold dilated at length upon the limited contributions made by the cotton lords to the relief funds[4] and indiscreetly revealed the extent of their profits during the crisis.[5] That work was bitterly resented in Manchester as 'a so-called history' written 'before events were completed or facts made clear',[6] so that the author was forced to withdraw in the second edition the original dedication to the members of the Central Relief Committee. Dr. Watts dismissed Arnold's book as 'a hurried compilation, got up to hit the humour of the passing hour'[7] and deliberately gave his own history the polemical title of *The Facts of the Cotton Famine* in order to rebuke Arnold and to vindicate the political economy of free trade, a task which he performed with all the fervour of a convert from the faith of Owenite Socialism. His work duly earned its meed of local praise[8] but remained powerless to stem the growing revulsion

[1] *The Times*, 18 Nov. 1862, 4i, 22 Nov. 5ii, C. Kingsley, 'North and South', criticized by *The Economist*, 22 Nov. 1862, 1289–90, and 29 Nov., 1319–20.

[2] *The Times*, 14 Mar. 1863, 14ii–iii, 20 Mar., 5v–vi, 4 Apr., 5vi; S. Liveing, *A Nineteenth Century Teacher. John Henry Bridges, M.B., F.R.C.P.* (London, Paul 1926), 96–103.

[3] *The Times*, 11 Aug. 1862, 8iv, 27 Aug., 8iv–v, 3 Sept., 6iv, 6 Sept., 6iv, 9 Sept., 6ii–iv, criticized by the *Spectator*, 30 Aug. 1862, 963–4, 6 Sept., 988–9, 22 Nov., 1292–3, 29 Nov., 1321–2.

[4] R. A. Arnold, *The History of the Cotton Famine* (1864), 196–243.

[5] Ibid. 77, 83.

[6] *Manchester Guardian*, 23 Jan. 1866, 3iv.

[7] J. Watts, *The Facts of the Cotton Famine* (1866), iii.

[8] *Manchester Guardian*, 23 Jan. 1866, 3iv–vi.

within Lancashire from the philosophy of economic and political liberalism.

Within the most central sphere of life the cotton operatives established their moral independence of their masters in a powerful Conservative reaction which manifested itself in the organization of Conservative Working Men's Associations, in an extensive revival of the Anglican Church, in an increase in popular hostility towards the Irish, and in the birth of an agitation in favour of reciprocity and against free trade.[1] The cotton lords paid a heavy price for their social abdication during the crisis of the 1860s. Firstly they were forced to increase wages by one-fifth between 1865 and 1868 in a labour market tightened by emigration, so setting in motion a long-term process increasing labour costs and labour's share of output. Then they suffered in the general election of 1868 the catastrophic loss of their political pre-eminence in so far as that was identified with the Liberal party. Lord Derby's grant of the vote to the artisans in 1867 paid a well-deserved tribute to the stoical bearing under privation of the cotton operatives of his home county and was justified by the sweeping Conservative victories in Lancashire in 1868[2] and in England in 1874, when the hopes of the Liberal Grant Duff were frustrated but his prophecy proved singularly true: 'What Lancashire thinks today, England thinks tomorrow.'[3]

[1] *Manchester Guardian*, 20 Sept. 1869, 3iii, 7 Dec. 1869, 5iii.

[2] W. A. Abram, 'Social Condition and Political Prospects of the Lancashire Workmen', *Fortnightly Review*, 1 Oct. 1868, 426–41; R. S. S. [Sowler], *The General Election in the Great Centres of Population* (London, Blackwood, 1869), 8–24; H. J. Hanham, *Elections and Party Management. Politics in the Time of Disraeli and Gladstone* (London, Longmans, 1959), 284–322, 'A Lancashire Election: 1868'; J. R. Vincent, 'The Effect of the Second Reform Act in Lancashire', *Historical Journal*, 1968, 84–94; J. C. Lowe, 'The Tory Triumph of 1868 in Blackburn and in Lancashire', *Historical Journal*, 1973, 733–48.

[3] *Manchester Guardian*, 10 Aug. 1868, 3iii, M. E. Grant Duff.

CHAPTER 5

The 'Great Depression' of 1873–1896 and the Challenge of Foreign Competition

> We have not been producing more than the world could really use, but more than the world, I suppose, could really pay for.
> *Second Report of the Royal Commission on the Depression of Trade*, 1886, Q.4315, Samuel Andrew of Oldham, 10 February 1886.

THE LONG deflation in prices from 1873 to 1896 resembled that of 1814–50 in its effects upon the economic world but cannot be arbitrarily isolated from the immediately preceding period and, since the revisionist studies of S. B. Saul, can no longer be considered as an indivisible unity. For the cotton industry as for the rest of the economy the decade of the 1880s rather than that of the 1870s seems to mark a turning-point in development. The decline in prices nevertheless proved more severe in the case of the cotton industry than in that of other industries. It also proved more prolonged since the decline in cotton prices began in 1864, was interrupted in 1869 and 1872, resumed its course from 1873 and lasted until 1898. During that period production expanded much less rapidly than formerly and suffered from three major cyclical depressions, in 1877–9, 1884–5, and 1891–3, and from a prolonged decline in its value. The gross value of production contracted unsteadily as prices sank and did not surpass the peak value attained in 1872 until 1904. That secular depression of prices reduced profits and prospects of future profit, so transforming the expectations of employers and checking the rate of expansion of the industry.

The decline in prices was a world-wide trend which coincided with and contributed to the relative industrial retardation of Britain. For the cotton industry it embodied a reaction from the rising prices of 1850–73 and especially from the massive inflation of prices during the Cotton Famine. The crisis of the 1860s had so distorted normal modes of business that a profound reaction therefrom was inevitable. The Cotton Famine had raised prices to such an extreme degree that it had helped to price the industry out of many of its markets, to the benefit of other textile industries. It had engendered a boom in the trade in raw cotton, especially in re-exports, and had tended to divert enterprise and capital from industry into commerce. The profits of merchants and manufacturers holding stocks or trading therein had been inflated to abnormal levels. Amongst such profit-takers patterns of high living, based upon the expectation of a continuing high level of profits, had been diffused whilst a curb had been imposed upon the income and the standard of living of the operatives. All those trends were reversed from 1864 as cotton prices began to decline and so transformed the economic environment of an intensely market-oriented industry. An extensive and continuous decline in prices was indeed essential to the industry to permit the reconquest of its lost markets but proved most unwelcome to employers and exerted immediate and growing pressure upon the costs of manufacture, so diverting interest from the sphere of commerce back to that of industry. Profits were placed under increasing pressure as wages proved resistant to reduction: even the high standard of living of employers seemed threatened.

The depression of 1873–96 embodied a reaction from the boom of 1870–3 as well as from the Cotton Famine. That boom was stimulated by the Franco-Prussian War and by the temporary upsurge in demand in the civilized markets of the world, particularly in Europe and the U.S.A. The expansion of the heavy industries in the service of those markets reduced the share of the cotton industry in total exports from 35·4 per cent in 1869 to 30·3 per cent in 1873 as exports of capital goods rose faster than those of cotton goods. The establishment of very high wage levels proved of great benefit to the home trade. The joint-stock mania of 1873–5 marked the culmination of that wave of prosperity in the cotton industry but increased productive power beyond the absorptive capacity of existing markets. Thus the way was paved for the subsequent reaction when supply was compelled reluctantly to adjust to demand through the medium of lower prices.

The decline in prices and profits was attributed by contemporaries to a variety of influences including overproduction, underconsumption, foreign competition, hostile tariffs, and fluctuations in the value of silver.[1] In the main it seems to have originated in a relative decline in demand coupled with an over-expansion of supply. The industry was influenced by the general trends affecting the emergent world economy and by factors peculiar to its own supply- and demand-schedules. The decline in the price of raw cotton seems to have reflected a more rapid expansion in the supply of the raw material than in the demand for cotton yarn and cloth. The extension within industry of cost-cutting technical innovations transmitted and reinforced the influence of the fall in the price of raw cotton. The mobilization of capital for investment by the joint-stock company facilitated that wave of technical innovation and depressed the return upon existing capital to the embarrassment and distress of established producers. Manufacturers and merchants painfully mastered once more the hard doctrine learned by the founders of the industry, that 'cheapness promotes consumption without any definite limit'.[2]

The demand for cotton manufactures had thitherto been more elastic than the supply of cotton but expanded less rapidly as other countries became more self-sufficient, as world trade in manufactures, especially in cotton goods, stagnated and as the British share declined. The cotton industry suffered first from the loss of the markets of industrial Europe and the U.S.A. and then from the resurgence of Oriental industry. At the same time the secular decline in the prices paid

[1] *A Few Original Ideas of a Manchester Man respecting our Bad Trade and Government Interference* (Manchester, Heywood, 1876, 32pp.), 2; J. Morley, 'An Economic Address', *Fortnightly Review*, Oct. 1878, 551–4; E. Guthrie, *Bad Trade considered in relation to the Present Condition of the Cotton Industry in England* (Manchester, Ireland, 1878, 24pp.), 21; E. Helm, 'The Depression of Trade', *Transactions of the Manchester Statistical Society*, 11 Dec. 1878, 48; F. Hibbert, *Bad Trade, and How to Avoid It. By A Cotton Spinner* (Manchester, Ireland, 1878, 31pp.), 19–31; *Manchester Guardian*, 13 Nov. 1878, 4v–vi, G. A. Southam, 'The Causes of the Depression of Trade'; E. Seyd, *The Decline of Prosperity: its Insidious Cause and Obvious Remedy* (London, Stanford, 1879, 104pp.), 25; A. J. Wilson, *The Resources of Modern Countries. Essays towards an Estimate of the Economic Position of Nations and British Trade Prospects* (London, Longmans, 1878), i. 126–30, 178; W. Hoyle, *Over-Production and the Present Stagnation in Trade* (Manchester, Heywood, 1878, 16pp.), 12, 15; idem, 'The Economic Conditions of Good Trade', *Transactions of the Manchester Statistical Society*, 12 May 1880, 107; idem, *Problems to Solve: Social, Political, and Economic* (London, Simpkin, 1883, 24pp.), 19.

[2] *Manchester Guardian*, 1 Jan. 1879, 5i, 'Review of the Cotton Trade of the Year 1878'.

for the staple exports of the primary producers, caused by the massive expansion of world trade in agricultural commodities and by the improvement of transportation facilities, reduced the purchasing-power of the great markets of Asia for the staple export of Lancashire. That restrictive influence was offset only in part by the continued reduction in transport costs and by the depreciation of silver, which enhanced rather than reduced the demand for cotton goods of the 70 per cent of the world's population upon the silver standard.[1] The favourable shift of Britain's terms of trade from the 1880s reflected that decline in prices and tended to restrict the demand for British exports but to facilitate the expansion of the home trade.

The decline in the price of raw cotton was no mere reflection of the general decline in the price of primary produce but represented an inevitable reaction from the concentrated price inflation of the Cotton Famine. Cotton had risen most in price during that inflation and declined most during the subsequent deflation, sinking between 1873 and 1896 50 per cent more than wholesale prices in general. That deflation took place in three successive swoops which reduced the price in 1876 to the level of 1860, in 1886 to the level of 1852 and in 1895 below the level of 1845 to an all-time low point. The slump in prices was in part a response to the increased production of cotton in Turkestan, China, India, and Egypt, to the effective establishment of a world market in cotton with the spread of the telegraph cable, to the reduction in the number of bales locked up at sea after the opening of the Suez Canal and the transfer to the steamship of the carriage of American cotton, and to the increasing use of future contracts, which served indefinitely to extend existing supplies. Above all, it reflected the triumphal re-entry of the Cotton Kingdom of the U.S.A. into the world market, the renewed eastwards expansion of the cotton belt,

[1] Joshua Rawlinson, 'Bimetallism for Beginners', *Transactions of the Burnley Literary and Scientific Club*, 8 Feb. 1887, 27–34 (reprinted, Manchester, Heywood, 1887, 24pp.); idem, 'The Silver Question. An Address', *Manchester Examiner and Times*, 21 Nov. 1889, 7iii, reprinted in full as *The Silver Question as it affects the Cotton Trade* (Manchester, Heywood, 1889, 26pp.); idem, 'Trades Union Leaders and Bimetallism. An Expository Address', *Manchester City News*, 17 Nov. 1894, 5iv–v, 24 Nov., 5iii–iv, reprinted as *Plain Words against Bimetallism. An Address delivered to the Blackburn Trades Council, November 13, 1894* (Manchester City News, 1895, 24pp.).

especially into Texas, and the trebling of the volume of U.S. cotton exports during the twenty years 1872–91. The supersession of the plantation by the less efficient share-cropping tenure did not prevent production from increasing faster during the 1870s than in any decade since the 1830s. The decline in prices produced by such a large expansion in supply was reinforced in the short term by the restriction of credit to planters after the financial panic of 1873 and the consequent increase in forced sales, and in the long term by the enlarged output and sale of the by-products of the cotton boll in cotton-seed oil and cakes and cotton stalks. Britain became the major beneficiary by the fall in the price of U.S. cotton, which supplied 67·5 per cent of its imports of cotton during the thirty years 1867–96.[1]

The decline in prices exerted a growing pressure upon the price of yarn and of cloth but affected the raw cotton market more than the yarn and cloth markets. Cotton lost all its power of attraction as an investment for capital. The holding of cotton became as unprofitable a venture as it had been a profitable one during the Cotton Famine, so that stocks sank from 27 weeks' supply at the close of 1864 and 15 weeks' supply at the end of 1871 to nine weeks' supply by 31 December 1877. The decline in prices and stocks was slightly steeper in Liverpool than in New York and encouraged repeated bouts of speculation for a rise in the market, especially by means of a corner. The corners of 1879 and 1881 were repeated in 1888 and 1889,[2] worsened the relations between Liverpool and Lancashire, and inspired the agitation for a Manchester ship canal as a means of ending the industry's dependence upon the Liverpool market. The extension of trading in futures, especially

[1] B. R. Mitchell and P. Deane (eds.), *Abstract of British Historical Statistics* (1962), 180–1.

[2] *Liverpool Daily Post*, 1 Nov. 1879, 8v; 31 Oct. 1883, 4vii; W. B. Halhed, 'On Commercial "Corners" ', *Nineteenth Century*, Oct. 1881, 532–7; E. Guthrie, 'The Effects upon Trade of the operation called Cornering, in relation to Commodities', *Transactions of the Manchester Statistical Society*, 30 Nov. 1881, 29–44; *Textile Manufacturer*, Sept. 1888, 432, Oct. 1888, 478, Aug. 1889, 382, Sept. 1889, 432, Oct. 1889, 483; T. B. Waters, *Cotton Facts and Lessons from the Past* (Manchester, Brook, 1889, 20pp.), reprinted from *Manchester Examiner*, 8 Jan. 1889, 4v–vi; W. W. Biggs, 'Cotton Corners', *Transactions of the Manchester Statistical Society*, 13 Mar. 1895, 123–34; T. Ellison, *Gleanings and Reminiscences* (Liverpool, Young, 1905), 337–56.

amongst spinners in self-defence during the 1880s, contributed to the increasing fluctuation in prices from 1886[1] which further undermined confidence in that market.

The cotton trade lost its position of primacy in the import and re-export trades, which were both dominated by raw cotton for the last time in 1873. The imports of grain exceeded in value those of cotton in 1874, so ending the era of forty-eight years, begun in 1825 and interrupted only in 1854, during which cotton had held the premier position in the import trade. As cotton prices sank faster than general prices the share of cotton in the value of merchandise imports shrank by almost 45 per cent from 14·8 per cent in 1873 to 8·2 per cent in 1896. The waning importance of cotton in the import trade markedly reduced the pressure upon import values thitherto exerted by the long-term increase in the imports of raw cotton and contributed to the favourable shift in the terms of trade during the 1880s. It also prevented the recurrence of any abnormal rise in import prices in general such as had been created in 1862 by the increase in price of a single commodity.

Re-exports of cotton had declined from their peak level of 1866 but reached in 1872 a secondary peak, which was surpassed in volume only in 1887 and in value only in 1910. From 1874 cotton was replaced by wool as the country's most valuable single re-export. The entrepôt trade of Liverpool was reduced by the competition of foreign ports, especially on the Continent, as the Suez Canal enabled new shipping lines to ply direct from India to the ports of the Mediterranean. Liverpool's re-exports of Indian cotton to Europe declined after 1872 and were surpassed from 1876 by the volume of imports direct from India to the Continent, suffering their sharpest proportionate reduction since 1830.[2] The stocks of Surat held in Liverpool declined much more sharply between 1873 and 1877 than the stocks of other varieties. The proportion of the imports of

[1] S. J. Chapman, 'The Conditions and Consequences of Market Developments in the Cotton Trade', *Transactions of the Manchester Statistical Society*, 14 Jan. 1903, 49–67; idem, 'Cotton: Marketing and Supply', *Encyclopaedia Britannica* (Cambridge University Press, 1910, 11th edn.), vii, 267–75; S. J. Chapman and D. Knoop, 'Anticipation in the Cotton Market', *Economic Journal*, Dec. 1904, 541–54; idem, 'Dealings in Futures on the Cotton Market', *Journal of the Royal Statistical Society*, June 1906, 321–73.

[2] W. B. Dana, *Cotton From Seed to Loom* (New York, Dana, 1878), 62, 66.

cotton re-exported declined from 20·6 per cent in 1850–72 to 13·5 per cent in 1873–96, and from 19·4 per cent in 1872 to 10·5 per cent in 1896. The decline in prices reduced the share of cotton in the total value of re-exports much more sharply from 25·2 per cent in 1850–72 to 8·2 per cent in 1873–96, and from 11·6 per cent in 1873 to 6·4 per cent in 1896, a decline virtually accomplished by 1878. The reduction in the share of cotton in the import and re-export trade contrasted sharply with the comparative stability of the cotton industry's share in domestic exports.

* * *

In foreign markets the export-oriented cotton industry of Britain suffered some loss of trade and especially a loss of incremental demand as cotton goods were supplied increasingly from rival centres of production. The competitive advantages of Lancashire proved in the long term to be essentially unstable and impermanent, save in specialized products of the highest quality. As an unnatural, exotic, and speculative graft upon English soil, the cotton industry was indeed doomed, in so far as it catered for foreign markets, to be fast exported to other lands and to become the first industry to be acquired by new states or to be regained by old ones. Its attrition first became apparent in a reduced rate of growth and was well-nigh inevitable, being much less remarkable than its relatively long career in England, but nevertheless disturbed profoundly a society accustomed to regard it as an asset of permanent and increasing value. The development of other cotton industries was encouraged by a wide range of influences which Lancashire could not hope to counteract and especially by the widespread distribution of supplies of the raw material, which was cheap to transport and lost little weight and consumed little power or other materials in the process of production. Thus raw cotton did not have to be manufactured near the source of supply but could be spun near a market or near a supply of labour, neither of which was transportable, as raw cotton was. The labour-intensive nature of the industry was almost as marked as that of cotton cultivation, made labour much more important as a factor of production than either capital or management, and thus benefited the lands of cheap labour and dear capital in the production of grey cloth, which was virtually a bundle of woven wages, at the expense of Lancashire with its commitment to high-cost mule-spinning and plain-loom weaving.[1]

The hand-loom weavers of Asia had survived the competition of the power-looms of Lancashire[2] because they enjoyed the effective protection of high inland transport costs, because their products were markedly preferred by consumers, and, above all, because their labour costs were low. The demand for cheap yarn generated by their hand-looms was met first by foreign imports and then by indigenous spinning mills, which were thus called into existence to supply an existing market and to replace imports by a local product. The successful establishment of such mills was facilitated by the simplicity of spinning technology, by the recuitment of unskilled labour to master an art no more difficult than that of hand-sewing, by the small scale of economic operation, and by the limited need for managerial expertise, especially in the spinning of coarse yarn. Their creation was also aided by the absence of any 'humane restrictions' upon hours of labour, by the removal of restrictions on the export of machinery from England, by the interest acquired in the export market by the textile engineers of Lancashire, reinforced by that of Manchester merchants and that of the Lancashire spinning industry in the replacement of its machinery and the resale abroad of its old equipment, and by the services of English foremen and managers as teachers of indigenous populations endowed with the imitative ability necessary to master a routine process of production. The large and expanding demand for cotton yarn and cotton goods, especially for cheap and coarse qualities, provided the local market necessary to such an industry, which tended only slowly to extend its range of production upwards from coarse to superior goods. Foreign states regarded the cotton mill as the great symbol of factory industry, wealth, power, and modern civilization on the English model: in the cotton industry they found a useful means of import-substitution and autarchic development in

[1] L. G. Sandberg, *Lancashire in Decline* (1974), 207–12.

[2] S. J. Koh, *Stages of Industrial Development in Asia. A Comparative History of the Cotton Industry in Japan, India, China and Korea* (Philadelphia, University of Pennsylvania Press, 1966), 48–52, 280, 370.

the interests of political and military, as well as of economic, independence. The grant of tariff protection provided additional encouragement in Europe, America, and Japan and proved essential to an infant industry because of the relative unimportance of maritime transport costs and the advantage thereby conferred upon the world's leading exporter of cotton manufactures. Such protection did not need to be high in order to be effective and was not extended to India before 1917 or to China before 1929, though its function was fulfilled in India by the national sentiment of 'swaraj' and in China by the levy of internal taxation. The effective incidence of specific import duties was raised by the fall in prices[1] and proved most protective in Europe and America.

The expansion of spindleage outside England, fostered by such influences, gradually reduced the British share of the mill spindleage of the world from 56 per cent in 1875 to less than half for the first time in 1893. The new cotton industries adopted the ring frame rather than the mule and employed thereon cheap unskilled labour, confirming their labour-intensive basis and differentiating themselves from the British cotton industry which continued to expand upon the basis of the mule. The consumption of cotton outside England increased and the British share of world cotton consumption shrank as foreign industries expanded and concentrated upon the production of coarse goods with a high cotton-content and as the British industry increasingly specialized in the spinning of fine counts and in the weaving of fine cloth incorporating a relatively large amount of skilled labour. The British share of America's expanding cotton exports was reduced from 69·3 per cent in 1850–72 to 60·3 per cent in 1873–96[2] and the supply of American cotton was increasingly diverted from England to Europe, which in 1888 for the first time consumed more cotton than Britain. In 1895 England first imported less than half of the cotton exported from the U.S.A. and in 1897 first consumed less cotton than the U.S. itself, thereby bringing to a close its century of pre-eminence as the largest single consumer in the

[1] J. C. Fielden, *Speech on Foreign Competition in the Cotton Trade* (Blackburn, Tiplady, 1879, 32pp.), 27.

[2] Excluding the years 1862–5 for which no data were available to M. B. Hammond, *The Cotton Industry—An Essay in American Economic History* (New York Macmillan, 1897).

TABLE 8

Factory Spindleage of the Cotton Industry of the World, 1832–1895

	Great Britain	Continent	U.S.A.	India	Total	British (%)
			millions of spindles			
1832	9	2·8	1·2		13	69·2
1845	17·5	7·5	2·5		27·5	63·5
1850	21	9·6	3·6		34·8	60·3
1861	30·3	10	5	0·34	45·64	66·4
1875	37·5	19·5	9·5	0·886	67·386	55·7
1877	39·5	19·6	10	1·23	70·33	56·3
1880	39·75	20·805	11·5	1·4	73·455	54·1
1881	40·6	21·215	11·375	1·496	74·686	54·4
1882	41	21·855	12	1·62	76·475	53·7
1883	42	22·5	12·66	1·7	78·86	53·3
1884	42·5	22·65	13·2	1·95	80·3	53
1885	43	22·75	13·25	2·05	81·05	53
1886	42·7	22·9	13·35	2·26	81·21	52·6
1887	42·74	23·18	13·5	2·42	81·84	52·3
1888	42·74	23·38	13·525	2·49	82·135	52
1890	43·75	25·46	14·55	3·27	87·03	50·2
1891	44·75	26·035	14·781	3·351	88·917	50·4
1892	45·38	26·405	15·278	3·402	90·435	50·2
1893	45·27	26·85	15·64	3·576	91·337	49·6
1895	45·4	28·2	16·1	3·8	96·04	47·2

Source: T. Bazley, 'Cotton Manufacture', *Encyclopaedia Britannica* (Edinburgh, Black, 8th edn., 1854), vii. 460, for 1850; *C.W.S. Annual*, 1884, 196, for 1881–3; T. Ellison, *The Cotton Trade of Great Britain* (1886), 348, for 1882–5; idem, 'Cotton', *Chambers's Encyclopaedia* (London, Chambers, 1889), iii. 515, for 1861, 1877, 1887; *The Economist*, 29 Oct. 1887, 1373, 'The Cotton Industry', for 1883–7, 3 Nov. 1888, 1380, for 1884–8; *Manchester Courier*, 30 Dec. 1893, 7viii, for 1890–3.

world. Increasingly Lancashire used specialized varieties of cotton appropriate to the high quality of its products, especially Sea Island and Egyptian cotton. As counts of yarn became finer the average consumption of raw cotton per spindle in Lancashire declined from the peak level reached in 1891.

* * *

The burden of readjustment to the growth of foreign competition was borne by exports rather than by the unprotected home trade. The secular reorientation of production towards the internal market took effect as Lancashire recovered from the Cotton Famine and reduced its export bias, especially after 1881. The home trade certainly declined more sharply than the export trade in each of the three cyclical crises between 1873 and 1893, especially in 1873–9 under the influence of the deep depression in the capital-goods industries. That market had indeed become much less important than the export trade but experienced a marked revival from the 1880s as purchasing-power was liberated by the decline in food prices, so progressively reducing the degree of its sympathetic slump in each successive cycle and facilitating its faster expansion in years of boom.

The exports of cotton manufactures entered in 1873 upon a period of thirty years of decline in value and did not surpass the level of 1872 until 1904. They increased in volume between 1873 and 1896 by 41 per cent but sank in value by 13·5 per cent, or by only three-fifths of the decline in value of the home trade, while their main constituent in piece-goods increased in volume by 50 per cent but sank in value by 9 per cent and declined in price by more than double the average decline in price of domestic exports in general. The industry developed the markets of Asia as those of the western hemisphere contracted during the first phase of the Great Depression and then faced during the second phase a slump in Asiatic demand. The proportion of the industry's exports shipped to Europe and the U.S.A. sank by over one-third between 1873 and 1896. That contraction proved slightly greater in volume than in value because of the increased export of thread. It proved much larger in the case of the U.S.A. than of Europe, whose imports of piece-goods reached their peak level in 1887 while those of the U.S.A. had reached their maximum amount in 1860. Demand suffered its greatest reduction in the important markets of France and Italy. The renewal of the Cobden-Chevalier Treaty in 1873 failed to prevent French imports of piece-goods declining from their peak level of 1874, a decade before French imports of yarn were reduced from their maximum by the tariff of 1883. Exports of piece-goods to Italy were drastically reduced by 65 per cent from their peak level of 1887 by the tariff of that year. The shrinkage in exports to the markets of Europe and the U.S.A. accounted for 60 per cent of the loss in exports by the industry in 1873–9, so afflicting most severely the centres of quality production in south-east Lancashire and Preston. The proportion of the industry's exports shipped to Asia increased from 31 per cent in 1873 to an all-time peak of 49 per cent in 1888, declining thereafter to 42 per cent in 1896. The volume of piece-goods exported to India in 1888 was surpassed in the bumper year of 1894 but the shipments of 1888 to China only in 1902. In the crisis of 1891–3 the marked decline in exports to Asia represented 62 per cent of the loss of exports by the industry. The incidence of that depression bore most heavily upon the centres of the India and China trade which had suffered least in the two preceding crises. The industry in partial compensation increased its exports to Latin America to a peak in 1895, especially of cheap sized and dyed goods, and to a lesser extent to the British colonies in Canada, Australasia, and South Africa. It also sought to expand its markets in the Levant and in Africa, where it hoped to discover a 'second India', first in the Congo and then in Nigeria.[1] A special interest in Africa was developed by the Manchester Geographical Society which was founded during the depression of 1885 for the study of the commercial geography of new markets and which reflected not only extensive lay interest in the wider world but also a traditional preference for market development by private rather than by public means.[2]

In Africa Egypt was absorbed only slowly and partially within the economic empire of Britain after its occupation in 1882, remaining relatively more important as a source of supply of raw cotton than as a market. It had found in England the largest customer since 1844 for its cotton and had supplied the mills of Bolton with the staple for their medium counts of

[1] *Cotton*, 6 Apr. 1878, 208, James Bradshaw, 'Trade in Africa'; *Manchester Examiner*, 7 Dec. 1878, 6vi, B. H. Thwaite, 'Trade with South Eastern Africa', 28 Dec. 1878, 3vi, idem, 'Africa our Future Hope'; *Oldham Chronicle*, 21 Dec. 1878, 3v–vi, A. Hatchard, 'Africa: the Future Market for Lancashire Cotton Goods'; *Textile Manufacturer*, Dec. 1878, 388, 'Africa and British Trade'; H. M. Stanley, *England and the Congo and Manchester Trade, and the Work and Aims of the International Association* (Manchester, Ireland, 1884, 39pp.), 12–13, 24–5; idem, *The Congo and the Founding of its Free State: a Story of Work and Exploration* (London, Low, 1885), ii. 364–77; W. L. Grant, 'The Development of Africa in its Relation to British Commerce', *Transactions of the Burnley Literary and Scientific Club*, 25 Nov. 1884, 86–8.

[2] T. N. L. Brown, 'The Manchester Society of Commercial Geography', *Journal of the Manchester Geographical Society*, 1952–4, 40–4; idem, *The History of the Manchester Geographical Society 1884–1950* (Manchester University Press, 1971, 102pp.)

yarn:[1] it had ranked in 1850 fourth in the quantity supplied and surpassed Brazil in 1852 but India only in 1891 when it assumed the second place to the U.S.A. as a source of supply of raw cotton. Unlike the U.S.A. it imported yarn and cloth in exchange for its cotton and had been the largest single market of Lancashire in Africa since 1835. Its import capacity however remained limited[2] and developed only from 1894, even though it did not imitate India in establishing its own spinning mills until 1901.

The main branches of the industry reached their maximum level of exports between 1882 and 1913.[3] The yarn trade bore the burden of depression earlier and more fully than the trade in piece-goods. The price of yarn declined more than the price of cloth, so placing the margins of spinners under greater pressure than the margins of manufacturers and exacerbating relations between the two main sections of the industry as each strove to secure the maximum share of the available margin. Yarn prices sank almost thrice as much as the price of piece-goods and almost sixfold as much as the average price of domestic exports in general as foreign spinners replaced British yarn by their own production and inflicted upon Lancashire its first great defeat. Exports of yarn had drained off 15 per cent of the total quantity spun between 1843 and 1884 and reached their peak value in 1872 and their peak quantity in 1884. They reached successive peaks to Germany in 1872, to Italy in 1876, to Belgium in 1878, to Russia in 1879, and to France in 1883. The watershed in the history of the trade occurred in 1884 when the volume of yarn exports to both Europe and Asia reached its all-time maximum. Thereafter those exports declined as the fears voiced in the years 1800–20 about the dangerous consequences of the traffic were finally realized. That decline proved steepest in the Far East where exports reached their peak to China in 1880 and to Japan in

[1] *Manchester Guardian*, 14 July 1882, 8v, John Slagg, 'English Trade in Egypt'.

[2] *Manchester Examiner*, 7 Nov. 1882, 4iii.

[3] The maximum volume of cotton hosiery was exported in 1882, that of yarn in 1884, that of sewing thread in 1900, and that of cloth only in 1913. Within the spectrum of piece-goods the peak volume of exports of printed cloth was recorded in 1911 and that of bleached cloth in 1912. Only in 1913 did exports of the great staple of Lancashire, unbleached cloth, reach their maximum, as did those of dyed goods, taking together yarn-dyed and piece-dyed cloth.

1881 and the combined share of both those markets in the total exports of British yarn declined sharply from 21·5 per cent in 1880 to 12·9 per cent in 1896. The loss of the incremental trade in yarn exports to China, first to India and then to Japan, dealt a serious blow to Lancashire since Japan continued to expand its imports of yarn until 1888, as did China until 1899.

The spinning industry achieved some diversification of its outlets in response to the curb imposed upon its trade with eastern Asia. It expanded its exports, especially of dyed yarn, to the Levant in the 1880s until they reached a peak for Egypt in 1891 and for Turkey in 1892. It also developed exports for the first time to Latin America, whose imports expanded rapidly to reach their maximum volume in 1896. Yarn exports had experienced, until 1880, a long-term process of decline in their quality, as measured by the fineness of their count and the degree of their finish. Their quality improved by 15·5 per cent between 1881 and 1894,[1] under the pressure of foreign competition, almost a decade before that of cloth exports. The growing demand for fine counts could not be met immediately by foreign mills which first produced coarse yarn and spun upwards in their range of counts only slowly. That demand was supplied by the spindles of Bolton and Manchester which made increasing use of long-stapled Egyptian cotton, especially from 1888, and so incorporated the skill and climatic advantages of the locality into their product.

As the share of yarn in the total value of exports of cotton manufactures declined from 36 per cent in 1842 to 20·4 per cent in 1884 and to 15·7 per cent in 1896, its function in the expansion of foreign markets was increasingly assumed by sewing thread. Exports of cotton thread continued to expand much faster than exports of yarn and reached their peak volume in 1900 at a level treble that of 1875. Those exports amounted in 1896 to less than 5 per cent of the total value of the exports of cotton manufactures and to only one-third of the value of yarn exports but were worth thrice the unit-value of yarn exports and thus revealed the industry's ability to enhance the value of its products and to tap the increasingly profitable markets opened, especially in the civilized Western world, by the spread of the steel needle as well as of the sewing-machine and by the

[1] Sandberg, 240–1.

extension of the influence of the fashion-cycle. The thread industry differed from the more plebeian branches of the cotton industry in that it remained in undisputed command of the world market but became, under the pressure of acute oligopolistic competition, the true pioneer of the trust movement within the industry.

Exports of piece-goods continued to expand for thirty years after exports of yarn had reached their peak in 1884. The new foreign producers of coarse cloth manufactured primarily for their home markets and so reduced the proportion of cotton goods entering into world trade but had much more difficulty in encroaching upon the great neutral markets of the world where the British hold was well established. Britain's share of the world trade in cotton goods nevertheless declined from 81·9 per cent in 1882–4 to 77·6 per cent in 1891–3 and to 69·9 per cent in 1909–13[1] in harmony with the decline in the rate of growth of British exports of cotton manufactures. The rate of increase in piece-goods exports slackened after 1888 and so suffered its first large reduction of the century. Exports of the great staple product of Lancashire in grey cloth reached their peak volume in 1890[2] and remained relatively stable until 1913 but formed a declining proportion of the total export of piece-goods as the shipment of bleached, printed, and dyed cloth increased. Thus Britain profited by the development of its finishing industries and increased the unit-value of its exports of cotton manufactures.

Textiles in general became less important in the export trade of the realm as production slackened and other industries expanded their output faster. Textile manufactures, including woollens, worsteds, linens, and silks as well as cottons, had reduced their share of domestic exports from the peak proportion of 1834 and supplied in 1873 for the first time less than half the value. Their average share sank by 27 per cent from 62·6 per cent in 1814–72 to 45·6 per cent in 1873–96 and by 30 per cent from 60 per cent in 1872 to 42 per cent in 1896. The exports of textiles declined in value between 1873 and 1896 by

[1] *Cotton Factory Times*, 6 May 1885, 8vi; F. Merttens, 'The Hours and Cost of Labour in the Cotton Industry', *Transactions of the Manchester Statistical Society*, 18 Apr. 1894, 174; R. Robson, *The Cotton Industry in Britain* (1957), 4.

[2] Of 2,325 million yards, exceeded only by the 2,336 million yards of 1905 and by the 2,357 million yards of 1913.

£32,100,000 or by double the decline in value of all domestic exports. That decline was however greater in the case of woollen than of cotton manufactures. The export of woollen goods reached their peak volume and value in 1872 and declined in value therefrom by 38 per cent, a decrease which was thrice the proportionate decline of 13·5 per cent in the exports of cotton manufactures, and represented 90 per cent of the decline in the total value of domestic exports while the decline in the value of the export of cotton manufactures represented only 67 per cent. As textiles ceased to dominate the export trade other industries expanded their exports and so insulated the economy from the effect of the relative decline in its staple exports. The volume of textile exports ceased to expand after 1888 in harmony with the reduced rate of growth of cotton textile exports and did not surpass the level of 1888 for seventeen years.[1] Those exports became increasingly exports of cotton manufactures, whose share rose from 64 per cent in 1873 to 68·5 per cent in 1896. The share of the cotton industry in domestic exports tended to decline and shrank especially during the three phases of economic expansion in 1880–4, 1886–90, and 1894–1900 whilst it expanded during the cyclical depressions of 1873–7, 1884–6, and 1890–4. Despite such fluctuations its share remained relatively stable and sank by only 5 per cent from 30·3 per cent in 1873 to 28·9 per cent in 1896, a much slighter reduction than the loss of a quarter which had taken place in 1850–73 from the 40 per cent of 1850. The industry nevertheless ceased to supply the increment in export values which it had thitherto furnished, especially in phases of cyclical expansion, and so ceased to operate as a stimulus to the expansion of exports and to the associated deterioration in the terms of trade. The dynamic function of the textile industry was inherited by the engineering industry. Exports of machinery expanded markedly as textile exports remained stagnant in the 1890s, so bringing about a major alteration in the structure of the export trade.[2] The export of machinery became increasingly a spur to industrial development abroad where earlier it had often been as unproductive

[1] S. B. Saul, 'The Export Economy 1870–1914', *Yorkshire Bulletin of Economic and Social Research*, 1965, 9.

[2] Ibid.

as the building of the Pyramids. At home textile engineering became a more profitable pursuit than the cotton industry and diffused the benefits arising from a highly skilled trade which required no factory legislation to maintain tolerable working conditions.[1] That industry effectively compensated Lancashire for the loss of its monopolistic position as the centre of the world's greatest cotton industry and laid the basis of its future industrial power through the export of machinery from 'the workshop of the world'.

* * *

The prolonged depression of prices between 1873 and 1896 ended the second main era in the history of the British cotton industry and ushered in a new phase wherein production adapted itself to the slower rate of market expansion and increased by an average annual rate of 1·4 per cent, or about a quarter of the rate sustained between 1780 and 1872. The decrease in the industry's rate of expansion was apparently the product less of any secular decline in the quality of entrepreneurship or of any shortage of capital than of the competition of low-cost competitors abroad, the long-term decline in profit expectations, and the secular shift towards more competitive spheres of production such as engineering. The decline of the industry was a relative rather than an absolute process but seemed to an expansion-oriented generation to mark the industry's entry upon the 'stationary state' anticipated by Smith and Mill and evoked gloomy forebodings of the doom of the cotton trade, of the factory system, and of Lancashire.[2]

Such a deceleration was much more marked than that experienced after 1839 and exerted its influence throughout

[1] H. Dietzel, *Bedeutet Export von Produktionsmitteln volkswirtschaftlichen Selbstmord? Unter besonderer Berücksichtigung des Maschinen- und Kohlenexports Englands* (Berlin, Simion, 1907, 65pp.), 18–31.

[2] W. A. Abram, 'The Prospective Decline of Lancashire', *Blackwood's Edinburgh Magazine*, July 1892, 1–17, reviewed in ibid., Aug. 1892, 284–92; *Cotton Factory Times*, 8 July 1892, 1i–ii, *Economic Journal*, Dec. 1892, 735–44 and Mar. 1893, 121–8, and *Textile Mercury*, 21 Jan. 1893, 42–6; 'Bonami', *The Doom of the Cotton Trade and the Fall of the Factory System* (Manchester, Heywood, 1896, 15pp.), reprinted in C. Allen Clarke, *The Effects of the Factory System* (London, Richards, 1899), 159–73, 'Decline of the Lancashire Cotton Trade'.

the whole of the industry and its dependent trades as the operation of the multiplier tended to move into reverse. New entrants to the industry were discouraged, depriving it of their rejuvenating influence. The channels of vertical mobility for successful entrepreneurs contracted. The number of giant firms ceased to expand and remained stable. The spinning industry of Scotland declined from 1874 and many country mills were pushed beyond the economic margin, especially in 1873–9 and in 1891–3, so furthering the process of regional concentration within the industry. Both the incentive and the opportunity to make innovations were reduced, crystallizing the investment of capital made in the perfected mule rather than in the imperfect ring-frame. The decline in the rate of profit discouraged new capital investment and encouraged capital-saving innovations and even the disinvestment of capital. Depreciation for purposes of replacement became less necessary at the same time as the real value of depreciation allowances increased with the fall in prices, so encouraging the 'mining' of assets for quick returns in the form of distributable profit and inspiring private spinners to make repeated complaints about the small allowance for depreciation made by their upstart rivals, the limited companies. The termination of the expansion of the spinning industry in north Lancashire reinforced the growing tendency for the processes of manufacture to be segregated upon a geographical basis. That trend weakened the competitive capacity of the industry in the world market by ossifying its structure and inhibiting innovation at a time when cost-cutting improvements in technology might perhaps have proved most beneficial.

The depression afflicted all the trades dependent upon the demand generated by the cotton industry.[1] Coal production in Lancashire expanded less rapidly and was surpassed in volume by that of four other regions in twenty years, so reducing Lancashire from the position of the second largest producer in 1882 to that of the sixth in 1901. Shipping tonnage clearing Liverpool also expanded more slowly and was exceeded from 1884 by that clearing from London, so reinforcing the port's opposition to the projected Manchester Ship Canal. On the

[1] *The Times*, 30 Aug. 1879, 7vi, 'The State of Lancashire'.

Rochdale Canal traffic declined from the peak tonnage reached in 1876 by 26 per cent during the next fifteen years.[1] The ancillary trades geared to the construction, equipment, and supply of mills for an expanding industry were threatened by the prospect of excess capacity generated by the slower rate of growth and were compelled where possible to discover new markets. The mill-building industries became more and more interested in supporting the flotation of new joint-stock companies which increased the supply of yarn as well as the intensity of competition within Lancashire. Both textile engineering and the chemical industry successfully established their independence of their parent trade by extending their production for other markets. Some diversification of occupational structure took place within the ambit of the textile industry through the development of paper manufacture in Bury, hosiery manufacture in Bolton, felt manufacture in Rossendale, and worsted spinning in Manchester and Stockport. Manchester extended its commercial influence without fear of any rivalry within Lancashire and secured some compensation for the decline in its share of the county's population and industry and for the waning prosperity of its home trade firms. The development from 1875 of a technical press[2] and of technical education endowed the city with the basis of a new ascendancy. The metropolitan influence of 'Cottonborough' was also extended through the increasing number of branch banks established in the cotton towns, though the spread of the tramway and the telephone from 1878, through the accelerated disturnpiking of main roads from 1879, and through the development of the city's distributive trades. The diversification of the regional economy widened the range of employment opportunities, reduced the degree of dependence upon a single trade by the 1890s, and was carried further by the development of engineering in the Mancunian renaissance fostered by the completion of the Ship Canal.

[1] *Report of the Joint Select Committee on Canal Rates, Tolls and Charges* [97 of 1894], 237, 28 June 1894, Q.2830, 253, 29 June, Q.3127, C. R. Dykes.

[2] *The Textile Manufacturer, A Monthly Review of the Cotton, Woollen, Silk and Linen Trades*, 15 Jan. 1875, published first in London and then from 15 Dec. 1875 in Manchester; *Cotton, its Growth, Manufacture and Commerce. The Journal of the Cotton Trade and its Allied and Auxiliary Industries*, 27 Jan. 1877, published first in London and then from 3 Nov. 1877 in Manchester, last appearing on 17 May 1879.

The slower rate of industrial expansion transformed the world outlook of operatives as much as of employers since it narrowed the available avenues for employment and for promotion, restricting the opportunities of children to profit by rapid vertical mobility and those of piecers to achieve full independence as mule-minders. The cotton industry ceased to fulfil its historic function as a vehicle of social mobility, as a stimulus to the increase of population, and as a magnet to attract immigrants. The pressure upon housing accommodation was eased and a decline occurred in the level of rents and in the building of houses, which reached a peak in the spinning towns of south-east Lancashire between 1875 and 1878.[1] Recruitment of labour from outside the county was last recorded in 1875[2] and complaints of labour shortage ceased for thirty years: emigration rose sharply in the 1880s and the rate of population increase declined after 1891. Workers were liberated from their reluctant bondage to the mill for employment in more congenial spheres. Their freedom of choice was indeed restricted not only by the threat to their traditional palladium in the small shop presented by the growing competition of co-operative stores but also by the decline of another popular occupation in hill-farming from the peak extent reached in the 1870s. Within the mill, cotton operatives became more resistant to change, more status-conscious, and more wage-oriented in their outlook, so enhancing their loyalty to the developing unions and even precipitating the establishment in 1890 of a separate piecers' union.[3]

The continuing decline in prices transformed conditions of production and sale throughout the cotton trade through its relentless pressure. The depression remained essentially one of prices rather than of production, affecting therefore the profit-oriented employer rather than the wage-earning employee.

[1] J. P. Lewis, *Building Cycles and Britain's Growth* (London, Macmillan, 1965), 122–3, 314–15, 317.

[2] *Reports of the Inspectors of Factories*, 31 Oct. 1875, 26.

[3] *Bolton Evening News*, 23 Sept. 1890, 3iii, 2 Oct., 2v, 19 Dec., 3iv, 28 Jan. 1891, 3iv, 30 Jan., 3iv, 3 Feb., 2vii, 6 Feb., 3v–vi, 25 Feb., 2v; *Cotton Factory Times*, 26 Sept. 1890, 5i, 3 Oct., 5i, 28 Nov., 1iv, 19 Dec., 5ii, 26 Dec., 4v, 9 Jan. 1891, 5i, 23 Jan., 5i, 30 Jan., 5ii, 6 Feb., 7iii; J. R. Clynes, *Memoirs 1869–1924* (London, Hutchinson, 1937), i. 47, which misdates the establishment of the union and places it in 1886.

Stocks of all kinds of cotton goods depreciated in value in sympathy with market prices. Merchants found it unprofitable to serve as a buffer between consumer and producer and so transmitted the impact of reductions in demand in a chain-reaction which bore most heavily upon spinners. Yarn prices sank less than cotton prices and grey cloth prices sank least of all so that margins became more favourable in weaving than in spinning.[1] The conflict between spinners and weavers for the available margin prevented their combination in any general trade association for the maintenance of prices and thereby of their own prosperity. The fall in prices reduced the cost of building and plant, depreciated the value of existing mills, and reduced the value of the capital invested in the industry especially during the successive cyclical depressions of trade, injuring the middling employer much more than either the very large capitalist or the small master, widening the gulf between the large and the small employer and inhibiting the growth of medium-sized firms into very large enterprises. The decline in building prices also encouraged the extension of existing mills as well as the erection of new ones, especially by companies. The reconstruction and re-equipment of mills was further facilitated by the growing frequency of mill fires occasioned by the increase in spindle speeds. The consequent extension in productive capacity so diminished the level of profits as to lead to the actual destruction of old mills and machinery. Private employers first criticized the new joint-stock companies and then themselves adopted the principle of limited liability, so successfully adopting the tactics of their foe in order to survive his onslaught.

The reduction in prices was effected by means of competition, whose efficacy was based upon such institutional factors as the ease of access to the industry, the small scale of economic operation, the divorce of textile engineering from cotton manufacture, the separation of spinning from weaving, the external economies available to a highly localized trade, and the extended use of credit. The central position of the merchants in such an atomized structure of trade was strengthened by the virtual destruction of the commission agents of Manchester by a legal decision in the case of *Williamson* v.

[1] Heylin, 12.

Barbour (1877).[1] Their systematic policy was to exploit their privileged access to the market and to accentuate competition between manufacturers through the imitation of successful products, the matching of patterns, and even the copying of trade-marks, so maintaining the commercial empire of Manchester over 'Cottonia'. The periodic waves of prosperity, the successive mill-building booms, the increased use of loan capital, and the advent of limited liability further intensified the competition experienced by established producers to the benefit of mercantile intermediaries and consumers. The pressure of fixed costs discouraged employers from resorting to short-time working so long as they could cover their variable costs. Such fixed costs weighed most heavily upon small producers and included interest on mortgages and loans and the rent paid for room and power so that the factors facilitating access to the industry also encouraged unremitting production by existing manufacturers. Competition was greatest within Lancashire and least within foreign markets until the depression of 1877–9 when the U.S.A. appeared as a rival,[2] followed by India in the 1880s, and by Germany and France in the 1890s. Within Lancashire competition was usually more intense in the weaving industry than in the spinning industry, in the export trade than in the home trade, despite the lack of tariff protection, and in the manufacture of prints and fancies than in that of domestics. It remained severest in its incidence where firms were most numerous and where the product was simplest, undifferentiated, easily graded, sold in bulk, and therefore substitutable. Thus it proved keenest in the standard plain-goods trade, where prices were fixed in the slaughter-house of the Manchester Exchange. Inevitably competition became less acute during phases of expansion than during periods of depression and over-production, when it was encouraged by the adaptability of machinery to the production of different goods and by the variation in labour costs between districts. No general trade association was ever formed and no price-fixing agreement was contemplated before the 1890s. Even a

[1] *Law Reports, Chancery*, 9, 1878, 529–38, *Williamson* v. *Barbour*, 28 Nov. 1877, M. R. Jessel.

[2] J. Thornely, *American Competition in the Cotton Trade: The Truth About It* (Manchester, Emmott, 1879, 71pp.), 14, 30, 40–1, 55–7.

local and temporary anti-union association maintained by the device of a penalty bond was discouraged by a hostile legal decision in the case of *Hilton* v. *Eckersley* (1855).[1] The severity of such competition made the life-span of the average firm relatively brief and produced a heavy mortality rate amongst businesses, a high rate of turnover of concerns, and a comparative shortage of old-established family dynasties.

The extent and intensity of competition within the industry should not be exaggerated and was in fact limited in a few favoured sectors. A wide and extending range of products dissolved the industry's superficial unity into a congeries of dissimilar and unconnected complexes of firms, producing different goods from different materials for different markets. In the most highly specialized branches of the trade a limited number of firms spun a limited supply of cotton for a restricted market, as in the fine spinning of Sea Island cotton in the mills of Manchester. In the home trade the increasing frequency of fashion changes in dress goods extended the range of differentiated products and so effectively partitioned the market. In the finishing industries competition by outsiders was precluded either by the immense capital necessary for entry, as in calico-printing, or by the control of the established firms over a limited supply of water, as in bleaching. Engineers and large manufacturers used patents with some success to preserve a monopoly of the most advanced technology, as in the development of the combing machine, the revolving flat-card, the self-acting mule, and the ring-spinning frame. Such firms maintained their rights by legal action and extended them by devising improvements sufficient to justify the grant of new patents. Competition was also restricted by the limited supply of highly skilled labour, which was invariably monopolized by the large firms of a district as in the fine trade of Manchester, Bolton, and Preston, and by the spread of the major wage lists which protected individual districts against internecine competition and enlisted the full support of the operatives for the differentials they embodied. A direct and secure market connection proved the most effective way of limiting competition

[1] T. F. Ellis and C. Blackburn, *Reports of Cases Argued and Determined in the Court of Queen's Bench* (London, Sweet, 1857), vi. 47–77, *Hilton* v. *Eckersley*, 20 June 1855.

and might be developed through the vertical extension of a firm's operations from manufacture into merchanting, through the establishment of a reputation-monopoly, as in the thread trade, or through the use of trade-marks for product-differentiation in perpetuity under the legal recognition granted in 1887. In sum competition proved least effective where an old-established market connection was essential to success, as in the Preston trade, where firms were few, long established, and protected by the reputation of their name and mark or where price-leadership by a single firm proved acceptable to a happy few oligopolists, as in fine-spinning and thread manufacture.

In those same few favoured niches of the industry the formal restriction of cut-throat competition was accomplished through the reorganization of business structures, undertaken by business politicians rather than by industrial statesmen and stimulated by the depression of 1891–3, which did not apparently diminish the prosperity of the giant firms within the industry. The creation of large-scale organizations was pioneered by Horrockses through amalgamation in 1887[1] and by Coats through the trust in 1895–6.[2] The Coats combine set a more acceptable example than that of Horrockses because it preserved the nominal independence of its member-firms, and stimulated a wave of emulatory foundations in 1897–1900, especially in the finishing trades. Such horizontal integration of separate firms reinforced the trend towards the vertical segregation of the processes of production and so permitted the interstitial survival of the small enterprise. The new trusts did not significantly reduce the costs of production. They neither launched the industry upon a new wave of expansion nor notably affected the course of trade in Manchester. Their influence upon the economy of Lancashire did not necessarily prove beneficial. The union of several mills under the control of a single firm inevitably attenuated the direct links between masters and men. The associated process of 'rationalization' in so far as it entailed the dismissal of employees further loosened those links, undermining local loyalties and weakening the local roots of the industry. The trusts did not prove financial

[1] *The Times*, 3 May 1887, 3i; *Textile Manufacturer*, May 1887, 195; *Textile Recorder*, 14 May 1887, 20iii.

[2] *Textile Manufacturer*, June 1895, 232, Aug. 1895, 313.

successes,[1] with one exception. The Fine Spinners' Association had the advantage of much younger member-firms than those of the printers' and dyers' associations but paid an average annual dividend of only 8 per cent between 1897–8 and 1917–8, or only a quarter of the 31·5 per cent paid by Coats.[2] The formation of such profit-oriented associations flagrantly flouted the faith of the Manchester School in competition and established no pattern for general imitation. The industry as a whole remained unorganized and condemned by the deep-seated individualism of its employers to undergo 'the ordeal of economic freedom'[3] within the open market. The strategic position of those employers was inevitably weakened by the creation of such combines, which elevated the finishing industries to a position of strength comparable to that of the Manchester merchants.

The cotton industry had become increasingly inclined to turn to the State for intermittent aid, first in order to improve the supply of cotton and to relieve distress during the Cotton Famine, and then to maintain through diplomatic or administrative action its markets abroad. In particular it relied upon the government to repeal or reduce the Indian import duties and to impose upon India such alien innovations as railways, factory legislation, and a gold-exchange standard. The industry nevertheless remained loyal to the service of the world market, the policy of free trade, and the faith of individualism through successive waves of crisis-generated criticism of the established commercial policy of the State, turning a deaf ear to the siren calls of fair trade, bimetallism, and tariff reform. Thus its representatives defended the good old cause before the protectionist-inspired Royal Commission on the Depression of Trade in 1885–6 and declined to permit the Bimetallic League, established in 1881 and based in Manchester from 1888, to repeat the success of the Anti-Corn Law League. Economic liberalism became, however, divorced from the cause of political liberalism under the influence of the Home Rule crisis. The Conservative cause advanced at Liberal expense in

[1] *Manchester City News*, 2 July 1904, 5ii–iii, 'Unfortunate Shareholders. Huge Losses: Results of the Textile Combines'.

[2] *Stock Exchange Official Year Book*, 1909, 1884, 1961; 1919, 1948–9, 2629.

[3] A. Marshall, *Principles of Economics* (London, Macmillan, 1907, 5th edn.), 11.

successive general elections between 1874 and 1895,[1] so making Lancashire a bastion of Conservative power second in importance only to London. The imperial, military, and naval renaissance of the 1890s further weakened the basis of a liberalism of interests rather than of ideas and strengthened the growing revulsion against 'Manchesterdom' (1882), 'Manchesterism' (1883), 'Cobdenism' (1887), and 'Manchesterianism' (1897).[2]

* * *

The pressure on prices and profits encouraged employers to seek to reduce costs in various ways, by the use of inferior cotton, by technical innovation, by the reduction of wages, and by efforts to cut mercantile charges and transport costs. The decline in cotton prices reduced the incentive to make cotton-saving innovations and permitted an increase in the amount of waste made in spinning from the low levels enforced during the 1860s. The increased use of inferior cotton, though not of cotton waste, became a common response by spinners to the pressure of declining prices. That trend necessitated further improvement in the preparatory processes of production and an increase in the spindle speeds necessary for the effectual conversion of such cotton into yarn but provoked growing complaints of 'bad spinning' from the operatives, worsened relations between employers and employees, and precipitated the great strikes of 1891–3. In weaving the fall in prices temporarily reduced the production of heavily sized fabrics[3] but the shrinkage in margins necessitated a reversion by 1877 to the use of cheap cotton-substitutes in order to produce a cloth of the same weight for the price, and extended in the long run the use of size,[4] so accentuating the problems created by the steaming of weaving sheds and the incidence of mildew in sized goods shipped through tropical seas to the distant markets

[1] *Spectator*, 26 July 1884, 972, 'Why Lancashire is less Liberal than Yorkshire'.
[2] Ibid. 12 Nov. 1898, 681–2, 'The End of the Manchester School'.
[3] *Manchester Guardian*, 1 Jan. 1875, 5vi.
[4] G. E. Davis, C. Dreyfus, and P. Holland, *Sizing and Mildew in Cotton Goods* (Manchester, Palmer, 1880), 255–81, 'The Manchester Goods Case. *Provand versus Langton and Riley*'; *Manchester Examiner and Times*, 23 Jan. 1883, 4iv–v, 'Vexed Questions in the Cotton Trade. Heavy Sizing'.

of Asia. The decline in mercantile profits encouraged a resort to the short-reeling of yarn and the short-folding of cloth, practices which were prohibited by legislation in 1887 and 1889.

Technical progress continued but no longer took the form of major innovations. It was rather embodied in the continued refinement of existing technology and in the more widespread diffusion of the most efficient machinery. Employers have indeed been criticized severely for their 'failure' to adopt the ring-frame, the automatic loom, and the electric drive. Such criticism was never apparently voiced at the time and seems to be in part an anachronistic quest for the causes of the later contraction of the industry, and in part a simple product of technological monomania. The policy of maintaining existing capital equipment in use was not founded in mere irrational inertia. The mule remained much more suitable than the ring-frame for the spinning of finer counts.[1] The increasing production of fancy cloths on the dobby and Jacquard loom similarly restricted the scope for investment in any automatic loom designed solely for the weaving of plain cloth. The use of the individual electric drive in place of the group drive from a steam-engine would have effectively transformed the whole internal economy of a mill from a monarchy into a democracy. The most significant technical progress was achieved less in the central processes of production than in the prosaic but vital preparatory processes through the perfection of the revolving flat card and combing machine, whose increasing efficiency improved the quality of rovings and so facilitated the spinning of superior yarn upon the improved self-acting mule.

Productivity continued to rise lowering real costs under the stimulus of the increasing scale of operation, the vertical separation of spinning and weaving, the wider diffusion of managerial talent, the spread of the Oldham and Blackburn piece-rate wage lists, and the increase in speeds of operation, which became the equivalent of a labour-intensive, capital-saving innovation. Productivity increased more slowly after

[1] L. G. Sandberg, 'American Rings and English Mules: The Role of Economic Rationality', *Quarterly Journal of Economics*, Feb. 1969, 25–43, reprinted in S. B. Saul (ed.), *Technological Change: The United States and Britain in the Nineteenth Century* (London, Methuen, 1970), 120–40, and in R. Floud (ed.), *Essays in Quantitative Economic History* (Oxford, Clarendon Press, 1974), 181–95.

1850 but rose much more after 1873 in spinning than in weaving. What seems to emerge most clearly from Table 9 is the absolute decline in the productivity of weaving, which apparently began after 1873 as production improved in quality and seems to have remained virtually unchecked until the increase in the number of looms per weaver in Burnley from 1929 onwards.[1] That increase in weaving costs was not enough to prevent a significant reduction in the total costs of production. Sandberg has effectively refuted the allegations of stagnant productivity by his critical examination of the Jones index of 1933[2] and has shown that output per worker grew between 1884 and 1896 by an average annual increment of over 1 per cent. The increase in productivity was all the more notable because goods did not become more standardized but became increasingly diversified in texture, colour, and finish as well as in length, width, and weight. It was even more remarkable because the quality of yarn exports improved by 8·3 per cent and that of cloth exports by 19·4 per cent between 1889 and 1896.[3] That improvement in quality reflected the growing shift from yarn to cloth, the spinning of finer counts, the boom in the manufacture of thread, the swelling output of fine cloth and fancy cloth, and the increasing export of fully finished cloth. Thus the industry produced new and better types of goods as well as introducing new and cheaper ways of making the old staples of production. The truth of Ellison's dictum was demonstrated anew: 'So far as the cotton trade is concerned periods of depression have always been periods of progress.'[4]

In the sphere of industrial relations employers sought to reduce wages with the same diligence which employers in Europe displayed in campaigning for protective tariffs. The trade unions in opposing such wage cuts extended their influence over the labour forces within the industry and successfully supplied them with a new sense of community and with new leaders as traditional faiths weakened in the 1890s.

[1] F. Merttens, 'The Hours and Cost of Labour in the Cotton Industry', *Transactions of the Manchester Statistical Society*, 18 Apr. 1894, 128; R. Robson, *The Cotton Industry in Britain* (1957), 342.

[2] Sandberg, 96–8.

[3] Ibid. 241.

[4] *Spectator*, 17 Sept. 1887, 1253, T. Ellison, 'The Cotton Trade of Great Britain'.

TABLE 9

Productivity in Spinning and Weaving, 1820–1896

Yarn Spun per Hand

	Yarn Spun lb.	*Hands Employed*	*Yarn per Hand lb.*	*Mean Annual % Increase in Productivity*	
1819–21	106,500	110,000	968		
1829–31	216,500	140,000	1,546		
1844–6	523,300	190,000	2,754		
1849–51	588,000	191,000	3,079	4·0	1820–50
1859–61	910,000	248,000	3,669		
1872–4	1,155,333	230,700	5,008	2·1	1850–73
1880–2	1,324,900	240,000	5,520		
1895–7	1,540,000	212,463	7,248	1·6	1873–96

Cloth Woven per Hand

	Cloth Woven lb.	*Hands Employed*	*Cloth per Hand lb.*	*Mean Annual % Increase in Productivity*	
1819–21	80,620	250,000	322·5		
1829–31	143,200	275,000	520·7		
1844–6	348,110	210,000	1,657·7		
1849–51	447,000	183,362	2,437·8	7·0	1820–50
1859–61	650,870	203,000	3,206		
1872–4	941,000	209,636	4,488·7	2·7	1850–73
1880–2	993,540	246,000	4,038·8		
1895–7	1,299,333	314,541	4,130·9	−0·37	1873–96

Source: T. Ellison, *The Cotton Trade of Great Britain* (1886), 68–9, for the estimates from 1819–21 to 1880–2, correcting his cloth-production figures for 1820 and 1845 and adding my own estimates for both spinning and weaving for 1849–51, 1872–4, and 1895–7; G. T. Jones, *Increasing Return. A Study of the Relation between the Size and Efficiency of Industries* (Cambridge University Press, 1933), 275, for estimates of yarn spun in 1849–51, 1872–4, and 1895–7. The most difficult column of the table to construct has been that estimating the number of hands in spinning and weaving, for which I have used the Factory Returns, allotting the hands of the combined factories in proportion to the spindles and looms operated, and S. J. Chapman, *The Lancashire Cotton Industry* (Manchester University Press, 1904), 179, for figures for 1896. I have raised the number of hands employed in weaving in 1849–51 by 40,000 in order to include the hand-loom weavers.

In the process of development they opened new avenues of social mobility at a time when opportunities for promotion within industry, and even more for self-employment, were declining. The cotton unions lost their control over the T.U.C. through the introduction of the bloc vote in 1890 but they still mustered the third largest group of members after the miners and the builders. In Lancashire they became more than ever before a cherished and unique repository of local power. They pioneered the organization of unskilled and women workers, especially from 1884–6, under the aegis of the adult male workers, whose superior status in the work-force they effectively maintained. They profited by the restrictions imposed on the employment of children in 1874 and 1891 as well as by the reduction in the hours of labour from 1874. They opposed tenaciously but quietly any attempt to lengthen the hours of work as well as any innovations tending to devalue the acquired experience and skill of their members. They preserved the pattern of single-shift working in the interests of their women members and so prevented the continuous use of capital equipment on the Japanese model. Above all, they maintained their standard rates of wages and levels of earnings above the minimum necessary for subsistence. In time of depression they sought to avoid the creation of unemployment by spreading the burden of adversity over the whole trade through the device of short-time working.

Each successive crisis in trade precipitated strikes, which were all non-political in origin and were concerned solely with the maintenance of wage rates. Those strikes opposed the attempt by employers to shift some of the burden of depression on to the shoulders of the operatives. In their outcome they simply served to strengthen the position of labour rather than that of capital, and to elevate labour from its subordinate status as a mere factor of production. The Great Strike of 1878 became the most violent since 1842 and lasted for nine weeks, revealing the dogged determination of the humble weavers of Blackburn to maintain their wage rates as a sacred and inviolable right.[1] The Oldham strike of 1885 was the longest in the history of the town and ended in a compromise after thirteen weeks.[2] The consciousness of the operatives was greatly

[1] *The Times*, 22 Apr. 1878, 6i, 27 Apr., 12iv–v; *Spectator*, 27 Apr. 1878, 528–9, 18 May, 627–8, 25 May, 661–2; *Co-operative News*, 8 June 1878, 369, 394, E. V. Neale, 'The Strike: its Motives and its Lessons'; *Cotton*, 29 June 1878, 397.

[2] *Manchester Guardian*, 20 July 1885, 4vii, 22 July, 4vi–vii, 1 Oct., 4iv, 17 Oct., 6vii; *Cotton Factory Times*, 31 July 1885, 1i, 4ii–iv, 23 Oct., 1i–ii; *Co-operative News*, 5 Sept. 1885, 816–7, 'The Oldham Strike and the Joint-Stock Mills'; *Saturday Review*, 24 Oct. 1885, 535, 'The End of the Oldham Strike'.

enhanced by the national recognition symbolized in the appointment of their union secretaries as magistrates and factory inspectors and by the foundation, under union influence, of the *Cotton Factory Times* in 1885. The extension of the influence of the unions and the organization of employers' associations in both spinning and weaving in 1888–9 paved the way for the great lock-out of 1892–3 in the spinning trade.[1] The Brooklands Agreement ending that conflict after twenty weeks enshrined the principle that wage rates could not be reduced unilaterally by employers and elevated the minority interest of labour to nominal parity with that of capital, through the institution of joint committees, in the process of collective bargaining.[2] That agreement helped to avert any recurrence of so extensive a stoppage until 1910. It reinforced the influence of the improving homilies read to employers by the German professor Schulze-Gaevernitz, arguing that short hours and high wages were as necessary as low labour costs and cheap food to the preservation of industrial supremacy and social peace. The unions maintained a common interest with the employers in the amicable division of the profits of industry and firmly opposed all hot-headed metropolitan proposals for the 'socialization' of the cotton industry.[3] They became 'the most powerful bulwark of conservative and opportunist progress in this country'[4] and faithfully reflected the views of the operatives, who remained perfectly content, even in wholly working-class constituencies, regularly to elect their employers as M.P.s[5] and dismayed the Webbs by their consistent and quasi-feudal conservatism.

The industry sought also to reduce the mercantile charges levied by brokers, agents, and merchants and the transport charges levied by railway companies. Such ambitious aspira-

[1] *Cotton Factory Times*, 5 Feb. 1892, 7iv; *Manchester Guardian*, 23 Apr. 1892, 5iii, 28 Apr., 4vii, 6 May, 4vi, 7 May, 5v, 7 Nov., 5iii, 25 Mar. 1893, 7iii.

[2] *Textile Mercury*, 25 Mar. 1893, 217, 'Settlement of the Cotton War'; *Cotton Factory Times*, 31 Mar. 1893, 1ii; *Textile Manufacturer*, Apr. 1893, 151–2, 'The Cotton Dispute'; J. H. Porter, 'Industrial Peace in the Cotton Trade 1875–1913', *Yorkshire Bulletin of Economic and Social Research*, May 1967, 53–4.

[3] *Cotton Factory Times*, 16 Jan. 1885, 1ii, J. Mawdsley; *Spectator*, 17 Oct. 1891, 529–30, W.W., 'Prosperous Lancashire'.

[4] D. F. Schloss, 'The Road to Social Peace', *Fortnightly Review*, Feb. 1891, 256.

[5] P. Joyce, 'The Factory Politics of Lancashire in the later nineteenth century', *Historical Journal*, 1975, 525–53.

tions were bound to be frustrated by the opposition of the mercantile élites and by the lack of general support from the industrial sector. No half-hearted effort could effectively reduce the influence of key mercantile intermediaries in an increasingly specialized trade. From 1885 the practice of direct dealing upon the German model was indeed adopted, especially by those large firms which could afford to dispense with middlemen much more easily than smaller firms. The agitation for the Manchester Ship Canal also succeeded in reducing the charges levied by Liverpool and the railway companies to such an extent that the completed canal found itself in dire financial straits by its failure to divert much traffic to the new port.[1]

As prices fell faster than the costs of production, especially in each successive cyclical crisis, profits per unit of production declined. The story of returns to capital is one chapter of history which remains to be written. It is however clear that the profits of individual firms and of separate sections, such as the thread trade, cannot be regarded as representative of the whole industry. In Lancashire the industry had created a new source of wealth which seemed all the more impressive in contrast to the earlier poverty of the region. The returns reaped by the generality of employers remained however moderate[2] as the large number of small firms spread the gains of industry fairly widely. The long-term contraction in those returns was reflected in the shift from private to joint-stock enterprise and helped to reduce the industry's rate of expansion. The history of gross returns suggests that there were three periods of relatively sharp decline in profits, in the 1820s, 1840s, and 1890s, and that there was a plateau of relatively gradual decline, 1845–1885. The reduction in average annual returns between 1850–72 and 1873–96 appears at first glance to have been only 5·1 per cent. That decline is however increased sevenfold to 35·4 per cent if the abnormally bad years of the Cotton Famine are omitted from the calculation and the years 1850–72 excluding 1862–3 are compared with the final bleak years of the depression, 1890–6.

[1] W. H. Chaloner and B. M. Ratcliffe (eds.), *Trade and Transport. Essays in Economic History in honour of T. S. Willan* (Manchester University Press, 1977), 173–213, 'The Manchester Ship Canal 1894–1913'.

[2] W. D. Rubinstein, 'The Victorian Middle Classes: Wealth, Occupation, and Geography', *Economic History Review*, Nov. 1977, 612.

TABLE 10

Average Annual Gross Return to Capital in the Cotton Industry, 1820–1896

	Pence per lb. of Cotton Consumed
1819–21	25·66
1829–31	13·57
1844–6	8·2
1850–72	6·49
1850–9	6·47
1860–9	5·46
1850–72 excluding 1862–3	6·99
1873–96	6·16
1870–9	7·75
1880–9	6·22
1890–6	4·52

Note: the balance shown comprises interest on capital, depreciation, and profits together with such minor costs as those for rent, rates, taxes, insurance, gas, coal, oil, flour, tallow, water, dyes, and repairs. It is a residual sum derived from the subtraction from the gross value of the industry's product of the cost of raw cotton and the cost of wages and from the division of that sum by the number of pounds of cotton consumed.

Source: T. Bazley, 'Manchester', *Encyclopaedia Britannica* (8th edn., 1857), xiv. 255, for 1850–56; I. Watts, 'Cotton', ibid. (9th edn., 1877), vi. 504, for 1867–76; T. Ellison, *The Cotton Trade of Great Britain* (1886), 69, 308–9, for 1820–45 and 1871–85. Deane & Cole, *British Economic Growth* (1962, 1967), 187, may be used, in conjunction with Mitchell and Deane, *Abstract of British Historical Statistics* (1962), 179, to supply confirmatory estimates for seventeen triennia from 1819–21 to 1899–1901.

Mill margins did not return to their level of 1872 until 1904 and reached their nadir during the crisis of 1891–3, when the value of gross production sank more sharply than in 1873–9, the volume of imports of raw cotton declined by 29 per cent, the value of yarn exports shrank by 26·6 per cent and the value of the exports of cotton manufactures to the Far East sank by 27 per cent. Even the favoured thread industry suffered a recession in the volume of its exports between 1889 and 1894. The severity of that particular depression was clearly manifested in the increase in cut-throat competition, in the unprecedented losses of the Oldham limiteds in 1892–3, in the reduction in the flow of funds available for the depreciation, renewal, and expansion of plant, in the marked loss of confidence in the future of the industry, in the prophecies made of its imminent doom, in the virtual cessation of investment in new plant, and in the prolonged pause in mill building. The extent and intensity of the crisis was also apparent in the deep distress suffered by the largest single concentration of cotton operatives in the Blackburn district, in the first recorded decline in the total number of operatives, in the reduction in the rate of population growth in Lancashire, in the increasing influence of London in Manchester, and in the outbreak of the costliest conflict between labour and capital which had ever divided the industry. That crisis inspired such remedial efforts as the conversion of the Manchester Ship Canal into a municipal enterprise. the extension of technical education, the agitation in favour of bimetallism, the campaign against the Indian import duties, the unprecedented mission sent to China in 1896 by the Blackburn Chamber of Commerce,[1] and the industry's acceptance of the cartel and the trust. The burden of the depression was borne by the capitalists alone and was not shared by the workmen. The declining rates of return upon their capital did not reduce employers to ruin or drive them out of the industry. The number of formal bankruptcies averaged only 31·6 per annum between 1873 and 1896, with one marked peak of 66 per annum in 1877–9,[2] and thus declined to one-third of the average annual rate of 101 during the deep post-Famine depression of 1865–9. Non-economic considerations apparently remained strong enough to retain employers within their chosen sphere of activity. The industry continued to serve its masters as a vehicle of power and status but became less remunerative in economic terms and served increasingly as a machine for the payment of wages rather than of profits. The declining returns to capital contrasted sharply with the rising returns accruing to labour. For the operatives the decline in prices proved an unmixed benefit since it reduced the price of their food and so raised their real wages, to the incidental

[1] *Report of the Mission to China of the Blackburn Chamber of Commerce 1896–7* (1898, 152pp., 386pp.).

[2] R. Seyd, *Record of Failures and Liquidations in the Financial, International, Wholesale and Manufacturing Branches of Commerce . . . in the United Kingdom, from January 1865 to July 1876* (London, Seyd, 1885), 374–6, 385–6, 395–6, 406–7, 419–21, 431–3, 440–1, for 1865–71; *Textile Manufacturer*, Feb. 1877, 62, for 1872–6; E. Guthrie, *The Cotton Trade: its Condition and Prospects* (Manchester, Ireland, 1883), 12, for 1874–82; H. B. Heylin, *Buyers and Sellers in the Cotton Trade* (1913), 91, for 1883–96.

benefit of the home trade. Thus the immediate burden of adaptation to the loss of the monopoly of the world market was borne by employers rather than by employees and the social benefits of falling prices were far more widely diffused than the economic costs.

PART THREE

The Structure of the Industry

MONEY WANTED

SUN MILL COMPANY LIMITED, OLDHAM

The LOAN ACCOUNT is NOW OPEN to the Public. Interest 5 per cent per annum. Office hours on Mondays and on the 25th of the month during mill hours, and on Saturdays from 8.30 to 12.30, and from 3 to 5 in the afternoon.

D. WILKINSON, Secretary.

THE UNITED SPINNING COMPANY LIMITED.

REGISTERED OFFICE:
Exchange Chambers, Bottom-o'th'-Moor, Oldham.
CAPITAL, £80,000, IN 16,000 SHARES OF £5 EACH.

This Company is now prepared to receive LOANS, withdrawable on demand. Interest five per cent per annum, from date invested to date withdrawn. Office Hours: Thursdays 9 to 8; Saturdays, 9 to 1; other days 9 to 6. Deposits may also be made at the Manchester and County Bank. Oldham and branches.

WILLIAM NUTTALL, Secretary.

CENTRAL MILL COMPANY LIMITED.

OFFICE: CENTRAL MILL, OLDHAM.

The above Company is now prepared to receive LOANS. Interest, five per cent per annum, to commence on the first day of each month. Office open during Mill Hours on Mondays and on the first day of each month; Saturdays, from three to five p.m.

ROBINSON TITHER, Secretary.

THE HOPE COTTON SPINNING COMPANY LIMITED.

The Directors of this Company are prepared to RECEIVE LOANS bearing interest at the rate of five per cent per annum from the date of deposit, repayable as follows, viz.: Sums under £20 at call; from £20 to £100 at seven days notice; and sums over £100 at one months notice. Loans can be deposited with the Secretary, at the undermentioned address, and he will also attend at No. 536, New-road, Failsworth, on Mondays between the hours of 6 and 8 p.m., for transacting Loan business and transferring Shares.

By order
WILLIAM KILNER, Secretary,
14, Church-lane, Oldham.

ROYTON SPINNING COMPANY LIMITED

Registered Office: High Barn-street, Royton.

The LOAN ACCOUNT is NOW OPEN to the Public. Interest 5 per cent per annum from the last Saturday in each month. Office hours: Monday, during mill hours; and Saturday, 9 to 12 a.m. and 3 to 5 p.m.

JOHN A. KERSHAW, Secretary.

LOCAL STOCK & SHARE LIST

J. Greaves, Sharebroker, 2 Clegg-street, has ON SALE Alberts, Boroughs, Croft Bank, Higginshaw, Windsor, Woodstock, Lees Union, Hollinwood, Commercial, Sun, Green-Lane, Phoenix, United, Horsedge, Parkside, J.K. Schofield, Belgian, Mossley, &c. WANTS Greenacres, West End, and Crimble.

A Sample of Advertisements for Loans and for Shares, from the *Oldham Standard*, 25 July 1874, 4vi–viii

CHAPTER 6

The Spread of the Joint-Stock Company in Lancashire

> The Joint Stock Companies Acts have been the salvation of the cotton trade. I do not think the cotton trade would have made one fourth part of the progress that it has done since 1870 had it not been for the operation of the Joint Stock Companies Act.
>
> *Royal Commission on Labour, Minutes of Evidence taken before Group 'C' (Textile Trades)* (C.6708-vi, 1892), i. 99, Q.2546, Joshua Rawlinson of Burnley, 11 July 1891.

THE REPRESENTATIVE unit of enterprise in the cotton industry was the small rather than the large firm and the representative employer was a yeoman of industry rather than a captain of industry. The seductive but misleading belief that large factories were typical of the industry stemmed from the obvious contrast between workshop and mill, from the impressions of visitors to the large but unrepresentative mills of Manchester, from the Victorian disposition to reify and magnify the power of 'capital', and from the obsessive association of the *Grossbetrieb* with the age of *Hochkapitalismus* by such German observers as Engels, Marx, Jannasch, Schulze-Gaevernitz, and Sombart. The rapid expansion of the industry had in fact been achieved by a myriad of small masters, unrestrained by any barriers to entry into the trade or by any restrictions upon sales and unembarrassed by the competition of large joint-stock companies. Such ease of access facilitated the increase in production, sales, and exports, the innovations in techniques of manufacture, and the social ascent of both masters and men, between whom it served broadly to maintain harmonious relations as sharers in a common ethic. Throughout the nineteenth century the typical firm continued to be the private enterprise rather than the public company because the scale of operations remained small, technology continued to change, capital requirements were limited, and the extension of credit from a variety of sources made the capital-raising capacity of the company unnecessary for some ninety years after 1780. The ranks of employers were swelled during each successive phase of expansion by a new influx of recruits with limited means and were then decimated during the subsequent depression, so creating a market in second-hand machinery, facilitating entry by new aspirants to fortune and exposing the trade to repeated bouts of over-production and under-selling. The inveterate tendency of such small masters to trade upon borrowed money enriched their creditors rather than themselves and kept them close to the margin of economic survival, so that they laboured to avoid bankruptcy rather than to make a profit. From its very origins the industry remained characterized by a large number of separate and relatively short-lived firms[1] and by the pervasive influence of the small employer and the self-made man.[2]

The industry remained readily accessible to the small capitalist because of its geographical concentration within the Lancashire area, the absence of any restrictions upon entry, the increasing separation of the spinning and weaving processes, the extension of the range of products manufactured by the industry, and the growth of a wide range of external economies offered by the auxiliary industries of the region, especially through the development of specialized markets for cotton, yarn, cloth, cotton waste, machinery, and mill stores. Employers could rent land and warehouses, obtain advances from agents, brokers, and banks, and secure long credit terms from machine-makers. Above all, they could rent room, power, and even machinery through a system which long remained the palladium of the small master, first in spinning and then in weaving. They could limit their fixed capital to some three-

[1] M. Lévy-Leboyer, *Les Banques européennes et l'industrialisation internationale dans la première moitié du XIXe siècle* (Paris, Presses Universitaires, 1964), 40, estimates the average age of 412 firms in 1844 to have been only sixteen years; K. Honeyman, 'The Self-Made Man: Myth or Reality? A Study of Social Mobility in the Industrial Revolution' (paper presented at the Economic History Society Conference, 3 Apr. 1977, 28pp.).

[2] V. A. C. Gatrell, 'Labour, Power and the Size of Firms in Lancashire Cotton in the Second Quarter of the Nineteenth Century', *Economic History Review*, Feb. 1977, 95–139.

fifths of that required for the establishment of a similar mill in Europe[1] and needed for working capital only one-fifth of the amount of their fixed capital. They might also buy second-hand machinery cheaply, sacrificing the increment of 10 per cent in production conferred by the use of new machines but acquiring the power to survive a depression better than a firm with expensive, new, and undepreciated plant. In times of bad trade they might easily adapt their machinery to the production of other types of goods and so encroach upon the sphere of other producers at the price of accentuating the industry's endemic tendency towards what Babbage called 'over-manufacturing'.[2] Their hands and their machinery might be of the poorest quality but they had in bad and good times alike the benefit of constant, direct, and self-interested supervision. They consistently opposed any reduction in the hours of labour or any resort to short-time working in order to spread their fixed costs over as much production as possible.[3] Their social myopia brought about the imposition upon the whole industry of what became the most rigorous factory legislation in the world. Their annual net profits might average only 10 per cent in contrast to the 30 per cent harvested by a first-class mill[4] but afforded them their necessary subsistence, especially in the years of prosperity which until the 1860s outnumbered those of depression by about ten to one. Such small concerns successfully coexisted with the large firms which surpassed them first in quality and then in quantity of production. Those great enterprises were more predominant in spinning than in weaving and supplied the industry with its permanent and relatively stable core, having found the key to long-term survival in self-financing and in independent marketing. Even those large firms were smaller than the large firms of the iron and steel industry but were still too large to inspire effective emulation by small masters.

[1] R. Jannasch, *Die Europäische Baumwollen-Industrie* (1882) 26–30, estimates 61 per cent.

[2] C. Babbage, *On the Economy of Machinery and Manufactures* (London, Knight, 1832), 193–7.

[3] W. Kenworthy, *Inventions and Hours of Labour. A Letter to Master Cotton Spinners, Manufacturers and Mill-Owners in General* (Blackburn, Walkden, 1842, 16 pp.), 9.

[4] J. C. Fischer, *Tagebücher* (Schaffhausen, Fischer, 1951), 289–90, G. A. Lee, cotton spinner of Salford in 1825.

The dominant tradition of the industry remained that of individual enterprise, unchecked by any countervailing tradition of corporate or co-operative activity. Such enterprise had supplied the magic key to expansion during the heroic age of the industry and had endowed the industry with its competitive superiority, serving as the sole source of wealth, power, and prestige. Bred in so proud a tradition, employers remained fully satisfied with the traditional form of firm and disliked intensely any idea of taking the world into partnership since the firm functioned, as Carlyle and Elizabeth Gaskell emphasized, as a structure of power and as a symbol of social status as well as a means of profit making.[1] 'Such an establishment is a sort of *imperium in imperio*—a model government on a small scale—a miniature kingdom, in which all the principles of an enlightened political economy receive the authority of a practical development.'[2] Inevitably such masters deemed the cotton industry an inappropriate sphere of operation for 'joint-stock schemers'[3] and regarded the principle of limited liability as anathema, being as jealous of their personal credit as aristocrats were of their honour and remaining consistently hostile to 'joint-stockism' (1856), 'joint-stockery' (1864), and 'promoterism' (1872). Some employers had established in the 1830s their own mill savings-banks and paid 5 per cent interest upon the loan capital placed upon deposit, but none had surrendered any control over management to investors from either inside or outside the firm. Unincorporated corporations called cotton-twist companies in spinning and cotton-mill companies in weaving were occasionally operated by private employers but no joint-stock company existed in the industry before 1845. Such a company lacked the ability, the knowledge, and the experience of the private employer and could not secure a manager endowed with as much vigilance, zeal, and prudence. It could not compete with the superior management or financial

[1] Richard Gardner, *The True Cure of Monopoly upon Radical Principles, suggested in an Address to the Master Spinners, Merchants and Manufacturers of Lancashire, &c. By a Son of Commerce* (Manchester, Gadsby, 1841, 15pp.), 12–13; E. Gaskell, 'North and South', *Household Words*, 21 Oct. 1854, 232, chap. 15, 13 Jan. 1855, 518, chap. 40, 27 Jan. 1855, 563, chap. 45.

[2] J. Baynes, *The Cotton Trade* (1857), 77.

[3] *Manchester Guardian*, 5 Nov. 1845, 4iv, 'Joint-Stock Spinning and Manufacturing Companies'.

probity of the private firm except with the artificial protection of limited liability. It was rightly deemed to be more appropriate to an industry based upon a trading monopoly, a fixed routine, and a stable technology than to one dependent upon a competitive market, upon a developing technology, and therefore upon the generalized ability of the entrepreneur.

The size of a firm was limited only by the capacities of an employer whereas the size of a mill was determined by the demands of technology. For most of the century the unit of ownership in the firm tended to remain broadly identical with the unit of production in the factory because employers had to remain on the spot in order to avoid any outbreak of 'trouble at the mill'. Firms could operate effectively on a very small scale only in the specialized spheres of waste spinning, doubling, and the manufacture of coloured goods. In all other sectors a minimum scale of operations was necessary and attainable since fixed costs did not bulk large in total costs in comparison to the cost of cotton and labour and proved no greater per employee in a large establishment than in a small one, so providing an exception to the general rule that large factories required more capital per head than small ones.[1] In particular the most economic use had to be made of prime movers and preparatory machinery in order to maintain the appropriate balance between the interlocking stages of spinning and to avoid the occurrence of bottlenecks in the production process. The capital cost of both steam-engine and self-actor became less as they became larger and even their running costs were reduced in proportion to the associated increase in output. A large steam-engine proved less extravagant in its consumption of coal than a smaller one as well as a more efficient supplier of power. The most expensive part of the automatic mule in the headstock became proportionately cheaper as the number of its dependent spindles increased. The spread of the long hand-mule, the self-acting mule and the steam-engine from the 1830s, coupled with factory legislation favouring the large employer, thus facilitated an increase in the size of the mill, which became general only in the 1870s, with the marked

[1] Alfred and Mary P. Marshall, *The Economics of Industry* (London, Macmillan, 1879), 54; A. Marshall, *The Principles of Economics* (London, Macmillan, 1890), 343 note.

increase in length of the self-actor and the adoption of the rope-race, which greatly increased the efficiency of power-transmission from a single prime mover.

The mechanization of the processes of production was achieved only gradually and imposed its own iron logic of size only slowly. The reduction in the price of cotton manufactures down to the 1860s had been caused as much by the reduction in the price of the raw material as by any reduction in the cost of production. The law of increasing return proved slow to operate in the industry,[1] returns to scale tended to be constant and the capital–output ratio may have remained relatively unchanged between 1815 and 1886.[2] The minimum scale of economic operation seems to have become for most employers a maximum since operation on a larger scale did not reduce costs in a degree commensurate with the additional outlay of capital involved. Those employers who extended their production capacity did so by adding new mills rather than by increasing the size of the old ones. When they did expand the size of their factories they did so to compete with one another for status as much as for profit.[3] Above all, the addition of a weaving shed to the spinning mill formed the most typical means of plant expansion during the middle third of the century, converting spinning-only firms into combined firms conducting an integrated process of manufacture. Some towns provided a more favourable environment to the development of large enterprises and so created a broad division between two types of factory town. Small employers remained characteristic of the industry in Stockport, Oldham, Rochdale, Bury, Heywood, and Rossendale while large firms evolved in Manchester, Ashton, Bolton, Blackburn, and Preston.

The average Lancashire spinning mill nevertheless increased

[1] J. Pope Hennessy, 'On the Causes of the Fall in the Price of Manufactured Cottons', *Proceedings of the British Association*, 1858, Miscellaneous Proceedings, 178–9.

[2] M. Blaug, 'The Productivity of Capital in the Lancashire Cotton Industry during the Nineteenth Century', *Economic History Review*, Apr. 1961, 369–70.

[3] T. H. Williams, *Observations on Money, Credit and Panics: to which are added, Strictures on Manchester Credits* (London, Simpkin, 1858, 43pp.), 28, reprinting on pp. 24–43 four letters from the *Manchester Guardian*, 3 Mar. 1858, 4ii–iii, 10 Mar., 4ii, 24 Mar., 4ii–iii; B. M. Ratcliffe and W. H. Chaloner (eds.), *A French Sociologist Looks at Britain. Gustave d'Eichthal and British Society in 1828* (Manchester University Press, 1977), 98.

only slowly in size before the 1870s, raising its spindleage by 45 per cent from 8,161 in 1811[1] to 11,818 in 1850 and then by 227 per cent, or fivefold as fast, during the next forty years, to 38,618 in 1890. During the last quarter of the century the size

TABLE II

Average Size of the Spinning Factory, 1850–1890

	Average Number of Spinning Spindles		Average Number of Employees
	England	*Lancashire*	*England*
1850	11,398	11,818	105·7
1856	16,770	20,494	109·5
1861	13,980	15,368	106·8
1867	15,827	17,000	88·4
1870	18,302	18,342	110·3
1874	21,452	23,872	123·5
1878	24,606	27,385	126·7
1885	28,552	32,437	137·2
1890	33,697	38,618	154·9

Source: Returns of the Factory Inspectors, 1850–90.

of the mill increased dramatically as the new mills of the 1870s adopted the standard size of 50,000 spindles and those of the 1890s that of 100,000 spindles. That sharp increase in scale of the mule-mill was not effectively counterbalanced by the spread of the ring-frame mill, which was invariably much smaller. Only in the closing decades of the century and only within the spinning sector did the large mill become typical of the industry, so making the joint-stock company an acceptable vehicle for the raising of the capital necessary for such large enterprises.

* * *

The first successful companies within the cotton industry were registered in 1845, not in Lancashire but in Hull, under the stimulus of the use of the new form of organization by the railways. Lancashire itself experienced no joint-stock boom until

[1] G. W. Daniels, 'Samuel Crompton's Census of the Cotton Industry in 1811' *Economic History*, Jan. 1930, 108.

1860. The spread of the limited company proved a slow process since only 1,046 companies were registered in the English cotton industry between 1856 and 1896, or 25 per annum on average in an industry with over 2,000 firms. Only 65 per cent of those companies proved to be effective flotations since 364 survived for less than ten years. Over two-thirds of the flotations were public companies while 33 per cent were private limiteds. Of the public companies mill-building companies alone introduced new capital into the industry and numbered only 155 or 15 per cent of the total number of flotations, while 544 or 52 per cent were turnover concerns. The dominant influence behind the joint-stock movement thus became the private employers who either turned over their mills to the public or adapted the company form of organization to their own ends. The hopes cherished in the 1850s that the spread of the company would emancipate labour from thraldom to the power of capital and to 'the system of competition' were thus frustrated by the influence of the dominant tradition elaborated under the aegis of the private firm.

Co-operative societies of producers were indeed established by working-class élites, especially in 1851 and in 1861. The first effective industrial associations of working men had been founded in 1848 in Bacup and Padiham in the very heart of ethnic Lancashire in Rossendale under the dual influence of the associations of artisans established in Paris to protect the right to work and of the assault launched by the Christian Socialists upon the philosophy of *laissez-faire*. The working men of Rossendale were rich and independent with a weak tradition of trade unionism and a strong tradition of co-operation matured in the most isolated communities of the shire. Their co-operative productive societies became the first successful ones since the baking and milling societies established during the dearth of 1795 and made Lancashire into the main centre of industrial association outside London. Those associations were founded in small centres of industry by homogeneous groups of workers for self-employment in harmony with the aspiration to independence common to the society of France and of Lancashire and in defiance of the dominant tradition sanctifying co-operation between masters and men rather than between workmen alone. They were encouraged to venture into the staple trade of cotton weaving by the success of the local co-operative stores, by the spread of building societies, by the availability of rented room and power, and by the influence of the great Preston strike of 1853–4.[1]

The founders of the new societies regarded co-operative production as the true means of social regeneration and won such support that their cause was championed by the Chartist Convention in 1851 and by the Parliament of Labour in 1854.[2] They acquired legal status under the Industrial and Provident Societies Act of 1852 whose provisions proved less restrictive than the Friendly Societies Acts and permitted them to borrow up to four times their subscribed capital. They followed the example set in Bacup in paying no bonus to labour but found it very difficult to secure credit from, or acceptance by, the cotton world, and were forced to make production an end in itself in order to survive in a competitive market. From 1856 onwards they turned themselves from associations into joint-stock companies and thus used the new company legislation to transform their original purpose from a means into an end in itself. Failing to remould industrial society they became assimilated to the conservative tradition of the community of the shire. They had however opened a new outlet to the savings of operatives as well as to their managerial capacity and encouraged the cultivation of thrift and sobriety by the example set by their members. Their limited success paved the way for the industry's first great joint-stock boom, centred in Rossendale.

During 1860 and 1861 92 companies were formed with an average capital of £35,000 under the stimulus of the rise in profits and wages, the increase in demand from India, and the high dividends paid with the aid of loan capital by established companies. The new companies were most heavily concentrated in Rossendale with its outliers in Rochdale, Bury, Heywood, Accrington, Hebden Bridge, and Halifax. Seventy seem to have been turnover concerns while only 22 built their own mills. Thirteen of the most distinctively co-operative in orientation proudly included the evocative word 'co-operative' in their registered titles and so explicitly dissociated themselves

[1] *The People's Paper*, 6 May 1854, 4vi–5i, 'The Preston Struggle'; *Manchester Guardian*, 31 May 1854, 1ii, J. Baynes, 'Proposed Remedy for Combinations and Strikes'.

[2] *Northern Star*, 12 Apr. 1851, 8iii; *The People's Paper*, 1 Apr. 1854, 1iv–vi.

from proprietary companies, of which twelve defiantly proclaimed themselves 'commercial' or 'industrial'. Such ostensibly non-competitive ventures were regarded by credulous middle-class 'friends of co-operation' and by educated working men as the harbingers of a new era in the organization of industry and as the most effective remedy for strikes and lock-outs.[1] Their offer of a 'joint-stock felicity' proved unacceptable to the individualistic middle class of the region. In fact they were co-operative only in name[2] and could not become true profit-sharing associations of producers because they sought primarily to make profit rather than to reform society. They were essentially associations of small capitalists, favouring the £10 share, offering no bonus to purchasers, and imposing no limit on the transferability of shares. They could not secure all the necessary capital from their own workfolk and admitted outside shareholders without making any provision for their re-education in co-operative principles. Thus they were insensibly transformed, like their precursors, from co-operative manufacturing associations into joint-stock companies with limited liability. They were forced to pay capital the dividends it demanded and therefore borrowed money on mortgage as well as on simple loan. The few associations that sought to maintain the principle of a bonus to labour were racked by internal dissension and denied commercial credit but were forced to compete with other producers in extending credit to their customers. They could not rival the energy and capital of individual employers in the task of production, and found managerial ability in short supply, especially in the face of insistent demands by shareholders for preferential employment. They were forced to reduce labour to the status of a mere factor of production and became even harder employers than other firms.[3] They lacked

[1] J. Watts, 'On Strikes and their Effects on Wages, Profits and Accumulations', *Journal of the Statistical Society*, Dec. 1861, 505; W. A. Jevons, 'Account of the Weavers' Strike at Padiham in 1859', National Association for the Promotion of Social Science, *Report of the Committee on Trades Societies and Strikes* (1860), 436; *Co-operator*, July 1860, 22, W. Cooper, July 1861, 26, J. H. Salkeld.

[2] J. Watts, 'Co-operative Societies', *Meliora*, Oct. 1861, 305–6; idem, *Co-operative Societies, Productive and Distributive: Past, Present and Future* (Manchester, Heywood, 1861), 80.

[3] H. W. McCready, 'The Cotton Famine in Lancashire, 1863', *Transactions of the Historic Society of Lancashire and Cheshire*, 1954, 132, quoting J. E. Edwards, 1 Apr. 1863.

the large reserve funds necessary to survive the great crises endemic to the cotton trade. The Cotton Famine brought to an end the first era of company formation in the history of the industry and forced half of the companies into liquidation, to the benefit of mortgagees and vendors. Forty-seven or 51 per cent of the 92 companies registered in 1860–1 were swept away by August 1871 while 72 or half of the 145 companies registered between 1856 and 1867 disappeared by that date. Bankruptcies were most numerous where the tradition of individualism was most deeply rooted. Thus the companies of Bolton and Blackburn suffered total liquidation while those of Rossendale and Bury survived the storm.

The Rochdale Co-operative Manufacturing Society (1854–1975), established by the Pioneers in 1854, weathered both the commercial crisis of 1857 and the Cotton Famine and paid a bonus to labour from 1856 until 1862.[1] From 1859 it expanded from weaving into spinning and set the example followed from 1860 by the Sun Mill of Oldham, established in 1858. It became the true pioneer of joint-stock enterprise in the cotton trade, though it did not register itself as a joint-stock company until 1916. The transition from the weaving industry requiring £20–50 per employee to the spinning industry requiring £250–300 per head condemned both companies to follow the proprietary pattern of private employers in taking all profit to themselves and enabled the Sun Mill to become the parent of the Oldham limiteds floated in 1873–5. The co-operative movement thus abandoned its original purpose in entering upon co-operative production, as the free-trade movement had become infected and perverted by the capitalist ethos.'Cotton manufactories, called co-operative, are generally, if not universally, simply joint-stock companies of limited liability, the capital of which has been subscribed in small shares, chiefly by workmen in the cotton districts, and which are often built and conducted with the aid of loans.'[2] Later joint-stock booms

[1] *Co-operator*, Dec. 1860, 92–3, July 1861, 25–6, Oct. 1861, 86–7, Apr. 1862, 19, May 1862, 210–13, June 1862, 6, 15, Sept. 1862, 70–1; P. Redfern, *John T. W. Mitchell, Pioneer of Consumers Co-operation* (Manchester, Co-operative Union, 1923), 29.

[2] J. Watts, *The Facts of the Cotton Famine* (1866), 84, Lord Derby, 12 Jan. 1863; W. T. Thornton, 'Strikes and Industrial Co-operation', *Westminster Review*, 1 Apr. 1864, 372–3.

similarly failed to place the trade upon any new and broad basis of co-operative association, despite the introduction of 'industrial partnership' shares in 1873–5 and the establishment of self-help manufacturing societies in the Burnley district in 1886–9. The industry remained more hostile to ventures in co-operative production than almost any other trade so that such societies as existed in the 1870s were very few in number, recent in origin, far apart in location, and quite unrepresentative of the general pattern of business organization.

Three further waves of company flotation in 1873–5, 1880–4, and 1889–92 extended the influence of the limited company within the industry and coincided with mill-extensions undertaken by private employers. The flotation mania of 1873–5 proved to be Lancashire's greatest joint-stock boom of the nineteenth century and assured the company of a permanent

TABLE 12

The Three Booms in Company Flotation, 1873–1892

	Total Number of Companies Registered	Average Capital	Proportion of Turnover Companies	Proportion of Private Limiteds	Proportion of Spinning Companies
		(£)	(%)	(%)	(%)
1873–5	226	57,500	77	14	66
1880–4	135	73,000	77	38	51
1889–92	181	46,000	88	48	35

Source: company files of companies registered in the English cotton industry.

place in the industrial life of the shire. In that wave of company promotion the ethos of co-operative production blended with and was overpowered by the desire of the non-commercial classes of society to share in the swelling profits of industry, as disclosed by the massive dividends paid by established companies with the aid of loan capital. Within three years 226 companies were registered with an average individual capital of £57,500 or 64 per cent more than the average capital of the companies of 1860–1. Almost two-thirds of the companies were spinning companies but only 53 or 23 per cent of the total number were mill-building companies, which were mainly established in the coarse spinning trade of south-east Lancashire and included 37, or 70 per cent of the 53, in Oldham. The Oldham model of a working-class limited with low share denominations and many shareholders proved less profitable than had been anticipated and took no extensive root outside its own immediate district, being imitated only in Darwen in 1874–5 under the influence of a demand unparalleled in its intensity even in Oldham.[1] No general share market was created since the companies remained essentially local enterprises and the savings of operatives could not be easily tapped outside Oldham and Darwen.

The flotation of 173 turnover companies, or 77 per cent of the total number, diffused the company form of business organization much more widely in Lancashire than it would otherwise have been. Such limiteds preserved particular localities, including Darwen, from the injury which the stoppage of a large factory might otherwise have caused. They might also pay respectable dividends over a long period of time if their cost per spindle was low and their management was skilful. Their primary function was however to transfer existing capital from established mill proprietors into the hands of new owners and to benefit the vendors by the sale to the public of businesses already in operation. They invariably enriched such private vendors and proved failures four times as often as new mills, very rarely surviving for as long as mill-building companies. Their influence undermined the spinning industry of north-east Lancashire through the transfer of old and dilapidated mills to companies at exorbitant prices.

The mill-building company made only a limited contribution in the 1870s to the extension of the industry's plant. Between 1870 and 1877 Britain added 7·5 million spindles, mainly in 1870–3, and Lancashire added 5 million spindles, so raising its spindleage by one-fifth. Of that increment of 5 million 2·7 million was furnished by mill-building companies and 2·2 million or 81·5 per cent was concentrated in the single town of Oldham. By 1877 mill-building companies controlled 10 per cent of Lancashire spindleage while turnovers and

[1] *Blackburn Times*, 17 Jan. 1874, 8iii, 9 May, 7iii, 11 July, 8iv; *Co-operative News*, 24 Jan. 1874, 40, 9 May, 258; *Oldham Chronicle*, 9 May 1874, 8v; *Preston Guardian*, 8 Aug. 1874, 7iii, 'Co-operative Enterprise in Darwen', reprinted in *Co-operative News*, 29 Aug. 1874, 104.

private limiteds operated another 20 per cent. The company secured a firm but restricted hold upon the industry of the shire, whose 270 companies in 1877 had on average 32 per cent more assets than the average private firm but controlled only 22·5 per cent of the industry's total capital of £65 million.[1] The depression of 1877–9 eliminated about one-fifth of the companies, increased the influence of the private firm at the expense of the company, and drastically reduced the average annual number of new registrations from 76 in 1873–5 to 13 in 1876–9. That depression was blamed upon the new companies, whose promoters were accused, like the early cotton masters, of 'headlong speculation'. The spread of limited liability began in fact to benefit wage-earners and the ancillary trades rather than shareholders.[2]

The next outburst of company promotion in 1880–4 did not become a boom on the scale of that of 1873–5 but none the less saw the registration of 135 companies. Their average capital was £73,000 or 27 per cent more than that of the companies formed in 1873–5. Companies were registered at only two-fifths of the average annual rate of 1873–5 and included the same proportion of mill-building companies but a lower proportion of spinning companies, a higher proportion of contractors' companies and of private limiteds, and the first room and power companies. No co-operative enterprises were launched because the depression of 1877–9 had discouraged the flotation of such ventures. The mill-building boom was concentrated particularly in south-east Lancashire, where local élites reacted strongly, under the influence of contractors and of high dividends, against the continued diversion of capital to Oldham. Joint-stock companies were founded, often at meetings held under the aegis of the local authority, in a conscious bid to emulate the mill-building enterprise of a town which enjoyed no exclusive advantage in respect of machinery, coal, transport, or even of labour. Those mills were intended to provide a local outlet for capital investment and a more satisfactory return thereon than a meagre 4 per cent, to extend the employment of local inhabitants, to fill empty cottages with occupants, to raise the value of land, and, above all, to pay wages, which

[1] *Textile Manufacturer*, June 1877, 183, R. Seyd, 'Capital in the Cotton Trade'.
[2] *Cotton*, 4 May 1878, 271, 'Limited Liability'.

were estimated in 1884 to amount to fourfold the amount of dividends distributed by existing companies. They would also contribute to the rates and increase the profits made upon the supply of gas, water, and coal. Under the influence of such hopes the first joint-stock limiteds were successfully floated in such established centres of the industry as Stockport, Stalybridge, Rochdale, Heywood, Dukinfield, and Bury as well as in Glasgow. Established limiteds also built new mills, financed by the issue of preference shares in the interests of existing shareholders, and even floated new companies. The new crop of companies enjoyed the advantage of latecomers in being able to build larger mills than those of the 1870s, usually of 75,000 spindles, and thus enlarged the size of the typical firm, under the influence of their contractor–promoters.

The depression of 1877–9 had deprived architects and builders of the contracts to which they had grown accustomed during the preceding period of expansion and embarrassed them acutely since they lacked the compensation of the overseas markets available to textile engineers. Those interests therefore allied with the suppliers of machinery and mill stores to float companies during the boom of 1880–4 in order to create a demand for their services. Such contractors' companies seem to have been peculiar to the cotton industry and were intended to supply its ancillary trades with profitable contracts, first for the construction of a mill and the installation of its machinery and then for the supply of cotton, coal, belting, or oil or for the sale of yarn or cotton waste. Their sponsors were not professional promoters but tradesmen who reversed the relationship thitherto customary with mill-owners by assuming the initiative in registering a company and in subscribing to its shares. Since they found their profits not in spinning but in building, equipping, and supplying a mill they could in practice pay for their shares out of their commission and profits and then dispose of them to the general public once the mill was at work. They took up shares in a new concern irrespective of its prospects or its cost and secured an additional bonus if they could dispose of their shares at a premium. They successfully extended their financial interests over a number of companies because shares were only part-paid and loan capital was available from investors with money deposited in the bank at an interest rate of 1½–2 per cent. Their interest in the extension of production was temporary rather than abiding and tended to divert the benefits of joint-stock enterprise from the investor to the contractor.

Contractors' companies had to pare their capital costs to the limit in order to avoid raising their costs of production. They could not however buy their machinery in the open market and were therefore burdened with higher costs of construction than other companies. They favoured the building of larger mills to spread those fixed costs over a larger number of spindles and to avoid reducing their profits. They might also be tied dangerously close to a particular cotton broker or waste dealer and so restricted in their access to the cotton and waste markets. The formation of such companies tended to diffuse a spirit of discreet corruption, encouraged excessive reliance upon loan capital, and aroused the violent indignation of private spinners. Such ventures not only accentuated the competition faced by existing mills but also forced other contractors in self-defence to sponsor similar flotations and so exposed the industry to the prospect of a continuing extension of capacity unrelated to the true level of demand.

The boom of 1880–4 neither reduced the importance of the Oldham limiteds nor prevented Oldham from further increasing its share of the industry's spindleage. Those companies formed outside Oldham were usually private, turnover, or short-lived ventures. Where they built mills they were less democratic in constitution than most of the Oldham limiteds: they restricted their shares to a small number of holders, excluded workingmen from their boards, and paid their directors high salaries. Nor did they publish their balance sheets or disclose information to the press. Thus they did not call into existence more sharebrokers or new local share markets. They proved however at least as successful financially as the Oldham limiteds. The increase in company flotation extended the sphere of influence of the corporate form of organization as the mill-building limiteds of 1881–4 laid down 1·94 million spindles, or 60 per cent of the 3·25 million spindles added in 1880–5. By 1884 mill-building limiteds had become responsible for the increment in the productive capacity of the industry and so encouraged the prophecy that the company would eventually absorb the greater part of the cotton industry.[1] In 1884 they controlled only 16 per cent of the industry's spindleage while private limiteds controlled another 16 per cent and turnover companies 3·9 per cent.

After the depression of 1884–5 a third joint-stock boom occurred in 1889–92 when 181 companies were registered, each with an average capital of £46,000. The reduction in the average size of the company by 37 per cent was caused by the increase in the number of small weaving companies of which 53 were registered in those four years. The proportion of new spinning companies, which had been 66 per cent in 1873–5 and 51 per cent in 1880–4, declined further to 35 per cent of the total number, or to the same proportion as in the boom of 1860–1. The last great mill-building boom of the Victorian age was inspired partly by existing limiteds and partly by contractors but proved less intense than that of 1880–4 since only 21 mill-building companies were registered instead of 31 and their proportion of the total number was halved from 23 per cent to 11·6 per cent. Contractors became for the first time the prime cause rather than the instrumental cause of mill construction. They raised the size of new factories to their optimum, equipped them with the latest technical devices and promoted the establishment of ring-spinning limiteds as well as of mills for spinning Bolton counts. They made the refitting of turnover mills with new machinery into a general practice, so generating a substantial replacement-demand and creating great prosperity within the textile engineering industry.[2] Companies began to compete for the possession of the largest mill and so swiftly raised the size of the largest new mill from 84,000 spindles in 1885 to 107,000 in 1889, to 116,000 in 1890 and to 132,000 in 1892. The average size of the new mule-mill rose to 100,000 spindles and that of the new ring-mill to 46,000 spindles. The new batch of mills installed 1·88 million spindles, or 70 per cent of the increment in spindleage, and helped to raise the industry's spinning-power by 6·2 per cent from 42·7 millions in 1888 to 45·38 millions in 1892. Those mills imposed for the first time a distinct check upon the industrial expansion

[1] *Textile Manufacturer*, Apr. 1884, 156, 'The Revolution in Cotton Spinning'.

[2] J. Nasmith, 'Recent Cotton Mill Construction and Engineering', *Textile Recorder*, May 1894, 1–51, reprinted (Manchester, Heywood, 1894, 1900, 284pp.).

Table 13

Number of Joint-Stock Companies Registered Annually in the English Cotton Industry, 1845–1896

Year	Tota	Effective	Abortive	Life-span of Ten Years or Less	Turnover	Mill Building	Spinning	Combined	Weaving	Private	Room and Power
1845	11	2	9		10	1	11				
1851	3	0	2	1	3				3		
1856	7	5	2		4	3	1	4	2		
1857	2	1	1		1	1	1		1		
1858	1	0	1		1			1			
1859	7	6	1		5	2	1	5	1		
1860	36	22	2	12	26	10	11	14	11	1	
1861	56	23	4	29	44	12	20	14	22		
1862	2	0		2	2				2		
1863	2	1		1	1	1	1		1		
1864	6	4		2	6		3	3		2	
1865	12	3	2	7	12		6	2	4	1	
1866	9	5		4	8	1	6	3			
1867	5	3		2	5			1	4		
1868	2	2			1	1	1		1		
1869	4	2	1	1	3	1	3	1			
1870	6	4		2	6		3	1	2	1	
1871	13	8	1	4	10	3	10	2	1	2	
1872	9	7	1	1	7	2	5	4		2	
1873	43	27	4	12	40	3	33	5	5	6	
1874	102	72	5	25	72	30	63	33	6	14	
1875	81	55	5	21	61	20	52	16	13	12	1
1876	17	8	1	8	16	1	8	6	3	5	
1877	20	13	1	6	17	3	8	7	5	5	
1878	10	5		5	10		3	2	5	4	
1879	7	4		3	7		2	5		1	
1880	21	7	6	8	21		12	4	5	5	3
1881	22	19	1	2	18	4	13	3	6	9	3
1882	24	20		4	20	4	14	8	2	16	2
1883	22	15	2	5	16	6	12	6	4	8	
1884	46	35	4	7	29	17	25	9	12	13	2
1885	21	11	3	7	20	1	12	5	4	9	2
1886	26	17	3	6	26		12	6	8	17	2
1887	32	22	4	6	29	3	9	8	15	16	5
1888	31	21	2	8	30	1	8	8	15	16	2
1889	40	26	2	12	34	6	21	10	9	21	4
1890	53	40	3	10	47	6	29	10	14	21	7
1891	52	36	5	11	45	7	29	7	16	27	4
1892	36	25	4	7	34	2	15	7	14	17	2
1893	35	25	3	7	34	1	12	7	16	23	1
1894	37	24	3	10	36	1	11	5	21	27	6
1895	35	25	2	8	35		10	6	19	19	1
1896	40	32		8	39	1	16	8	16	27	1
	1,046	682	90	274	891	155	512	246	288	347	48

Note: private limited companies, unlike room-and-power companies, are included in the totals and in the three main subdivisions of the table.

The figures for mill-building companies in 1845, 1859–61, and 1873 are estimates.

Source: company files of companies registered in the English cotton industry.

of Oldham: they reduced its share of the increment in spindleage from 51 per cent in 1881–4 to 42 per cent in 1889–92 and checked any further increase in its share of the industry's spindleage after it had reached the peak proportion of 27 per cent in 1893. Mill-building limiteds increased their share of the total spindleage from 16 per cent in 1884 to 26 per cent in 1896 while turnover companies raised their share from 4 per cent to 10 per cent and private limiteds almost doubled their share from 16 per cent to 30·7 per cent, so that by 1896 66·7 per cent of the industry's spindles were operated by limited companies.

The flotation boom of 1889–92 undoubtedly stimulated the construction industries but was not apparently justified by the legitimate needs of trade because existing mills could produce finer and better fabrics as well as the newer ones.[1] The failure of the new limiteds to produce impressive financial results could not be fully concealed by the increasing popularity of semi-private limiteds which published no accounts. Many new mills fared so badly in the depressed years of 1891–3 that they could not unload their shares except at a great loss: they therefore encouraged workers to take up shares as the price of obtaining work and eked out their capital by the use of preference shares, mortgage debentures, and commercial credit. Many established mills could not afford to re-equip with new machinery and instead cut their prices to the limit, reducing the profits of the newer mills and forcing some older mills to the wall. The new mills began in effect to replace the older plant thitherto retained in use in the spinning trade, especially in Ashton and Bury, and brought about the permanent stoppage in 1895–6 of 1,943,000 spindles or 4·5 per cent of the total number in the industry.[2] The decline in returns to the spinning trade precipitated the prolonged industrial disputes of 1892–3 and inhibited any further creation of new mill-building companies until the boom of 1904–7.

* * *

[1] *Textile Mercury*, 4 Oct. 1890, 227, 'The Extension of Spinning and Weaving'; *Textile Recorder*, Dec. 1891, 170–1, 'The Limited Liability Acts', Mar. 1892, 243, 'Mill Floating', Dec. 1896, 223, 'The Pause in Mill Building'.

[2] *Manchester Courier*, 26 Dec. 1896, 6iv.

The three successive waves of company flotation between 1873 and 1892 did not remould the economy of Lancashire upon the pattern of Oldham. The new limiteds were founded in only four of the six main spinning towns, i.e. in Oldham, Rochdale, Ashton, and Stockport, and in six smaller centres. Within those towns their influence was restricted by the abiding presence of the private firm and by the preference of investors for employers' companies, so that the Oldham model of the working-class limited remained largely confined to its birthplace. Rochdale became the second largest centre of the joint-stock company in Lancashire after Oldham, securing the advantages of limited liability without its disadvantages and building its new company mills at the very moment when they were necessary after the acute depression suffered first by its coarse and heavy trade in 1877–9 and then by its flannel trade in 1881.[1] Rochdale was encouraged to imitate Oldham by its proximity, by a strong civic spirit fostered by a low municipal franchise and a highly effective local authority, and by a traditional preference for co-operation rather than for trade unionism.[2] The coarse counts spun in the locality were as well adapted as Oldham counts to production by joint-stock companies. The town had the river and the canal lacked by Oldham, together with cheaper land and water, lower rents and wages and weaker unions to offset its high rates and less productive workmen. Its abundant capital had been notably increased by the woollen boom induced by the Cotton Famine and was exported to Oldham before 1882. Unlike Stockport or Ashton, Rochdale had not only two successful limiteds established in the boom of 1861 but also six efficient turnover companies incorporated in 1874–5. Above all, in the Rochdale Co-operative Manufacturing Society it had created the true parent of the joint-stock limiteds and the most successful dividend-paying machine in the county, whose average dividend rose from 6·4 per cent in 1862–82 to 8·25 per cent in 1886–96.[3]

Rochdale adopted the joint-stock company later and slower

[1] *Rochdale Observer*, 28 Dec. 1878, 5v–vi, 27 Dec. 1879, 5iv–v; *Textile Manufacturer*, Dec. 1882, 439–40, 'The Trade of Rochdale'.

[2] J. Vincent, 'The Electoral Sociology of Rochdale', *Economic History Review*, Aug. 1963, 76–90, reprinted in *The Formation of the Liberal Party, 1857–1868* (London, Constable, 1966), 96–118.

[3] *C.W.S. Annual*, 1883, 165–7, 1884, 174.

than Oldham but earlier and faster than Bolton in harmony with its position midway between the two great centres of the spinning trade. Under the guidance of local flannel manufacturers the Rochdale limiteds were established in the cotton industry and not in the woollen trade.[1] Those manufacturers thereby safeguarded their own trade from joint-stock competition, created a useful diversification of their interests, and secured a remunerative return on their capital. Between 1882 and 1892 seven mill-building limiteds installed 613,700 spindles or 32·8 per cent of the spinning plant of Rochdale and a higher proportion than in either Ashton or Stockport, whose limited mills were larger. The size of the average spinning firm rose by 48 per cent between 1884 and 1896 but remained smaller than in any other major spinning town apart from Stockport. The limiteds established model spinning mills, ended a decade of depression in the district, and ushered in a new era of expansion. They introduced more new trades than in any other centre and attracted industry to the town from the surrounding countryside. Local trade revived under the beneficial influence exerted by the advent of the new limiteds, the growth of spinning-only firms, the spread of ring-spinning at the expense of throstle-spinning, the competition of cotton flannelette with the old staple of flannel, and the stimulus given to the local manufacture of textile machinery.[2]

The Rochdale limiteds created local outlets for capital thitherto exported to Oldham, provided employment, paid out wages and dividends, and reduced the heavy burden of the rates. They did not however succeed in their attempt between 1888 and 1895 to enter the weaving trade[3] and were thus

[1] 'The Rise and Progress of the Rochdale Limiteds', ten articles in the *Rochdale Observer*, 10 May 1890, 5i–ii, 'Mitchell Hey', 17 May, 5i, 'Crawford Spinning Co.', 24 May, 4vi–vii, 'Rochdale Spinning Co.', 31 May, 4vii, 'Arkwright Spinning Co.', 7 June, 4vii–viii, 'Standard Spinning Co.', 14 June, 5vi, 'Union Manufacturing Co.', 21 June, 5v–vi, 'Milnrow Spinning Companies', 28 June, 4vi–vii, 'Milnrow Ring Spinning Companies', 5 July, 4vii–viii, 'Norden Fustian Companies', 19 July, 4vi–vii, 'The Limited Mills in the Whitworth Valley'.

[2] G. B. Williamson, 'Steam Engine Building in Rochdale', *Transactions of the Rochdale Literary and Scientific Society*, 19 Nov. 1943, 7–18; E. Smalley, 'History of Textile Machinery Making in Rochdale', ibid. 18 Feb. 1960, 65–8; *Textile Manufacturer*, Jan. 1889, 15, Nov. 1892, 524, Dec. 1893, 569–72; R. D. Mattley, *Annals of Rochdale* (Rochdale, Clegg, 1899), 99, 104.

[3] *Rochdale Observer*, 15 Oct. 1887, 4vii, 22 Oct., 4vi, 29 Oct. 4vi, 30 Mar. 1889,

restricted in their capacity to create jobs. They could not prevent a decline in the population of the town during the 1880s nor do much to raise the submerged eleventh of its inhabitants from the verge of pauperism.[1] They did not revive the woollen industry but they provided some compensation for its decline to almost a quarter of the size it had reached during the boom of the 1860s.[2] The town enhanced its position as a centre of the spinning trade, increased its share of the total spindleage of Lancashire, and rose in status, at the expense of Ashton, from the sixth largest spinning town in 1884 to the fifth largest in 1894, with the seventh largest population of cotton operatives. A greater proportion of its spindles and looms passed under corporate control than in any other major cotton town but the dominant role played in Oldham by the mill-building limited was performed in Rochdale by the turnover company and the private limited. The mule-spinning limiteds won a good name for their yarn while the ring-spinning limiteds helped to endow the town between 1884 and 1886 with a higher proportion of ring-spindles than any other cotton town and became models to the rest of Lancashire.[3] The Rochdale limiteds raised two-thirds of their capital in loans and paid high dividends to their discreet shareholders. The town was spared the influence of contractors' companies and was blessed with profitable turnover companies. Between 1886 and 1896 19 Rochdale limiteds paid an average annual dividend of 5·46 per cent: six mill-building limiteds paid 5·6 per cent, three ring-spinning limiteds paid 7·2 per cent, and nine older turnover companies paid 4·8 per cent. The most successful limited in Lancashire proved to be the Rochdale Spinning Company Ltd., which was established in 1884 and paid an average dividend of 10 per cent between 1886 and 1896.[4] The Rochdale limiteds estab-

5iii, 28 Dec., 6vi, 22 Jan. 1890, 2v, 14 June, 5vi, 14 Jan. 1891, 3ii, 9 Oct. 1895, 3ii, 19 Oct., 5iii, 13 Nov., 3ii, 'Union Manufacturing Company'.

[1] R. Veitch, 'Our Local Problem of Poverty', *Transactions of the Rochdale Literary and Scientific Society*, 8 Jan. 1892, 25.

[2] *Textile Manufacturer*, June 1890, 267.

[3] *Cotton Factory Times*, 31 Dec. 1886, 4v, 'The Development of Ring Spinning in Rochdale'; S. E. Boyle, 'The Development of Ring Spinning: its Present and Future Position', *Textile Manufacturer*, Dec. 1889, 567–9; idem, 'Ring Spinning and its Development with especial reference to its introduction into Rochdale', *Rochdale Observer*, 21 Dec. 1889, 6ii, 4 Jan. 1890, 6iv.

[4] *Rochdale Observer*, 24 May 1890, 4v–vi; G. W. Daniels, 'The Balance Sheets of

lished a clear financial superiority in the trade from 1892 and paid between 1893 and 1896 a return on their total capital, loan and share, which far exceeded that of the Oldham limiteds.[1]

Ashton-under-Lyne became almost as notorious as its neighbour Oldham during the boom of 1873–5 for gambling in shares and acquired between 1874 and 1891 five mill-building limiteds,[2] including the very high proportion of three contractors' companies. The town nevertheless remained beneath the influence of its private employers, whose bitter opposition to the new limiteds was forcefully expressed by Hugh Mason as President of the Manchester Chamber of Commerce,[3] so bringing to an end the limited boom of 1873–5. Ashton benefited more from the advent of the limited company than its neighbours in the Tame valley, Dukinfield, Hyde, Stalybridge, or Mossley. Between 1874 and 1894 its five limiteds installed 504,000 spindles or 28·2 per cent of the spinning power of the town and helped to raise the average size of its spinning firms by 22 per cent between 1884 and 1896, or almost to the level of Manchester firms. The Ashton limiteds expanded and diversified the trade of a town hitherto dependent upon one branch of a single industry. From 1892 Ashton spun Bolton counts from Egyptian cotton, so ceasing to be solely a spinner of medium counts from American cotton. Its limiteds succeeded in the spinning trade but not in the weaving trade. Their function was to replace and rejuvenate plant rather than to expand it since their competition brought 28 per cent of Ashton's spindles to a permanent halt by 1896. They proved slightly more profitable than the limiteds of Oldham, Bury, Heywood, or Middleton but much less profitable than those of Rochdale or Stockport, presumably because of the influence of the contractors' companies.

Three Limited Companies in the Cotton Industry', *Manchester School*, Autumn 1932, 77–84. 'C' Company is the Rochdale Cotton Spinning Company Ltd., registered on 28 March 1884.

[1] *Manchester Courier*, 22 Dec. 1893, 4vii, 29 Dec. 1894, 7vi, 28 Dec. 1895, 7v, 26 Dec. 1896, 6v.

[2] *Ashton Reporter*, 28 Nov. 1874, 6v–vi, 23 Jan. 1875 5vii–viii, 30 Jan.,, 6iv, 8 Jan. 1876, 5vii–viii, 19 Feb., 3v–vi, 22 Mar. 1884, 5iv, 13 Dec. 1890, 4viii, 20 Dec., 4viii, 21 Feb. 1891, 7vi–viii.

[3] *Manchester Guardian*, 2 Feb. 1875, 6ii.

Private companies became more important than public companies as the combined firms of Ashton responded to the challenge of the limiteds, imitating the response of Bolton rather than that of Oldham or Stockport and making private limiteds and turnover companies as relatively important in its spinning trade as in that of Rochdale. In that response they resembled the firms of Hyde, Mossley, and Glossop but differed markedly from those of Stalybridge, whose combined firms remained largely unincorporated, despite the establishment of the first successful limited in the town in 1882. The family firms of Hyde preferred individual to joint-stock enterprise and distrusted limited companies. Local capitalists acquired in Ashton an object of investment nearer to hand than Oldham and so diverted their capital from local investment, delaying the flotation of any mill-building company in Hyde until 1905. The combined firms of the township adopted the form of private limited more extensively than in any other cotton town in order to limit their liabilities and proved unable to prevent the absolute decline of both their spindles and looms under the impact of the competition of their neighbours as well as of the weaving towns of north-east Lancashire.

Stockport remained a bastion of private enterprise, especially of old-established firms, and exported much capital to Oldham which had surpassed it as a spinning town, as Blackburn had as a weaving centre. Its trade had stagnated since the 1840s and had suffered more severely during the depression of 1877–9 than that of any other town in south-east Lancashire,[1] but was revived by the establishment of three mill-building limiteds in 1881, 1884, and 1891[2] and the consequent cessation during the 1880s of the emigration of labour and the decline in population. The three companies installed by 1894 370,400 spindles, or 18·4 per cent of the spinning plant of the town and a lower proportion than in Oldham, Rochdale, or Ashton. The Stockport limiteds were however much larger in their average size than those of the other three towns and they built in 1893 the largest ring-mill in the industry. They mustered fortifold the spindleage

[1] *The Times*, 7 Sept. 1878, 11ii.

[2] *Stockport Advertiser*, 3 Mar. 1881, 4vi, 4 Mar., 8v, 11 Mar., 2vii, 18 Mar., 7iv–v, 25 Mar., 5vi, 1 Apr., 5iv, 8 Apr., 2v, 22 Apr., 8v–vii, 28 Oct., 5i, 4 Nov., 8viii, 11 Nov., 5iii, 29 May 1885, Supplement, 4ii, 4 Sept., 4i–iv, 1 July 1887, 7iii–iv, 2 Jan. 1891, 8ii.

of the numerous small cotton doublers and candlewick makers but could not prevent the average size of spinning firm from declining between 1884 and 1896 in a process without parallel in any other cotton town. Stockport did not adopt the Oldham model of the limited company and did not attract operative shareholders to its companies. Nor did it try to apply the principle of limited liability to either the weaving trade or the hatting trade.[1] Its adoption of the Oldham list from 1883 did not raise wages from their below-average level and did not prevent its cotton operatives from once more declining in number after a decade of revival during the 1880s. Its private firms, especially in the spinning trade, became private limiteds from 1881 under the stimulus of the new limiteds and upon the model of Bolton. The influence of private employers in diffusing the corporate form of organization proved far greater than in Oldham, Rochdale, or Ashton. Under their aegis the expansion of the local spinning trade raised Stockport from the fifth largest spinning town in 1884 to the fourth largest in 1894, an ascent achieved at the expense of Preston.

In the other two main spinning towns of Bolton and Manchester joint-stock enterprise failed to flourish in a hostile environment. In the second largest centre of the spinning trade the vast majority of companies registered were private limiteds which became as characteristic of Bolton as public companies were of Oldham, spreading faster amongst its combined firms than amongst its spinning firms. The town had been the birthplace of the industry's most distinguished entrepreneurs and remained the great citadel of private enterprise, the seat of the aristocracy of the spinning trade, and the main preserve of the family firm. Its fine trade was only conquered by the self-acting mule in the 1880s and was much less suited to joint-stock enterprise than the coarse trade of Oldham. Only five mill-building limiteds were formed, one in 1874, one in 1889, and three in 1892–4 under the stimulus of the profitability of Bolton counts and the guidance of local spinners. Those companies installed by 1896 484,000 spindles or 10 per cent of the town's spindleage. They gave Bolton larger companies and larger limited mills than those of Oldham and so confirmed it in the possession of the largest spinning firms in the industry outside

[1] Ibid. 12 June 1891, 5ii, 10 July, 5v, 17 July, 4vi–vii, 31 July, 2vii.

Leigh, with sixteen of the eighty leading firms in the trade. They imported mill architects from Oldham but made no attempt to introduce Oldham counts into the home of medium-fine spinning. Their mills served as models of their kind to the industry and paid to their shareholders treble the returns paid by the Oldham limiteds between 1884 and 1904.

The third largest spinning centre in south Lancashire in Manchester remained wholly unaffected by the successive joint-stock booms and did not create any viable mill-building company. The companies registered in its cotton industry down to 1896 were fewer in number than those registered in either Oldham, Bolton, Rochdale, or Blackburn and increasingly comprised private limiteds, wholly free from the embarrassing proximity of working-class limiteds. The local labour force lacked the unity of that of Oldham, being fragmented, deferential, and mobile while the cotton operatives seem to have had neither the resources nor the will to float their own limiteds. Thus Cottonopolis built no joint-stock mills to stem the decline of its spindles from their peak level of 1885 and expanded its looms through the medium of its private employers. It had no need to imitate Oldham in the formation of companies since it concentrated within its boundaries the most profitable sections of the trade and the largest loomage within the spinning district. The corporate form of organization was adopted by private employers, first by combined firms and then especially from 1885 by spinning firms, but spread more slowly than in any other spinning centre and was put to wholly new use in the profit-oriented trust movement of 1897–9.

The limited company thus found its most congenial seat in the highly urbanized spinning district of south-east Lancashire and exerted a regional influence which was strictly limited in extent. The small country mills and the towns on the periphery of the cotton region from Clitheroe in the north around through Golborne in the west to Glossop in the south-east remained untouched by the joint-stock movement. The weaving district similarly remained broadly unaffected, though in two small centres mill-building companies had installed by 1884 34 per cent of the spindles in Accrington and 26 per cent of those in Darwen, the enterprise of companies in spinning being there combined with that of private employers in weaving. In

Rossendale the companies only replaced private firms and erected no new buildings: they neither increased the output of local industry nor prevented the industrial decline of the valley from the 1870s. In south-east Lancashire the influence of the limiteds undoubtedly arrested the decline of Stockport, Stalybridge, and Heywood and contributed to the expansion of the spindleage of Middleton and Dukinfield. They did not prevent the decline in the spindleage of Bury or the decline in the population of Bacup and Mossley. Their advent did not usher in a new era of general competition outside the sector spinning Oldham counts.

* * *

The limiteds undoubtedly transformed the industry's image and provided in 1891 222 of the 457 members of the United Cotton Spinners' Association established in 1888.[1] They created a whole new generation of firms which built mills much larger in size than the average private concern. That increase in the scale of operations did not present any real threat to the competitive structure of the industry but may well have inspired the quest undertaken by Marshall and Chapman for the representative size of firm in an effort to save appearances. By 1896 thirteen companies nevertheless ranked amongst the eighty largest enterprises in the industry and had an average age of 22 years, or one-third of the 63 years averaged by the 63 largest private firms. Their average spindleage was 160,735, which was less than the average size of the 22 largest private spinners but almost fourfold the size of the average spinning mill. Those large companies contributed to the functional separation of spinning and weaving and to the geographical divorce of the spinning and weaving areas since they were all spinning companies located in the spinning district of south-east Lancashire, Bolton having the largest number of great firms, both public and private. Only in the three small centres of Heywood, Middleton, and Slaithwaite in the Colne valley east of Oldham did a company establish the largest single enterprise in a cotton town. The limiteds did not alter the fundamental pattern of industrial location and created only a marginal

[1] *Textile Manufacturer*, Sept. 1891, 426.

alteration in the hierarchy of rank amongst spinning towns with the ascent of Stockport and Rochdale. They were not pioneers or innovators: usually they extended the production of established staples rather than introduced wholly new branches of trade. Thus they introduced the spinning of Oldham counts into Ashton from 1875 and into Rochdale from 1882 and the spinning of Bolton counts into Oldham from 1883, into Rochdale from 1890, and into Ashton and Heywood from 1892, so broadening the area of inter-centre competition. They extended the sphere of influence of established techniques rather than introduced new ones, enlarging the role of ring-spinning where it had already taken root. In no case did they spin the highest grades of yarn or manufacture the finest products.

The cotton industry adopted the company more extensively than any other branch of the textile industry and much more rapidly than the woollen and worsted industry. Its companies undoubtedly attracted capital into the spinning industry in south-east Lancashire, especially in Oldham and Rochdale, which would never have been so embarked without the protection of limited liability and the consequent division of risk amongst many investors. The corporate form of organization enabled small capitalists to band together, as the amount of fixed capital necessary for spinning grew, in order to compete with the giant firms of the industry. It made possible the aggregation of small savings to such effect that Lancashire acquired the largest number of small joint-stock companies in the whole country and thus preserved an industrial structure based upon the small unit of enterprise. The ownership of the limited spinning companies was diffused much more widely than had been that of their private predecessors. The capital resources of the industry were extended more broadly than those of its foreign competitors through the use of loans, preference shares, mortgages, and debentures. Lancashire experienced no large scale influx of capital from outside its borders, least of all from London, and retained full control over its staple trade. The spread of the company prevented the rate of investment from declining as rapidly as it might otherwise have done, strengthened the role of capital within the industry, and encouraged the more intensive use of existing plant.

The mill-building limiteds installed 10·982 million spindles between 1860 and 1896, so increasing the industry's plant by about one-third and supplying one quarter of the total spindleage in existence in 1896. Three-fifths of that increment was added during the three booms between 1873 and 1892 and three-quarters was laid down in seven towns. Increasingly the companies supplied the bulk of new investment in spinning plant and their contribution thereto rose from 54 per cent in 1873–5 to 70 per cent in 1889–92. The building of the new limited mills undoubtedly benefited the construction industries and the operative population but increased the competition faced by private spinners. The use of loan capital horrified private employers who, with growing support from shareholders in established companies and from trade-union leaders, vainly tried in 1877, 1887, and 1891 to secure the imposition of some statutory restraint upon the borrowing powers of limited companies. The only effective restrictions were in fact placed not upon promoters, directors, or subscribers but upon mortgagees and especially upon their right to distrain for interest.[1] Freed from any such restraint, the limiteds fulfilled a function of creative destruction, driving out of use at least two million spindles, or as much as was laid down by private spinners between 1873 and 1896.

The grant of legal personality to joint-stock companies in 1844 and to trade unions in 1871 eroded the moral foundations of individualism. The spread of the limited company represented a triumph over the theory of individual competition but not over the principle of competition as such. It did not moderate the influence of competitive individualism nor revolutionize the structure of industry. It simply enhanced the intensity of competition amongst firms for labour and for profits. The resulting relentless pressure for the manufacture of dividends prevented the limiteds from permanently improving industrial relations or from transforming the pattern of production into one based upon producers' co-operatives, co-partnerships of labour, or even profit-sharing associations. The advent of the joint-stock company did not necessarily entail the

[1] *Law Reports, Chancery,* 35 1887, 656–68, *In re* Lancashire Cotton Spinning Company. *Ex parte* Carnelley, 4 and 5 May 1887, Sir Henry Cotton and Sir Nathaniel Lindley; ibid. 1896, ii. 544–51, *In re* Higginshaw Mills and Spinning Company, 2 July 1896, Sir Nathaniel Lindley.

more efficient organization of industry, a faster rate of industrial expansion, or a new stimulus to economic growth.

Ownership was separated from control as the proprietor was replaced by a corporation and the employer by a manager. The creation of a new career for the professional mill manager did not transform the social hierarchy of Lancashire as much as that of Oldham. The typical manager differed sharply from the traditional employer, who hazarded both his fortune and his reputation on the commercial battlefield. He lacked the permanent and profound pecuniary interest in an enterprise possessed by an owner, his drive to succeed in the acquisition of profit, and his large reserves of moral strength.[1] Such a salaried employee tended to seek maximum income, security, and status rather than maximum profit and sought to further his own career rather than the interests of his company. Measuring status by the size of the unit of management, he encouraged both the enlargement in size of the firm and the movement towards horizontal integration within the spinning industry. The key position of a manager within a company enabled him to divide and rule his shareholders, to conceal the true financial state of his company even from his own directors, and to reduce his auditors to the status of dependent clients, whose functions were restricted to a formal minimum. In such a task he was aided by the authoritative judgement of Sir Henry Lopes in 1895 that auditors were not officers of a company within the meaning of the Companies Acts and could not therefore be prosecuted for negligence. 'An Auditor is not bound to be a detective . . . He is a watch-dog, but not a bloodhound.'[2] The spread of the limited company extended the career opportunities for the emerging class of mill managers but may well have reduced the quality of entrepreneurship within the industry in so far as really good managers were in very short supply and could pursue more profitable prospects in other fields. The company may indeed have been the form of organization best suited to an industry experiencing a slower rate of growth than formerly: its diffusion undoubtedly

[1] J. W. Cross, 'Poor Lancashire', *Nineteenth Century*, Nov. 1903, 866, reprinted in *The Rake's Progress in Finance* (Edinburgh, Blackwood, 1905), 107–28.

[2] *Law Reports, Chancery*, 1896, i. 6–19, *In re* Kingston Cotton Mill Company, 2 and 22 Nov. 1895; ibid. 1896, ii. 288, *In re* Kingston Cotton Mill Company (no. 2), 19 May 1896, Sir Henry C. Lopes, L.J.

coincided with the deceleration in the industry's rate of expansion from 1877. Thus it could be deemed to have 'devitalized the soil of Lancashire'[1] and to have set in motion the trend carried further by the spread of the trust.

The capital investment undertaken by the limiteds was made in an age of declining returns, which they themselves in part occasioned. They extended the influence of financial considerations at the expense of purely industrial factors and expanded the sources of funds from fixed-interest loans to dividend-reaping shares by the sale of promises and the inculcation of hope. They could not however afford purely passive investors the same return upon their capital that employers secured for their capital, labour, and zeal in combination. Thus they failed to generate the financial returns anticipated by their credulous shareholders. The average dividend paid between 1882 and 1896 by 112 limiteds publishing their dividends was 4 per cent, with 72 mill-building limiteds paying 4·1 per cent, and 40 turnovers paying 3·9 per cent.[2] Such returns cannot be regarded as representative of the spinning trade or even of spinning companies because of the exclusion of both private firms and of semi-private limiteds. The 39 most successful companies of the 112 paid an average dividend of 6·95 per cent and comprised 21 Oldham limiteds, 13 Rochdale limiteds, two from Ashton, and one apiece from Heywood, Dukinfield, and Stalybridge. The companies outside Oldham proved more profitable than the Oldham limiteds but achieved their financial success on a different basis. Of the 33 limiteds outside Oldham paying on average 4·74 per cent, or over a quarter more than the 3·66 per cent of the Oldham limiteds, 13 turnover companies, mainly in Rochdale, paid 4·86 per cent, or almost a twentieth more than the 4·65 per cent paid by the twenty mill-building companies. Of the mill-building limiteds five contractors' companies paid on average 3·42 per cent, or 31 per cent less than the average return of the other 28 while six other contractors' companies floated in 1889–91 preferred to remain semi-private and to avoid disclosing their profits. The true

[1] W. H. Mills, *Sir Charles W. Macara, Bart.: A Study of Modern Lancashire* (1917), 27–8, 65.

[2] *Oldham Standard*, 26 Dec. 1891, 8v, for 1884–91, 26 Dec. 1896, 7iii, for 1884–96; *Rochdale Observer*, 31 Dec. 1890, 3vi, for 1883–90, 26 Dec. 1896, 4ix, for 1888–96.

financial function of the limiteds was to devalue the capital of private spinners, forcing them to depreciate their plant more thoroughly and reducing the rate of return on capital invested in the cotton industry towards the level of that paid on bank deposits or on consols.

* * *

The company did not displace the private firm from the commanding heights of the regional economy nor from the local domination of the cotton industry because established firms themselves became private companies in response to the growing competition of the limiteds and so appropriated for their own convenience the privilege of limited liability intended by Parliament to protect associations of small capitalists in the establishment of a new business. Such private limiteds gave to the Companies Acts a new function which was given legal recognition only in 1907. They usually had £100 shares held by the seven statutory holders. They were rarely abortive foundations and were usually effective and long-lasting. Their longevity contrasts sharply with the brevity of existence of turnover companies. Of the 347 private limiteds registered between 1860 and 1896 239 or 69 per cent still existed at the end of 1896. Those companies discreetly combined public privilege with the pursuit of private profit and set the example followed by the equally secretive semi-private limiteds.

The first private limiteds incorporated in 1864 were large and old-established enterprises in the capital-intensive industry of spinning on the fringe of ethnic Lancashire. The joint-stock boom of 1873–5 markedly increased the number of that type of company and enlarged its functions since it was used by some leading firms to effect the amalgamation of separate businesses and also to establish industrial partnerships, as facilitated by an amendment of the Companies Act secured in 1865 by the 'friends of co-partnership'. Such schemes reflected the enthusiasm for shareholding diffused from Oldham and provided for the acceptance of loan capital on deposit, for the grant of a bonus to labour, or for the offer of shares to employees, often on credit extended at 5 per cent interest, so effecting the gradual conversion of loans into share capital. They were quite distinct from producers' co-operatives in so far as they reserved the function of management to the managers, debarred wage-earners from sharing in decisions, and imposed no limits upon the power of managers, on the number of their shares, or on the size of their dividends. They succeeded in improving industrial relations and in discouraging strikes against such firms but they remained untypical because proprietary concerns preferred to become private rather than public companies.

The new institution spread relatively slowly but surely until the 1880s. The first private limiteds were incorporated in Manchester in 1864, in Blackburn in 1868, in Wigan in 1870, in Oldham and Glossop in 1872, and in Bury, Bolton, and Ashton in 1874. From 1876 the number of private limiteds registered regularly exceeded (save in 1884) the number of new mill-building companies and the private limited established itself firmly in Lancashire three decades before its formal legal recognition. Rochdale had no such firms before 1878 because its businesses tended to be small in size. In the boom of 1881–4 the private limited appeared in Stockport, Leigh, and Chorley in 1881 and in Preston and Heywood in 1882. The spindleage of existing private limiteds first exceeded that in the control of mill-building limiteds during 1885 when they became the dominant force in the joint-stock movement. During the 1880s large firms, especially those with assets of £200,000 and more, limited their liability in increasing numbers. By the close of 1889 35 or more than half of the 63 largest firms had become private limiteds and by 1896 only 15 or 24 per cent of those 63 giants remained unincorporated. In the weaving district of north-east Lancashire the progress of the private limited proved much slower: it appeared first in Burnley, Nelson, and Haslingden in 1886 and first secured widespread acceptance during the booms of 1889–92 and 1893–4, proving most popular in Blackburn, Burnley, and Nelson and least acceptable to patrician Preston. In the main spinning centres it was adopted most extensively by the combined firms of Bolton, Glossop, Ashton, Hyde, and Bury and by the spinning firms of Oldham, Stockport, Stalybridge, Mossley, Heywood, and Leigh whilst both combined and spinning firms adopted it in Manchester, Rochdale, and Wigan, leaving the unincorporated private firm dominant among the great combined firms of Stalybridge,

Oldham, and Leigh. The spindleage of private limiteds increased half as fast again as that in mill-building limiteds and rose from 44·4 per cent of the total number of spindles in joint-stock companies in 1884 to 46·06 per cent in 1896, while the share of mill-building limiteds declined from 44·7 per cent in 1884 to 38·9 per cent in 1896. Those private limiteds increased their share of the total spindleage from 16 per cent in 1884 to 30·7 per cent in 1896, so supplying much of the 67 per cent of spindles under the control of companies.

The continuing advantages of incorporation were considerable for the management and financing of a large firm.[1] Registration as a company gave to a business artificial immortality through the perpetual succession conferred by statute. The use of shares facilitated the division of interests among partners and the apportionment of an inheritance amongst members of a family. Such shares could be transferred in the event of the death, bankruptcy, or lunacy of a leading shareholder without dislocating a concern through an enforced liquidation and ruinous sale of assets. Incorporation thus enabled a proprietor to retire from business, to provide for the contingency of his own death or that of a partner, to associate his sons in the management of a firm, and to capitalize the goodwill which he had built up for the business. It did not restrict the freedom of the managing partners in any way and entailed the minimal intrusion on the privacy of a firm. Incorporation also conferred the privilege of limited liability and so enabled a partner to leave capital in a business without risking all his savings and to free himself wholly from further liability by taking fully paid-up shares. It also permitted the legal separation of businesses actually under one control as an insurance against the transmission of shocks and failure, a device employed especially by large spinning firms in Manchester and Bolton. The corporate form of organization was also used in 1895–9 for the amalgamation of businesses in the thread and fine-spinning trades.

The greatest single advantage of incorporation was to enable

[1] C. W. Turner, *Treatise on the Conversion of a Business into a Private Limited Company* (London, Solicitors' Law Stationery Society Ltd., 1907, 146pp.), 67; H. W. Jordan, *How to Form a Company* (London, Jordan, 1913, 80pp.), 54–8, Appendix on Private Companies; idem, *Private Companies* (London, Jordan, 1916), 14–25.

a private firm to issue debentures which constituted a formal acknowledgement of debt by the shareholders.[1] Such bonds were given full legal protection from 1891 and enabled a company to give security to creditors without publicity since they lay outside the scope of the Bills of Sales Acts of 1878 and 1882 and thus, unlike mortgages, did not need to be registered. Those bonds could be issued with the minimum of interference with a business and provided a far-reaching and effective mortgage security on the undertaking and property of a company issued under its seal. They yielded a lower interest rate than shares because their holders avoided the risks of being held liable as partners. Thus debentures could replace the share capital of retiring partners as effectively as the loan capital of creditors. They were more easily obtainable, transferable, and marketable than an ordinary mortgage. A company might thereby raise more money than an ordinary partnership by extending the charge from its fixed stock to its floating stock or even to its uncalled capital. Thus a company could extend its capital resources cheaply but effectively and pay high dividends upon its ordinary shares on the model of the successful Oldham limiteds. It could also avoid giving its creditors any share in management, so setting the example followed by the trusts in the textile industry. Private firms extended their financial resources in this way without being compelled to publish balance sheets. Their prosperity thus remained concealed from public scrutiny in contrast to the financial losses suffered in time of depression by the Oldham limiteds.

[1] H. W. Jordan, *Debentures and Other Charges* (London, Jordan, 1913, 3rd edn. 1914, 45pp.).

CHAPTER 7

The Emergence of the Oldham Limiteds, 1874–1890

> Private enterprise decays and dies, but companies may live for ever.
> William Marcroft, *Sun Mill Company Limited. Its Commercial and Social History from 1858 to 1877* (Oldham, Tetlow, 1877), 3, Preface.

> There is here no conciliation of competing interests; no recognition by the individual of the general good as the true end of his own life and work; no security against the tricks of trade by the removal of those influences which tend to produce them; no attempt to apply the principles of justice for the protection of the classes who are not strong enough to protect themselves; no tendency to form bodies of workers proud of the establishment in which they work as their own, jealous of its honour, bound up with its success, who might use their accumulated profits to cover the country with Saltaires, and unite, through the combination of agriculture with manufacture, the advantages of town and country life; no attempt to subject the natural force of competition to that control of reason indispensable to make any natural force truly serviceable to man.
> Thomas Hughes, Report of the Central Co-operative Board, 30 March 1875, in the *Co-operative News*, 10 April 1875, 194.

THE TRANSFORMATION of Oldham from 'the pariah of the cotton trade'[1] into the very hub of the spinning universe was rapid and unexpected, astonishing the old-established spinners of Lancashire. In the 1860s the town became the largest centre of cotton spinning in the world: in the 1870s its new spinning

[1] *Chambers's Repository of Instructive and Amusing Tracts* (Edinburgh, Chambers, 1852), i. 28, 'The Cotton Metropolis'.

companies made it the largest centre of joint-stock enterprise in the cotton industry. Those companies were launched in the first of a series of successive waves of feverish flotation in a town endowed with few apparent natural advantages for the pursuit of industry. Oldham was a frontier town within a frontier community, sited on a high hill on the easternmost edge of the county. It lacked any strategic function and acquired no nodal significance, lying distant from both of the main trans-Pennine routes from south-east Lancashire to Yorkshire via the Roch or Tame valleys. It possessed no visible natural resources or advantages since it was not located on a stream or served by a canal. Its frontier location left it a hamlet in the seventeenth century when Rochdale, Bury, and Bolton had become thriving market towns. Those considerable disadvantages were overcome only during the nineteenth century through a combination of industrial, technological, social, and conjunctural influences.

The process of 'proto-industrialization' had, from the seventeenth century, separated the cottagers of the locality from its farmers. The spread of factories from the 1790s occurred relatively late in the history of Oldham, as in that of Manchester: they derived their power from the steam-engine in the complete absence of the water-wheel, so valorizing the concealed coal seams of the district. The local textile industry was transformed from the manufacture of woollens and fustians into coarse spinning and velvet weaving but remained marginal to the staple trade of Lancashire. To what extent the distinctive pattern of a society of small landowners, small employers, and small shopkeepers was transformed by the emergence of a small class of large employers, or 'jenny-gentry',[1] and a substantial working class, remains a debatable issue. The room and turning system seems however to have maintained the small firm as the typical unit of production and prevented the large employers from monopolizing the profits of industry. That system reduced the amount of capital necessary to begin business and enlarged the opportunities for social mobility: it moderated the social antagonisms which, as John Foster has shown,[2] sorely divided

[1] H. Bateson, *A Centenary History of Oldham* (Oldham Borough Council, 1949), 83, quoting Edwin Butterworth.

[2] J. Foster, 'How Oldham's Working-Class Leaders Managed to Avoid Reformism 1812–1847', *Bulletin of the Society for the Study of Labour History*, Spring 1968,

the town until 1850. It also fostered the rapid expansion of the spinning industry and especially of the coarse spinning which was most suited to the small firm as well as to the high level of local humidity. It accentuated the degree of competition amongst employers, reduced the level of individual profits, and increased the mortality rate amongst factory masters, so preventing the family firm from establishing an hereditary monopoly of local industry under a separate caste of employers.[1]

The engineering industry expanded markedly from the 1850s when the population of the town entered upon a phase of sustained expansion lasting until the 1880s and carrying it to an all-time peak level in 1911. The consequent competition for labour with the cotton industry created an endemic shortage of piecers, who were essential in coarse spinning and could therefore secure for their services the payment of higher rates than elsewhere. The cotton operatives of the locality worked harder than others, under the influence of the almost continuous rainy season of the foothills of the Pennines. They benefited by the competition for their labour, produced more yarn per spindle than elsewhere, and received from 1841 onwards the highest gross earnings in Lancashire.[2] The engineering trade employed in the 1870s nearly 20,000 prosperous workers who formed a stronger union than that of the spinners, earned even higher wages, and notably enhanced the industrial consciousness of the working class. That industry supplied foreign mills with managers as it developed the export of machinery, so calling into existence an abundant supply of mill managers drawn from the working class. The perfection of the self-acting mule by local engineers for the spinning of coarse counts completed the mechanization of the central process in spinning and freed the industry from the fear of technical change as well as from the need for the constant

6–10; idem, 'Nineteenth Century Towns—A Class Dimension', in H. J. Dyos (ed.), *The Study of Urban History* (London, Arnold, 1968), 281–99, reprinted in M. W. Flinn and T. C. Smout (eds.), *Essays in Social History* (Oxford, Clarendon Press, 1974), 178–96; idem, *Class Struggle and the Industrial Revolution* (London, Weidenfeld, 1974), discussed in *Social History*, Oct. 1976, 335–66, by A. E. Musson and the author.

[1] E. Butterworth, *Historical Sketches of Oldham* (Oldham, Hirst 1856), 118–19, 139, 183.

[2] G. H. Wood, *Wages in the Cotton Trade* (1910), 116.

application of inventive skill. The extensive adoption of the self-actor from 1867 ushered in a decade of unprecedented expansion of spindleage but threatened to undermine the position of the small employer in so far as it entailed an enlargement in the size of the mill.

Oldham lay near enough to Manchester to use its market but sufficiently distant for land to remain cheap, for capital to prefer local investment and for local customs to remain largely uncontaminated by alien influence. Those traditions comprised the 'great tradition' of individualism and the 'little tradition' of co-operation, developed amongst a largely paganized working class. The outlook of its employers inculcated pride in the achievements of individual enterprise and inhibited the development of civic consciousness, corporate institutions, and municipal utilities. Thus Oldham had no public property after the enclosure of its common lands in 1807 and no public buildings until 1841. It lagged behind other towns in the development of social amenities: its railway station and its town hall remained the most modest in all Lancashire since it was bypassed by the Manchester–Leeds railway in 1841 and was not incorporated as a borough until 1849. The dominant ethos of competitive individualism was moderated by the radical co-operative tradition of the working class whose opposition delayed the introduction of the Poor Law Amendment Act of 1834 until 1847. In the 1850s the growing wealth of the working population encouraged a general efflorescence of friendly societies, building societies, sick clubs, funeral clubs, permanent money clubs, and, above all, of co-operative stores. Oldham acquired two co-operative societies, where Rochdale and Manchester were content with only one, and became a co-operative centre second in importance only to Rochdale. Those societies fostered the joint-stock movement in industry by providing an effective model for imitation, especially in relation to methods of organization, management, and accounting. They also supplied capital, promoters, directors, and the ideal of the reconstruction of society upon a non-competitive basis. That inspiring ideal was transformed under the pressure of industrial competition so that what had been a means to an end became an end in itself.

The process of transformation is exemplified in the history of the pioneer limited which was founded in 1858 as the Oldham

Building and Manufacturing Company Ltd.[1] in an attempt to reform society by uniting the pursuit of agriculture and industry in a co-operative village. That company built no cottages but extended its operations from weaving into spinning, quintupled the denomination of its shares from £1 to £5, and built the Sun Mill (1860–2) with 60,000 spindles, or more than treble the average size of local mills, so ushering in a new era in the history of mill building in the district. As it expanded its capital and drew largely upon investors from outside Oldham it abandoned its co-operative ideals and concentrated upon maximizing the return to capital, for which purpose it used loans from 1864. In 1867 it abandoned weaving, renamed itself the Sun Mill Company Ltd., and omitted from its new rules both the objective of building and the bonus to labour, which it had never in fact paid. Thus it became what Gladstone described in 1867 as 'an association of small capitalists employing other work-people'.[2] The Sun Mill was the first joint-stock mill in Oldham and also the first successful one, finding spinning more profitable than weaving and earning a high reputation in the Manchester market for the quality of its 32s twist. Its success proved wrong the prophecies of its detractors and made straight the path for its imitators, especially through the publication of quarterly balance sheets from 1864 and the payment of quarterly dividends from 1867. It gave working men experience as secretaries, salesmen, managers, and directors, so demonstrating their capacity and creating a cadre of company promoters. It made average profits on its capital of 8·67 per cent and, with the help of loans, paid between 1863 and 1873 an average annual dividend of 12⅓ per cent. The average dividends of 25 per cent paid in 1871–3 exceeded the annual wage bill and aroused much local envy, because of the large number of outside shareholders. Such dividends revealed the size of the profits being made by private employers and the ability of companies to tap those gains through good management and the use of loans, which were however employed as a supplement to, rather than as a substute for, share capital. By adopting the

[1] W. Marcroft, *Sun Mill Company Limited* (1877); R. E. Tyson, 'The Sun Mill Company Limited—A Study in Democratic Investment, 1858–1959' (M.A. thesis, University of Manchester, 1962).

[2] Marcroft, 8.

corporate form of organization the Sun Mill created an entity freed from the curse of mortality which dogged the private employer and marred the sublime prospect of a never ending succession of dividends of 25 per cent. In the sphere of employment its sole innovation was to end work on Saturdays one hour earlier than other mills. It survived without a single strike until 1873 when it joined the local employers' association and so finally abandoned its original purpose. By raising its spindleage in 1875 to 142,000 it became the largest mill in the district and the equivalent in size of three modern mills, with a capital investment of £237 per employee. Thus the Sun Mill became the parent of the limiteds floated in 1873–5 and Oldham became the birthplace of the limited company in cotton spinning, as Rochdale was of consumers' co-operation.

During the crisis of the Cotton Famine Oldham adapted its mills to the consumption of Surat in place of American cotton and benefited from the perfection of the self-acting mule for the spinning of coarse counts. In that decade it seems to have acquired the largest spindleage of any cotton town, silently surpassing Manchester in the early 1860s and Bolton in the later 1860s to become the leading mill town in Lancashire. In the boom of 1870–3 its mills reverted from the consumption of Surat to that of American cotton as production recovered in the South, supply returned in 1871 to its pre-war level, and the U.S.A. regained its competitive power in price. The demand for yarn increased as weaving capacity expanded in north-east Lancashire to meet the swelling demand for India and China shirtings and as yarn exports rose towards the all-time peak value attained in 1872. Profit rates reached in 1871 their highest level of the whole period from 1850 to 1900 and profit expectations soared ahead even of those margins. The high dividends paid by the Sun Mill and the creation of co-operative workshops by the Paris Commune encouraged a miniature boom in 'co-operative spinning companies' in Oldham and the formation in 1871 of five more companies, increasing the number of its companies in the cotton industry from eight in 1870 to fifteen in 1872. Those companies included seven turnover concerns and remained peripheral to the local cotton industry, whose spindleage was doubled by private employers from three millions in 1866 to 6·5 millions in 1872, or from 12 per cent to

24 per cent of the total in Lancashire.[1] As pathfinders for their successors, they nevertheless enlarged the local sphere of joint-stock enterprise, established the company securely within the spinning industry, and generalized the use of the £5 share. They raised 75 per cent of their nominal capital from the working classes,[2] especially from engineering operatives, and paid high dividends with the aid of loans which co-operative societies preferred to shares, after the establishment in 1871 of the legality of their investment in joint-stock companies.[3] Allotting all of their dividends to capital and none to labour,[4] they proved financially successful and thus differed from the successor companies which they helped to call into existence but which were forced to build at far higher prices.

The coal famine of 1872–3 precipitated the launching of fifteen turnover concerns in 1873 as proprietor–lessors of mill space sought to regain the profits eliminated by the sharp rise in the price of fuel and as shrewd vendors sought to capitalize upon the windfall gains made possible by the concomitant rise in the price of machinery. The influence of the coal shortage proved much greater in the sphere of coarse spinning than in that of fine spinning and encouraged smaller spinners to respond to the challenge of the perfected self-actor and to the shortage of room and turning[5] by evolving through the use of the joint-stock company from lessees into full corporate proprietors. Thus employers became, after the co-operative stores, the true originators of the local joint-stock movement. The flotation of those turnover concerns precipitated a keen debate over the profitability of the cotton spinning companies of Oldham.[6] Such companies added nothing to the means of production in existence and were soon overshadowed by the mill-building concerns created in 1874–5. The boom of 1873–5 proved to be the greatest in the history of Oldham and lacked any local precedent. During those three years seventy limiteds were established, including 37 mill-building companies, and

[1] *C.W.S. Annual*, 1884, 186–7, 'Growth of the Cotton Business in Oldham'.

[2] *Co-operative News*, 8 Aug. 1874, 63.

[3] Ibid., 2 Sept. 1871, 3, 27 Jan. 1872, 41, 20 July 1872, 377.

[4] Ibid. 19 Oct. 1872, 530, W. Nuttall, 'Productive Associations'.

[5] *Oldham Chronicle*, 29 Mar. 1873, 7iii.

[6] *Manchester Examiner*, 22 Nov. 1873, 7v–vi, 26 Nov., 7iv–v, 27 Nov., 7iv, 29 Nov., 7iv–v, 5 Dec., 7v.

representing 31 per cent of the total number of companies registered in those years in the English cotton industry. When the boom ended in February 1875 a hundred companies had been created in the hundred months since the beginning of 1868. Thereafter five long years passed, from 1876 to 1880, without the flotation of a single mill-building company as existing limiteds became, during the deep depression of 1877–9, machines for the payment of wages and loan interest rather than of dividends. Two more booms followed the reappearance of high dividends and spawned ten more mill-building companies in 1883–4 and another nine in 1889–90. In sum Oldham formed between 1858 and 1896 154 companies in the cotton industry, or more than twice as many as the 76 registered in Bolton, the second largest centre of company registration. Of the 154 companies 68 or 44 per cent were mill-building ventures, a proportion almost thrice the general average of the industry and representing 44 per cent of the total number launched within the industry. Those massed companies became a socio-economic force, both as construction enterprises and as spinners of yarn. In both respects they created a demand for the factors of production and especially for capital.

* * *

The mill-building companies of 1873–5 had an average nominal capital of £54,190 divided usually into £5 shares on which the first call was normally one of 5*s*. Their average number of shareholders was 343 with an average nominal holding of £158. The turnover companies were smaller, with 17 per cent less nominal capital, 27 per cent fewer spindles, 45 per cent fewer shareholders, but with an average shareholding 50 per cent higher, almost 60 per cent less loan capital, and a much higher proportion of share to loan capital. They included some of the most profitable companies in the borough, with a very low cost per spindle, but they were in general poorer investments than the new companies and proved much more short-lived, being burdened by older buildings and machinery, heavier promotion expenses, and a higher capital–spindleage ratio. The mill-building companies survived the depression of 1877–9 much better than the turnover companies and found more favour in later flotations.

Investors increased in number from one-twelfth of the population of Oldham in 1873 to one-fifth in 1875[1] but still remained a small minority. As local inhabitants they subscribed to shares in a distinctively familiar enterprise in the hope of reaping high dividends but also sought to speculate in premium-taking and simply to follow the fashion. Usually one-third of a company's capital was drawn from persons engaged directly in the cotton industry while the remainder came from those in dependent and associated trades. The share of the working classes in a vastly expanded capital was reduced from above 75 per cent in 1872 to about one-half in 1875 as investment increased by shopkeepers and private spinners, who each supplied about a quarter of the capital. Working men comprised at least three-quarters of the shareholders even if they provided only half of the capital. Cotton operatives supplied some 30 per cent of the shareholders and spread their investments so widely that no working class company as such existed. They preferred not to invest in the mills where they worked: they sought work where they could obtain the highest wages and invested where they could obtain the highest return, so recognizing the divorce between labour and capital. Such wage-earning shareholders were not the low-paid and representative mill-hands but the most highly paid operatives such as mule-minders, overlookers, and roller-coverers from the card-room, together with mechanics, joiners, and masons. They diverted their savings from building societies, loan societies, savings banks, and co-operative societies and their expenditure from clothes, footwear, and hats, especially at Whit and the Wakes, so evoking complaints of bad trade from shoemakers, hatters, and clothiers. Thus a new and democratic source of capital was opened to the local cotton industry through the combination of wage-earners with small capitalists to work a business which might otherwise have been increasingly left to large capitalists. The new companies helped to bridge the gap between such capitalists and mere wage-earners and to prevent any recurrence of the social conflicts characteristic of Oldham before 1850.

The traffic in shares was encouraged by sharebrokers whose

[1] *Co-operative News*, 21 Mar. 1874, 133; *C.W.S. Annual*, 1884, 11.

numbers swelled dramatically to some forty in the boom of 1873–5.[1] That new trade attracted many seekers for an Eldorado in the 'Oldham share Utopia':[2] it lay open to democratic recruitment from almost all walks of life and therein differed markedly from sharebroking outside Oldham, whose first sharebroker established in 1859 had never secured the national recognition allotted to the brokers of Preston or Rochdale.[3] The brokers of Oldham mostly dealt in shares on a cash basis and relied, in the tradition of the Manchester Exchange, upon a simple verbal agreement since they did not use contract-notes. They made the purchase and sale of shares into a regular trade, acted as intermediaries between buyers and sellers, and so encouraged the transfer of shares which earlier co-operators had deemed immoral. No company ever refused to register a transfer of shares and very few limited the number which might be held by any one shareholder since such a provision would have reduced the demand for shares. That demand was stimulated by the use of loans to pay hypnotically attractive dividends, by the general use of the £5 share denomination, and by the charging of the small sum of 5*s*. on initial application for a share. The demand became so great during the flotation fever that it placed a premium upon the value of a share even before allotment and in extreme cases upon a mere share application form. The demand was inflated even further from those seeking a profit from premiums rather than from dividends, which offered far smaller prospective gains. The appetite for such quick profits proved congenial to the local tradition of small-scale capitalism and to the local taste for gambling. It remained unchecked by any legal restrictions since no stamp duty was paid on the transfer of shares before 1884.[4] It was undoubtedly encouraged by the sharebrokers whose activity was condemned as unproductive by hard-headed economic men since it encouraged margin-trading by impecunious speculators and

[1] W. A. Thomas, *The Provincial Stock Exchanges* (London, Cass, 1973), 145–68, 'The Oldham Stock Exchanges and the "Limiteds" '.

[2] *Oldham Chronicle*, 2 Jan. 1875, 8vi, 'A Night with the Share-brokers'.

[3] *Oldham Standard*, 20 May 1876, 8iv, Jonathan Greaves; *The British and Foreign Stock Exchange and Joint Stock Directory* (London, Mann, 1863), 9, 70.

[4] *Oldham Standard*, 5 May 1883, 8ii, 12 May, 8iii, 19 Jan. 1884, 7v; *Textile Manufacturer*, May 1883, 166, 'The Revenue Office and the Oldham Spinning Companies'.

so unduly inflated the demand for shares, pushing the price well above their true economic level. The brokers nevertheless effectively served the new companies as missionary preachers and incited emulation by investment companies and even by land companies. A share exchange was first established in April 1874 and a share list was first published on 2 May 1874.[1] The commission of brokers was kept low by the intense competition within a new trade unconfined by professional restrictions or by the physical limits of a formal stock exchange. Brokers established successive associations in 1874, 1875, and 1890 but failed to establish any control over company flotation[2] or any authority to arbitrate in disputes. The first attempt to build a stock exchange by the Oldham Share Exchange Company Ltd. (1874–6) proved a total failure,[3] apparently because the promoters sought to separate their trade from the taverns where it flourished best in an intoxicating atmosphere. The Lancashire Sharebrokers' Association was established in 1880 but did not secure its own premises until 1883 and did not close its market to the public until 1888. That exchange preserved its independence during the century of its independent existence and did not become a member of the Council of Associated Stock Exchanges formed at Liverpool in 1890.[4]

The limiteds had been created to pay high dividends comparable to those paid in 1871–3. They borrowed money at fixed interest, used it make higher profits, and then paid dividends which were at least twice as high as they could have paid without its aid. From the beginning they issued part-paid shares and used loan capital in the same way and to the same degree as paid-up share capital, i.e. to finance the creation of their fixed capital in mill and machinery. They secured loans even before they began spinning and so departed from the example of the Sun Mill which used loan capital to supplement and not to replace its fully paid-up share capital. They also abandoned the banker's principle of liquidity despite their lack of any of his distinctive resources, especially in mercantile bills, with which to meet any sudden demand for capital.

[1] *Oldham Standard*, 2 May 1874, 5i.
[2] *Oldham Chronicle*, 9 May 1874, 8iv, 10 July 1875, 8v, 17 July, 8vi, vii.
[3] Ibid. 18 Mar. 1876, 8iv.
[4] Thomas, 150–1, 194.

Loans remained quite distinct in law from share capital in so far as they embodied a debt incurred by a company's directors on behalf of its shareholders. They were a liquid investment made by lenders without any legal security other than the good faith of the directors who remained free to mortgage their property up to its full value. They conferred no vote since they did not represent proprietary capital. Their service imposed no prior charge upon assets and their depositors ranked amongst the ordinary unsecured creditors of a company. Loans could however be withdrawn at short notice and were nearly always in practice repayable on demand. The local population welcomed the expansion of such deposit accounts as outlets for their savings and the regular payment thereon of 'use brass' at 5 per cent, providing on those terms half the capital of the spinning companies. Thus the Oldham limiteds were freed from dependence upon the banks by turning themselves into 'informal banks'.[1] They became 'the bankers of the manufacturing population' and 'the savings banks of their several localities'.[2] 'People were beginning to look upon these companies as more in the nature of a bank, where they could bring their surplus capital for investment for a short or long period, and withdraw it when they required it.'[3] The limiteds were able to add the profits of the banker to those of the spinner, so long as their rate of profit exceeded 5 per cent, and to distribute the gains of industry more widely than had thitherto been customary.

Loan capital had long been used in both the commerce and the industry of the region. In the cotton industry credit was used by most private spinners in a variety of forms and at all stages of their operations. In Lancashire co-operative societies had become in effect working-class banks while municipal boroughs, led by Manchester from 1872, began to imitate the example set by Liverpool in 1850 and to borrow small sums against the security of the local rates. The potentialities of loan capital were first fully developed by the Oldham limiteds and to a far greater extent than in any other industry, so creating a

[1] *Oldham Chronicle*, 6 Feb. 1875, 5iv.

[2] *The Times*, 18 Aug. 1875, 10ii. See the advertisements for loans on p. 208 above.

[3] *Oldham Chronicle*, 20 June 1874, 8vi, W. Nuttall.

form of industrial finance peculiar to the cotton trade.[1] That new development was encouraged by the rising wages of the local population and by the birth of interest in industrial shares with their lure of high dividends. Loan accounts were favoured by those investors who were too timid or too prudent to venture their capital in ordinary shares and who therefore preferred security and liquidity to the high but risky returns of shareholders. They afforded a safe investment for the ideal type of the passive rentier in the small saver and the institutional investor such as a co-operative society, a limited company, or a 'going-off club', which could secure the institutional privilege of an additional 1 per cent interest upon their larger deposits. The working classes were especially impressed by such advantages and held a higher proportion of loan capital than of share capital. Their middle ranks thereby secured for the first time a satisfactory investment outlet in their own neighbourhood, offering almost double the 2¾ per cent paid by a savings bank. Loan-holders were drawn mainly from the ranks of small shopkeepers, publicans, engineers, and the leading hands in a cotton mill. The loan accounts of the limiteds became the equivalent of the building society account in the West Riding, attracted investment from outside the borough, and so discouraged the spread of the building society in Lancashire. Within Oldham their success forced into liquidation in 1884 the Oldham Trustee Savings Bank established in 1840.

Companies accepting such loans might borrow on easy terms and at 1 per cent less than the rates available to private spinners, the rate of return on whose capital their competition reduced from 1875. Under the expansive influence of prosperity companies sought to keep their share capital as low as was practical and to swell their loan funds as much as possible. Some security was in effect given to loan-holders in the uncalled portion of share capital, whose existence reflected the survival of the old principle of unlimited liability and provided a reserve

[1] *Manchester Guardian*, 29 Jan. 1875, 4iii, 5 Feb. 1875, 4iv; T. Vogelstein, *Organisationsformen der Eisenindustrie und Textilindustrie in England und Amerika* (Leipzig, Duncker, 1910), 116–22; C. W. von Wieser, *Der finanzielle Aufbau der englischen Industrie* (Jena, Fischer, 1919), 393–423, 'Die Aktienspinnereien von Lancashire'; F. Jones, 'The Cotton Spinning Industry in the Oldham District from 1896 to 1914' (M.A.Econ. thesis, University of Manchester, 1959, 229pp.), 34–62.

fund in case of dire need. The delicate balance between shares and loans varied with the state of trade and the fortunes of the individual company. The uncalled portion of share capital could not be too great lest it should discourage shareholders but could not be too low lest it should fail to reassure loan-holders. In 1877 41 new companies held almost twice as much of their capital in loans as in shares and the full complement of 72 companies derived over 56 per cent of their total capital from loans.[1] The use of such funds became an institution because banks paid too low a rate of interest to depositors and not because they restricted the supply of credit to spinning companies. Loan accounts did not compete directly with bank deposits and in fact made it necessary for companies to maintain an overdraft at the bank in order to meet day-to-day calls and to receive deposits. Thus to a large extent their use created custom for the banks, especially for the C.W.S.,[2] and made their business more profitable and safe than ever before. Loans served as a substitute not for bank credit but for debentures and preference shares, to which they were no legal equivalent since they conferred only a claim upon earnings without any prior charge on assets or any proprietary rights.

The rate of interest paid was sanctioned by custom and could not be reduced from its traditional level of 5 per cent by the unilateral decision of any single company. That rate did not vary with the condition of the money market in England but with the condition of that in Oldham, with the general state of trade, and, most of all, with the position of the individual company. Companies could attract capital on favourable terms if their mills lay within rather than outside the borough, were not saddled with a mortgage or with preference shares, had leading shareholders well known to be solvent, had a large depreciation fund, and did not require long notice before repaying deposits. Above all, companies could always secure loans if they were efficient and competitive and were known so to be. Such companies might borrow at 3 per cent when less efficient companies had to pay the full 5 per cent or even 6 per cent. The extensive use of loan capital was thus as much a sign of strength and a testimony of local confidence in the

[1] *Textile Manufacturer*, June 1877, 180; *Manchester Examiner*, 14 July 1877, 4v.
[2] *Oldham Chronicle*, 15 Sept. 1877, 6vi.

limited companies as it would have been a sign of weakness in a private firm.[1] Some first-class companies preferred to confine the privilege to their own shareholders and then paid them the full 5 per cent, so securing to them the best of both worlds. Others found it useful in time of prosperity to have more loan capital than they needed and reinvested it in other less credit-worthy companies at the same interest rate, so as to avoid keeping idle capital in hand whilst maintaining their prestige. In so confidently relending they fulfilled the function of a bank but did so at the risk of the directors rather than of the shareholders and renounced the higher interest rate which a bank would have exacted. The practice of relending undoubtedly inflated contemporary estimates of the total amount of loan capital and exaggerated the degree of dependence of the limiteds upon borrowed money.

Some companies could limit the amount loanable by any one person or institution, in order to protect themselves from the possibility of any undue pressure. Loan-holders in general remained isolated and unorganized, like consumers, and lacked any organization comparable to an association of sharebrokers or shareholders but became in the mass almost as important as shareholders in supporting their company and its share prices. They bore the risks of poor management and bad trade in a degree second only to the shareholders. Their influence proved beneficial in bringing to bear the judgement of outsiders upon the trading career of a company. The limiteds never defaulted in the regular payment of interest which became in effect a primary charge upon their profits, since failure to pay would have been tantamount to a declaration of bankruptcy. They readily accepted the risk of a possible panic efflux of capital which might compel them to suspend operations because the profits accruing from the use of loan capital were deemed to be an ample compensation. The use of loans constrained companies to maintain their market quotation at all costs and may have tempted some to take stock incorrectly in order temporarily to increase their dividends for purposes of speculation. The high dividends made possible in good times by the use of loans gave a fictitious appearance of prosperity to the cotton trade, to the alarm and horror of private spinners who regarded such divi-

[1] A. D. Shaw, *The Cotton Goods Trade of Lancashire* (1883), 17.

dends as monstrous. Those artificial dividends exaggerated not only the level of profits in the industry but also any increase in their level, so attracting into the trade new masses of blind and hungry capital and stimulating successive waves of mill building. The use of loan capital nevertheless opened a new source of finance to industry, and reduced the barriers to the entry of new talent created by the increasing capitalization of industry.

The depression of 1876–9 provided the new system of industrial finance with its first severe test. The reliance upon loan capital eliminated all dividends as soon as profits sank below 5 per cent because loan interest maintained a prior claim upon earnings and few companies had the reserve funds from which to pay dividends. Loans were not however withdrawn despite the drastic depreciation in share prices[1] because investors with eminent sobriety deemed their money to be as secure as investments in real estate or in the public funds, so enabling the depression to be borne with fewer failures than had thitherto been customary and proving wrong the doom-laden prophecies made by private spinners. Most companies benefited by the presence of many shareholders among their loan-holders and their aversion to further calls in the event of any drain on the loan account. Some were able to issue preference shares to their shareholders but 31 out of 71 companies were forced to effect mortgages at rates as high as 6 per cent or even 7½ per cent, in order to avert further calls and so avert imminent collapse. Such mortgages increased the burden of fixed costs involved in interest payments and deterred institutional lenders, especially co-operative societies. No company dared to repudiate either loans or the interest thereon, despite the heavy and growing burden of the fixed interest. The limiteds became in effect machines for paying interest to loan-holders rather than dividends to shareholders as they could not afford to resort to short-time working.

When interest rates rose during 1876 to 6 per cent only the best companies could restrict payment of the new rate to investors of large amounts above £500 for six months at three months' notice. Other less fortunate companies vainly proposed the formation of an association to reduce the rate to 5 per cent

[1] *Oldham Chronicle*, 29 Dec. 1877, 7ii, 28 Dec. 1878, 6vi; Ellison, 137, transposes the figures for 1877 and 1878.

but were forced to pay the price demanded by loan-holders.[1] Companies were reluctantly forced to call up more capital from their shareholders in order to reduce the burden of loan interest and to give added security to loan-holders. The tendency to expand the use of loan capital characteristic of the preceding boom was thus checked and reversed: the proportion borne by share capital to total capital rose from 44 per cent in 1877 to 55 per cent in 1881.[2] In the later booms and slumps the same pattern recurred, of an increased use of loan capital during prosperity and its decreased use during depression, but the average proportion of share capital never sank after 1886

TABLE 14

Proportion of Share Capital to Total Capital of the Oldham Limiteds, 1877–1896

Year	Number of Companies	Total Capital	Paid-up Share Capital	Proportion of Total (%)	Source
1877	72	4,120,000	1,787,000	43·37	*Textile Manufacturer*, June 1877, 180
1881	70	5,340,827	2,936,099	55	*Co-operative News*, 12 Aug. 1882, 543
1882	69	5,281,422	2,892,248	54·76	*Manchester Guardian*, 30 Dec. 1882, 4v
1883	72	6,234,006	3,843,256	61·65	*The Statist*, 2 Feb. 1884, 127
1885	73	6,691,212	3,145,851	47·01	*Business History*, Dec. 1961, 52–3, R. Smith
1886	90	6,891,103	3,455,676	50·15	*Royal Commission on the Depression of Trade and Industry, Third Report*, 1886 Appendix A.viii, 308, J. Kidger
1890	88	6,711,436	3,491,851	52	B. Jones, *Cooperative Production* (1894), i. 304–5
1891	101	8,908,456	5,029,861	56·5	*Oldham Standard*, 26 Dec. 1891, 8vi
1892	99	7,255,732	3,692,635	50·9	Ibid., 31 Dec. 1892, 2vii
1893	99	7,720,904	3,960,153	51·3	Ibid., 23 Dec. 1893, 8v
1894	94	7,100,073	3,823,252	53·8	Ibid., 29 Dec. 1894, 7iv
1895	94	6,700,906	3,662,164	54·6	Ibid., 28 Dec. 1895, 7iv
1896	94	6,766,407	3,852,274	56·93	Ibid., 26 Dec. 1896, 7iv

[1] *Textile Manufacturer*, Feb. 1877, 48; *Manchester Examiner*, 14 July 1877, 4v.

[2] *Textile Manufacturer*, June 1877, 180; *Manchester Guardian*, 30 Dec. 1882, 4v; see Table 14.

below half the total for the remainder of the century. The use of loan capital provided the cotton trade of Oldham with a stable financial basis until the 1920s but undoubtedly accentuated competition because it was attracted more easily to new than to old companies and because its rigid demands discouraged mills from resorting to short-time working as a remedy for overproduction.

Capital remained far more important than labour as a factor of production in cotton spinning and frustrated by its pervasive influence any attempt to remould the limiteds upon a co-operative basis. To some idealists the new companies seemed to represent a form of producers' co-operation, to portend the emancipation of the operatives from their occupational thraldom, and to bring nearer the advent in the greatest of modern industries of a working-class millenium based upon industrial partnership. Certainly the limiteds might have created an identity of purpose and interest and a community of advantage and risk between employer and employee by encouraging their operatives to acquire shares or at least by paying a symbolic bonus to labour. Such a gesture would have been quixotic and uneconomic in companies investing £400 in capital for each employee. The limiteds therefore remained true to their nature as associations of capitalists dedicated to the making of private profit and compelled to compete with private firms and with other limiteds. They were all registered under the Companies Acts rather than under the Industrial and Provident Societies Acts: they all excluded the word 'co-operative' from their titles and, if they advertised in the *Co-operative News*, did so under the rubric of 'Public Companies' and not under that of 'Co-operative Production'. They adopted no constitutional guarantees either against the transfer of shares or against their accumulation into very few hands during the course of time. None paid more than the market price for labour and none offered to take their hands into industrial partnership. Not one offered a bonus to labour or limited its dividends to shareholders.[1] All of their profits they gave to capital, which they

[1] *Co-operative News*, 21 Sept. 1872, 483, W. Nuttall, 'Co-operation and Social Science'; J. Watts, 'Co-operation considered as an Economic Element in Society', *Transactions of the Manchester Statistical Society*, 13 Nov. 1872, 11, reprinted in *Co-operative News*, 30 Nov. 1872, 602, and separately (Manchester, North of

could secure upon no other terms. Their shareholders declined to share those profits with non-shareholding workers since profits were largely independent of the work of the mill-hands and payment by piece-work already provided the greatest incentive to application. Thus the limiteds exalted the financial above the moral benefits of co-operation, fostered individual selfishness, and created a new class of small capitalists, so facilitating the elevation of the few rather than the many.

The new companies were not in fact intended to elevate the masses and were expressly welcomed by *The Times* as 'voluntary missionaries of capital among the mass of labourers' and as an aid to the conservation of order in English society.[1] In following the example of Bacup rather than that of Rochdale they became *Gesellschaften* rather than *Gemeinschaften*, hybrid products of co-operative productive societies and joint-stock companies. Using the principles of association in the interests of individualism and recognizing the cash-nexus as the sole link between their members they could not introduce any higher morality into ordinary life. Oldham in fact fragmented the very principle of co-operation in creating 'its joint-stock "tubs", each standing on its own bottom, with their separate stock and their separate boards of directors, and their separate dividends'.[2] The function of the limiteds seemed to older co-operators to be to 'multiply organisations for the individual rather than the common profit, and enlarge the field of strikes, and prepare ground for contests between capital and labour more furious and savage than any which have hitherto occurred'.[3] Above all, such companies encouraged the spirit of speculation and discouraged the growth of true producers' co-operatives by attracting investment by co-operative societies. Thus they

England Co-operative Printing Society, 1872, 24pp.), 20; idem, *The Working Man: a Problem. A Lecture delivered at the Mechanics' Institution, Manchester, November 6th, 1875* (Manchester, Central Co-operative Board, 1875, 24pp.), 23, reprinted in *Co-operative News*, 19 Feb. 1876, 87; Lloyd Jones, 'Letters to the Co-operators of the United Kingdom No. VI—Banking, &c.', *Industrial Review*, 26 May 1877, 3, reprinted as *Co-operation; its Position, its Policy and its Prospects* (London, Potter, 1877, 31pp.), 24–6.

[1] *The Times*, 18 Aug. 1875, 9iii.

[2] *Co-operative News*, 22 July 1876, 395, E. V. Neale, 'Oldham and Co-operation', by the General Secretary from 1873 to 1891 of the Central Co-operative Board.

[3] G. J. Holyoake, *The History of Co-operation in England: its Literature and Advocates* (London, Trübner, 1879), ii. 123.

effectively closed and barred the door to any seekers for a new moral world. The wish to reaffirm the original principle of co-operation inspired the projection of a Co-operative Village Company Ltd., which was designed to undertake co-operative cotton spinning and farming on the sea-coast of Lancashire and so to crown the whole structure of the limiteds in a more congenial atmosphere than that of Oldham.[1] The formation of that company was frustrated by the depression of 1877–9.

The later joint-stock booms of 1883–4 and 1889–90 aroused new waves of censure from co-operators, especially at the seventeenth Co-operative Congress, held at Oldham in 1885. The sturdy local defenders of the limiteds remained wholly unabashed by the criticism that their dividends had become an end in themselves and urged in reply that 'capital had its rights as well as labour'[2] and that the joint-stock company remained far superior to the private firm as a social entity and as an economic unit. In their eyes the limiteds were managed by working men and were 'co-operative in everything but the name'[3] and had proved the best, surest, and most successful form of co-operative production so far instituted. The limiteds had enabled small capitalists to break the industrial monopoly of large capitalists and had taught others how best to invest their savings. They had built lofty, well-ventilated buildings with every care and consideration for the labourers, so extending to them an indirect share in profits.[4] Such pleas largely ignored the main reproach that the limiteds gave the workman as such little hope for the future unless he became a capitalist since they recognized not him but only the capitalist. That defence nevertheless embodied the true spirit of co-operation in Oldham which seemed to prefer pure capitalist companies to middle-class companies and middle-class companies to working-class companies. Oldham became 'Diviborough' rather than 'a practical commercial democracy'[5] and oscillated sharply between the Liberal and Conservative poles in its

[1] W. Marcroft, *A Co-operative Village: How to Conduct It and Where to Form It* (Manchester, Central Co-operative Board, 1878, 20pp.).

[2] *Co-operative News*, 30 May 1885, 483, J. F. Brearley.

[3] Ibid. 7 Apr. 1883, 292, T. R. Marsden, 30 May 1885, 477, Lloyd Jones.

[4] Ibid. 7 Apr. 1883, 286, 291, 292, 30 May 1885, 477, 483–6.

[5] W. Marcroft, *The Companies Circular. Part First* (Oldham, Clegg, 1879, 16pp.), 16; *Textile Mercury*, 3 June 1893, 417.

choice of parliamentary representatives, returning two Conservative M.P.s in the prosperous years of 1874–7, 1886–92, and 1895–9. Its companies were discounted by the new generation of intellectuals as not even partially co-operative concerns and as mere 'working class limiteds'.[1]

* * *

The limiteds were inevitably less important as employers of labour than of capital but nevertheless opened up to the indigenous working class new opportunities for employment. The number of hands employed in the mills of Oldham rose from 23,000 in 1872 to 36,000 in 1883 and to 49,000 in 1896. The operative population of the borough surpassed that of Bury, Preston, Stockport, Manchester, and Ashton to rank third after that of Blackburn and Bolton. The total population of Oldham rose during the boom of the 1870s by 35 per cent from 82,628 in 1871 to 111,343 in 1881[2] and surpassed that of Blackburn to become the first town of 100,000 inhabitants on the Pennine frontier of Lancashire. During that period of expansion the power of the local trade unions was undermined by the increase in capital invested in the cotton industry, by the introduction of outside labour, by the extension of the employment of women, by the persistent competition of the engineering industry for juvenile labour, and by the continuing increase in the length of mules as well as in their speed of operation, encouraged especially by the Factory Act of 1874. The operative spinners lost ground to the piecers between 1871 and 1875 but secured the fundamental principle of gross earnings in the Oldham spinning list of 1875[3] and gained all the speed-allowance paid thereunder at the expense of the piecers, raising their earnings with the increase in output. Until 1877

[1] B. Potter, *The Co-operative Movement in Great Britain* (London, Sonnenschein, 1891), 126–33; A. Marshall, *Principles of Economics* (London, Macmillan, 2nd edn., 1891, omitted from 1st edn. of 1890), i. 364; R. H. I. Palgrave (ed.), *Dictionary of Political Economy* (London, Macmillan, 1894), i. 417–18, E. B. Osborn, 'Co-operation, Partial (Oldham Cotton-Spinning Companies)'.

[2] *Textile Manufacturer*, May 1881, 165.

[3] *Oldham Standard*, 15 Jan. 1876, 8vi; H. Sidgwick, 'The Regulation of Wages by means of Lists in the Cotton Industry', *Report of the British Association*, 1887, 311; J. Jewkes and E. M. Gray, *Wages and Labour in the Lancashire Cotton Spinning Industry* (Manchester University Press, 1935), 66–71.

they enjoyed a prosperity absent elsewhere in Lancashire and were then forced to accept four successive wage reductions in two years, not regaining the list prices of 1876 until 1900. The reduction in wage rates by 20 per cent effected a lasting lowering of costs since the limiteds had become during the depression machines for paying wages and loan interest rather than dividends and had revealed both their incapacity to maintain wage levels and their essential similarity to private employers. Thereafter no fresh influx of working-class capital took place into the new limiteds of the 1880s and the town became a battleground between capital and labour as the Oldham Spinners' Union organized from 1880 the spinners of American cotton throughout south-east Lancashire and extended the influence of the Oldham List. The spinners successfully resisted attempts by the masters to reduce them to the level of superior piecers and forced their employers to accept compromise settlements in the strikes of 1885 and 1893, so making Oldham the home of the standard wage rate and of collective bargaining. By extending the demand for labour the limiteds compelled capital to compete for its services, to pay more for increased production, and to become more of a constitutional monarch than an autocrat.

The limited spinning companies became vehicles for the education of 20,000 shareholders as well as for the employment of 500 directors. Most companies were democratic in organization but a minority were oligarchic from their inception. Most allowed shareholders to own as many shares as they wished but adopted the principle of 'one man, one vote' and, unlike the Sun Mill under its rules of 1867, did not permit votes to be weighed in proportion to the number of shares held. Such a principle assumed that the company was a union of persons in accordance with the tradition of Roman law and of the medieval corporation but in defiance of the modern principle of the joint stock, which remained a union of capital and not of persons. The allotment of equal votes to the nine-tenths of the shareholders outside the oligarchic companies was in profound agreement with the radical egalitarian spirit of the 'Oldham rough-heads' who would tolerate no pretensions by others to superiority. Such a democratic principle worked very well in practice, prevented control from passing into the hands of the few, enlisted the moral support of the many, and permitted attendance even by women at the quarterly meetings. Shareholders took great pride in their mill and had extensive technical knowledge of the industry, as well as an insatiable hunger for dividends. Their reluctance to countenance any separation of control from ownership and their relentless supervision of the directors and principal servants fulfilled an educational function and proved all the more effective because the companies were local entities constantly under their eyes, quarterly meetings were frequent, and relevant information might be gleaned from the published balance sheets, the local press, and dissident directors or employees. Such shareholders proved to be the strictest of economists and were prepared to oust a whole board which failed to produce an acceptable balance sheet, displaying as much ruthlessness as the Athenian Ecclesia or the leaders of the French Revolution towards their unsuccessful generals. Thus they never found it necessary to take criminal action against any director for the abuse of his trust. They never subscribed however to the democratic principle of 'one man, one directorship' and failed to curb the pluralistic proclivities of the promoter–directors of the 1880s, being compelled to form in protest a Shareholders' Protection Association in 1889.[1]

The depression of 1877–9 marked the end of the golden age of the working-class limiteds but proved their capacity for survival. That crisis inflicted heavier losses through depreciation of their share values on working men's companies than on oligarchic companies with their higher share denominations. It discouraged working men from investing in shares, diverted their expenditure back to consumer goods, and attracted their investments back to the traditional sphere of cottage property, supplemented by insurance companies and building societies. The new companies of the 1880s were much more oligarchic than their predecessors and tended, especially in Shaw, to be semi-private limiteds, launched by cliques of mill officials, and financed by wealthier investors. The ten mill-building companies of 1883–4 had an average nominal capital of £81,000 or 48 per cent more than that of the limiteds of 1874–5. Their average number of shareholders was 125 or only one-third of that of

[1] *Oldham Chronicle*, 9 Feb. 1889, 8vi.

their predecessors and the average nominal holding of each investor was £650 or fourfold that in their forerunners. Six of the ten companies preferred the £100 share to the much more marketable £5 share and insisted on a minimum subscription to at least five shares. Five companies carried the desire for privacy to the extent of not publishing their accounts and so inaugurated a new and secretive trend away from the publicity essential to democratically financed companies. The nine mill-building companies of 1889–90 had an average nominal capital of £83,500 in £10 shares but only on average 83 shareholders,[1] or 35 per cent less than that of the limiteds of 1883–4, with an average nominal holding of £1,000 or half as much again as that typical of the companies of 1883–4. Seven of the nine were in fact semi-private limiteds which did not publish their accounts or mould their policy in accordance with a market quotation but quietly maintained a respectable level of dividend payments. By 1894 94 companies published their accounts while 16, including 13 established in 1889–91, did not. Such semi-private limiteds increased notably in popularity during the boom of 1904–7.

In general the Oldham limiteds of 1873–89 failed to produce the anticipated returns of 25 per cent which did not reappear until the booms of 1904–7 and 1918–20. Inevitably they paid much lower dividends than their precursors. Even with the aid of loan capital the average dividend paid upon the share capital of 79 limiteds over the twenty years 1877–96 was only 3·7 per cent,[2] or a quarter of the dividends paid by the local co-operative societies and one-eighth of the amount paid out in wages.[3] Their published trading profits were some 90 per cent higher than their distributed dividends and averaged 7 per cent during 1877–96, including the interest paid on share and loan capital. Those profits exclude the gains made by private spinners and by semi-private limiteds and cannot be taken as representative

[1] Excluding the Holly Mill of 1890 which with 341 shareholders, each with an average holding of £205, reverted to the democratic pattern of 1874.

[2] *Oldham Chronicle*, 13 June 1885, 8vi, for 1877–84, 22 Dec. 1900, 8vi, for 1877–99; *Oldham Standard*, 31 Dec. 1887, 8iv, for 1877–87; 26 Dec. 1891, 8v, for 1884–91, 31 Dec. 1892, 2vi, 23 Dec. 1893, 8iii, 29 Dec. 1894, 7iv, 28 Dec. 1895, 7iii, for 1884–94, 26 Dec. 1896, 7iii; *Discussion on International Bimetallism at the Manchester Chamber of Commerce. Full Report of the Three Days' Debate April 13th and 27th, and 4th May 1892* (Manchester, Cornish, 1892, 96pp.), 66, J. C. Fielden, 4 May 1892.

[3] *Oldham Standard*, 17 Aug. 1894, 3v.

either of the Oldham spinning trade or of the spinning industry as a whole. Of the 79 limiteds 27 turnover companies paid an average of 3·34 per cent while 52 mill-building companies paid a dividend one-sixth higher, of 3·9 per cent. The later companies proved more successful, six limiteds of 1883–4 paying an average dividend of 6·34 per cent and two limiteds of 1889–90 paying one of 6·6 per cent. Those concerns achieved their success however over a much shorter period of time and purchased it at the expense of the older companies, especially during the unprecedented depression of 1892–4 when the limiteds suffered an average annual net loss on their paid-up capital of 1·7 per cent. In general the limiteds remained machines for the payment of interest on loans, for the creation of employment, and for the production of yarn. They had however succeeded in their primary aim of survival at the price of transforming the local spinning trade into 'a huge machine for paying wages'.[1]

The erection of the new mills strained the capacity of the construction industries to the limit and created pressing new demands for land and for real capital. Land was cheaper in Oldham than in any neighbouring town: it was not locked up in great estates but was split up into many separate properties, because of the hilly nature of the locality, and was thus easily purchasable. The mill-building boom placed a premium on favourable sites with access to roads, a railway station, coal, good clay, and the abundant water so necessary in Oldham. The exhaustion of suitable sites within a radius of one mile from the town's centre shifted the centre of mill flotation in the 1880s northwards to Shaw, or Crompton, on the road to Rochdale. The rental and rateable values of land near the mills was permanently raised as house building soared to a peak level of activity in 1877. Cottage property reached its peak value in 1876 but thereafter relapsed by 1882 to a level 6 per cent below its value in 1872.[2] The boom brought wealth to landowners, increased the commissions of estate agents, and even led to the formation of land companies, which sought to create chief rents rather than profitable spinners of yarn, so saddling some unfor-

[1] *Oldham Chronicle*, 19 Jan. 1889, 6iii, 26 Jan., 6v, J. Taylor, chairman of the Sun Mill Company.

[2] *Oldham Standard*, 26 Aug. 1882, 4vi, 'The Value of Property in Oldham. Ten Years Ago and Now'.

tunate companies with a heavy chief rent or with high transport costs. The increase in the sale and lease of land benefited accountants, auctioneers and valuers, and, above all, solicitors. The subsequent liquidation of turnover companies in 1877–9 proved almost as profitable to accountants as their earlier flotation had been. The limited mania endowed Oldham with a substantial professional class, geared to the service of local industry.

The building boom stimulated the production and sale of building materials, creating employment for brick-makers and stone merchants, timber merchants and saw-mill proprietors, joiners and builders, slaters and labourers. The basic material used in mill building was brick rather than the dearer stone favoured in Yorkshire. Bricks were made first by the companies themselves on the site and then by brick-makers, who increased more rapidly than the members of any other trade and almost trebled in number between 1870 and 1875. A large new market was opened up to mill-furnishers and to all the ancillary trades. The engineering trades benefited directly as machinery prices rose in 1877 to a peak one-third higher than in 1869. Platt Brothers could not keep pace with the demand for machines, even by the use of night shifts, but were protected against competition by their well-established reputation in the market and by the large capital necessary to enter the trade. They benefited by the local patriotism of the shareholders in the limiteds, including their own employees, and succeeded in extending the period of mill building from one to two and even to three years, so that they could profitably equip the mills of Bombay at the same time as those of Oldham. They increased the number of their hands by 29 per cent from 7,000 in 1871 to 9,000 in 1880[1] and established the undisputed primacy of Oldham in machine-making as well as in cotton spinning. Thus they reaped quasi-monopoly profits on their sales from 1872, and even more from 1875. Their net profits during the five years ending at Easter 1877 averaged 34 per cent per annum or fivefold those of the spinning mills they equipped.[2]

* * *

[1] *Co-operative News*, Sept. 1871, 10; *Textile Manufacturer*, Nov. 1880, 401.

[2] Annual Reports of Platt Brothers & Co. Ltd., 1869–80, in the Archives Department of the Manchester Central Library.

As specialized spinning firms the limiteds made a large addition to the spinning power of the industry, especially in the production of counts of 32, and notably extended the area of the best technical practice, so deriving a substantial incremental advantage from the possession of new machinery. They built tall and wide mills,[1] installed high-pressure horizontal compound steam-engines to drive wider cards and longer mules than had hitherto been customary, and ensured the mass triumph of the self-actor in the Oldham district. The mills of 1874–5 raised the normal size of a modern mill from 20,000 to 50,000 spindles, or to double the size of the average Lancashire mill. The mills of 1883–4 had an average spindleage of 75,000 and those of 1889–90 one of 90,000. The average size of the Oldham limited rose by over a third from 59,000 spindles in 1883 to 81,000 in 1896, or to eightfold the average size of the mills of Japan, and the average size of the Oldham mill surpassed that of Manchester to approach that of Bolton. The machinery of the limiteds was operated at faster speeds, especially after the introduction of the speed list of 1875 which penalized employers preferring to work with short and slow mules rather than to renew their machinery. Their 'mushroom managers', recruited from the indigenous working class rather than from the immigrant Irish, competed to excel one another in the quality of their yarn and the level of their dividends.[2] Their directors were skilled and experienced, having mostly been brought up in the business of cotton spinning. They paid no unnecessary managerial salaries, sought to reduce the commissions earned by cotton brokers and yarn agents,[3] and invited tenders for the purchase of their cotton waste, so compelling the waste dealers in self-defence to form the Cotton Waste Dealers Association Ltd. (1883–91). Their shrewd and able salesmen and buyers were as gregarious as shipowners and quickly diffused a knowledge of improvements and economies. Their accounts were usually balanced quarterly and the results

[1] *Textile Manufacturer*, June 1876, 153–7, 'Modern Mill Architecture' (The Abbey Mill Spinning Company Ltd., Oldham).

[2] *Cotton Factory Times*, 4 Dec. 1885, 1i, 'Then and Now, or Oldham Slave Driving', 24 Feb. 1888, 1i, iii, 'Minders' Wages in the Oldham District', 5 July 1889, 1i, 5 Feb. 1892, 1i, 19 Jan. 1894, 1iii, 'The Limited Companies not a Blessing'.

[3] Ibid., 1 May 1885, 5v, 'Commissions in the Cotton Trade. Yarn Agents'; *Textile Manufacturer*, Aug. 1885, 364–6, 'The Yarn Agent'.

published within three days. Such publication was exceptional in Lancashire but became the rule in Oldham as the necessary adjunct to a share market. The limiteds were not models of the best financial practice of the day: they used single-entry book-keeping or the simple cash accounts favoured by the local co-operative societies,[1] accumulated no reserves, and made a low allowance for depreciation as the mania for dividends triumphed over the old concept of ownership.

The limiteds ushered in a new era of competition in the spinning industry of Oldham and Lancashire. They flung down a direct challenge to the private spinner because they did not lease room and turning in the Oldham tradition but built new mills of the largest possible size and used loan capital to the utmost feasible extent. Their competitive advantages were reinforced by their limited liability, their jealousy of each other, and their inability in times of recession to agree to work short time. The private spinners believed that working men might make retail stores pay but could not manage spinning mills: they were shaken in their self-esteem by the success of the limiteds and harassed by the consequent decline in their profit margins. They therefore criticized them with the same fervour as shopkeepers had abused the co-operative stores in the 1850s and charged them with a whole variety of financial malpractices. They declared that the companies cooked their balance sheets, underdepreciated their plant, overestimated their stock, distrusted their buyers, salesmen, and managers and paid them comparatively poor wages. The loan capital on which they relied to excess seemed to their critics a fair-weather source of funds, would be withdrawn when bad trade came and would so force the limiteds to sell their mills to private employers.[2] Those eager prophets of doom were proved wrong by the demonstration that wage-earners could make industrial production profitable under their own control as managers.[3] The private spinners of Oldham still added to their plant during the 1870s but lacked the resilience of their counterparts in Bolton, Stockport, Ashton, or Rochdale and lost much of the family fortunes locked up in combined mills as they reduced their spindleage

[1] *Oldham Chronicle*, 12 Oct. 1889, 6v.
[2] *Co-operative News*, 7 Apr. 1877, 167, W. Nuttall.
[3] Ibid. 22 July 1876, 395, E. V. Neale.

from the 1880s.[1] Their spindles declined between 1884 and 1896 by 413,000 or by 6·4 per cent of the 6·5 million private spindles in Oldham in 1884. Their share of the total spindleage declined from 67 per cent in 1884 to 55 per cent in 1896. But they still retained control of a majority of the spindles of the borough and of the greatest single units of local enterprise. Eleven of the eighty largest firms in the industry were located in Oldham but included only two limiteds. The other nine were all private firms and six were still unincorporated in 1896. The largest local firms were indeed small in comparison to those elsewhere, especially after Samuel Radcliffe & Sons Ltd., one of the industry's twelve leading firms, disintegrated between 1890 and 1892 under the competition of the limiteds of Shaw. The private firms remained unchallenged in the manufacture of those specialized products which conferred prestige upon Oldham in the trade. They preserved their own employers' association and admitted the limiteds to membership from 1875[2] but sabotaged every short-time movement begun by the limiteds and prevented them from forming their own association until 1877. They formed their own private limiteds, especially from 1888, and so strengthened their competitive position.

The limiteds supplied more of the increment in the spinning power of Oldham from 1874 than in any other town. They installed some 68 per cent of the increment in the spindles of Oldham between 1870 and 1890 and some 46·3 per cent of the increment in spindleage laid down by all mill-building limiteds in the cotton industry between 1860 and 1896. The mill-building limiteds added 2·2 million spindles or 73·4 per cent of the three million laid down in Oldham between 1870 and 1877. Between 1884 and 1896 sixteen new mill-building limiteds added another 1·53 million spindles or 87 per cent of the 1·754 million added therein. Their achievement nevertheless remained circumscribed by the abiding presence of the private firm. The 3·222 million spindles of the mill-building limiteds in 1884 represented 68·6 per cent of the spindleage in spinning companies

[1] *Oldham Chronicle*, 22 Dec. 1900, 8vi, S. Andrew.

[2] According to Samuel Andrew in the *Oldham Chronicle*, 22 Dec. 1900, 8vii, the proportion of limited companies in the Oldham Master Cotton Spinners' Association rose from 60 or 34 per cent of the total membership of 177 firms in 1875 to 116 or 76 per cent of the total number of 153 in 1900.

(including turnover and private limiteds) but only 39·4 per cent of that in spinning firms and only 33·2 per cent of the total spindleage of Oldham. Their spindleage of 5·08 million in 1896 represented 66 per cent of the spindles in spinning companies but only 51 per cent of those in spinning firms and only 45 per cent of the total spindleage. Such mill-building companies became more important in Oldham than in any other cotton town and limited the share of the corporate spindleage controlled by turnovers and private limiteds to only 31·4 per cent in 1884 and to 33·8 per cent in 1896. They increased the importance of the specialized spinning firm and helped to raise the proportion of Oldham's spindleage in spinning-only firms from 84·3 per cent in 1884 to 88·7 per cent in 1896 as combined firms reduced their spindleage. The relative importance of spinning in the local cotton trade increased as the looms of Oldham declined from their peak level of 1886.[1]

Oldham became the birthplace of the mill-building company, erected thrice as many mills as churches and chapels, and constructed them as though they were little more than new houses. It added 5·5 million spindles or 34·4 per cent of the 16 million spindles laid down in Lancashire between 1870 and 1890, increasing its share of the industry's spindleage to a peak of 27 per cent in 1893. The town became the hub and pulse of the spinning trade and its share market became the best barometer of the state of trade. It extended its influence in south-east Lancashire, especially in Ashton and Rochdale, through the medium of its engineers, its mill architects, its functional type of mill, its counts of yarn, its cotton buying company, its spinners' union, its speed-spinning list of 1875, its mode of payment by the yarn indicator, and its hours of work. The spinning power of Oldham contributed to the contraction of spinning in Rossendale and north-east Lancashire,[2] to the decline of the combined firm, and to the geographical segregation of the spinning industry in south-east Lancashire. Its limiteds became increasingly blamed from the 1880s for the greater frequency, duration, and influence of commercial

[1] *Manchester Guardian*, 11 Jan. 1886, 4v, 'Oldham as a Weaving Centre'.

[2] *Manchester Guardian*, 2 Oct. 1882, 4iii, 11 Jan. 1884, 4v, 5 Oct. 1885, 4v; *Textile Manufacturer*, May 1884, 216, July 1884, 316; *Rochdale Observer*, 6 Dec. 1884, 2v.

depressions. The rise of Oldham did not however retard the expansion of the spinning industry of Bolton, which preserved its family firms, the largest mills in the industry, and its medium-fine trade, which produced value where Oldham produced weight.

Oldham became in 1873–5 the leading centre of the joint-stock company in England, with more limited companies than any other manufacturing town in the country and with thirty turnover companies outside the cotton industry. 'The whole town is rapidly becoming one huge joint stock concern.'[1] The limiteds followed the example of the co-operative societies and took the very bold step of investing the funds of their stockholders in the establishment of new companies outside the field of cotton spinning, so extending the influence of 'joint-stockism' and erecting a secondary structure of dependent companies. The leading limiteds formed the Federative Insurance Company Ltd. (1875–97) on the American model of a mutual insurance association under the pressure of the increased frequency in mill fires caused by the increase in the running speeds of machinery: they thereby secured a reduction in mill insurance rates by a half between 1876 and 1885. They formed their own Limited Liability Association in 1877[2] but proved unable to reduce wages except by reaching agreement with the private employers. The Oldham Joint Stock Bank Ltd. was however formed in 1880 by the leading private spinners and not by the limiteds. It was the first truly local bank possessed by Oldham since 1847 and preserved its independence until 1898: it drove a rival to the wall within four years, expanded its interests to Rochdale in 1882, and freed the private firms from dependence on the Manchester banks, as the limiteds had emancipated themselves by the use of loan capital. The Oldham Incorporated Chamber of Commerce was also established by private spinners, for the yarn trade, in 1882 and was registered as a company in 1883:[3] its creation enlarged the local sphere of corporate action and brought the limiteds into closer association with the private spinners. Thus the cause of the limiteds was ably defended by the spokesmen of the Oldham Employers'

[1] *Manchester Examiner*, 1 Feb. 1875, 3v.
[2] *Oldham Standard*, 4 Aug. 1877, 3vii, 8 Sept., 8iv.
[3] *Textile Manufacturer*, Sept. 1881, 338, Jan. 1883, 29.

Association before the Royal Commission on the Depression of Trade in 1885.

The boldest feat of the new companies was to engage in the corporate purchase of raw cotton in a bid to reduce the high commissions charged by the brokers of Liverpool on deliveries to the largest single centre of consumption. The Cotton Buying Company Ltd. (1881–1928) was established by 16 of the wealthiest limiteds on the model of the C.W.S.[1] and enlarged its membership almost fivefold by 1889 to 75 companies, of which nearly half lay outside Oldham in Ashton, Royton, Shaw, Rochdale, and Bury. The new company divided its profits on the co-operative principle as a bonus to customers and paid a double bonus to shareholding clients. After a slow start its sales increased even more rapidly than its membership, compelling brokers to compete for the custom of spinners and to mitigate the deplorable practice of charging double brokerage. It took up shares in the Manchester Ship Canal Company in 1890, so financing a tertiary structure of investment on behalf of the shareholders in the member companies. The company never handled more than a minor share of Oldham's cotton but achieved such success within its own sphere as to encourage demands for admission by the private spinners of Oldham and the projection of similar companies for Rochdale in 1887 and for Bolton in 1890. It gave only a restricted impulse to unity amongst the Oldham limiteds since it excluded over half of them, embraced companies from outside the borough, and employed as its secretary from 1882 until 1916 Samuel Andrew, the secretary of the Oldham Master Cotton Spinners' Association. It successfully resisted a proposal in 1890 by the Rochdale limiteds to introduce district representation upon its board and so to end the control of its policy by Oldham directors, remaining thereafter a unique creation and instrument of the élite of the Oldham limiteds.

The depression of 1884–5 encouraged the limiteds to consider a number of other projects for cutting costs such as a new

[1] Ibid., May 1881, 182, Nov. 1881, 418, Jan. 1882, 9, Feb. 1882, 43; *Co-operative News*, 7 Jan. 1882, 13; *C.W.S. Annual*, 1884, 195, 'Wholesale Cotton Buying Company'; *Manchester Guardian*, 14 July 1884, 4v, 'Cotton Buying in Liverpool' 19 July, 6v, 'Buying and Selling Brokers', 21 July, 4v, 'Cotton Buying'; *Cotton Factory Times*, 13 Feb. 1885, 7v–vi, T. Ashton, 'Oldham Cotton Buying Company: its Difficulties and Triumphs'.

bank, an insurance company, a mill-furnishing company, a mill-stores company, a yarn-selling agency, a co-operative manufacturing shed, and even a merchanting company to supply foreign customers direct with manufactured goods and so to bypass the Manchester merchants. None of those schemes bore fruit save that for manufacture in 1884 and that only within the familiar field of the weaving of velveteens, wherein local manufacturers enjoyed a quasi-monopoly. Oldham became a highly developed centre of industry but remained very specialized and restricted to its own staple trade. It could not repeat its success against the brokers of Liverpool with the merchants of Manchester for the same reason that it could not import cotton direct from the U.S.A.: it could never have secured the necessary financial support for such risky operations from the banks. Thus Oldham failed to deprive Manchester of any of its mercantile functions just as it could not challenge the power of Bolton in the spinning of medium counts. The limiteds of 1889–90 gave no new impulse to corporate action as their predecessors had done in 1875, 1877, and 1881.

The Oldham limiteds fulfilled their historic function at the expense of their shareholders, benefiting third parties such as machine-makers, loan-holders, and cotton operatives. They confirmed the supremacy of the locality in the spinning trade and, reinforced by the turnover concerns, gave the town the veneer of a joint-stock community. Many-milled Oldham passed increasingly under the spell of the limited company: it became the ideal type of a purely industrial community and appeared a more probable prototype than London of the society of the future, with its highly developed power of associated action and its aggressively industrial atmosphere.[1]

[1] *Manchester Guardian*, 9 July 1889, 7i; A. Shadwell, *Industrial Efficiency* (London, Longmans, 1906), i. 84.

CHAPTER 8

The Revolution in Weaving and the Horizontal Reorganization of the Structure of Industry

> However convincing may be the proofs of the division of labour among the cells of the organisms we investigate, man, as long as he is not deprived of reason, will still say that no one ought to have to weave cotton cloth all his life long, and that such an employment is not a division of labour but an oppression of men.
>
> Tolstoy, *What Then Must We Do?* 1886, in *Works* (London, Oxford University Press, 1934), Vol. 14, 253.

THE MECHANIZATION of weaving was the major technical achievement of the nineteenth century as the development of machine-spinning had been that of the eighteenth century. It was effectively accomplished in the 1840s, seventy years after the advent of machine-spinning and almost sixty years after the invention of Cartwright's 'weaving mill' in 1785. The transformation of spinning had been relatively rapid but that of weaving was long drawn-out because of technical, economic, and social obstacles. The technical hindrances to the mechanization of the loom were far greater than in the case of the spinning wheel because the basic reciprocatory picking-motion of the shuttle obstinately resisted the application of power as much as the rotary motion of the spindle lent itself to it so that weaving inspired the invention of more mechanical appliances than any other craft.[1] The economic obstacle consisted simply in the limited returns accruing from power-looms and in the continuing competitive capacity of the hand-loom. The social opposition to mechanization stemmed from the vested interest of the community of weavers in preserving a monopoly of a labour-intensive occupation, which handled the central process

[1] A. Barlow, 'Weaving', *Engineering*, 25 June 1875, 536.

in the manufacture of cloth and was almost as much a male preserve as spinning had once been a female one.

Those weavers enjoyed their golden age during the 1780s as the output of machine-spun yarn swelled rapidly. They became a new aristocracy of labour and increased their earnings in harmony with the mounting demand for their services. Their numbers trebled from 75,000 in 1795 to 225,000 in 1811[1] and a civilization of farmer-weavers extended throughout two-thirds of the 68 parishes of Lancashire. Their numbers stabilized in the 1820s but did not begin to decline until after the commercial crisis of 1825 and the riots of 1826 and 1829,[2] although their average earnings had been declining since the 1790s and had been exceeded since 1816 by the earnings of the factory operatives. Their labour raised the cotton industry to the peak of its importance in the export trade and made its greatest contribution in the climactic year 1830 when the exports of cambrics, their major product, reached their all-time peak volume. Between 1831 and 1840 all the other hand-woven cloths attained their peak volume in the export trade.[3] The decline of the weavers took place largely between the 1830s and the 1860s. From 1834 their numbers were exceeded by those of the factory operatives in the cotton industry and from the 1840s the number of hand-looms was surpassed by the number of power-looms. New hand-looms ceased to be assembled after the 1830s and hand-loom cottages ceased to be built after the 1850s. The weavers themselves gave vent to sporadic protests between 1808 and 1842 but thereafter disappeared silently from the industrial scene as their trade was finally mechanized from 1841 onwards.

The decline in their earnings was caused by the expansion in their numbers and by the increase in alternative outlets for yarn, first abroad and then at home. The large-scale export of yarn began in 1792, when their earnings reached their peak, and exposed them to the indirect competition of foreign weavers working up English-spun yarn. No restrictions were placed upon that trade and such restrictions became impossible after the repeal in 1824 of the prohibition upon the export of

[1] S. D. Chapman, *The Cotton Industry in the Industrial Revolution* (1972), 60.
[2] D. Bythell, *The Handloom Weavers* (1969), 264.
[3] R. Burn, *Statistics of the Cotton Trade* (1847), tables 6 and 9.

wool and woollen yarn. Exports of yarn expanded faster than exports of cloth up to 1842 and drained off a substantial proportion of all the yarn spun. The development of other internal markets for yarn, especially from the 1820s, in the hosiery trade of Nottingham, the lace trade of Leicester, the mixed goods trade of Bradford, and the thread trade of Glasgow further reduced the demand for the services of the weavers of Lancashire at the very time that their numbers had reached a maximum.

The growth of the population of weavers was facilitated by the absence of any restrictions upon entry to the trade and by the ease with which the rudiments of the craft could be learned, within half the time necessary to master the art of mule-spinning. The very high birth-rate of a peasant society populated the 'naked and desolate hills' of east Lancashire to their very tops with 'the habitations of a swarming population of weavers'.[1] The influx of Irish labour has been unfairly blamed for depressing the earnings of weavers and affected their trade much less in ethnic Lancashire than in Manchester,[2] where their survival power was enhanced by the continuing demand for fancy cottons and mixed goods, by the large number of fent-dealers, by the payment of outdoor relief, and by the extensive charitable resources and non-economic perquisites of a large city. The influx of demobilized soldiers after Waterloo and their exchange of the musket for the shuttle was probably more influential than the immigration of Irish in expanding their numbers. Women were however attracted to the trade by the equal rates paid to both sexes. The position of the weavers was aggravated by their comparative longevity and immobility which contrasted with the brevity of life and the mobility of the factory operative. Their trade was sanctioned by the tradition of the master–manufacturers of the past and offered all the satisfactions, save one, which factory employment denied. The possession of a loom gave to weavers control of the basic instrument of production, guaranteed their independence, and made them embryonic capitalists, since they rarely rented their looms and sold their cloth rather than their labour. As masters of their

[1] W. Howitt, *The Rural Life of England* (London, Longman, 1838), i. 286, 'Nooks of the World—Life in the Dales of Lancashire and Yorkshire'.

[2] Bythell, op. cit. 63–5.

fate, they could combine the self-sufficiency of the peasant and the pride of the craftsman with the vitality of the frontiersman. The loom also served as an 'heirloom' and provided their wives with a virtual insurance policy. As a propertied order of society the weavers supplied the foundation of the conservative alliance of altar, throne, and cottage and served as a seed-bed of loyalist sentiment in fundamental opposition to the radical factory operatives, being regarded until 1816 as a bulwark of their country, much as the husbandmen had been in the sixteenth century. Thereafter their image was debased by progressive journalists into one of 'men of idle, irregular and dissipated habits', most like unto poachers or smugglers.[1] The extent to which they prized their independence more than their standard of living was measured by their reluctance to quit the trade and by their continued patient acceptance of declining rates of pay. The social role of weaving inspired the use of the loom, especially from the 1820s, as an instrument of the penal code and of the poor law to enable prisoners and paupers to become self-supporting. Weavers supplemented their declining income in a variety of ways, by sending their children into the mill, by taking in lodgers, by carrying on dairy farming, or by working as agricultural labourers and thus maintaining the traditional links between industry and the land.

The improvement of the power-loom in 1822, combined with the boom in the demand for hosiery yarns, seems to have been effective enough to check any further increase in their numbers and to begin to force them into other occupations such as the weaving of silks or woollens. The steam-loom provoked however, as in 1812, a strong conservative reaction in the loom-breaking riots of 1826 and 1829, whose failure marked a turning-point in the history of the weaving community. Then from 1827 combined spinning and weaving factories developed in south-east Lancashire in response to a sharp fall in the price of yarn and benefited by the development of the self-acting mule in 1831, the repeal in 1831 of the excise on printed cloth, and the expanding demand from the printing works for cheap power-woven calico. As the Tame valley and especially Stalybridge became the headquarters of power-weaving as well as of power-spinning the competition of its machine-woven cloth

[1] E. Baines, *History of the Cotton Manufacture* (1835), 495.

undermined the position of the hand-loom weavers on coarse goods throughout south-east Lancashire. The power-loom remained imperfect and confined to the production of three types of plain goods in printers, domestics, and shirtings so that it did not compete with the hand-weaving of superior and fancy goods. The spread of the new machine was also limited by the capital cost, which was double that of a hand-loom, by the difficulty experienced by power-loom weavers in supervising more than one loom, and their steadfast refusal to supervise more than two, by the low and declining rates paid to hand-loom weavers, and by the continued competitive capacity of their craft.

The hand-loom itself experienced a technical renaissance in the invention in 1802 of the compact iron-framed dandy loom and in the application in 1803 of the time-saving preparatory technique of warp-dressing. Such machines were assembled in 'loom-shops' and even in sheds, in association with sizing shops, and increased the productivity of shop-weavers substantially. The adoption from 1834 of the elaborate Jacquard apparatus for controlling the shedding of the warp notably extended the competitive position of the hand-loom in the weaving of fancy and figured cloth. Thus the hand-weavers benefited by the slow pace of development of the power-loom, by the extensive demand for fancy cloth, and by the development from the 1830s of the manufacture of such luxurious mixed goods as *mousseline de laine* which combined a cotton warp with a worsted weft to create a woollen muslin.

The true industrial revolution in weaving was ushered in by the perfection of the Blackburn plain loom, which was the first great innovation in the sphere of power-weaving made within north-east Lancashire. It had been invented in 1827 but was only made effectively automatic in 1841,[1] enabling a weaver to mind more than one loom and produce more cloth of a

[1] C. G. Gilroy, *The Art of Weaving, by Hand and by Power* (New York, Baldwin, 1844), 416; J. Latham, *The Art of Managing the Patent Power Loom* (Bury, Trimble, 1855), 43; J. Baynes, *The Cotton Trade* (1857), 29; W. Harrison, 'Cotton Weaving and Lancashire Looms', *Macmillan's Magazine*, Oct. 1862, 451–2; J. Watson, *The Theory and Practice of the Art of Weaving by Hand and Power* (Glasgow, Watson, 1863), 125–6; D. Morris, *The Past and Present Productive Power of Cotton Machinery* (Manchester, Guardian Press, 1865), 32–4; A. Barlow, *The History and Principles of Weaving by Hand and by Power* (London, Low, 1878), 306.

better quality, admirably adapted to Eastern markets, than he could from any other loom. The full productive capacity of the power-loom was realized through the application of the new techniques of power-warping, invented in 1843, and, above all, of slasher-sizing, invented in 1853. Its capacity for the weaving of high-quality dyed and figured fabrics was extended by its successive application from 1843 to the manufacture of coloured goods, through the use of multiple shuttle-box motions, and from 1845 to the weaving of quilts: its full potential was developed during the next fifty years. The dobby, or small Jacquard for the control of warp shedding, was not applied in the cotton industry to the weaving of bordered goods until 1858, although it had been patented in 1824. The Jacquard proper was applied to the fancy power-loom only between 1860 and 1890, was never adopted as extensively as the dobby, and did not become as important in the cotton industry as in the silk industry. Thus the history of the power-loom furnishes a perfect example of the very slow spread of new inventions.

The new power-loom imparted a great stimulus to the expansion of coarse spinning rather than of fine spinning and extended its production at the expense of the hand-loom weavers, whose decline became very rapid in the 1840s and 1850s, especially in the large towns where alternative employment was available. The weavers had become the victims of technological unemployment and had formed since the 1820s a useful auxiliary labour force, so providing the model for Marx's reserve army of labour. In each revival of trade between the 1820s and the 1850s they benefited from the expansion of demand and secured a rise in piece-rates which was invariably lost in the ensuing depression. The long-term decline in their earnings was moderated by the decline in prices so that their real wages declined between 1815 and 1849 much less than their money-wages, which sank however fourfold as much as those of factory operatives. The debate on the responsibility of the power-loom for their plight[1] favoured the meliorist con-

[1] H. Rose, *Manual Labour versus Brass and Iron* (Manchester, Pratt, 1825, 8pp.), 6, 7; E. Baines, *History of the Cotton Manufacture* (1835), 498–501; W. C. Taylor, *The Hand Book of Silk, Cotton and Woollen Manufactures* (London, Bentley, 1843), 171–2, 199, 209; T. C. Banfield, *Four Lectures on the Organisation of Industry* (London, Taylor, 1845), 73; G. W. Hilton, 'The Controversy concerning Relief for the Hand-Loom Weavers', *Explorations in Entrepreneurial History*, Winter 1964, 164–86.

clusion that they supplied almost the sole exception to the rule that most operatives gained by the introduction of mechanical inventions.[1]

The weavers had debarred themselves from the mills and therefore from the monetary benefits accruing to the factory operatives but they had proved wholly unable to preserve their own monopoly gains. They had been virtually created by the revolution in machine-spinning and lacked the support of any deep-rooted tradition of home-spinning. They could not form trade unions because they cherished their tradition of independence and respectability and were in any case too widely scattered to conduct successful strikes or prolonged shuttle-gathering. Even for self-protection they could not control their own numbers and thereby the level of their earnings, either by combination or by emigration. The co-operative manufacturing societies formed between 1830 and 1861 failed to moderate their sturdy individualism, to compete successfully with private employers in the slaughter-house of the Manchester market, or to emulate the success of the co-operative stores, which were often pioneered by weavers. Without political power or support they could not secure any legislative remedy for their plight. Their demands for political reform through the Hampden clubs, the Peterloo demonstration, the anti-Poor Law movement, and the Chartist agitation were essentially conservative pleas for a return to a vanished golden age rather than a programme for a radical reconstruction of society upon a new basis. The weavers failed to secure any political concessions as they failed to obtain a ban on the export of yarn, a tax upon power-looms, or a restriction upon the hours of work in steam-loom factories. Least of all could they secure a minimum wage, especially after the repeal in 1824 of the Spitalfields Acts, or a compensatory remission of taxes. They nevertheless displayed remarkable tenacity in the face of long-sustained adverse pressure upon their way and standard of life. They survived longest in the villages and small townships of rural Lancashire, especially in the Ribble valley. The last hand-loom weavers disappeared from Rossendale and the Blackburn district in the early 1880s and from Ribblesdale in 1893.[2] Their last stronghold was

[1] S. Smiles, 'Strikes', *Quarterly Review*, Oct. 1859, 504.

[2] *Textile Manufacturer*, Jan. 1883, 3, Mar. 1884, 97, Aug. 1887, 426; J. L. Green,

Bolton where shop-weaving ended in 1895 and the hand-loom weavers' union, registered in 1883, was dissolved in 1899.[1] The decline of their trade marked a stage in the urbanization of the cotton industry and withdrew an important source of livelihood from the population of the weaving townships of north-east Lancashire,[2] leaving some to revert to purely agricultural pursuits but wholly depopulating none.

* * *

Power-loom manufacture inherited from hand-loom manufacture its fundamental pattern of organization and developed upon different lines from those of machine-spinning. Spinning and weaving became increasingly interdependent but remained almost as distinct from each other as were the cotton and woollen industries. Weaving differed profoundly from spinning in its technical and commercial basis, especially in the ease of access which it offered to small capitalists in the age of the power-loom as much as in the age of the hand-loom. Looms were much cheaper than mules and quicker to instal than self-actors. Thus a manufacturer could begin operations within a few months where a spinner might require up to three years. He required less technical knowledge and less floating capital to operate a weaving shed than a spinner needed to run a spinning mill of corresponding size. He could conduct his business on a much smaller scale than was possible to a spinner who required, especially from the 1860s, a large capital, both fixed and floating, and could no longer easily begin in a small way with hired spindles. A manufacturer might hire both looms and power, might secure yarn on credit more easily than a spinner might secure raw cotton, and might even obtain an advance from a Manchester cloth agent which would be made upon the

The Rural Industries of England (London, Marlborough, 1895), 90; E. W. Abram, 'The Last Lancashire Hand-Loom Weavers', *The Leisure Hour*, Nov. 1893, 737–41.

[1] *Report by the Chief Labour Correspondent of the Board of Trade on Trade Unions in 1899 with Comparative Statistics for 1892–1898* (Cd. 422 of 1900), 52–3, 306; *Report by the Chief Labour Correspondent of the Board of Trade on Trade Unions in 1901* (Cd. 1348 of 1902), 46–7; J. Conrad (ed.), *Handwörterbuch der Staatswissenschaften* (Jena Fischer, 2te Auflage, 1900), iv. 1157, W. Sombart, 'Hausindustrie'.

[2] W. A. Abram, *A History of Blackburn, Town and Parish* (Blackburn, Toulmin, 1877). 236, 425, 587, 644, 657. 681.

security of cloth to be produced and would suffice to pay wages for the first two or three weeks of business. Thus any operative weaver who had acquired a knowledge of the basic techniques of the industry and had saved a few hundred pounds could begin business on the merest fraction of the capital necessary to become a spinner.[1]

The tradition of small-scale enterprise was inherited from the age of the master-manufacturer and carried on into that of the power-loom as weaving increasingly developed upon its own specialized lines, separate from spinning. The number of weaving firms was only one-third of the number of spinning firms in 1850 and one-half in 1874 but rose to surpass their number by 1890 and to become the most numerous single group of enterprises within the industry, trebling their share of the total number of firms from 13 per cent in 1850 to 38·6 per cent in 1890. The weaving trade expanded through an increase in the number of manufacturers rather than through an increase in the size of the individual units of production. Weaving firms certainly laid down more looms in response to the increase in the productivity of the sizing machine between 1850 and 1870 but grew much less rapidly in size than spinning firms, although the process of primary mechanization had begun in the spinning trade some sixty years ahead of the same trend in the weaving trade. The average weaving firm functioned as an agent for the employment of labour rather than of capital: it increased the number of its hands faster than those of the average spinning firm, surpassing it by 1867, but increased its plant at only two-thirds of the rate of the average spinning firm between 1850 and 1874 and at only half the rate between 1874 and 1890. Thus it declined to follow the pattern of expansion set in spinning and its estimated average capital suffered a proportionate decline from one-third of the capital of the average spinning firm in 1850 to one-quarter in 1890.[2] The aggregate capital invested in weaving rose from 25 per cent of that invested in spinning in 1874 to 34 per cent in 1890 but the amount of capital employed per operative increased four times

[1] *Manchester Guardian*, 3 Mar. 1858, 4iii, T. H. Williams; T. H. Williams, *Observations on Money, Credit and Panics: to which are added Strictures on Manchester Credits* (1858), 26–7.

[2] £4,000 or 36 per cent in 1850 and £9,150 or 27 per cent in 1890.

as fast in spinning as in weaving so that spinning became by 1890 an industry more than fourfold as capital-intensive as weaving. The small firm thus remained typical of the weaving trade, especially in Blackburn, Darwen, Burnley, and Rossendale: the only large firms in the weaving district were built up in Preston and Chorley. The limited scale of operations presented few barriers to beginners in the trade. That remarkable freedom of access to the industry was reflected in its typically small units of business, its rooted aversion to a capital-intensive technology, its endemic inefficiency, its quick response to a

TABLE 15

Average Size of the Weaving Factory, 1850–1890

	Average Number of Power Looms	Average Number of Employees
1850	160	97·8
1856	157	100·4
1861	182	87·5
1867	218	115·3
1870	270	123·5
1874	284	136·1
1878	299	140·2
1885	332	156
1890	366	173

Source: Returns of the Factory Inspectors, 1850–90.

favourable commercial conjuncture, its capacity for rapid expansion, its dependence upon mercantile intermediaries, the precariousness and brevity of its conjunctural prosperity, its very moderate profitability, its liability to internecine competition, over-production, and deep depression, and the very heavy mortality amongst manufacturers and their very low status in the hierarchy of rank within the cotton industry.[1]

Manufacturers did not in the long run benefit from the ease of entry into the industry but suffered from the severity of the consequent competition and from the determining influence

[1] *Spectator*, 27 Oct. 1883, 1372, 'The Crisis in the Cotton Trade'; *Textile Manufacturer*, Feb. 1884, 78, 'The Past Year in the Cotton Trade', reprinted in T. Ellison, *The Cotton Trade* (1886), 78–9.

exerted upon their whole business strategy by their lack of capital. They found it difficult to expand their range of production and they remained confined within the bounds of their own specialized vocation. They never scaled the commanding heights of the industry nor even realized the modest ambitions which they shared with other small employers in the industry. They remained in the weakest position within the cotton trade with the least control over the price of a finished cloth. The average manufacturer could never afford to spin his own yarn. He therefore became more dependent upon the spinner than the spinner was upon him since he lacked the spinner's freedom of choice amongst several different markets and produced for a more specialized and restricted outlet. In order to maintain his looms at full capacity throughout the year he had constantly to vary his output, especially in the quiet interval between the busy seasons of spring and autumn. Since he ran more risks than a spinner in producing for stock he had to engage in the unremitting pursuit of a full order-book. He could not insure himself against a rise in the price of yarn since spinners refused to accept orders on the basis of a future contract. In order to secure his raw material he had to pay whatever price the spinner or his agent demanded, once new looms had come into operation and had so extended the spinner's market. The manufacturer also lacked the comparable advantage of integration with a merchanting firm and was forced to depend wholly upon his cloth agent for secure and uninterrupted access to the cloth market as well as for the supply of credit.

As a class manufacturers were the first to benefit from any revival of demand and could certainly make money under such favourable conditions and invest it in the hire or purchase of more looms. They fared better than spinners during the first portion of a boom but were plagued by a greater and more constant tendency to undue expansion and thus by severer competition and lower profit margins. As the barometers of trade, they were the first to feel the approach of any depression and to suffer the loss of their margins as more looms came into operation and benefited the spinners, who could retain a margin of profit for some time after that of manufacturers had vanished. The passage of such an initial wave of prosperity left manufacturers buying yarn in a firm market but selling cloth in a weak one. Usually they did not know the identity of the merchant–buyer of their cloth and were thus powerless to protect themselves from the monopolistic pressure exerted in a variety of ways by the cloth agents.[1] Thus they became subject to relentless pressure from both ends of the trade and were squeezed as dry as lemons by yarn agents and cloth agents, who as creditors became the main beneficiaries by the increase in their number of debtors. Inevitably manufacturers resorted to forced sales and when business became too bad they suffered bankruptcy. Such bankrupts compounded with their creditors, paid them a dividend, and left their looms to stand idle awhile before they passed into the hands of another manufacturer. They might even resume business almost immediately since the barriers against re-entry to the industry were as low as they were to initial entry.

The peculiarly heavy mortality amongst firms within the weaving industry benefited new entrants by enabling them to buy serviceable machinery at rock-bottom prices. Looms were not as good as spindles when new but their economic lifespan was twice as long as that of mules and could extend up to sixty years or more, so halving the charges for depreciation. Investment in weaving tended to be more continuous and less concentrated in particular years than that in spinning plant because looms were cheaper than mules and operated on a much smaller scale. The weaving industry expanded most when spinning was depressed as in the years 1858–62, 1868, 1870, 1874–7, 1880–3, 1886–8, 1890–1, and 1894. The secular depression in the spinning trade after 1875 cheapened yarn more than cloth and maintained margins of manufacturers at a higher level than those of spinners, so encouraging a massive expansion in loomage in successive waves of investment. Those periodic spurts reacted upon the spinning industry and encouraged the reactive extension of spinning plant, especially when spinning margins were inflated at the expense of manufacturers. Each period of prosperity in the weaving industry ended in a bout of over-production as the spinning industry regained its preferential margins.

* * *

[1] *Textile Manufacturer*, Aug. 1882, 283, 'Responsibilities of Agents and Manufacturers', Nov. 1882, 392, 'Manufacturers and Cloth Agents', Dec. 1882, 433, 'Manufacturers and Cloth Agents'; *Manchester Guardian*, 30 Dec. 1882, 4viii, 'Yarn and Cloth Commission Agents'.

The primary instruments in the expansion of cotton manufacturing were private employers rather than joint-stock companies. The limited company proved less necessary and less popular in the weaving industry than in the spinning industry. The weaving companies floated between 1880 and 1896 mustered twice the capital of the average unincorporated manufacturer but usually suffered a high rate of abortion and had a short corporate life. The company became proportionately more important in the older and smaller centres of the weaving industry such as Haslingden. There the population was enterprising, industrious, and economical, bred better weavers than elsewhere, and retained an aversion to trade unions: there companies had since 1851 embodied the co-operative tradition of Rossendale and became in proportion to the population more influential than in any other town, controlling 69 per cent of its looms in 1896 and making it more of a true industrial democracy than Oldham itself.[1] The limited company was much less important in the main weaving towns and least important of all in the most rapidly developing centres such as Burnley and Nelson. In none of the six main centres of weaving did companies, even including private limiteds, control more than one-fifth of the looms in 1884 or more than one-third in 1896. The suggested contrast between the faster spread of the company in the towns dependent upon the relatively stable Eastern trade and its slower spread in the centres of the more volatile fancy trade[2] is controverted by the statistics available for the period down to 1896 since Blackburn had almost the same proportion of looms in companies as Burnley and Nelson and a lower proportion than Preston or Accrington. In Preston an aristocratic prejudice against limited liability, working-class limiteds, and contractors' companies was reinforced by the peculiar demands of the local fine trade, which required closer attention to detail than spinning as well as an established selling connection, so effectively discouraging the promoters of limited companies before 1874.[3] The private limited type of company was slowly adopted from 1882 but proved less popular in

[1] *Textile Manufacturer*, Jan. 1884, 30, Feb. 1885, 77, Feb. 1888, 50, 'Weaving Companies'; B. Jones, *Co-operative Production* (Oxford, Clarendon Press, 1894), i. 272–6.

[2] Schulze-Gaevernitz, op. cit. 68–9.

[3] *Preston Guardian*, 29 May 1875, 6i.

Preston than in any other weaving town. In Accrington from 1860 and in Darwen from 1874 the company developed with great success but did so in the spinning trade, which had been mechanized sixty years before weaving and spun fine yarns resistant to the competition of Oldham.

Weaving remained easily accessible to small capitalists and proved a far riskier investment than spinning in terms of both technology and marketing.[1] The technology of weaving had not acquired the stability appropriate to its operation under a joint-stock company but developed much faster than that of spinning between 1860 and 1900. Weaving required greater diligence, skill, and resource, especially in the trades in fine, fancy, and coloured goods, than was necessary in the routine management of a spinning mill. Even in the plain trade it required much more judicious handling of the operatives than was necessary in the spinning room. It was in short an industry unsuited to the talents of a remote board of directors and best carried on by one-man firms under the autocratic control of 'laborious, strong and inventive men' springing from the ranks of the operatives.[2] Such yeomen-farmers of industry cherished their privacy and independence more than they valued or needed the capital-raising facilities of the joint-stock company. They supplied the enterprise essential to the expansion of the weaving industry which working-class associations in general could not. Such employers were inspired by the memory of the golden decade of the 1850s and were moved by social as much as by economic ambition. The weaving industry rivalled shop-keeping as an attractive vehicle of social mobility and enhanced its competitive attraction as the co-operative stores began to reduce the profits of the small trader. Aspiring entrants to the trade wished to acquire a passport to social distinction and to embed themselves in the thin upper crust of local society.[3] In that society there were no gentry to rebuff intruders and the poor quality of the local land restricted the sphere of economic achievement to industrial activity. Within the weaving industry

[1] *Textile Recorder*, 15 June 1883, 26–7, 'The Defects of Limited Liability Companies'.

[2] E. Helm, 'The Alleged Decline of the British Cotton Industry', *Economic Journal*, Dec. 1892, 743; *Textile Mercury*, 15 Dec. 1894, 464, 'Joint-Stock Weaving Companies'.

[3] *Textile Manufacturer*, Aug. 1882, 276, 'The State of the Cotton Trade'.

employers remained free from any specific interference by the State before 1889 and from the oppressive presence of mass unionism before 1890.

The most acceptable form of the joint-stock company in the cotton manufacturing industry proved to be the room-and-power company which fulfilled a dual function. In origin it was a contractors' company which built a weaving shed and then became a landlord by renting space and supplying power to tenants. The proprietors did not require either the technical or the commercial ability necessary to carry on manufacture but they provided employers with the basic overhead capital, leaving them to bear the risks of trade. Thus they secured the maximum of profit with the minimum of risk over the longest period of time. The practice of renting room and power, or 'space and turning', had provided an important financial basis for industrial development in the midlands and the north during the eighteenth century and had been especially common within the textile industries. In the cotton industry it declined markedly in importance in spinning but assumed a new intensity in weaving, spreading in north-east Lancashire particularly from the 1850s as the new building societies made available local credit for the expansion of local trade. Room and power was provided first by unincorporated firms or companies and then from 1875, after the end of the cost-raising coal famine, by joint-stock companies and especially by small private limiteds. Between 1875 and 1896 48 room-and-power companies were registered, mainly in the most rapidly developing area: they included 15 in Burnley, 10 in Nelson, 7 in Colne, and 7 in Skipton. Such companies were established in growing numbers from 1880 when the first effective companies were established in Burnley, Nelson, and Colne. The average capital of the 48 was £13,700, or 12 per cent less than the £15,500 of the average weaving company established between 1880 and 1896, and was generally held by seven promoter–shareholder–directors. Usually they were promoted and financed by local engineers, builders, contractors, and cotton manufacturers under the guidance of a solicitor or accountant. In order to secure loan capital they mortgaged their sheds to local building societies and so succeeded in extending their own outlay of capital over the largest number of similar safe investments.

They made the office of a solicitor or accountant into their registered office and eluded the attention of the compilers of directories so that their influence upon industrial development has understandably been neglected.

The justification of the room-and-power system lay in the comparative poverty of north-east Lancashire, the profitability of the local trade, the stabilization of steam-power technology in contrast to the comparative imperfection of power-loom technology, and the substantial difference between the optimum size of a weaving shed and that of a weaving firm, which made it economical for several firms to share the same shed and source of power. The weaving firm required no major investment of capital apart from its preparatory machinery: it had simply to have enough looms to keep in full employment and to make the most economic use of its winding, warping, and sizing machines and of its supervisory staff. In contrast a weaving shed had to be large enough to spread its costs of construction over the area of land rented, to enclose an economic number of looms within four walls, and to make full use of the power generated by a steam-engine. Such a shed was rarely liable to burn down since the machinery to be turned was lighter than in a spinning mill, its motions were comparatively slow, and the fire-risk from friction was therefore reduced to a very low degree so that premiums had to be lowered almost to the level of those upon a dwelling-house in order to persuade manufacturers to take out insurance policies.[1] Such sheds enjoyed a longer life than fire-prone spinning mills and a longer life than the looms they housed so that they could maintain a separate economic existence from that of the firms which they sheltered.

Usually room and power companies leased space and power in their sheds to tenants who installed their own looms. Their sheds were not in general giant structures comparable to the large spinning mills of Shaw, near Oldham. On average they housed four firms and encouraged the maximum use of space through the close-packing of looms. The system reduced the amount of capital necessary to begin weaving, opened new opportunities for self-employment to small capitalists, and facili-

[1] J. H. Bagshaw, 'Cotton Factories and Sheds', *Journal of the Federation of Insurance Institutes of Great Britain and Ireland*, 1900, 119–20.

tated the entry of new firms to the trade whenever the commercial conjuncture was propitious. Such an influx was certainly facilitated by the secular expansion of the weaving trade and by its rapid extension into the country townships of the Calder valley where both land and labour were cheap. In Burnley the weaving industry expanded upon the basis of the room and power system and of the narrow 36-inch-wide loom since rent was charged upon the basis of the 40-inch-wide loom and not upon that of the actual number of looms in the shed. The system proved more useful to the fine-weaving industry of Nelson and Colne than to the coarse trade of Blackburn where firms were larger than in the Calder valley but nevertheless increasingly resorted to leasing space and even spindles and looms.[1] The practice increased horizontal as well as vertical mobility by facilitating movement by manufacturers from shed to shed.

The economic and social benefits of relatively free entry into the weaving industry were notably exaggerated by Frederick J. Marquis,[2] whose thesis influenced the interpretation of the origins of the Industrial Revolution made by his colleague T. S. Ashton. Marquis estimated that 63 per cent of the employers in Burnley in 1911 owning 49 per cent of the total number of looms had begun life as wage-earners and therefore belonged to the first generation of employers. The slender statistical basis of his brief investigation aroused immediate criticism of his conclusions by expert statisticians and was aggravated by his total reliance upon unverified verbal responses to leading questions in the simplest of questionnaires. Marquis erred in identifying the fast-developing Burnley district with the weaving industry and even more in identifying it with the cotton industry as a whole. He made his survey before Sorokin in 1927 had placed the study of social mobility as a historical phenomenon upon a firm scientific foundation. The incidence of vertical mobility within the industry was in fact almost impossible to assess accurately and its extent could easily be exaggerated under the influence of a predisposition in

[1] *Report of the Chief Inspector of Factories*, 31 Oct. 1890, 5.

[2] S. J. Chapman and F. J. Marquis, 'The Recruiting of the Employing Classes from the Ranks of the Wage-Earners in the Cotton Industry', *Journal of the Royal Statistical Society*, Feb. 1912, 293–313, reprinted in F. J. Marquis, *Upward Mobility of Labour as Evidenced in the Lancashire Cotton Industry* (Liverpool, Northern Publishing Company, 1912, 24pp.).

its favour. Marquis's reaffirmation of his Fabian faith in the continuing existence of an industrial career open to talents may well have been an intellectual response to the contemporary outburst of syndicalist agitation, which established its provincial headquarters in Manchester. The survival of such opportunities would prevent the crystallization of a separate caste of capitalists, link together the worlds of capital and labour, moderate the intensity of the class war, extend the area of social peace, and undermine the whole basis of the pessimistic forecasts about the future of industrial society then flourishing amidst the Edwardian revival of agrarian sentiment. Such a belief in the beneficial function of vertical mobility conformed to the ethos of liberalism and was especially cherished by members of the Manchester Exchange. It was however misleading in so far as it imposed a superficial Smilesian ethic upon a trade where both success and failure were apportioned in flat defiance of all rational expectation.[1] Moreover it cloaked the reality of the dominance of the family firm and concealed the steady diversion of the profits of manufacture into the pockets of the agents. The insistent increase in competition undoubtedly tended to impoverish manufacturers as a class. For their part the operatives remained uninspired by the opportunities which ostensibly remained open to them but which necessarily appealed to the few rather than to the many. The workfolk in general could not assimilate such a pessimistic world outlook which offered them little hope for the future within their own station in society and rewarded them only when, at high psychosomatic cost, they abandoned that status. They accepted both the structure of society and their place within it, embalming their own long-term historical perspective in the comforting local proverb 'from clogs to clogs is only three generations'.[2]

The room-and-power system fulfilled its essential function through the manufacture of rent. The rents charged were as high as tenants could bear to pay and served to create a structural impediment to the adoption of short-time working in time of bad trade since rents remained due whether looms worked

[1] *Royal Commission on Labour, Minutes of Evidence taken before Group 'C'*, i. 103, Q.2637, Joshua Rawlinson, 11 July 1891.

[2] *Notes and Queries. A Medium of Intercommunication for Literary Men* (London, The Office), Fourth Series, VII, 3 June 1871, 472.

or stood idle. They represented a prior charge which had to be met before wages were paid: they were even blamed for encouraging employers by their relentless pressure to resort to unacceptable wage cuts.[1] As proprietors, room-and-power companies undoubtedly benefited by the preferential position enjoyed by the landlord in English law, especially in relation to distraint,[2] and by the general reluctance of rents to follow prices, especially coal prices, in their downward movement. With such a large and secure income they very rarely proved abortive and usually enjoyed an even longer existence than private limiteds, proving to be the most stable type of company in the whole range of limiteds within the industry.

* * *

The story of the expansion of the weaving trade has never been fully told because it affected the most humble of industries and aroused no interest amongst outside observers. In the semi-rural folk society of north-east Lancashire an educated middle class was non-existent or uninterested in the process of industrial development while its labouring members could not fully comprehend the transformation of their way of life caused by the industry's voracious demands for labour. The civilization of the region was quite distinctive but could hardly be classified as a sub-culture in the virtual absence of any superior cultural tradition. Nor was it a 'culture of poverty' such as the English disciples of Oscar Lewis have sought to unearth in native soil.[3] Its basic units remained the family and the church, which bound their members closely together in mutual protection against the hostile influence of Nature and of the industrial machine. Family structures were not weakened under the pressure of a marginal existence: they were rather strengthened by the absence of immigrants and lodgers, by the presence of a higher proportion of children and of unmarried daughters than

[1] *The Times*, 24 Dec. 1883, 7vi, 12i.

[2] R. C. Richards, 'A Consideration of Some of the Effects of the Landlord's Preferential Position upon Commerce and Agriculture', *Transactions of the Manchester Statistical Society*, 11 Jan. 1888, 50–2.

[3] J. Seabrook, *City Close-Up* (London, Lane, 1971), 38, on Blackburn; Eleanor B. Leacock (ed.), *The Culture of Poverty. A Critique* (New York, Simon and Schuster, 1971).

in the spinning district, and by the customary employment of children as assistants, or tenters, to their parents. The family was almost as authoritarian in structure as the occupational hierarchy of the mill and socialized its members neither to failure nor to success but simply to survival, transmitting to them a rigid system of values, a deeply conservative disposition, and a longing for material independence as keen as that of the hand-loom weavers. Church and chapel satisfied a whole spectrum of otherwise repressed emotions, linked their members to a wider world, and imbued them with an abiding sense of community which was extended, as traditional faiths weakened in the 1890s, to democratically organized trade unions and even to political parties. To such institutions outside the walls of the factory the population habitually reserved its deepest loyalty, restricting the role of industry to the instrumental function of providing employment.

The demand for labour was great because cotton manufacture required fivefold as many operatives in proportion to the capital invested as did spinning, being as labour-intensive an industry as spinning was capital-intensive. Labour costs formed 77 per cent of the cost of production in weaving but only 47 per cent in spinning: they amounted to 50–60 per cent of the weaving margin but only to 32–40 per cent of the spinning margin[1] so that a manufacturer required a margin large enough to pay as much to his weavers as to himself. The labour required was essentially the unskilled labour of machine-minders at relatively low rates of pay since the power-loom reduced the direct demand for skilled labour as much as the spinning mule had increased it. The demand for such labour could be satisfied without much difficulty in north-east Lancashire, because employment opportunities were restricted in the absence of a diversified economy to agriculture and weaving, the prevalent standards of living and of wages were low, restrictions upon entry to the weaving trade were absent, and unions did not develop their influence until 1890. Cotton manufacture could not afford to compete for labour with any other industry apart from agriculture and drew upon an ample supply of relatively immobile labour, with an old tradition of weaving and less aversion in Blackburn or Burnley to steam-looms than that once

[1] Schulze-Gaevernitz, op. cit. 158.

held by the skilled weavers of Bolton or Manchester. The rural population had a high birth-rate, a low death-rate and a higher rate of natural increase than the population of south-east Lancashire.[1] It had been stimulated to expand by the great boom of the 1850s and could supply in abundance the cheap labour of women, girls, and children, so leaving the menfolk free to follow the equally labour-intensive pursuit of agriculture. The wage differential between the north-east and the south-east of the county was based upon the lower cost of living in the rural north, the superior strength of the local employers' associations, and the absence before 1870 of any district associations of power-loom weavers. That differential had been maintained after the north-east had first surpassed the south-east in 1850 in the number of its factory operatives. It narrowed and vanished between 1860 and 1871 and was then restored after the failure of the great strike of 1878, being thereafter maintained until 1906 by the shrinkage of the local spinning industry which ceased to compete for labour as it did in the south-east.

The weaving industry fulfilled its social function even more effectively than its economic function. It expanded its share of the industry's labour force in both weaving and combined firms to exceed half of the total by 1878 and in north-east Lancashire to exceed four-fifths by the 1890s. Most weavers remained unskilled wage-earners throughout their lives, working hard for relatively low wages. 'The sons and daughters of the loom'[2] needed no strength, knowledge, art, or skill but only manual dexterity: they were little better than machine-tenders and had little opportunity to use their initiative. They had much less hope of promotion than piecers since the weaving shed had no superior caste of employees comparable to the self-actor minders of the mule mill. The higher supervisory positions were very few in proportion to the number of weavers in a shed and were often hereditary, descending from father to son, while the executive posts of salesman, manager, manufacturer, or agent were beyond the aspirations or the resources of most weavers,

[1] R. Lawton, 'Population Trends in Lancashire and Cheshire from 1801', *Transactions of the Historic Society of Lancashire and Cheshire*, 16 Nov. 1961, 204, 212.

[2] *Manchester Examiner*, 22 Aug. 1860, 3i, Abraham Pinder.

even with the aid of technical education. Attempts to transform the dominant system of production through enterprises based upon co-operative production, especially in the boom of 1886–9,[1] sought to bridge the gulf between the subsistence-ethic of local society and the market economy of the cotton trade. Almost always such ventures failed to fulfil their anticipated role of profit-sharing and were reduced in a hostile market to the role of wage-paying and loss-sharing associations.

The operative weavers were condemned to occupy a subordinate role in the industrial structure, becoming neither partners in a common pursuit nor sharers in the profits of a common enterprise and being denied even the receipt of a symbolic bonus to labour. Their sole return from the industry remained the wages they earned. It was their achievement to make a virtue out of adversity, to preserve their trade as a palladium of labour, and thus to make it into a virtual emanation of their own folk society. Lacking any schooling in habits of deference by a resident gentry, they regarded the industry differently from the masters. They viewed it as essentially 'co-operative, not competitive—a partnership of all masters and all workpeople with one another' and as 'an estate, not to be worked by each party for itself, or by individuals competitively, but by each party for the other, and on the plan of a close corporation'.[2] The weavers tended to consider the masters as the directors of a company and themselves as the paid-up shareholders: they insisted that the masters should so conduct the business as to satisfy all engaged and should always preserve its *raison d'être* in the employment of labour. Such a world outlook explains their intrinsic hostility to labour-saving devices, their rooted objection to minding more looms, their successful restriction of six-loom working to the districts of Burnley and Nelson, their predictable boycott of automatic looms, their opposition to the speeding-up of production, their readiness to work short-time in a period of depression even at the cost of

[1] *Textile Manufacturer*, Sept. 1891, 407, L. Katscher, 'Profit-Sharing in the Textile Industries'; *Royal Commission on Labour. Minutes of Evidence taken before Group 'C'* (C.6708. vi, 1892), Q.2550–78, Q.2587–2637, Q.2901–8, J. Rawlinson 11 July 1891; B. Jones, *Co-operative Production* (1894), i. 315–29; H. D. Lloyd, *Labor Copartnership: notes of a visit to Co-operative Workshops . . . in Great Britain* (New York, Harper, 1898), 154–65.

[2] *The Times*, 27 Dec. 1883, 2i, 'Cotton Trade Socialism'.

sacrificing one-third of their earnings, and their receptivity after 1885 to the preaching of the 'new unionism'.

The weaving industry increased the productivity of its looms far less than the spinning industry increased that of its spindles and even raised its labour costs per pound of woven cloth as fancy weaving spread while labour costs in spinning continued to fall:[1] it remained on the whole far more profitable to its workfolk than did the spinning industry and furnished during the Civil War the main reservoir of pro-Southern sentiment in Lancashire. Industrial relations remained better in weaving than in spinning because the scale of operations was smaller, unions were weaker, and masters were free from the incubus of a relatively small, highly skilled, and tightly organized key group of operatives such as the self-actor minders. Unlike the spinners, the weavers were far too weak to control entrance to their trade and therefore sought to control the level of their wages through the large-scale organization of unskilled labour,[2] which was effected first informally through the local community and then formally through the union. The great strike of 1878 had revealed the vast powers of resistance of the folk community of the weaving district.[3] Thereafter employers and unions recognized their mutual bargaining-strength and established in 1881 a joint negotiating committee, creating a recognized procedure for the peaceful conciliation of the conflicting interests of capital and labour, following the example set in the iron and steel industry in 1869 and establishing a precedent imitated by the spinning industry in 1893. Thus the weaving industry suffered from more disputes than the spinning industry because of its larger number of workfolk but successfully contained those differences within an established framework for conciliation and in consequence suffered from far fewer strikes.

Women supplied most recruits to the labour force of the industry because no sex differential existed in weaving wage rates[4] and few men wished to remain 'only a weaver' through-

[1] W. Whittam Jr., *Report on England's Cotton Industry* (Washington, Government Printing Office, 1907), 15.

[2] H. A. Turner, *Trade Union Growth, Structure and Policy. A Comparative Study of the Cotton Unions* (London, Allen, 1962), 128–35, 150–7.

[3] *The Times*, 28 Aug. 1878, 4iv.

[4] S. Webb, 'The Alleged Differences in the Wages Paid to Men and to Women for Similar Work', *Economic Journal*, Dec. 1891, 640.

out their working life. Female weavers proved punctual, regular, and zealous in their application to labour: they were more docile than men and more easily encouraged to increase production under the competitive slate system. With energy and deftness, they could attain the coveted status of a four-loom weaver and so become rich, proud, independent, and highly marriageable. The local womenfolk adapted their pattern of life to the demands of industry: they usually married late after saving for a dowry and gave up weaving after the birth of their first child: they did however bring up their daughters to enter the shed and provided a useful reserve supply of labour able to undertake 'weaving for sick' when necessary. Lancashire thus retained the highest proportion of half-timers, working girls, and working women in the whole country. The weaving towns had the highest proportion in the county of women to men and the highest proportion of working women: they also had lower fertility ratios and higher infantile death-rates than the spinning towns.[1] The dominant role of women within the labour force maintained the social pattern of single-shift working, limited the economic use of capital equipment, and raised the cost of production. It also increased the liability of women to suffer wage cuts since they were helpers in the family rather than its chief support. It served to maintain the generally low level of wages in the cotton industry and in particular in the weaving section, to reinforce the conservative attitudes of operatives, and to retard the spread of unionism.

The labour-intensive process of weaving was able to recruit an ample supply of cheap labour and to increase the proportionate share of such labour within the industry's work-force. The share of women and girls in the labour force of weaving firms rose only from 59 per cent in 1850 to 62 per cent in 1890 but their total number first exceeded those employed in spinning firms in 1867 and so established the pattern followed by children in 1885 and by men and youths in 1890. As weaving became the main employer of half-timers, the share of children in the labour force of weaving firms increased from 0·5 per cent

[1] T. A. Welton, 'Forty Years' Industrial Changes', *Transactions of the Manchester Statistical Society*, 9 Mar. 1898, 158; idem, 'Notes on the Census Report (1901) for the County of Lancaster', ibid. 19 Nov. 1902, 9, 12; A. Shadwell, *Industrial Efficiency* (1906), i. 96–9; B. L. Hutchins, 'Statistics of Women's Life and Employment', *Journal of the Royal Statistical Society*, June 1909, 226, 239.

in 1850 to a peak of 13·5 per cent in 1874. Their numbers would have increased even faster if the minimum age for half-timers had not been raised in 1874 from eight to ten and, against the stout opposition of the adult weavers to such a social revolution, from ten to eleven in 1891. The number of children employed in weaving firms exceeded the number employed in spinning firms in 1885 and the number employed in combined firms in 1890. Weaving firms increased their share of the total number of children employed in the whole industry from 1 per cent in 1850 and 10 per cent in 1861 to 43 per cent in 1890. Factory legislation does not seem to have increased the demand for male labour but may well have prevented a decline in its employment after 1874. The competition of men with women for employment undoubtedly became important in north-east Lancashire in proportion to the absence of alternative employment for males. Thus Preston, Chorley, and Accrington employed a higher proportion of female labour than Burnley or Blackburn while Nelson and Colne employed more men than women in their cotton industry in the complete absence of alternative employment in coal-mining or engineering.

* * *

The emergence of a horizontally organized structure of industry, with its major sections located in two different geographical areas, was caused by the expansion of the spinning trade in the south and its decline in the north and by the growth of the weaving industry in northern Lancashire as both regions developed their comparative advantages for the pursuit of different trades. The superiority of southern Lancashire in the spinning industry was based upon both technical and commercial advantages and especially upon the early establishment of the factory system in spinning, the invention and improvement of the mule, the adoption of the steam-engine, and the expansion of the textile engineering trade. The spinning firms of the south had always been more numerous than those of the north. They enjoyed convenient access to the cotton market of Liverpool and the yarn market of Manchester. They spun yarn for sale in the open market because it was produced for other trades as well as for the weaving industry, either for export or for the yarn trade of Nottingham, Leicester, Bradford, or Glasgow. They concentrated in particular upon the manufacture of high counts which were unsuitable for use in the power-loom. They set the example followed by the doublers of high-quality yarn who developed their trade upon a similar specialized basis. The textile engineers of the main spinning centres of Oldham and Bolton established their superiority with the advent of the self-actor and the long mule in the 1830s and thereafter developed the capacity of the mule to the highest degree until it had conquered the bulk of the trade by the 1880s.[1] The spinning mills of the south benefited from a more highly developed network of communications and from the growth of an active market in cotton waste. The advent of the Oldham limiteds in 1874–5 and the introduction of the Oldham spinning list in 1876 with its built-in incentive to the speedier production of yarn further enhanced the advantages of the south. The new limiteds exploited the economies of scale to the limit: they adopted longer mules and wider cards than their predecessors and employed a superior class of operatives who earned more but worked better and harder than their northern counterparts. They made their full technical superiority apparent only slowly but nevertheless reduced yarn prices and the profit margins of their competitors, so ushering in the great depression of 1877–9. They gave a great impetus to the development of specialization by process in both north and south since the yarn they spun was high in value in relation to its weight and thus could bear the cost of additional transportation to the weaving sheds of the north. Nor did their cops deteriorate during carriage since they were regularly and firmly wound during the process of spinning on the self-actor. Such specialized spinning firms remained the most numerous group of firms within the industry until 1890: they reduced the comparative importance of the combined firm in the spinning trade much more than in the weaving trade and increased their share of the industry's spindles from 45 per cent in 1850 to 70 per cent in 1890. In the spinning area their share rose from 72 per cent in 1884 to 76 per cent in 1896.

Between 1882 and 1896 the spindles of Lancashire increased by 14 per cent but those in the south increased by 6,460,000

[1] *Preston Guardian*, 3 July 1875, 6ii, T. Banks; *Bolton Chronicle*, 13 Mar. 1880, 5iv.

or by 23 per cent while those in the north decreased by 1,324,500 or by 15 per cent. The south raised its share of the county's spindleage from 77 to 83 per cent and preserved a widely distributed and well-balanced spinning industry in six main centres. The average size of spinning firm remained much larger in Bolton, Oldham, Manchester, and Ashton than in Rochdale and was least of all in Stockport, with its large

TABLE 16

Distribution of Lancashire Spindles, 1882–1896

	Total	Spinning District	Proportion (%)	Weaving District	Proportion (%)
1882	37,545,344	28,872,202	76·9	8,673,142	23·1
1884	40,656,662	31,814,186	78·25	8,842,476	21·75
1885	41,298,110	32,693,635	79·16	8,604,475	20·84
1886	40,993,386	32,683,523	79·73	8,309,863	20·27
1887	41,032,021	32,836,193	80·03	8,195,828	19·97
1888	41,284,088	33,237,064	80·51	8,047,024	19·49
1890	41,544,829	33,510,541	80·66	8,034,288	19·34
1891	42,529,151	34,635,755	81·44	7,893,396	18·56
1892	41,872,783	34,151,243	81·56	7,721,540	18·44
1893	42,970,528	35,361,327	82·29	7,609,201	18·15
1894	43,186,647	35,730,443	82·73	7,456,204	17·27
1896	42,681,081	35,332,427	82·78	7,348,654	17·22

Source: J. Worrall, *The Cotton Spinners' and Manufacturers' Directory*, 1882–1896.
The towns of the spinning district comprised Ashton, Bolton, Bury, Dukinfield, Farnworth, Glossop, Golborne, Heywood, Hyde, Leigh, Manchester and Salford, Middleton, Mossley, Oldham, Radcliffe, Rochdale, Stalybridge, Stockport, Uppermill, Warrington, and Wigan.

number of small doubling firms. The broad pattern of specialization between the different centres remained unchanged, with the coarse and coarse-medium trade centred in Oldham, the medium and medium-fine trade located in Bolton, and the fine and extra-fine trade based in Manchester, whose old buildings remained best suited to the needs of that branch.[1] The new technique of ring spinning was most readily adopted in the coarse spinning districts of Rochdale, Heywood, and Wigan and further enhanced the superiority of the south, reducing the north to the role of an exporter of ring spindles, especially from

[1] B. A. Dobson, *Humidity in Cotton Spinning* (1897), 8–9, 34.

Accrington, and to that of an importer of yarn. The main exporters of yarn to the north became the towns of Oldham, Bolton, Ashton, and Stockport while Manchester, Rochdale, and Bury maintained a more balanced ratio of looms to spindles and consumed most of their own yarn.

In the north of Lancashire beyond Bolton and Rochdale spinning continued to expand until the 1860s and in Darwen and Accrington until 1875. There the spinning trade had developed from the 1830s under the aegis of the combined firm rather than under that of the specialized spinning firm but had always been relatively inferior to that of the south and suffered an absolute decline after 1875. The depression of 1877–9 precluded the possibility of any further investment in spinning mills. Thereafter no new mill was built in the north until 1901, not even under the auspices of the limited company: proposals for such ventures were not implemented, even during the prosperity of 1890. New capital ceased to be invested in the local spinning trade as its yield declined below that on consols and well below that accruing to investment in weaving. The mills of the district remained too old, small, and narrow to adapt to the requirements of improved machinery and especially of long mules. They were saddled with higher insurance premiums, higher transport costs, and less efficient labour than the mills of the south. The northern mills were invaded by inferior Irish labour after the Irish Famine, first in Blackburn and then in Preston,[1] and suffered the cumulative loss of the hereditary skill of their spinners, who were attracted to the mills of the south, especially of Bolton, by higher wages than those paid under the Preston list of 1859 or the Blackburn list of 1867. The cost structure of northern mills was further inflated by the turnover joint-stock companies of 1873–5 which charged exorbitant prices for old mills. The local engineering industry failed to adapt to the transition from the hand-mule to the self-actor and declined under the competition of the great firms of the south, becoming specialized in the manufacture of looms. The competition of the mills of the south was reinforced from the 1870s, especially in Rossendale, by the competition of the mills of Bombay in the market for T-cloths and domestics. Many old mills were burned down and not rebuilt while others were

[1] *Textile Mercury*, 27 Apr. 1889, 2.

converted to alternative uses or even demolished, after the sale of their old machinery as scrap.

The spindleage of the northern mills declined while that of the southern mills continued to increase for another fifty years until 1927. The decline was greatest in the east, least in the west of the northern district and slowest of all in Rossendale. Between 1882 and 1896 the three largest spinning centres, Preston, Blackburn, and Burnley, bore most of the total loss of spindles in the region, losing respectively 18, 20, and 36 per cent of their total spindleage. The reduction in spinning capacity was accomplished at the expense of the combined firms and not at that of the spinning firms. The district did not become wholly dependent upon the import of yarn but continued to spin one-quarter of its consumption of yarn because its labour force was less strongly unionized than that of south-east Lancashire and accepted lower wages. Attempts to enhance the competitive power of the short mules in northern mills were made by the use of coarse cotton and by the reduction of labour costs through the coupling (or 'double-decking') of mules or the joint minding of a pair of mules by two adults, practices opposed by southern operatives. The employment of female piecers was however resisted by male spinners in the north, although it was tolerated in the south. The ring-frame could be effectively used in old and narrow mills but was adopted in the south rather than in the north. The balance of industry between the two districts was fundamentally altered. Between 1884 and 1896 Burnley sank in status from the eleventh to the seventeenth largest centre of spinning, Blackburn from that of seventh to that of ninth, while Preston was surpassed in spindleage by both Stockport and Rochdale and reduced in status from the fourth to the seventh of spinning towns. The share of northern Lancashire in the total spindleage of the county was reduced from 23 per cent in 1884 to 17 per cent in 1896 and the share of the combined firm in its spindleage declined by 23 per cent or by exactly the same proportion.

North-east Lancashire found in specialization the key to rapid if unbalanced industrial expansion and regained the supremacy in manufacture lost during the great era of the combined firm. The Calder valley which extended from Burnley to Colne became the scene of the greatest expansion in population and industrial production as new specialized weaving firms and communities arose from the 1870s onward beneath the shadow of Pendle. That predominantly rural region lacked resources for the pursuit of arable farming but had the endowment necessary for industrial development in its abundant coal, stone, clay, and water as well as in the facilities of the Leeds and Liverpool Canal. It had an old-established tradition of weaving woollens and worsteds developed under the influence of Bradford, a population growing faster than anywhere else in Lancashire, and had no district associations of power-loom weavers before 1870. The climate of the region was more humid than that of south-east Lancashire. Its valleys were sheltered from the dry east winds most harmful to good weaving but lay open to the moist southwesterlies and had a clayey subsoil which preserved its moistness even in hot weather.

The poor quality of a rough, hilly, and humid land reduced its price well below the levels reached in south-east Lancashire, where urbanization had raised rentals, increased the height and cost of buildings, and multiplied the number of restrictive by-laws. The low price of land had facilitated the building of large cloth warehouses during the great age of the hand-loom: in the age of the power-loom it made possible the construction of large numbers of weaving sheds which were single-storeyed, since looms unlike mules did not work well upon upper floors, and therefore became as prodigal in their use of land as multi-storeyed spinning mills were economical. The modern type of weaving shed developed from 1850 in the Burnley district[1] and proved much better adapted to the wide spaces and cheap land of the north-east of the county than to the restricted confines and dear land of the south-east. The north-light roof truss of such sheds and their ancillary warehouses created their characteristic saw-toothed profile[2] and distinguished them sharply from the box-like multi-windowed structure of the spinning mill. The shed was as superbly functional a building as the mill. The windows in the roof eliminated the need for windows in the wall, transmitted from the north the maximum

[1] W. Fairbairn, *Treatise on Mills and Millwork. Part II On Machinery of Transmission and the Construction and Arrangement of Mills* (London, Longman, 1863), 115–16.

[2] *Textile Recorder*, May 1894, 14–17, reprinted in J. Nasmith, *Recent Cotton Mill Construction and Engineering* (Manchester, Heywood, 1894), 40–1, 90.

amount of clear and steady light at the working level of each loom, excluded the bright direct rays of the sun harmful to coloured cloth, and eliminated the deceitful shadows cast by direct light.

TABLE 17

Distribution of Lancashire Looms, 1882–1896

	Total	Weaving District	Proportion (%)	Spinning District	Proportion (%)
1882	465,454	292,678	62·88	172,776	37·12
1884	534,493	327,116	61·2	207,377	38·8
1885	546,118	333,913	61·14	212,205	38·86
1886	550,077	338,302	61·5	211,775	38·5
1887	582,307	370,091	63·56	212,216	36·44
1888	597,287	388,938	65·12	208,349	34·88
1890	614,964	397,832	64·69	217,132	35·31
1891	620,437	403,532	65·04	216,905	34·96
1892	625,217	404,278	64·66	220,939	35·34
1893	602,627	395,271	65·59	207,356	34·41
1894	631,302	416,506	65·98	214,796	34·02
1896	637,631	423,384	66·4	214,247	33·6

Source: J. Worrall, *The Cotton Spinners' and Manufacturers' Directory*, 1882–1896.
The towns of the weaving district to the north of Rochdale comprised Accrington, Bacup, Blackburn, Burnley, Chorley, Clitheroe, Colne, Darwen, Great Harwood, Haslingden, Littleborough, Nelson, Newchurch and Rawtenstall, Padiham, Preston, Ramsbottom, and Todmorden.

The growth of separate weaving firms specializing in the production of grey calico was facilitated by the perfection in 1841 of the strong and heavy Blackburn loom and by the adoption from 1858 of the slasher sizing machine. The process of vertical disintegration within the cotton industry was furthered by the expansion of the specialized trade in coloured goods, by the growth of loom-manufacture, and by the adaptation of the loom to the particular products of each locality. Under such influences the loomage of north-east Lancashire increased between 1882 and 1896 by 45 per cent while its spindleage declined by 15 per cent: the net addition of 130,000 looms, or more than thrice the number added in the south during the same period, represented a capital investment of some £3,300,000 which far outweighed the loss of capital invested in its ancient spindles. That process of expansion was wholly the work of weaving firms which added some 153,600 looms or fivefold the 29,800 looms lost by combined firms in the area. As looms were added out of all proportion to the spindleage existing in the north, the local ratio of spindles to looms declined sharply[1] and thus afforded a striking indication of the advance of specialization by process. The district increased its proportion of the looms of Lancashire from 63 per cent in 1882 to 66·4 per cent in 1896 and increased its imports of yarn from the spinning district from two-thirds to three-quarters of its total consumption. The most specialized centres of weaving became most dependent upon such imports. By 1896 Nelson imported 98 per cent of its yarn, Burnley 95 per cent, and Blackburn 90 per cent while Preston imported only some 55 per cent since its spindles produced fine counts with which Oldham could not compete. Thus the spinning industry acquired a vast local market, internal trade flourished between the two districts, and the yarn and cloth agents became essential intermediaries therein. Rossendale became increasingly more important as a transit-region between the two districts than as an independent centre of production as its mills suffered the blight of competition from Oldham and Bombay in the 1870s.

* * *

The main product of the revolution in weaving was not cloth but weavers and weaving communities. The economic returns of the industry were paid in profit, rent, and, above all, in wages. The greatest expansion of population and production in north-east Lancashire occurred first in the Blackburn district between 1840 and 1880 and then in the Burnley district. Blackburn remained the seed-bed of invention in power-weaving from the 1820s until the 1880s and became the true pioneer of specialization by process, importing yarn from the 1820s in increasing volume. It became the world's main centre of cloth production as its Eastern markets expanded. It benefited from the negotiation of the Blackburn list in 1853 and

[1] According to Worrall's *Directories* the spindle–loom ratio decreased in the north from 29·6 in 1882 to 17·4 in 1896, in the south from 168·5 to 165, and in Lancashire as a whole from 80·5 to 67. The northern ratio thus sank from one-sixth of the southern ratio in 1882 to one-tenth in 1896.

became more dependent upon the cotton industry than any other town.[1] The development of calico-manufacture, especially in the boom of the 1850s, compensated the district for the loss of its calico-printing industry to south-east Lancashire, with whose weaving industry it began increasingly to compete. It captured the cotton shirting trade of Stalybridge, Hyde, and Stockport and prevented any further increase in their power-looms after the 1840s. Blackburn became the seat of the greatest yarn market in Lancashire and stimulated the internal trade in yarn, to the especial benefit of Oldham. It preserved its primacy as the capital of the weaving kingdom even after the development of the towns of the Calder valley. It remained the home of the largest single population of cotton operatives in all Lancashire, the main centre of the vast India trade, and the headquarters of the Weavers' Amalgamation established in 1884 as well as of the United Cotton Manufacturers' Association established in 1889. The Blackburn weaving list of 1853 regulated by 1883 nearly two-thirds of the wages earned upon 600,000 power-looms[2] and became the basis of the new list of 1892, which superseded all other local lists and transferred to the operatives most of the benefits of increased output in the form of higher earnings.[3]

Burnley became the great boom town of Victorian Lancashire, having displaced Colne by the 1830s as the most populous centre of the Calder valley. It did not have a single specialized weaving firm in 1850 but began to convert its spinning mills into loom sheds during the weaving boom of 1858 and benefited by its abundant supply of labour, its low standard of living, its low wages, and its lack of any wage list before 1873. In the 1870s and 1880s it expanded its weaving industry rapidly, captured from Blackburn the trade in cheap, narrow printers with the aid of the light fast-running Burnley loom and of the Burnley list of 1880, and acquired a monopoly of their production as Oldham acquired a monopoly of the spinning of the

[1] *Blackburn Standard*, 28 Sept. 1864, 2i.

[2] J. C. Fielden, 'A Sketch of the British Cotton Industry', *C.W.S. Annual*, 1887, 322.

[3] *Textile Recorder*, May 1892, 18, 'The New Weaving List'; R. Marsden, *Cotton Weaving* (London, Bell, 1895), 355, 497–509; E. M. Gray, 'Wage Rates and Earnings in Cotton Weaving', *Transactions of the Manchester Statistical Society*, 9 Nov 1938, 14–15.

American yarn used in their manufacture. It also developed the manufacture of fancy goods from 1887 under the stimulus of a four months' strike in Ashton and profited from the negotiation of the North Lancashire Fancy Weaving List of 1887. The average size of its weaving firms grew faster than in any other weaving town. In 1894 the number of its looms first surpassed the number of looms in Blackburn and the membership of the Burnley Weavers' Association first equalled that of the Blackburn Weavers' Association, giving it the fourth largest population of cotton operatives in the county after Blackburn, Bolton, and Oldham. The trade of the largest textile manufacturing town in Europe employed the highest proportion of married women weavers and paid by 1885 the highest average wages in Lancashire,[1] in testimony to the productivity of its weavers and the militancy of their union.

Nelson and Colne developed their weaving trade and began to manufacture Manchester goods in place of mixed goods for the Bradford trade but still preserved a finer trade than that of Blackburn or Burnley, beginning to import Egyptian yarn from Bolton. Nelson developed the manufacture of sateens from 1882 and that of coloured goods from 1887, benefiting from its access to the dyeing industry of Bradford as well as to cheaper labour than that of Radcliffe. It lost its last spinning firm in 1887 and its spindles were first surpassed in number by its looms in 1896 in a county which mustered on average 67 spindles to every single loom. It increased its looms at thrice the rate of north-east Lancashire as a whole and rose in status from the twelfth largest weaving centre in 1882 to the fourth largest in 1891. The town enjoyed the highest rate of growth of population in all Lancashire and became far more dependent upon weaving than any other town as well as far more dependent upon the cotton industry than Burnley since it lacked coal-mining or engineering industries.

Preston had enjoyed its greatest wave of industrial expansion between 1820 and 1850 and remained the only town beyond the limits of the Lancashire coalfield with a substantial cotton industry. It preserved its historic superiority to the inland towns, based upon its nodal position for communications at the

[1] *Returns of the Rates of Wages in the Principal Textile Trades of the United Kingdom* (C.5087 of 1889), viii; G. H. Wood, *Wages in the Cotton Trade* (1910), 83.

lowest bridging-point of the Ribble, its ready access to the cheap food and labour of the fertile Fylde, its great agricultural market, its diversified economy, and its role from 1888 as the administrative headquarters of the new county council. Its firms were large, old, and wealthy, enjoying an international reputation and adding value to their cloth where Blackburn created weight and Burnley produced length.[1] Its cotton industry was more diversified than that of any other town: it retained the largest spindleage in the north and the fifth largest population of cotton operatives and ranked third in loomage after Burnley and Blackburn, with the support of the largest engineering industry in the weaving district.

The spinning district successfully adapted its substantial weaving industry to the new division of labour brought about by the growth of cotton manufacture in the north-east. It retained five of the county's eleven largest centres of weaving, dominated by combined firms which controlled two-thirds of the looms of the area. Moreover it expanded its loomage even faster than its spindleage in the 1880s and 1890s, increasing it between 1882 and 1896 by 24 per cent, or at about half the rate of the weaving district. Thus the weaving trade of the south did not suffer a general decline comparable to that of spinning in the north but survived and prospered with the aid of the peculiar advantages of the region. The supply of yarn was much closer to hand than in the north and afforded some compensation for the shortage of competent weavers. Weaving became more dependent than spinning upon the Manchester market whose proximity reduced the carriage costs entering into the price of cloth. The loom manufacturers of Bury and the Jacquard loom-makers of Manchester came to rank amongst the most highly specialized of textile engineers. The local unions of power-loom weavers were relatively few, new, and weak and their influence was further reduced by the failure of the Ashton strike of 1887. Capital was more abundant than in the north and had no need for the facilities supplied by room-and-power companies. Nor were the weaving sheds of the south afflicted and destroyed by fires, like the spinning mills of the north. The combined firms of the area had old-established market connections and continued profitably to produce

[1] *Textile Manufacturer*, Feb. 1881, 41, 'Weaving in Preston'.

printers and shirtings while specialized manufacturers maintained their output of such local specialities as counterpanes, quilts, and fancy goods in Bolton, towelling in Heywood and Droylsden, velveteens in Oldham, fancies in Ashton, and coloured goods in Manchester, Radcliffe, and Bury. The south indeed remained the home of the most valuable weaving trade and relegated plain weaving to the north. The expansion of its loomage was the achievement of separate manufacturing concerns even more than of the combined firms. It was also the work of private employers rather than of companies which failed in Stalybridge (1883–9), Ashton (1884–97), and Rochdale (1888–95) to compete with north-east Lancashire in the manufacture of plain goods. Private firms became private limiteds and so expanded the role of the company in weaving especially in Rochdale, Bolton, and Bury, to a much greater degree than in the north-east.

There was certainly a shift in weaving capacity within the spinning area as the loomage of the Ashton district declined, especially after the failure of the strike of 1887, and that of the Bolton–Bury district expanded. South-east Lancashire did not in fact include any major centre of the weaving industry but suffered a decline in its loomage, save in Stalybridge and Glossop where the weavers remained un-unionized, and became increasingly a specialized spinning district. Oldham declined in status from the seventh largest centre of weaving in 1882 to the eleventh largest in 1892 while Manchester similarly declined from the fourth largest to the sixth largest in 1890. The loss of 9,900 looms in seven towns of the south-east was however far outweighed by the addition of 51,400 looms in nine other centres within the belt of land extending eastwards from Bolton and Leigh to Heywood and Middleton, especially in the coloured and fancy goods trades. Bolton, the oldest centre of weaving, the home of the fancy trade, and the centre of production of the industry's most valuable single output of cloth, increased its loomage by 32 per cent and surpassed Oldham from 1891 as a weaving centre. In the heart of the spinning district Radcliffe and Walkden remained thriving specialized centres of weaving, especially of coloured goods. The south retained in 1896 the sixth largest centre of weaving in Manchester, the eighth largest in Rochdale, and the next three largest in Bury, Bolton, and Oldham. Its share of the total loomage of Lancashire sank only from 37 per cent in 1882 to 33·6 per cent in 1896. Thus weaving remained far less localized within the cotton districts than spinning.

The geographical segregation of the major processes of production was inevitably achieved only by reducing the role of the firm which combined weaving with spinning. Such firms had appeared first in south-east Lancashire and then during the 1830s in the north-east, where they had established a relatively stronger position than in the Stalybridge area. By 1841 they employed more workers than the separate spinning and weaving firms in every cotton town except Rochdale. Thereafter they increased in importance and embraced by 1850 31 per cent of the firms but 52·5 per cent of the spindles, 60·8 per cent of the labour force, and 82·6 per cent of the power-looms employed in the English cotton industry and an even higher proportion of those employed in Lancashire.[1] That trend towards the concentration of industrial capital remained subject to technological constraints. Such firms controlled only coarse spinning and plain weaving and could not develop in the medium and fine trade while the power-loom remained comparatively imperfect. They were outnumbered two to one by the separate spinning and weaving establishments, whose continued development checked the movement towards vertical integration after it reached its peak during the 1840s. The combined firms declined earlier and faster within Lancashire than outside the heartland of the industry. They were surpassed in importance by the faster growing specialized firms, first in spinning in south Lancashire during the 1850s and then in weaving in north Lancashire during the 1880s as the power-loom was brought to technical perfection and revived the tradition of small-scale enterprise. Their number reached its peak in 1861. They increased their employees until 1861 at less than one-third the rate of other firms. They increased their spindles until 1870 at only half the rate of spinning firms, and their looms until 1878 at only one-seventh the rate of weaving firms. They were surpassed by the separate spinning firms in their aggregate spindleage between 1850 and 1856 but not in their average spindleage until 1874 in Lancashire or until 1885

[1] Respectively 38, 56, 62·6, and 82 per cent.

in England as a whole. In 1884 they still dominated the spinning trade of north Lancashire, controlling 81 per cent of its spindleage, and the weaving trade of south Lancashire, operating 66 per cent of its loomage. In that year they controlled only 28 per cent of the spindleage in south Lancashire but 50 per cent of the loomage in north Lancashire.

During the weaving boom of the 1880s the combined firms finally lost their supremacy in manufacture, especially in the weaving district. They were surpassed by the specialized weaving firms in their aggregate loomage by 1885 though not in their average loomage because of their immense superiority in capital. Their share of the total number of looms in Lancashire declined, according to the returns made to the Inspectors of Factories, from 52 per cent in 1878 to 46·5 per cent in 1885 and to 38·8 per cent in 1890 or, according to the more reliable figures in *The Cotton Spinners' and Manufacturers' Directory* of John Worrall, from 57 per cent in 1884 to 42 per cent in 1896. The decade of the 1880s thus completed the work of the 1850s in dethroning them from their eminence within the industry, a process accomplished during the weaving boom of 1886–90. In north Lancashire their decline began earlier than in the south, was much greater and was more apparent in the sphere of weaving than in that of spinning. Between 1884 and 1896 the number of looms in the combined firms of the north sank by 30,476 of which 70 per cent were lost by the combined firms of Blackburn, Preston, and Burnley. Their share of the loomage of the weaving district sank from 49·7 to 31·2 per cent while that of the specialized weaving firms increased in corresponding proportion. The combined firms reduced their loomage in fourteen out of eighteen weaving towns. Those of Burnley suffered the greatest losses, of 51 per cent of their spindles and 68 per cent of their looms. The combined firms still dominated the spinning trade of the area and controlled 75 per cent of its spindles, particularly in the great centres of Preston and Blackburn. They still remained the basis of the cotton manufacture in the older and smaller centres, above all in Rossendale.

In south Lancashire the combined firms were older and larger, especially in loomage, than in the north and they declined far less. Between 1884 and 1896 they reduced their spindleage by 5·5 per cent against a reduction of 24 per cent in the north, and their loomage by 4 per cent against a reduction of 27 per cent in the north. Those firms still operated 62 per cent of the looms in the spinning district in 1896. They continued to control the coarse spinning trade of Bury, Ramsbotton, Radcliffe, and Wigan as well as the weaving trade of the three large centres of Oldham, Rochdale, and Bolton. In Leigh and Bolton they expanded their relative share of both the spinning and weaving plant. The original home and unchallenged domain of the combined firms remained however in the south-east, where they controlled the trade of Glossop, Stalybridge, Hyde, Ashton, and Mossley in high-class Cheshire printers. There the firms were old-established, deep-rooted, and strong in capital resources as much as in market connections. There the pure manufacturing firm had never established itself and the combined firms virtually monopolized the manufacture of printing cloths. Hyde indeed suffered a loss of both spindles and looms as its combined firms declined under the competition first of Blackburn and then of Burnley: it lost 28 per cent of its spindleage and 12 per cent of its looms between 1884 and 1896 and became the only cotton town to suffer such a double loss in the process of vertical disintegration, expanding its hatting trade as the cotton industry declined. In Glossop however the great combined firms, headed by the concerns of John Wood and Francis Sumner, were relatively more important than in any other cotton town because of the total absence of small firms. They were the peers of the firms of Preston in weaving and were even more important in the field of spinning, where they ranked with the large firms of Bolton and Leigh. Nine firms controlled all the looms of Glossop and expanded without the spur of competition from limited companies felt in Ashton. Between 1884 and 1896 they increased their spindleage by 16 per cent and their loomage by 18 per cent to reach the giant average size of 116,000 spindles and 2,026 looms, or nearly fourfold the size of the average combined firm.

Combined firms had been originally created in order to reduce the pressure on profits created by falling prices. They apparently declined least during the period of falling prices from 1873 to 1896 and most rapidly during the rising prices of 1850–73 and 1896–1914. They were affected earlier and more severely by the competition of specialized spinning firms than

TABLE 18

Average Size of the Combined Spinning and Weaving factory, 1850–1890

	Average Number of Spinning Spindles	Average Number of Power-Looms	Average Number of Employees
1850	18,621	342	327·4
1856	16,979	336	314·4
1861	19,634	351	321·3
1867	25,433	328	298·6
1870	31,494	460	413·4
1874	24,451	427	344·4
1878	25,955	466	348·3
1885	26,678	533	389·5
1890	30,169	574	437

Source: Returns of the Factory Inspectors, 1850–90.

by that of weaving firms and reduced their share of the total spindleage in the industry from 39 per cent in 1884 to 33 per cent in 1896. Their share of the spindleage in the spinning district declined from 28 to 24 per cent as spinning firms continued their expansion. They adapted to the growth of their specialized rivals and achieved a new balance between their departments by basing their operations increasingly upon manufacture rather than on spinning. They did not become more but less specialized and increased the variety of their products in order to keep pace with the frequent changes of fashion in dress goods, particularly in the home trade. Instead of making the same cloth year in and year out and piling up stocks in recession until demand revived, as they had done down to the 1870s, they moved away from the American pattern of product standardization. They became much more responsive to fluctuations in demand and employed their massed looms upon a whole range of different fabrics, often making fifty to a hundred varieties and qualities within the course of a few weeks. They did not lag behind their competitors in the adoption of new machinery but kept pace with the flow in innovations in the spinning industry and ahead of it in the weaving industry.

In their aggregate of employees the combined firms were outnumbered by the spinning firms only in 1890, when they still employed 38 per cent of the industry's labour force. By then they had ceased to be the representative firms of the industry such as they had been in 1850 when the average combined firm operated 18,600 spindles and 342 looms or 64 per cent more spindles than the average spinning firm and

TABLE 19

Decline of the Combined Spinning and Weaving Factory, 1850–1890

	Spindles	% of Total	Looms	% of Total	Employees	% of Total
1850	10,055,410	52·5	184,816	82·6	176,776	60·8
1856	10,577,799	41	209,609	74·9	195,893	57·4
1861	13,274,346	41·8	235,268	63·9	215,577	52·9
1867	16,022,831	49·3	206,827	60	188,126	52·7
1870	16,155,290	44·8	235,904	57·4	212,078	51·1
1874	14,917,362	37·3	260,724	60·6	210,073	47·7
1878	15,106,601	32·4	271,062	55·3	202,721	44·9
1885	13,205,795	30·6	263,892	49·9	192,789	41·4
1890	12,912,170	29·9	245,877	42	187,033	38

Source: Returns of the Factory Inspectors, 1850–90.

114 per cent more looms than the average weaving firm. In 1890 it controlled 30,000 spindles and 574 looms, being 10 per cent smaller[1] than the average spinning firm of 33,700 spindles but still 57 per cent larger than the average weaving firm of 366 looms. It mustered 437 employees in contrast to the 173 hands of the average spinning firm and the 155 hands of the average weaving firm, or 33 per cent more than both such firms together: it even employed a total capital some 4 per cent greater than the joint capitals of the average spinning firm and the average weaving firm. By 1896 the combined firms were fewer than one-fifth of the total number of firms in the industry and employed only 10 per cent of its doubling spindles but 33 per cent of its spinning spindles and 42 per cent of its looms.[2] The powers of survival of such firms were greater than those of their specialized competitors because their managerial ability was more generalized, their operations were geared to the stable home trade rather than to the fluctuating export trade, and

[1] In Lancashire 24 per cent smaller, where in 1850 it had been 50 per cent larger.

[2] J. Worrall, *The Cotton Spinners' and Manufacturers' Directory*, 1896.

their structure afforded protection against the impact of cyclical depression. Combined firms continued to function as the main sphere of private enterprise, the preserve of the leading industrial clans of the county and the seed-bed of the greatest of its firms, of which the nine largest were all combined enterprises. They survived in every single one of 42 cotton towns except for Middleton after 1887. They formed the greatest obstacle to the progress of the public company as well as to the onward march of specialization by process.

* * *

The specialization of the northern and southern halves of the cotton district in different industrial processes ushered in from the 1880s a new era in the history of the cotton industry: it produced a peculiarly English pattern of industrial organization unknown in any other cotton industry or in any other branch of the British textile trade since no geographical segregation of processes developed in the worsted industry to reinforce its horizontal structure. The cotton industry became increasingly organized upon horizontal lines with specialist firms engaged in buying cotton, spinning, weaving, finishing, and marketing. The core of that structure was however the divorce of spinning from weaving which developed not by a process of fission within the combined firm but appeared only with the rise of separate spinning firms in the 1850s and of separate weaving firms in the 1880s. It was not the logical development of tendencies long present in the structure of the trade and it reversed the trend towards the vertical integration of processes which had been characteristic of the period 1830–50. The new trend was indeed interpreted at first as a sympton of decline rather than of progress[1] and was only reappraised in optimistic terms by a bankrupt manufacturer turned publicist, the Arthur Young of the cotton industry.[2] The new form of industrial

[1] W. A. Abram, 'The Prospective Decline of Lancashire', *Blackwood's Edinburgh Magazine*, July 1892, 3–6.

[2] Elijah Helm, 'The Alleged Decline of the British Cotton Industry', *Economic Journal*, Dec. 1892, 738; idem, 'Commercial and Industrial Manchester' in B.M.A., Manchester Meeting, 1902, *Handbook and Guide to Manchester* (Manchester, Ireland, 1902), 120–1; idem, 'The British Cotton Industry', in W. J. Ashley (ed.), *British Industries* (London, Longmans, 1903), 80.

organization undoubtedly developed in response to the world-wide demand for the cotton goods of Lancashire but survived only because the industry had become so concentrated and had inspired the intense development of ancillary facilities for transportation, communication, marketing, and banking.

The new structure of industry was assumed to increase both external and internal economies through an enhanced degree of local specialization by ancillary industries and through intensified specialization by separate firms enforced by the beneficial influence of competition and rationalized in terms of the division of labour. In theory such a horizontal organization gave to both spinning and weaving a free choice of markets and so facilitated the specialization of management, machinery, and labour, enhancing productivity as capacity was adapted to function. Such specialization would improve the quality of the product, increase its quantity, and minimize its cost. The functional division of labour between the processes would also limit the risks involved in the investment of capital and moderate the adverse influence of seasonal and cyclical fluctuations in trade. Such theoretical advantages were however exaggerated at the expense of the practical disadvantages of specialization. They were greatest in respect of skilled labour and remained least in the manufacture of plain calico which became the main sphere of such specialization. In effect the process made resources increasingly specific to limited tasks and made the industry less flexible and less responsive to market pressures at the very time when it needed to become more responsive. It failed to engender any major cost-cutting innovations in spheres where there was still vast scope for such inventions. It embodied an unproductive form of over-specialization which deprived the world of any model for emulation, limited the range of expectations of such specialized firms, and thereby reduced the rate of growth of the industry as a whole. By compartmentalizing technical knowledge it accentuated the vertical ignorance of both spinners and manufacturers who became sundered by more than thirty miles of physical distance. It insulated spinners from the ultimate market for woven goods, hindered them from producing the yarns best suited to specific types of cloth, and so prevented them from serving manufacturers to the best of their ability.

Cloth agents usually lacked the technical knowledge of manufacturers and often failed to convey to them the detailed instructions of merchants. The quality of yarn also deteriorated through the damage suffered in transit, which increased the amount of waste by some 2½ per cent.[1]

Specialization not only worsened the quality of products but also raised their cost of production. Spinners were burdened with the costs of dampening their yarn, of packing and carting it as well as with the commission on its sale. The reduction of costs through technical innovation was also hindered since the ring-frame offered the greatest economies to combined firms but was restricted in its spread by the cost of transport of the bobbins on which its yarn had to be spun. Thus horizontal segregation of the processes reinforced the dominance of the mule, whose cops were superbly made for the necessary handling and packing in skips and could be skewered directly on to the shuttle-tongue without rewinding. For their part manufacturers were precluded from exploiting the economies of scale to the same extent as the spinners. The combined firm in contrast retained a whole range of cost advantages denied to separate firms. Its weaving shed could be conveniently sited beneath the lee of its tall mill so as to protect it from the cost-raising blast of the dry east wind. Its costs of production remained lower because it saved upon the commission paid and the discount allowed upon the sale of yarn, acquired no bad debts, and required neither packers nor yarn agents. It also saved on the repair of skips, on carriage costs, and on the interest of money during the time lost in transit because the yarn was woven into cloth more quickly than would otherwise have been the case. Its yarn suffered no damage through excessive damp and no delay or injury in transit so that a smaller stock could be kept and less waste was produced in weaving. Its final products were superior to those of specialized firms which could neither design each process of manufacture in relation to the end in view nor control quality at every stage of production.

The geographical separation of spinning from weaving ben-

[1] *Textile Manufacturer*, June 1878, 179, 'The Improvement of our Cotton Textiles'; *Manchester Guardian*, 17 Nov. 1882, 4v, 'The Condition of the Cotton Trade'.

efited commerce much more than industry. It created a vast transport industry to carry the cotton on six separate and successive journeys, so increasing the burden of transport charges upon the industry. Those charges were less competitive in the north of the cotton district than in the south because of the less developed nature of transport facilities: they weighed more heavily on yarn and cloth than on raw cotton and thus doubly favoured the south against the north. Moreover they were much more important in the plain trade of the north than in the fancy trade of the south, which could more easily afford to absorb high transport costs into the high prices paid for its products.

The horizontal organization of industry helped to employ an increasing proportion of the population of Lancashire in the cotton trades as distinct from the cotton industry. In particular it consolidated the position of yarn and cloth agents as semi-parasitical middlemen who earned commissions totalling double the costs of carriage and equal to 10–15 per cent of the total wages bill of the industry.[1] Cloth agents acted as bankers and financed manufacturers as yarn agents financed spinners but enjoyed much higher incomes than their clients whom they reduced to the level of virtual piece-workers, cut off from direct contact with the ultimate buyers of their half-finished goods. The prosperity of each of the two separate branches of the industry became dependent upon the existence of excess capacity and overproduction in the other branch so that commercial fluctuations did not diminish in intensity but tended to extend their influence. The resistance of both spinners and manufacturers to cyclical depression was reduced in so far as their products were suited only to a limited market, since long runs of production to standard specifications became more difficult to achieve. Thus competition for the available margin of profit engendered jealousy and friction, reducing the possibility of co-operation within the industry even at a purely economic level. The position of both spinners and manufacturers was weakened in relation to the merchants whose dominant position and high profits were partly maintained by their tactics of 'divide and rule'.

[1] *Cotton Factory Times*, 24 Apr. 1885, 4v, 8 May 1885, 4ii, 'Commissions Paid in the Cotton Trade'.

The new pattern of industrial organization impressed progress-oriented minds as peculiarly appropriate to a concentrated, differentiated, and integrated organism and as more clearly illustrative of Herbert Spencer's principles of biology than the organization of any other industry.[1] Nevertheless it remained a wasteful and expensive pattern which paradoxically developed at a time of declining profits.[2] The division of function reduced the profits of specialized producers while combined firms continued to reap the rewards appropriate to their greater skills of management. Both spinning and weaving towns were debarred from the possibility of the balanced employment of their men in spinning and of their women in weaving. Both spinning and weaving areas were denied the full independence so highly prized locally and were condemned to depend upon interregional trade. The spinning towns were deprived of the profits of plain weaving and the weaving towns of the profits of spinning as well as of the trade in cotton waste. The burden of progress was however unequally distributed between the two areas. The weaving district paid a much higher price than the spinning district in the destruction of the capital invested in its spinning plant, in the devaluation of the capital of the manufacturers of Preston and Blackburn, in the precipitation of many failures in the weaving trade, in the unnecessary investment of capital in Burnley and Nelson, in the reduction of the economy of the weaving towns to total dependence upon a single industry, and in the perpetuation of the status of manufacturers in general as the most impoverished members of the whole cotton trade. Blackburn in particular was reduced to the level of 'a struggling town, with one branch only of a great trade, and the most elementary department of that branch'[3] and voiced its opposition to such a fate most strongly during the depression of 1891–3. The yarn imported by Blackburn would, it was estimated, if spun locally require 35 100,000-spindle mills, which would cost £3,500,000, employ 3,500 men, and pay £564,200 in wages as well as £350,000 or 10 per cent in profits, in notable benefits to the local economy.[4]

[1] Schulze-Gaevernitz, op. cit. 65–6.

[2] *Textile Recorder*, Nov. 1885, 147, 'Spinning and Weaving'.

[3] *The Bee. The Magazine of the Blackburn Technical School*, Mar. 1891, 27, 'The Blackburn Ship Canal. An Argument in Three Chapters'.

[4] Ibid., Mar. 1891, 27–8, Apr. 1891, 46–7, 'Jennv', 'Neither Do We Spin',

The extent of specialization was often exaggerated by outside observers and undoubtedly became most marked in the small centres of the industry. It became extreme in Burnley, Nelson, and Colne and their dependent townships, but was never general throughout the cotton districts. The whole area of east Lancashire remained closely united by a delicate web of social, cultural, and religious relationships as well as by a network of capital investments, the omnipresence of the combined firm, and the indivisible unity of Rossendale. That unity masked however a broad socio-cultural difference between the developed south and the 'undeveloped' north, between the Liberal–Nonconformist culture of the *Gesellschaften* of the south and the Conservative–Anglican tradition of the *Gemeinschaften* of the north. It also concealed the extension of the imperial influence of Manchester and its adjacent spinning towns. The weaving district acquired a majority of the population of cotton operatives but remained in commercial thraldom to south Lancashire which retained control of the commanding heights of the regional economy through its great banks, its extensive markets for cotton waste, yarn, and cloth, its possession of the great bulk of the finishing and engineering trades, and its more developed and competitive transportation facilities, which were further extended by the successful completion of the Manchester Ship Canal. The ancillary industries of hard-waste spinning and skip manufacture generated by the structural reorganization of industry tended to settle in the south rather than in the north. The export trade in spindles remained far greater than that in looms to the benefit of the south which also remained the home of the leading family dynasties of the industry and became the main seat of the private limited company as well as of the trust. The weaving towns in contrast had only eight of the leading eighty firms in the industry. The increasing emphasis placed by publicists upon the north–south division of Lancashire between the Ribble and Irwell basins in effect diverted attention from the historic east–west division of the shire between the frontier communities of the Pennine region and the metropolitan cities of the plain with their flourishing commerce, their accumulated wealth, and their declining birth-rates.

May 1891, 50–1, 'Our Disappearing Spindles', May 1891, 52, 'Why Not Bleach?'

Conclusion

> I hope that cotton will eventually be spun and woven where it is grown—or at least by races capable of no manlier business.
>
> Ruskin, 'General Statement Explaining the Nature and Purposes of St. George's Guild, 1882', in *The Works of Ruskin*, edited by E. T. Cook and A. Wedderburn (London, Allen, 1907), Vol. 30, 52.

FRONTIER SOCIETIES have often been military societies and have made their impact upon the world through the force of arms. The influence of Lancashire, 'the America of England',[1] was confined to the economic sphere but was perhaps more pervasive than any military hegemony during the era of its maturity. A barren and isolated region erupted suddenly into a fury of productive power of which its previous history had given but faint promise and of which its later history showed but little trace. Its cotton industry was the creation of the three generations between 1780 and 1840 and grew to maturity during the next three generations from 1840 to 1913, transforming the life of the nation as well as of the region. In a longer perspective that industry may be seen as the dominant theme of an important phase in English industrial history and of a relatively brief episode in British textile history, whose fundamental course was determined by the native raw material of wool.

The overwhelming dependence of the industry upon foreign trade prevented the cotton industry from sinking its roots as deep as those of the woollen industry. The mere import of raw material committed it to the export of its products in order to maintain the balance of trade. During the abnormal conjuncture of the mid-nineteenth century the creation of a large-scale factory economy, the rapidity of the expansion in production, and the generation of a near-universal commerce not only established an entrenched industrial tradition but also fostered a widespread acceptance of the industry's permanent role in

[1] *Chambers's Edinburgh Journal*, 17 Apr. 1858, 251, 'The City of Men'.

the British economy as well as in the life of Lancashire. Contemporary observers tended to exaggerate the significance and the antiquity of the industry and even well-informed foreign observers believed it to be the basis of an 'enduring manufacturing power'.[1] Thus the industry assumed the guise of 'the most indigenous of English manufactures'[2] and of 'a great national property', which would provide future generations with a secure livelihood and conferred, as in a trust, a mere life-interest upon the existing generation.[3] Its fragile dependence upon free trade, free ports, and universal peace and its essentially, nomadic, and ephemeral nature were concealed from all but the most percipient observers.[4]

As a producer of yarn and cloth the industry expanded its output with such unprecedented rapidity that it could not retain the same markets in perpetuity and therefore shifted its outlets throughout the century. In defiance of all rational expectation it found in India its ideal predestined vent, free from the climatic constraints of European markets, and acquired a reassuring belief in the permanence of its democratic mission to clothe the tropical two-thirds of the world's population. The relationship of Lancashire to India never became a true symbiosis since India did not become a substitute for the U.S.A. as a source of raw cotton despite the hopes centred around such a consummation during the Cotton Famine. Lancashire thus developed an inherently unstable entrepôt commerce between the U.S.A. and Asia, working up the raw material imported across the Atlantic and re-exporting it in manufactured form to the markets of Asia. Its power to exploit the largest of those markets was limited by the resistance of an even more archaic peasant society than that of Saxon Lancashire, since the demand of the ryot for loincloths could be met most effectively by the local manufacture of native cotton by local labour. No reduction in costs could have been

[1] F. List, *The National System of Political Economy* (1885), 43.

[2] L. Levi, 'On the Cotton Trade and Manufacture, as affected by the Civil War in America', *Journal of the Statistical Society*, Mar. 1863, 37.

[3] R. Marsden, *Cotton Weaving* (1895), vi.

[4] Malthus, *Essay on the Principle of Population* (5th edn., London, Murray, 1817), ii. 428, 'Of Systems of Agriculture and Commerce Combined'; *Journal of the Society of Arts*, 27 Jan. 1854, 168, W. B. Adams, 'English Cotton Trades, Indigenous or Exotic?'; *Spectator*, 27 Dec. 1862, 1444–5, W. B. Adams, 'The Political Economy of the Cotton Manufactures', 1433–4, 'An Engineer's View of the Cotton Question'.

large enough, as Sandberg has cogently argued, to permit the industry to retain for ever its tropical markets.

Costs of production were undoubtedly reduced under the pressure of competition, less from abroad than from within. 'It is the competition of Lancashire with Lancashire which controls the price.'[1] Strict limits upon the reduction of costs were however imposed by the industry's lack of control over its supply of raw cotton, by its growing dependence upon imported dyestuffs, by its increasing specialization, and by its inelastic wage levels. The industry suffered from increasing pressure upon its supply of raw material from 1898 and could not really fulfil its appointed function of clothing the poorer populations of the world by spinning progressively finer counts. Its commitment to intermittent spinning upon the mule, reinforced by the consistent failure of employers to replace men by women as mule-minders, placed it at an ultimate technological disadvantage in a world market served increasingly by cheap continuous production upon the ring-frame. Costs were also made less flexible by the survival of small-scale production, by the progress of specialization, by the separation of spinning from weaving, and by the crystallization of mercantile intermediaries in the interstices of the trade. Above all, wages proved inelastic as wage lists became more influential and limited the freedom of action of capital through the massive inertia of a quasi-peasant society, which became increasingly geared to a rising level of expectations and earnings as it became more urbanized, commercialized, and monetized. The cultural conservatism of the operative population inspired their hostility to wage cuts and to labour-saving devices. The maintenance of single-shift working imposed a further restraint upon the reduction of costs. The successful maintenance of levels of earnings ensured that from 1891 the gross returns accruing to labour in the industry surpassed those accruing to capital.

From the 1880s the markets of Asia began to be lost, first in the yarn trade and then in the grey cloth trade. The loss of the yarn trade undermined the whole position of the industry in the world market since the supremacy of Lancashire had always been much more marked in spinning than in weaving. The

[1] *Royal Commission on the Depression of Trade and Industry, Second Report*, 1886, Q.5909, J. Rawlinson 18 Feb. 1886.

demand for cotton goods did not prove as elastic, especially after 1888, as had been anticipated and failed to increase in proportion to the increase in world incomes, as other consumer goods and even other textiles proved more attractive, so reducing the share of textiles entering into world trade. The delusory hope that 'a second India' might be opened up in either China or Africa remained unfulfilled. Lancashire attained its peak proportion of the total population of the realm in 1901 and experienced an Indian summer of prosperity during the Edwardian boom. Thereafter its protracted decline set in motion 'the most terrible retreat in the history of industry',[1] precipitated by the Great War, by the post-war diversion of interest to the artificial silk industry and then by the world depression. The passage of 'Lancashire under the hammer'[2] took place amidst profound local incomprehension but represented a triumph for the gospel of economic liberalism. The deep-rooted aversion to state aid had been so deeply imprinted upon the mind of Lancashire that the cotton unions demanded nationalization only from 1935 while employers sought protection from foreign competition only from 1958.

The industrial population of Lancashire remained willing captives to the delusion spun by the spell of the world market. They remained in cultural isolation from the rest of England and retained in full measure the spiritual insularity of the Saxon, being largely uninfluenced by the globe-spanning commerce generated by their labours. 'They preserve the old British feeling of contempt and indifference for the rest of mankind.'[3] Their culture had been overlain but not destroyed by the upsurge of an economic civilization. They had never been as attached as their employers to the staple industry of the shire. Nor had they dedicated their lives wholly to the worship of the economic calculus. The spinning and weaving of cotton had simply furnished one particular mode of earning a living to a population capable of adapting itself, as in the past, to other modes. From the 1880s their cultural life began to develop

[1] G. Armitage, 'The Lancashire Cotton Trade from the Great Inventions to the Great Disasters', *Memoirs and Proceedings of the Manchester Literary and Philosophical Society*, XCII, 1950–1, 34.

[2] B. Bowker, *Lancashire under the Hammer* (London, Hogarth, 1928).

[3] Havelock Ellis, *The Nineteenth Century. A Dialogue in Utopia* (London, Richards, 1900), 22, on 'the Lancashire Enclosure'.

a renewed dedication to non-economic pursuits, especially to music and sport.

The role of the staple industry of the shire remained strictly confined to the economic sphere and separated from the mainstream of national existence. The cotton industry supplied no spokesman to the British Association after the time of Bazley, no recruits to the peerage between 1856 and 1910,[1] and no spinners eminent in their trade alone to the new *Dictionary of National Biography*. Nor did 'Cottonia' contribute much to the cultural life of the country before the Lancashire renaissance of 1908–12, when its authors first began to win a national market in place of a purely local one. Until that time the inhabitants of industrial Lancashire were burdened by the incomprehension of the outer world,[2] like the fellahin of the Nile or the *contadini* of the Mezzogiorno. Even the reduction of the cultural barriers between 'North and South' was purchased at a high price: a profound aesthetic revulsion to banausic pursuits emerged in Manchester during the 1890s and reinvigorated the original negative image of modern industry. Thus Ancoats, the 'horrible' industrial township of the city, seemed to presage the very 'doom of civilisation'[3] while industrial Lancashire seemed best designed to serve the future only as a dramatic example of pure barbarism, 'a piece of ancient life carried on into the present in all its nakedness, and untouched by contact with the outside world'.[4]

[1] R. E. Pumphrey, 'The Introduction of Industrialists into the British Peerage', *American Historical Review*, Oct. 1959, 11–12.

[2] Ruskin, 'The Crown of Wild Olive' (1866), in *The Works of Ruskin* (1905), Vol. 18, 513, for the confusion of Lancashire with Yorkshire; *The Times*, 28 Aug. 1878, 7ii, for the confusion of Blackburn with Bolton.

[3] *Manchester Guardian*, 16 Oct. 1894, 12ii, T. C. Horsfall, 'Modern Life and Civilisation in Cities'.

[4] H. Ellis, *The Nineteenth Century* (1900), 21.

Select Bibliography

INTRODUCTION

The historiography of the cotton industry may be divided into five main periods, the era of controversy (1806–34), the age of the heroic synthesis of Baines (1835–85), the period of the economic synthesis of Ellison (1886–1930), the historical era (1931–61) dominated by the work of Wadsworth and Mann, and the era of the quantitative revolution detonated in 1962 by the work of Mitchell, Deane and Cole and extended by Anderson in 1971 to the sphere of social history.

Almost all histories of the industry have been largely derivative and have rarely been free from bias, of which the main types seem to have been the technological, the free-trade, and the Marxist. The technological bias has tended to exaggerate the role of machinery in reducing production costs at the expense of agriculture, that of the factory at the expense of the shop and home, that of the large firm at the expense of the small firm, and that of capital investment at the expense of labour organization. The free-trade bias has tended to magnify the role of economic man at the expense of socio-political man and of a market economy at the expense of all non-market oriented ventures, especially into co-operative production. It has sacrificed the history of the operatives to that of their employers. It has encouraged the reinterpretation, undertaken since 1971, of the social history of the factory towns of Lancashire in terms of an idealized *Gesellschaft*, based upon individualized and monetarized relationships. The Marxist bias has inspired the interpretation of the cotton industry as the prototype of modern capitalism and as the parent of a new class-structured society. Its dominant theme has been that of exploitation, both of operatives within the mill and of rival producers within the world market. All three types of bias have tended to identify Lancashire and Manchester in their development and world outlook. All have helped to reinforce the polemical tradition established in the early apologias for the industry by Baines (1835) and Ure (1836).

Such bias was not expressed in any strident form in the three monographs produced by Ellison (1886), Schulze-Gaevernitz (1892), and Chapman (1904)[1] which have largely moulded the

[1] T. Ellison, *The Cotton Trade of Great Britain* (London, Wilson, 1886; Cass, 1968), reviewed in *Textile Manufacturer*, Sept. 1886, 408–9, and in *Schmollers Jahrbuch für Gesetzgebung*, 1890, 107–26, by C. J. Fuchs, 'Die Organisation des Liverpooler Baumwollhandels in Vergangenheit und Gegenwart'; G. von Schulze-Gaevernitz, *Der Grossbetrieb, ein wirtschaftlicher und socialer Fortschritt. Eine Studie auf*

interpretation of the history of the cotton industry during the nineteenth century. Two were the work of young scholars while the third was that of a mature businessman. The work of the cotton broker Ellison lacked the ostentatious footnotes of the other two books but was more solidly based and proved in the long run to have far greater survival power. It was a study in pure economic history, unlike the socio-political history of Schulze-Gaevernitz or the socio-economic history of Chapman. Ellison devoted a whole chapter to a critical discussion of source material and adopted a wide perspective, placing the industry within the spectrum of the whole textile trade and studying its comparative development, outside as well as inside England. Above all, he gave his work a firm quantitative foundation lacking in the other two books. His statistical compilations have never been amended nor even criticized and gave his work its permanent value to all later writers. *The Cotton Trade of Great Britain* became an indispensable source of reference to the 'new economic historians' of the 1960s and was the first of the three books to be reprinted, in 1968.

* * *

The discussion of four main sources will serve as an introduction to the bibliography, which is based mainly upon private rather than on public sources in the belief that such sources give a truer picture of an industry which operated to a large degree independently of the State.

COMPANY FILES

Three main sources of information exist upon the joint-stock

dem Gebiete der Baumwollindustrie (Leipzig, Duncker, 1892), reviewed in *Revue d'économie politique*, Oct. 1892, 1137–53, by W. Lotz, in the *Zeitschrift für die gesamte Staatswissenschaft*, 1892, 730–7, by F. Wörishoffer, in *das Handels-Museum*, 6 Oct. 1892, 521–3, by H. Herkner, in *Preussische Jahrbücher*, 1893, 71:i, 156–9, by G. Schmoller, and in *Economic Journal*, Dec. 1892, 691, by J. E. C. Munro; translated as *The Cotton Trade in England and in the Continent. A Study in the Field of the Cotton Industry* (London, Simpkin, 1895), reprinted from eight weekly articles in *Textile Mercury*, 22 Dec. 1894, 488–9, to 9 Feb. 1895, 109–10; and reviewed in *Manchester Guardian*, 19 Aug. 1895, 5ii, in an article reprinted in *Textile Mercury*, 31 Aug. 1895, 167–8, *Textile Manufacturer*, Aug. 1895, 292–3, and *Textile Recorder*, 15 Aug. 1895, 131–2, by J. Nasmith; S. J. Chapman, *The Lancashire Cotton Industry. A Study in Economic Development* (Manchester University Press, 1904; Clifton, N. J., Kelley, 1973), reviewed in *Manchester Guardian*, 24 Oct. 1904, 5i–ii, *Economic Journal*, June 1905, 215–19, by F. J. Faraday, and *Economic Review*, Oct. 1905, 497–9, by H. du Parcq. A comparative study of the three authors may be found in *Textile History*, 9, October 1978, 75–89, 'Three Historians of the Cotton Industry: Thomas Ellison, Gerhart von Schulze-Gaevernitz and Sydney Chapman'.

companies registered in the cotton industry, the company files, the classified index of companies, and the published parliamentary returns. The manuscript files of the 1,094 companies registered in the English cotton industry between 1845 and 1896 were all, until 1953, in the custody of the Registrar of Companies and were used by H. A. Shannon in the preparation of his pioneering articles of 1932 and 1933. The file of each company includes its memorandum and articles of association, its certificate of registration, an annual return of shareholders, and any winding-up resolution or order of court for compulsory liquidation. These files are more reliable for purposes of research than either the classified index or the parliamentary returns. The manuscript classified index contains a brief history of each company in terms of the contents of its file but furnishes no details of shares or of shareholders. The returns of joint-stock companies registered under the Act of 1856, made annually to Parliament from 1862 and published amongst the parliamentary papers of each session, were based upon the classified index and were thus twice removed from the ultimate source of information in the files. They contain no details of shareholders and give no information about the origin, industrial history, or life-span of a company.

The files are subject to certain administrative limitations:

1. They relate only to companies registered under the Act of 1856 and exclude unincorporated companies, companies incorporated by charter or by special statute, and associations registered under the Industrial and Provident Societies Act.
2. They relate only to companies registered in England and exclude those registered in Scotland and Ireland.
3. Both the classified index and the files for unlimited companies registered before 1856, including fourteen in the cotton industry, are not available for public inspection.
4. The custody of the files has been divided since 1953 when four out of every five annual returns in the files of 'dead' companies were destroyed in order to reduce their bulk. The drastically thinned-out files of the 'dead' companies were then transferred to the care of the Public Record Office, leaving those of 'live' companies in the custody of the Registrar of Companies.

The files provide a central source of information upon the spread of the limited company. The articles of association reveal whether a company was a mill-building or a turnover concern. The annual returns record the number of shares issued and the names, addresses, and occupations of shareholders, so making possible an estimate of the main sources of share capital, the size of an average shareholding, and the proportion of paid-up capital to nominal capital. The returns relate however only to share capital and supply no information upon loan capital so that they cannot be used to measure the total capital employed by a company. They give no details of the industrial or financial history of a company and must be supplemented by the study of local directories etc., in order to ascertain the functions fulfilled in practice by any company.

The interlocking relationships between groups of promoters and directors, especially in south-east Lancashire, reduce the utility of the study of a single company and enhance the value of a study of all the companies registered within a particular town or district. Thus the spread of the company in four main spinning towns has been traced, with the supplementary aid of Worrall's *Directories*. In the case of Oldham the large number of shareholders in the working-class limiteds contrasts sharply with the seven statutory shareholders of the typical private company and makes the estimate of capital invested by various socio-economic classes a tedious task. The files have proved of most use in the study of the spinning industry, where the amount of capital invested has been estimated from the spindleage laid down by mill-building companies. They have proved least useful in the study of the less-capitalized weaving industry, where the files of the room-and-power companies have however thrown light upon the adaptation of the company to the peculiar requirements of that branch of the cotton trade.

The 1,094 companies have been classified into four main categories:

1. 727 effective flotations and 367 companies which survived for less than ten years;
2. 699 public companies (including 'semi-private' ones) and 395 private companies, including 48 room-and-power companies;
3. 891 turnover companies (including 347 private companies) and 203 mill-building companies, including 48 room-and-power companies;
4. 512 spinning companies, 288 weaving companies, 246 spinning and weaving companies, and 48 room-and-power companies.

The company files were supplemented from two other sources, the files of the Registry of Friendly Societies and an index of some 637 private firms, including 83 unincorporated 'companies'. The individual files of friendly and provident societies, including the 27 formed in the cotton industry between 1851 and 1888, date back to 1852 and contain copies of rules and regulations and, from the 1890s, of liquidation accounts but include no annual returns before 1916. A statistical survey based upon these files was made by William Nuttall, 'Failures of Co-operative Productive Societies, 1850 to 1880', *C.W.S. Annual*, 1883, 168–80.

WORRALL'S DIRECTORIES

The printing firm of John Worrall was established in Oldham between 1865 and 1868, extended its activity during the boom of 1870–3, and published a series of local directories for the cotton towns of Lancashire, including Wigan (1869, 1872, 1881), Blackburn and Darwen (1870), Bolton (1870), Warrington (1871, 1876), Bury (1871), Burnley (1872), Stockport (1872), Rochdale (1873, 1885), and Lancashire (1879) as well as Oldham (1871, 1875, 1880, 1884, 1888, 1891). It then published in 1882 *The Cotton Spinners' and Manufacturers' Directory*, which contained the first enumeration ever made of the spindles and looms operated by individual firms. The information was collected by agents of the firm, aided by the local connections established during the 1870s, but was, according to the preface, 'not so complete as we could have wished it to be', lacking the necessary information for 111 firms or 5·7 per cent out of a total of 1948 and being especially weak on the firms of Oldham, Rochdale, Manchester, Leigh, and Preston. In the second edition of 1884 the contents of the *Directory* were made more complete and more accurate by the inclusion of missing firms and by the avoidance of any duplication. Thereafter the *Directory* was published upon an annual basis[1] and supplied a continuous annual census of the same statistical population. The statistics were indeed more accurate in the 1880s and 1890s than they became in the twentieth century when the publishers placed more emphasis upon the revenue-yielding advertisements placed in what they renamed from 1931 *The Lancashire Textile Industry*.

The Cotton Spinners' and Manufacturers' Directory contains information on the whole of the Lancashire cotton region, including Glossop in Derbyshire, Stockport and Hyde in Cheshire, and Todmorden but not Skipton in Yorkshire. The Lancashire *Directory* was supplemented by the publication of one for Yorkshire from 1883, with statistics in its edition of 1885, and of another for Scotland from 1889 as well as by the compilation of a *Steam Users' Directory* in 1888, covering the textile districts of Lancashire and Yorkshire. The Lancashire *Directories* remain the most valuable of the series but are unfortunately only reliable from 1884. Moreover they give no information upon employees or upon mills as distinct from firms, since their principle and mode of compilation differed from that of the factory returns.

The work nevertheless forms an indispensable and authoritative source for the historian and is wholly free from the imprecision of

[1] The volumes for 1889 and 1896 were published in the December of the preceding year.

the factory returns. The *Directories* have been used by Ellison (1886), Chapman (1904, 1914), Ashton (1914, 1926), Jewkes (1930), Jones (1933), Robson (1957), and Mitchell and Deane (1962) as well as by such geographers as Ogden (1927), Beaver (1933), and Smith (1941, 1948). They give details of the spindles, looms, and products of the firms in each cotton town of the Lancashire region and enable scholars to make their own calculations and draw their own conclusions as they cannot from the factory returns. Thus one may trace from 1884 the pattern of local industrial development, the history of individual firms, the degree of concentration of productive capacity in each town, and the evolution of specialization by process. In chapters 6, 7, and 8 of the preceding work the various estimates made of the progressive concentration of spindles in the spinning district and of looms in the weaving district as well as of the spindle–loom ratio in each of the main cotton towns have been derived from these *Directories* which have also been used to measure the decline of the combined firm and the progress of the limited company within the main spinning towns.

FACTORY RETURNS

The Annual Report of the Chief Inspector of Factories for 1896 (C.8561 of 1897), 135–6, gives a brief account of the thirteen returns made between 1835 and 1890. These returns were distinct from those made under the Act of 1844 requiring notification to the factory inspectors of the opening or occupation of any factory. They were intended to be complete returns of the number of factories and of employees, together with, from 1850, the number of spindles and looms. They classified factories from 1850 into three main types, spinning, weaving, and spinning and weaving. Their statistics can be used only with caution and with an understanding of four fundamental limitations:

1. The returns were concerned solely with 'factories' and defined a factory as a unit of production rather than as one of ownership, i.e. as a separate building in one locality irrespective of occupation or ownership. In 1837 and 1838 they did indeed record firms rather than mills but in 1835 and from 1850 they recorded mills and not firms. Thus they took no account of the room-and-power system or of the horizontal integration of several mills under a single proprietor. They are more reliable for the estimation of the size of mill than for that of the size of firm and they have been used for this purpose in chapter 8. They are less reliable for the weaving industry than for the spinning industry because of their implicit exclusion of the room-and-power system. By definition the returns excluded workshops which did not come within the scope of the Factory Acts and

were mostly occupied by weekly tenants. The return of 1870 did indeed include information on loom-shops and on the extent of the survival of shop-weaving as distinct from domestic weaving. Information on domestic hand-loom weavers was however never presented in the returns which are therefore less representative of the capacity of the weaving industry in the years 1835–60 than they became later. The figures of factory employees are markedly fewer than those recorded in the census returns as engaged in the 'cotton manufacture' and including those outside as well as inside the factories.

2. The preparation of the returns was not a primary function of the factory inspectors but an incidental task imposed upon them at irregular intervals of time. The returns were thus non-consecutive and lack the value of a continuous annual series. A regular annual survey was indeed recommended in 1886 by Ellison and again in 1895 by a departmental committee of the Home Office but was never instituted, perhaps because that task was already being performed by John Worrall of Oldham. Because the returns were prepared under different conditions, they do not necessarily always relate to the same statistical population. The 1856 return apparently failed to classify spinning and combined factories by the same criterion used in 1850 and 1861 and thus showed that spinning factories in Lancashire had almost doubled their average spindleage between 1850 and 1856 while combined factories had reduced theirs by 11·7 per cent. The 1861 return reverted to the criteria of 1850 and corrected the error made in 1856 but first used real (or indicated) instead of nominal horse-power in its return of moving-power installed and so implied an increase in the amount of steam h.p. installed between 1850 and 1860 by 318 per cent in England and by 332 per cent in Lancashire, an increase fivefold that in machinery during the same decade. Figures for motive-power were last included in the return for 1870, which has been examined by A. E. Musson, 'Industrial Motive Power in the United Kingdom, 1800–70', *Economic History Review*, August 1976, 415–39.

3. The inspectors assumed that firms failing to answer their questionnaire did not exist. Thus the returns of 1868, 1878, and 1885 were incomplete because they were collected during periods of severe commercial depression when many firms closed down. The 1868 return recorded an apparent decline since 1861 in the number of power-looms in England by 23,405 or by 6·4 per cent and must have excluded many closed mills which were either empty or had stationary machinery, especially weaving sheds. That particular return was excluded by Ellison from his scrupulously careful calculations but was incautiously used by Marx to illustrate the

effects of the improvement in machinery. The 1870 return first distinguished working spindles, which formed 94 per cent of the total number recorded, and set the example followed in the returns of 1874 and 1878. The 1885 return however excluded closed mills as well as new mills in course of erection and omitted from its purview 4,002,000 spindles and 41,735 looms, so underestimating the number of spindles in the U.K. by 9 per cent, the number of spinning spindles by 7·2 per cent, and the number of looms in Lancashire by 8·95 per cent.[1]

4. The returns give information only on the basis of counties rather than of firms, towns, or districts and thus preclude the drawing of any conclusions about the progress of specialization by process between the spinning and weaving districts within Lancashire. The 1870 return was exceptional in so far as it included a supplementary return of the occupations carried on in certain large towns, including Ashton, Blackburn, Manchester, Oldham, and Stalybridge. The unpublished 1897 returns used by Brodnitz (1902) do give information on the local distribution of machinery and employees but, like the 1836 return of power-looms, lump the statistics of the combined firm inextricably together with those of specialized spinning and weaving firms: the appendices to his work nevertheless remain a primary source containing material which is now apparently no longer available elsewhere.

The inherent inaccuracy of the returns has always been stressed by informed observers as in the *C.W.S. Annual*, 1884, 677, in Ellison, 325–8, and in *The Accountant*, 30 Oct. 1886, 606, 'The Companies Acts and Cotton Mills' which thought that the 1870 return purporting to be more than usually comprehensive was in fact very badly collated, utterly unreliable, and generally useless. The return for 1890 was equally defective in the view of Elijah Helm, 'The Alleged Decline of the British Cotton Industry', *Economic Journal*, December 1892, 737. The returns for the textile districts were nevertheless superior to those for other industrial areas and, in the official opinion expressed in the *Report of the Departmental Committee* [of the Home Office to Mr. Asquith] *on Factory Statistics* (C.7608 of 1895), 14, 'so far as they have been carried, may be taken to be tolerably reliable'. This judgement may be accepted for the five returns of 1850, 1861, 1870, 1874, and 1890 but not for those of 1856, 1868, 1878, and 1885. The limits of the statistical utility of the returns have been examined by M. Blaug, 'The Productivity of Capital in the Lancashire Cotton Industry during the Nineteenth Century', *Economic History Review*, April 1961, 379–81 and by D. T.

[1] Ellison, 327.

Jenkins, 'The Validity of the Factory Returns 1833–50', *Textile History*, October 1973, 26–46. The return for 1841 has been the subject of an elaborate analysis by V. A. C. Gatrell, 'Labour, Power, and the Size of Firms in Lancashire Cotton in the Second Quarter of the Nineteenth Century', *Economic History Review*, February 1977, 95–139. The deductions that may safely be drawn from the returns have been discussed by Robert Baker in the *Reports of the Inspectors of Factories*, 31 October 1862, 60–2, in the *C.W.S. Annual*, 1883, 288–335, 'The Progress of the Cotton Trade from 1697 to 1881', and by Ellison (1886), 65–9, 71–7, 325–8. In general they have proved most useful for the study of the period 1850–84, before their supersession by Worrall's *Directories*, and for the study of the history of the combined factory.

STATEMENTS OF TRADE

The official *Annual Statements of Trade* published from 1854 contain extensive statistics of the foreign trade generated by the cotton industry and have been supplemented by the *Tables of the Revenue, Population, Commerce &c. of the United Kingdom*. They have been used by generations of scholars, especially by Bazley (1854), Mann (1860), Ellison (1886), Fielden (1887), Heylin (1913), Smith (1954), Robson (1957), Mitchell, Deane (1962), and Sandberg (1968, 1974), whose published statistics have made any repetition unnecessary. The *Statements* supply information in terms of volume and value on the import of raw cotton and on its re-export and thus furnish invaluable data upon the consumption of raw material by the industry. Above all, they supply similar details for the export of yarn and cloth. The use of these statistics was developed to its highest point by Ellison, whose tabular return of the development of the industry's yarn and cloth markets between 1820 and 1884[1] was extended to 1910–11 by the Balfour Committee of 1928.[2] These statistics have been used in the first four chapters to place the role of the cotton industry in the economy upon a quantitative basis, especially in relation to imports, re-exports, and exports. They illuminate the trends and cycles in the history of the industry, the development of its markets and its products, and the influence of foreign tariffs. They have supplied the material for the cogent analyses of the industry's market performance made by Sandberg (1968) and by Marrison (1975). Their utility will be enhanced by bearing in mind that:

[1] *Second Report of the Royal Commission on the Depression of Trade and Industry*, 1886, Appendix C.13, 143.

[2] Committee on Industry and Trade, *Survey of the Textile Industries* (London, H.M.S.O., 1928), 148–9, Tables 7 and 8.

1. the trade statistics of importing countries form a complementary source of information;
2. the influence of entrepôts reduced the nominal imports of countries served by them and increased their own imports beyond their true domestic needs. Most British possessions seem to have fulfilled such an entrepôt function, so raising the nominal share of the industry's exports taken by the Empire at the expense of foreign destinations;
3. many mixed goods were until 1883 wrongly recorded as cotton manufactures instead of as woollen and worsted piece-goods;
4. bleached and unbleached cloth was lumped together, as was printed and dyed cloth, and was recorded separately only from 1889 at the request of the Manchester Chamber of Commerce.

BIBLIOGRAPHIES OF THE COTTON INDUSTRY

Beales, H. L., 'The "Basic" Industries of England, 1850–1914' (Studies in Bibliography, iv), *Economic History Review*, April 1935, 108–10.

Chaloner, W. H., 'Bibliographical Introduction' to E. Baines, *History of the Cotton Manufacture in Great Britain*, 5–14, London, Cass, 1966, 2nd edn.

Henderson, W. O., *The Lancashire Cotton Famine 1861–1865*, 133–70 in 1st edn., ix–x and 157–94 in 2nd edn., Manchester University Press, 1934, 1969.

Horrocks, S., *Lancashire Business Histories*, 115 pp., Manchester, Joint Committee on the Lancashire Bibliography, 1971.

Juraschek, F. von, 'Baumwollindustrie (Geschichte und Statistik)' in J. Conrad (ed.), *Handwörterbuch der Staatswissenschaften*, ii. 508–9, 515, Jena, Fischer, 1899, 2nd edn.

Oppel, A., *Die Baumwolle nach Geschichte, Anbau, Verarbeitung und Handel*, 719–28, Leipzig, Duncker, 1902.

Patent Office, *Subject List of Works on the Textile Industries and Wearing Apparel . . . in the Library of the Patent Office*, Patent Office Library Series No. 10. Bibliographical Series No. 7, 127 pp., London, H.M.S.O., 1902.

Woodbury, C. J. H., *Bibliography of the Cotton Manufacture*, 213 pp., Waltham, Mass., Barry, 1909; New York, Franklin, 1970, listing 5,074 titles.

THE COTTON INDUSTRY AND THE ECONOMY

STATISTICAL SURVEYS

Bazley, T., 'Cotton Manufacture', *Encyclopaedia Britannica*, 8th edn., vii. 437–60, Edinburgh, Black, 1854.

—— 'Manchester', *Encyclopaedia Britannica*, 8th edn., xiv. 250–60, Edinburgh, Black, 1857.

Blaug, M., 'The Productivity of Capital in the Lancashire Cotton Industry during the Nineteenth Century', *Economic History Review*, April 1961, 358–81, reprinted in K. A. Tucker (ed.), *Business History. Selected Readings*, 91–125, London, Cass, 1977.

Brodnitz, G., *Vergleichende Studien über Betriebsstatistik und Betriebsformen der englischen Textilindustrie*, 93 pp., Jena, Fischer, 1902.

Burn, R., *Statistics of the Cotton Trade*, 35 pp., 27 tables, London, Simpkin, 1847.

Ellison, T., *The Cotton Trade of Great Britain*, 355 pp., London, Wilson, 1886; Cass, 1968.

FORWOOD, W. B., 'On the Influence of Price upon the Cultivation and Consumption of Cotton during the Past Ten Years', *Journal of the Statistical Society*, September 1870, 366–83.

HAMMOND, M. B., *The Cotton Industry—An Essay in American Economic History*, 382 pp., New York, Macmillan for American Economic Association, 1897; Johnson, 1966.

HEYLIN, H. B., *Buyers and Sellers in the Cotton Trade*, 234 pp., London, Griffin, 1913.

HOFFMANN, W. G., *British Industry 1700–1950*, 338 pp., Oxford, Blackwell, 1955.

JONES, G. T., *Increasing Return. A study of the relation between the size and efficiency of industries, with special reference to the history of selected British and American Industries, 1850–1910*, 100–19, Cambridge University Press, 1933.

MCCULLOCH, J. R., *A Descriptive and Statistical Account of the British Empire*, 4th rev. edn., i. 673–703, 'Cotton Manufacture', London, Longmans, 1854.

MACGREGOR, J., *Commercial Statistics. A Digest of the Productive Resources . . . of All Nations*, iv. 780–815, 'Miscellaneous Statements of the Prices and the Progress of Cotton Fabrics', London, Whittaker, 1848.

M'QUEEN, J., *General Statistics of the British Empire*, 95–110, 'Manufactures. Cotton Manufacture', London, Fellowes, 1836.

MANN, J. A., *The Cotton Trade of Great Britain*, 134 pp., 36 tables, London, Simpkin, 1860; Cass 1968.

MERTTENS, F., 'The Hours and the Cost of Labour in the Cotton Industry at Home and Abroad', *Transactions of the Manchester Statistical Society*, 18 April 1894, 125–90.

MITCHELL, B. R. AND DEANE, P., *Abstract of British Historical Statistics*, 513 pp., Cambridge University Press, 1962.

PENDER & CO., JOHN, *Statistics of the Trade of the United Kingdom with Foreign Countries from 1840*, 134 pp., London, Simpkin, 1869.

POOLE, B., *Statistics of British Commerce*, 107–18, London, Smith 1852, by the general goods manager of the L.N.W.R.

Return of the Number of Cotton, Woollen, Worsted, Flax and Silk Factories subject to the Factories Acts in the United Kingdom (745 of 1850, 7 of 1857, 23 of 1862, 453 of 1867–8, C.440 of 1871, C.393 of 1875, C.324 of 1879, C.340 of 1885, C.328 of 1890).

ROBSON, R., *The Cotton Industry in Britain*, 331–59, London, Macmillan, 1957, by the intellectual heir of Thomas Ellison.

SHAPIRO, S., *Capital and the Cotton Industry in the Industrial Revolution*, 230–66, Ithaca, Cornell University Press, 1967.

WATTS, I., 'Cotton', *Encyclopaedia Britannica*, 9th edn., vi. 482–508, Edinburgh, Black, 1877.

WORRALL, JOHN, *The Cotton Spinners' and Manufacturers' Directory*, Oldham, Worrall, 1882–96, 12 vols.

—— *Textile Directory of the Manufacturing Districts in Ireland, Scotland and Wales and the Counties of Chester, Derby, Gloucester, Leicester, Nottingham, Worcester*, Oldham, Worrall, 1889–96, 7 vols.

—— *The Yorkshire Textile Directory*, Oldham, Worrall, 1883–96, 10 vols.

GENERAL HISTORIES

ANDREW, S., 'Fifty Years' Cotton Trade', *Oldham Standard*, 17 September 1887, 4i–v, 21 September, 4i–iii, reprinted, 12 pp., Oldham Standard, 1887, not reprinted in the Report of the British Association, before the Economic Section of which the paper was read at Manchester on 5 September 1887. For the obituary of Samuel Andrew (1837–1916) see *Oldham Chronicle*, 29 April 1916, 3i–v.

ASHWORTH, H., 'Cotton: its Cultivation, Manufacture and Uses', *Journal of the Society of Arts*, 10 March 1858, 256–70, 289, reprinted, 64 pp., Manchester, Collins, 1858.

——*Historical Data chiefly relating to South Lancashire and the Cotton Manufacture*, 26 pp., Manchester, Ireland, 1866.

AXON, W. E. A., 'A Century of the Cotton Trade', in *Companion to the British Almanac*, 1886, 100–15, reprinted with bibliography in *Stray Chapters in Literature, Folk-Lore and Archaeology*, 277–302, Manchester, Heywood, 1888.

BAINES, E., *History of the Cotton Manufacture in Great Britain*, 544 pp., London, Fisher, 1835; Cass, 1966. A polemical defence of working conditions in manufacturing industry by a young journalist, who was criticized for his optimism by L. Faucher, *Études sur l'Angleterre* (1845), i. 380, 417. For his obituary see *Manchester Guardian*, 3 March 1890, 5 iv, 8 iii–iv.

BAYNES, J., *The Cotton Trade: Two Lectures*, 111 pp., Blackburn, Haworth, 1857.

BAZLEY, T., *Cotton as an Element of Industry; its Confined Supply, and its Extending Consumption by Increasing and Improving Agencies*, 70 pp., London, Longman, 1852, reprinted in Society of Arts, *Lectures on the Results of the Great Exhibition of 1851*, 347–67, London, Barclay, 1853.

—— 'Trade and Commerce the Auxiliaries of Civilization and Comfort', *Report of the British Association*, 1858, 169–70, reprinted, 15 pp., Manchester, Ireland, 1858.

BYTHELL, D., *The Handloom Weavers. A Study in the English Cotton Industry during the Industrial Revolution*, 302 pp., Cambridge University Press, 1969.

—— 'The Hand-loom Weavers in the English Cotton Industry during the Industrial Revolution: some Problems', *Economic History Review*, December 1964, 339–53.

CHAPMAN, S. D., 'Fixed Capital Formation in the British Cotton Industry, 1770–1815', *Economic History Review*, August 1970, 235–66, reprinted in revised form in J. P. P. Higgins and S. Pollard (eds.), *Aspects of Capital Investment in Great Britain, 1750–1850*, 57–119, London, Methuen, 1971.

—— *The Cotton Industry in the Industrial Revolution*, 80 pp., London, Macmillan, 1972.

CHAPMAN, S. J., 'The Cotton Industry' in W. Farrer and J. Brownbill (eds.), *The Victoria History of the County of Lancaster*, ii. 379–93, London, Constable, 1908.

—— *The Cotton Industry and Trade*, 175 pp., London, Methuen, 1905.

—— 'Cotton Manufacture', *Encyclopaedia Britannica*, 11th edn., vii. 281–301, Cambridge University Press, 1910.

—— *The Lancashire Cotton Industry. A Study in Economic Development*, 309 pp., Manchester University Press, 1904; Clifton, N. J., Kelley, 1973.

CRICK, W. F. AND WADSWORTH, J. E., *A Hundred Years of Joint Stock Banking*, 140–66, 'Cotton Banks', London, Hodder, 1936.

ELLISON, T., 'Cotton', *Chambers's Encyclopaedia*, 3rd edn., iii. 506–16, London, Chambers, 1889.

HAUSE, J. M., *English Cotton-Goods Trade*, 11 pp., Department of Commerce and Labor, Bureau of Manufactures, Special Agents Series No. 47, Washington, Government Printing Office, 1911.

HELM, E., 'The British Cotton Industry' in W. J. Ashley (ed.), *British Industries. A Series of General Reviews for Business Men and Students*, 68–92, London, Longmans, 1903.

—— 'The Cotton Industry' in H. Cox (ed.), *British Industries under Free Trade. Essays by Experts*, 1–20, London, Unwin, 1904.

JANNASCH, R., *Die Europäische Baumwollen-Industrie und deren Productionsbedingungen mit besonderer Berücksichtigung des Oberrheins*, reprinted from *Zeitschrift des königlich preussischen statistischen Bureaus*, 1881, 112 pp., Berlin, Allgemeine Verlags-Agentur, 1882, in the British Library.

LANDAUER, E., *Handel und Produktion in der Baumwollindustrie unter besonderer Berücksichtigung der lohnindustriellen Organisationsform*, Archiv für Sozialwissenschaft und Sozialpolitik, Ergänzungsheft VII, 1912, 183 pp.

MALLALIEU, A., 'The Cotton Manufacture', *Blackwood's Edinburgh Magazine*, March 1836, 407–24.

—— 'The Cotton Manufacture, and the Factory System', *Blackwood's Edinburgh Magazine*, July 1836, 100–21.

Riddell, H., 'The Textile Industries 1815–1851' and 'The Textile Industries 1851–1885' in H. D. Traill (ed.), *Social England. A Record of the Progress of the People*, vi. 69–74, 589–92, London, Cassell, 1897.

Schulze-Gaevernitz, G. von, *Der Grossbetrieb, ein wirtschaftlicher und socialer Fortschritt. Eine Studie auf dem Gebiete der Baumwollindustrie*, 281 pp., Leipzig, Duncker, 1892, translated as *The Cotton Trade in England and on the Continent. A Study in the Field of the Cotton Industry*, 214 pp., London, Simpkin, 1895.

Shaw, A. D., 'The Cotton-Goods Trade of Lancashire' in *Cotton and Woollen Mills of Europe*, U.S. Consular Reports No. 23, September 1882, 1–62, Washington, Government Printing Office, 1882, reprinted as *Extracts from a Special Report on the Cotton Goods Trade of Lancashire*, 55 pp., Manchester, Ireland, 1883, written by the U.S. Consul in Manchester, 1878–85, with the help of Samuel Andrew and Elijah Helm, being a revised and expanded version of the following report.

—— 'The Cotton Manufactures of Lancashire', in *The Cotton Goods Trade of the World, and the Share of the United States Therein*, U.S. Consular Reports No. 12, October 1881, 127–33, Washington, Government Printing Office, 1881.

—— 'Manchester Made Goods. Figures from Consul Shaw and a Talk with him', *New York Times*, 8 February 1883, 7 iv–vi, discussed in *Manchester Examiner and Times*, 6 March 1883, 4 iv, J. C. Fielden, 'The Cotton Trade and its Critics'.

Slagg, J., 'The Cotton Trade and Industry' in T. H. Ward (ed.), *The Reign of Queen Victoria. A Survey of Fifty Years of Progress*, ii. 153–95, London, Smith, 1887.

Smelser, N. J., *Social Change in the Industrial Revolution. An Application of Theory to the Lancashire Cotton Industry 1770–1840*, 440 pp., London, Routledge, 1959, discussed by M. M. Edwards and R. Lloyd-Jones in N. B. Harte and K. G. Ponting (eds.), *Textile History and Economic History* (Manchester University Press, 1973), 304–19 and by M. Anderson in *Social History*, October 1976, 317–34.

Smith, R., 'A History of the Lancashire Cotton Industry between the Years 1873 and 1896', 752 pp., Ph.D. thesis, University of Birmingham, 1954.

Taylor, A. J., 'Concentration and Localisation of the British Cotton Industry 1825–1850', 251 pp., M.A. thesis, University of Manchester, 1947.

Vogelstein, T., *Organisationsformen der Eisenindustrie und Textilindustrie in England und Amerika*, 105–32, Leipzig, Duncker, 1910.

WADSWORTH, A. P., 'Lancashire in Prosperity and Adversity', *Manchester Guardian Commercial*, 5 May 1934, 4–5.

WHITTAM JR., W., *Report on England's Cotton Industry. With Brief Notes on Other Industries*, 54 pp., Department of Commerce and Labor, Bureau of Manufactures, Special Agents Series No. 15, Washington, Government Printing Office, 1907.

WILHELMSEN, L. J., *English Textile Nomenclature*, 229 pp., Bergen, Beyer, 1943.

THE LOCALIZATION OF THE INDUSTRY

ATWOOD, R. S., 'Localization of the Cotton Industry in Lancashire, England', *Economic Geography*, April 1928, 187–95.

—— *The Localization of the Cotton Industry in Lancashire England*, 48 pp., Ph.D. thesis, Gainesville, University of Florida, 1930.

BEAVER, S. H., 'The Textile Industries: Cotton', in L. D. Stamp and S. H. Beaver, *The British Isles. A Geographic and Economic Survey*, 473–500, London, Longmans, 1933.

CHAPMAN, S. J., *The Lancashire Cotton Industry*, 148–64, Manchester University Press, 1904.

HYDE, F. E., *Liverpool and the Mersey. The Development of a Port 1700–1970*, 269 pp., Newton Abbot, David and Charles, 1971.

JEWKES, J., 'The Localisation of the Cotton Industry', *Economic History*, January 1930, 91–106.

OGDEN, H. W., 'The Geographical Basis of the Lancashire Cotton Industry', *Journal of the Manchester Geographical Society*, 1927, 8–30, reprinted in *Journal of the Textile Institute*, xviii, 1927, T 573–94 and discussed on pp. 47–51 of the present work.

ROBERTSON, A. J., 'The Decline of the Scottish Cotton Industry 1860–1914', *Business History*, July 1970, 116–28.

ROBSON, R., 'Location and Development of the Cotton Industry', *Journal of Industrial Economics*, April 1953, 99–125.

—— *The Cotton Industry in Britain*, 28–42, 'Changes in Location', London, Macmillan, 1957.

RODGERS, H. B., 'The Lancashire Cotton Industry in 1840', *Transactions and Papers of the Institute of British Geographers*, 28, 1960, 135–53, reprinted in A. R. H. Baker, J. D. Hamshere, and J. Langton (eds.), *Geographical Interpretations of Historical Sources*, 337–56, with supplementary note on p. 356, Newton Abbot, David and Charles, 1970.

SMITH, W., 'Trends in the Geographical Distribution of the Lancashire Cotton Industry', *Geography*, March 1941, 7–17.

—— *An Economic Geography of Great Britain*, 462–99, 'Cotton Manufacture', London, Methuen, 1948.

TAYLOR, A. J., 'Concentration and Specialization in the Lancashire Cotton Industry, 1825–1850', *Economic History Review*, 1949, 114–22.

WILLIAMS, D. M., 'Liverpool Merchants and the Cotton Trade 1820–1850', in J. R. Harris (ed.), *Liverpool and Merseyside. Essays in the Economic and Social History of the Port and its Hinterland*, 182–211, London, Cass, 1969.

MANCHESTER

ASHTON, T. S., *Economic and Social Investigations in Manchester, 1833–1933. A Centenary History of the Manchester Statistical Society*, 179 pp., London, King, 1934; Brighton, Harvester, 1977.

AXON, W. E. A., *The Annals of Manchester*, 456 pp., Manchester, Heywood, 1886.

—— 'Manchester', *Encyclopaedia Britannica*, 9th edn., xv. 459–65, Edinburgh, Black, 1883.

BAKER, H., 'On the Growth of the Commercial Centre of Manchester, Movement of Population, and Pressure of Habitation—Census decenniad 1861–71', *Transactions of the Manchester Statistical Society*, 14 February 1872, 87–106.

—— 'On the Growth of the Manchester Population, Extension of the Commercial Centre of the City and Provision for Habitation—Census Period 1871–81', *Transactions of the Manchester Statistical Society*, 9 November 1881, 1–27.

BRIGGS, A., *Victorian Cities*, 83–135, 'Manchester: Symbol of a New Age', London, Odhams, 1963.

CHADWICK, D., *On the Progress of Manchester During the Twenty Years from 1840–60*, 14 pp., Manchester, Ireland, 1861, abridged in *Report of the British Association*, 1861, 209–16.

CHALONER, W. H., 'The Birth of Modern Manchester' in C. F. Carter (ed.), *Manchester and its Region*, 131–46, Manchester University Press, 1962.

'The City of Men', *Chambers's Edinburgh Journal*, 17 April 1858, 251–4.

'The Cotton Metropolis', *Chambers's Repository of Instructive and Amusing Tracts*, i. 1–32, Edinburgh, Chambers, 1852; Manchester, Shipperbottom, 1972, 32 pp.

ENGELS, F., *The Condition of the Working Class in England*, trans. and ed. W. O. Henderson and W. H. Chaloner, 50–87, 'The Great Towns', Oxford, Blackwell, 1958, 1971.

FAUCHER, L., 'Études sur l'Angleterre, iv Manchester', *Revue des deux mondes*, 15 Mars 1844, 1041–77, 1 Avril 1844, 118–62, trans. by J. P. Culverwell as *Manchester in 1844; its Present Condition and Future Prospects*, 152 pp., London, Simpkin, 1844; Cass, 1969.

Fraser, D. D., 'A Decade of Manchester Banking, 1896–1905', *Transactions of the Manchester Statistical Society*, 14 November 1906, 1–36.

Gatrell, V. A. C., 'A Manchester Parable' in J. A. Benyon, C. W. Cook, T. R. H. Davenport, K. S. Hunt (eds.), *Studies in Local History. Essays in Honour of Professor Winifred Maxwell*, 28–36, Cape Town, Oxford University Press, 1976.

Grindon, L. H., *Manchester Banks and Bankers: Historical, Biographical and Anecdotal*, 333 pp., Manchester, Palmer, 1878.

Helm, E., 'Commercial and Industrial Manchester' in B.M.A., Manchester Meeting, 1902, *Handbook and Guide to Manchester*, J. H. Ray (ed.), 120–38, Manchester, Ireland, 1902.

—— 'The Export and Home Trade of Manchester', *Trade and Industry*, 31 March 1900 (Manchester Number), 411–16.

—— 'The Middleman in Commerce', *Transactions of the Manchester Statistical Society*, 16 January 1900, 55–64.

Hertz, G. B., *The Manchester Politician, 1750–1912*, 101 pp., London, Sherratt, 1912.

Kay-Shuttleworth, J., *Public Education as Reviewed in 1832–39—1846–1862*, 87–170, 'Sketch of the Progress of Manchester in thirty years, from 1832 to 1862', London, Longman, 1862; Brighton, Harvester, 1973.

Kellett, J. R., *The Impact of Railways on Victorian Cities*, 150–74, London, Routledge, 1969.

Kohl, J. G., *Ireland, Scotland and England*, iii. 106–46, London, Chapman, 1844, reprinted in *England, Wales and Scotland*, i. 106–46, London, Chapman, 1844.

[Lamb, Robert], 'Manchester, by a Manchester Man', *Fraser's Magazine*, June 1853, 611–26, reprinted in *Free Thoughts on Many Subjects*, i. 131–71, London, Longmans, 1866. The author was an Oxonian, a Tory, and an Anglican clergyman who became in the 1860s, according to Charles Rowley, *Fifty Years of Work Without Wages* (London, Hodder, 1912), 32, the 'idol and chief' of the Ancoats reformers. The brief review in *Manchester Guardian*, 19 June 1866, 7i, concluded that 'to the genuine Manchester man, his criticisms will be unpalatable'.

'The Manufacturing Districts. Manchester', *Morning Chronicle, Supplement*, 21 December 1849, liii–vi, 2vi–3iv.

Marcus, S., *Engels, Manchester and the Working Class*, 271 pp., London, Weidenfeld, 1974.

Marshall, L. S., 'The Emergence of the First Industrial City: Manchester, 1780–1850' in C. F. Ware (ed.), *The Cultural Approach to History*, 140–61, New York, Columbia University Press, 1940.

MONKHOUSE, A. N., 'Cotton Goods and Yarn', *Encyclopaedia Britannica,* 11th edn., vii. 275–81, Cambridge University Press, 1910.

MORTIMER, J., *Mercantile Manchester Past and Present,* 146 pp., Henry Bannerman & Sons Ltd., Diary and Buyers' Guide for 1896, Manchester, Palmer, 1896.

MOXON, T. B., 'The Manchester Joint-Stock Banks', *Manchester Guardian,* 11 March 1882, 12iv, reprinted, 8 pp., Manchester, 1882.

PARSONS, J. G. C., *The Centenary of the Manchester Royal Exchange 1804–1904; Historical Sketch,* 34 pp., Manchester Royal Exchange, 1904.

PATMORE, J. A., 'The Railway Network of the Manchester Conurbation', *Transactions and Papers of the Institute of British Geographers,* 34, June 1964, 159–73.

'Provincial Society, Manchester', *Whitehall Review,* 31 August 1882, 11–12, in Guildhall Library.

RODGERS, H. B., 'The Suburban Growth of Victorian Manchester', *Journal of the Manchester Geographical Society,* 1962, 1–12.

SCHULZE, H. J. F., *Nationalöconomische Bilder aus Englands Volksleben mit besonderer Berücksichtigung der landwirthschaftlichen und industriellen Verhältnisse,* 271–96, 'Die Verarbeitung der Baumwolle der Höhepunkt der englischen Industrie. Manchester, die Königin der Baumwollenstädte', Jena, Mauke, 1853, by the father of Schulze-Gaevernitz.

SHAW, W. A., *Manchester Old and New,* ii. 1–72, 'The Trade of the City', London, Cassell, 1894.

SIMPSON, E. F., *A Sketch of the History of the Manchester Royal Exchange,* 36 pp., Manchester, Guardian Letterpress, 1875.

SMITH, R., 'Manchester's Changing Role in the Lancashire Cotton Trade 1820–30', 120 pp., B.A. thesis, University of Birmingham, 1950.

—— 'Manchester as a Centre for the Manufacture and Merchanting of Cotton Goods, 1820–30', *University of Birmingham Historical Journal,* 1953, 47–65.

SPENCER, R., *The Home Trade of Manchester, with Personal Reminiscences and Occasional Notes,* 278 pp., London, Simpkins, 1890.

STEWART, C., *The Stones of Manchester,* 144 pp., London, Arnold, 1956.

SWINDELLS, T., *Manchester Streets and Manchester Men,* 5 vols., Manchester, Cornish, 1906–8.

TURNER, R. E., *James Silk Buckingham 1786–1855. A Social Biography,* 390–402, 'Manchester: the New Industrial Civilization', London, Williams, 1934.

—— 'The Cultural Significance of the Early English Industrial

Town', in C. W. de Kiewiet (ed.), *Studies in British History (Presented to H. G. Plum)*, 32–77, University of Iowa, Studies in the Social Sciences, xi: 2, January 1941.

WADSWORTH, A. P., 'Manchester in 1830', in M. Anderson (ed.), *The Book and Programme of the Liverpool and Manchester Railway Centenary. L.M.R. 1830–L.M.S. 1930*, 53–59, Liverpool Organization Ltd., 1930.

LANCASHIRE

ASHMORE, O., *The Industrial Archaeology of Lancashire*, 352 pp., Newton Abbot, David and Charles, 1969.

ASHWORTH, H., 'Statistical Illustrations of the Past and Present State of Lancashire and more particularly of the Hundred of Salford', *Journal of the Statistical Society*, October 1842, 245–56, reprinted, 24 pp., London, Madden, 1842.

ASPIN, C., *Lancashire, the First Industrial Society*, 190 pp., 49 illustrations, Helmshore Local History Society, 1969.

BAINES, E., *History, Directory and Gazeteer of the County Palatine of Lancaster*, 3 vols., Liverpool, Wales, 1824, 1825.

—— *History of the County Palatine and Duchy of Lancaster*, 4 vols., London, Fisher, 1836; 2nd edn., J. Harland (ed.), 2 vols., London, Routledge, 1868, 1870; 3rd edn., J. Croston (ed.), 5 vols., Manchester, Heywood, 1886–93.

BARKER, W. H., 'The Towns of South-East Lancashire', *Journal of the Manchester Geographical Society*, 15 November 1927, 31–54.

BOYSON, R., 'The New Poor Law in North-East Lancashire, 1834–71', *Transactions of the Lancashire and Cheshire Antiquarian Society*, 1960, 35–36.

BRYCE, J., 'General Report on the County of Lancaster', *Schools Inquiry Commission*, ix. 425–899, London, Eyre, 1868.

BUTTERWORTH, E., *A Statistical Sketch of the County Palatine of Lancaster*, 168 pp., London, Longman, 1841; Manchester, Lancashire and Cheshire Antiquarian Society, 1968.

BUXTON, D., 'On the Rise of the Manufacturing Towns of Lancashire and Cheshire', *Transactions of the Historic Society of Lancashire and Cheshire*, 8 May 1856, 199–211.

CLARKE, P. F., *Lancashire and the New Liberalism*, Cambridge University Press, 1971.

DANSON, J. T., 'On the Area and Population of the Manchester District', *Transactions of the Historic Society of Lancashire and Cheshire*, 14 February 1856, 165–80.

DANSON, J. T. AND WELTON, T. A., 'On the Population of Lancashire and Cheshire and its Local Distribution during the Fifty Years 1801–51', *Transactions of the Historic Society of Lancashire and*

Cheshire, 23 April 1857, 195–212, 10 December 1857, 1–36, 13 January 1859, 31–70, 9 February 1860, 35–74.

[Easby, J.], *Manchester and the Manchester People, with a Sketch of Bolton, Stockport, Ashton, Rochdale, and Oldham, and their Inhabitants. By a Citizen of the World*, 36 pp., Manchester, Literary Agency Office, 1843.

Fairbairn, W., 'The Rise and Progress of Manufactures and Commerce, and of Civil and Mechanical Engineering', in T. Baines, *Lancashire and Cheshire, Past and Present*, iv. i–cclx, London, Mackenzie, 1867.

Fitzgerald, W., 'The Ribble Basin (The Geography of Industrial Development)', *Journal of the Manchester Geographical Society*, 13 March 1928, 75–96.

Freeman, T. W., Rodgers, H. B., and Kinvig, R. H., *Lancashire, Cheshire, and the Isle of Man*, 308 pp., London, Nelson, 1966.

Grindon, L. H., 'Illustrations of Lancashire', twelve articles in *The Portfolio*, January 1881, 1–7, to December 1881, 194–9, reprinted as *Lancashire: Brief Historical and Descriptive Notes*, 355 pp., London, Seeley, 1892.

Houghton, D. S., 'An Historical Geography of Oldham', *Northern Universities' Geographical Journal*, 5 February 1964, 15–22.

Howitt, W., *The Rural Life of England*, i. 285–92, 'Nooks of the World:—Life in the Dales of Lancashire and Yorkshire', London, Longman, 1838.

Jones, F. M., 'The Aesthetic of the Nineteenth-Century Industrial Town', in H. J. Dyos (ed.), *The Study of Urban History*, 170-87, London, Arnold, 1968, a notable reinterpretation, performing for Lancashire what the work of Cecil Stewart (1956) did for Manchester.

Jones, L. R., *North England: An Economic Geography*, 256 pp., especially 157–253, London, Routledge, 1921.

Law, Alice, 'Social and Economic History' in W. Farrer and J. Brownbill (eds.), *Victoria History of the County of Lancaster*, ii. 261–329, London, Constable, 1908.

Lawton, R., 'Population Trends in Lancashire and Cheshire from 1801', *Transactions of the Historic Society of Lancashire and Cheshire*, 16 November 1961, 189–213.

Midwinter, E. D., *Law and Order in Early Victorian Lancashire*, 42 pp., Borthwick Papers No. 34, University of York, 1968.

Millward, R., *Lancashire. An Illustrated Essay on the History of the Landscape*, 128 pp., London, Hodder, 1955.

Niven, J., 'On the Statistics of Some Lancashire Industries', *Transactions of the Manchester Statistical Society*, 12 April 1899, 107–54.

PELLING, H., *Social Geography of British Elections 1885–1910*, 239–87, 'Lancastria', London, Macmillan, 1967.

REACH, A. B., *Manchester and the Textile Districts in 1849*, C. Aspin (ed.), 122 pp., Helmshore Local History Society, 1972.

REDDING, Cyrus, *An Illustrated Itinerary of the County of Lancaster*, 286 pp., London, How, 1842, reprinted as *The Pictorial History of the County of Lancaster*, 376 pp., London, Routledge, 1844.

SHADWELL, A., *Industrial Efficiency. A Comparative Study of Industrial Life in England, Germany and America*, i. 48–102, 'Industrial Districts in England', London, Longmans, 1906.

TAYLOR, W. C., *Notes of a Tour in the Manufacturing Districts of Lancashire; in a Series of Letters to His Grace the Archbishop of Dublin*, 331 pp., 2nd edn., London, Duncan, 1842; Cass, 1968.

WALLWORK, K., 'Aspects of the Modern Economic Geography of the Calder-Darwen Valley', 2 vols., 172 pp., 63 maps and 4 figures, M.A. thesis, University of Manchester, 1955.

WARNES, A. M., 'Early Separation of Homes from Workplaces and the Urban Structure of Chorley, 1780 to 1850', *Transactions of the Historic Society of Lancashire and Cheshire*, 1970, 105–35.

WELTON, J. A., *England's Recent Progress. An Investigation of the Statistics of Migrations, Mortality, &c. in the Twenty Years from 1881 to 1901*, 207–63, London, Chapman, 1911.

—— 'Forty Years' Industrial Changes in England and Wales', *Transactions of the Manchester Statistical Society*, 9 March 1898, 153–342.

—— 'Notes on the Census Report (1901) for the County of Lancaster', *Transactions of the Manchester Statistical Society*, 19 November 1902, 1–48.

—— 'The Occupations of the People of England and Wales in 1911, From the Point of View of Industrial Developments', *Transactions of the Manchester Statistical Society*, 10 February 1915, 47–176.

—— 'Some Published Results of the Census of 1871', *Transactions of the Manchester Statistical Society*, 13 December 1871, 41–68.

—— *Statistical Papers Based on the Census of England and Wales, 1851, and relating to the Occupations of the People and the Increase of Population 1841–51*, 168 pp., London, Savill, 1860.

LABOUR

ABRAM, W. A., 'Social Condition and Political Prospects of the Lancashire Workmen', *Fortnightly Review*, 1 October 1868, 426–41.

ANDERSON, M., *Family Structure in Nineteenth Century Lancashire*, 230 pp., Cambridge University Press, 1971.

—— 'Urban Migration in nineteenth-century Lancashire. Some

insights into two competing hypotheses', *Annales de démographie historique*, 1971, 13–26.

—— 'Household structure and the industrial revolution; mid-nineteenth century Preston in comparative perspective', in P. Laslett and R. Wall (eds.), *Household and Family in Past Time*, 215–35, Cambridge University Press, 1972.

ASHWORTH, H., *The Preston Strike, An Enquiry into its Causes and Consequences*, 98 pp., Manchester, Simms, 1854.

BEVAN, G. P., *The Industrial Classes and Industrial Statistics*, 7–34, 'Cotton', vol. 13 of *British Manufacturing Industries*, London, Stanford, 1877.

BOWLEY, A. L., *Wages in the United Kingdom in the Nineteenth Century*, 115–19, Cambridge University Press, 1900.

BRIDGES, J. H. AND HOLMES, T., *Report to the Local Government Board on Proposed Changes in Hours and Ages of Employment in Textile Factories*, 62 pp., C.754 of 1873.

BURGESS, K., *The Origins of British Industrial Relations. The Nineteenth Century Experience*, 231–303, 'Cotton Textiles', London, Croom Helm, 1975.

CHADWICK, D., *The Expenditure of Wages, 1839 to 1887. Read at the British Association, Manchester Meeting, Section F, on Monday 5 September 1887*, 11 pp., London, Wertheimer, 1887.

——'The Rate of Wages, in Two Hundred Trades and Branches of Labour in Manchester and Salford and the Manufacturing District of Lancashire during the Twenty Years from 1839 to 1859', *Journal of the Statistical Society*, March 1860, 1–36, reprinted, 36 pp., London, Harrison, 1860.

CHAPMAN, S. J., *The Lancashire Cotton Industry*, 179–276, Manchester University Press, 1904.

—— 'The Regulation of Wages by Lists in the Spinning Industry', *Economic Journal*, December 1899, 592–9.

—— 'Some Policies of the Cotton Spinners' Trade Unions', *Economic Journal*, December 1900, 467–73.

——'An Historical Sketch of Masters' Associations in the Cotton Industry', *Transactions of the Manchester Statistical Society*, 13 February 1901, 67–84.

—— 'Some Theoretical Objections to Sliding-Scales', *Economic Journal*, June 1903, 186–96.

—— 'The Cotton Industry', in *Work and Wages. In Continuation of Lord Brassey's 'Work and Wages'*, Vol. i, *Foreign Competition*, 139–85, London, Longmans, 1904.

CHAPMAN, S. J. AND ABBOTT, W., 'The Tendency of Children to Enter their Fathers' Trades', *Journal of the Royal Statistical Society*, May 1913, 599–604.

CHAPMAN, S. J. AND MARQUIS, F. J., 'The Recruiting of the Employing Classes from the Ranks of the Wage-Earners in the Cotton Industry'. *Journal of the Royal Statistical Society*, February 1912, 293–313, reprinted by Marquis, F. J., *Upward Mobility of Labour as Evidenced in the Lancashire Cotton Industry*, 24 pp., Liverpool, Northern Publishing Company, 1912, in the British Library of Economics and Political Science.

The 'well-known cotton manufacturing town with 100,000 inhabitants' where Marquis carried out his survey was identified as Burnley in *The Memoirs of the Rt. Hon. the Earl of Woolton*, 12–13, London, Cassell, 1959. The author's argument is discussed on pp. 293–4 of the present work.

CHAPMAN, S. J. AND SHIMMIN, A. N., 'Industrial Recruiting and the Displacement of Labour', *Transactions of the Manchester Statistical Society*, 11 March 1914, 93–147.

CLARKE, ALLEN, *The Effects of the Factory System*, 178 pp., London, Richards, 1899, translated into Russian under the auspices of Tolstoy as *Fabrichnaya zhizn' v Anglii*, Moscow, Posrednik, 1904.

COLLET, C. E., *Report by Miss Collet on the Statistics of Employment of Women and Girls. Board of Trade—Employment of Women (Labour Department)*, 152 pp., especially 30–40, 52–65, 106–9, 120–38, C.7564 of 1894.

FOSTER, J., *Class Struggle and the Industrial Revolution. Early Industrial Capitalism in Three English Towns*, 346 pp., London, Weidenfeld, 1974.

FRASER, W. H., 'The Glasgow Cotton Spinners, 1837', in J. Butt and J. T. Ward (eds.), *Scottish Themes. Essays in honour of Professor S. G. E. Lythe*, 80–97, Edinburgh, Scottish Academic Press, 1976.

GASKELL, P., *The Manufacturing Population of England, its Moral, Social and Physical Conditions, and the Changes which have arisen from the use of Steam Machinery*, 361 pp., London, Baldwin, 1833; New York, Arno, 1972, reprinted in revised form as *Artisans and Machinery*, 399 pp., London, Parker, 1836; Cass, 1968.

GIBSON, R., *Cotton Textile Wages in the United States and Great Britain. A Comparison of Trends, 1860–1945*, 137 pp., New York, King's Crown Press, Columbia University, 1948.

HENDERSON, W. O., 'The Labour Force in the Textile Industries', *Archiv für Sozialgeschichte*, 1976, 283–324.

HEWITT, M., 'The Effect of Married Women's Employment in the Cotton Textile Districts on the Organisation and Structure of the Home in Lancashire, 1840–1880', 329 pp., Ph.D. thesis, University of London, 1953.

—— *Wives and Mothers in Victorian Industry*, 245 pp., London, Rockliff, 1958.

HOPWOOD, E., *A History of the Lancashire Cotton Industry and the Amalgamated Weavers' Association. The Lancashire Weavers' Story*, 200 pp., Manchester, Amalgamated Weavers' Association, 1969.

HUTCHINS, B. L., 'Statistics of Women's Life and Employment', *Journal of the Royal Statistical Society*, June 1909, 223–47.

JEWKES, J. AND GRAY, E. M., *Wages and Labour in the Lancashire Cotton Spinning Industry*, 222 pp., 9 charts, Manchester University Press, 1935.

JEVONS, W. A., 'Account of the Weavers' Strike at Padiham in 1859', in National Association for the Promotion of Social Science, *Report of the Committee on Trades Societies and Strikes*, 433–72, London, Parker, 1860; New York, Kelley, 1968.

JEVONS, W. S., 'Married Women in Factories', *Contemporary Review*, January 1882, 37–53.

JOYCE, P., 'The Factory Politics of Lancashire in the Later Nineteenth Century', *Historical Journal*, 1975, 525–53.

KIRBY, R. G. AND MUSSON, A. E., *The Voice of the People. John Doherty, 1798–1854. Trade unionist, radical and factory reformer*, 474 pp., Manchester University Press, 1975.

[LAMB, R.], 'The Manufacturing Poor', *Fraser's Magazine*, January 1848, 1–16.

—— 'The Manufacturing Poor: the Means of Elevating their Moral Condition—Education', *Fraser's Magazine*, February 1849, 127–43, reprinted, with the preceding article, in *Free Thoughts on Many Subjects: a Selection from Articles Contributed to 'Fraser's Magazine' By a Manchester Man*, i. 1–40, 'A Manufacturing District: a Sketch from Nature', 41–82, 'Our Manufacturing Populations,—The Educational Agency Among Them', London, Longmans, 1866.

LAW, ALICE, 'The People of the Valley', *Independent Review*, March 1904, 266–77.

LEVI, L., *Wages and Earnings of the Working Classes*, 76–80, 'The Cotton Manufacture', London, Murray, 1867.

NEWBIGGING, T., 'Lancashire Factory Doffers', *East Lancashire Review*, 1890, 20–4, reprinted in *Lancashire Characters and Places*, 49–55, Manchester, Brook, 1891.

POTTER, E., 'Trades' Unions and their Tendencies', *Transactions of the National Association for the Promotion of Social Science*, 1860, 755–62, reprinted with discussion in National Association for the Promotion of Social Science, *Report of the Committee on Trades Societies and Strikes*, 597–623, London, Parker, 1860.

READE, A., 'Life in Lancashire', *London Society*, January 1885, 25–32.

REDFORD, A., *Labour Migration in England 1800–1850*, 209 pp., Manchester University Press, 1926, 1964.

Report to the Board of Trade on the Relation of Wages in Certain Industries to the Cost of Production, 196 pp., especially 25–7, C.6535 of 1891.

Return of Rates of Wages in the Principal Textile Trades of the United Kingdom, with Report thereon, 152 pp., C.5087 of 1889.

Royal Commission on Labour, *Minutes of Evidence taken before Group 'C' (Textile . . . Trades)*, C.6708–vi of 1892, i, Textile.

SANDERSON, M., 'Education and the Factory in Industrial Lancashire, 1780–1840', *Economic History Review*, August 1967, 266–79.

SCHULZE-GAEVERNITZ, G. VON, *Zum socialen Frieden. Eine Darstellung der socialpolitischen Erziehung des englischen Volkes im neunzehnten Jahrhundert*, ii. 290–329, 'Die Textilgewerbe', Leipzig, Duncker, 1890, translated in part as *Social Peace. A Study of the Trade Union Movement in England*, 138–69, London, Swan, 1893.

SIDGWICK, H., FOXWELL, H. S., ACLAND, A. H. D., CUNNINGHAM, W., AND MUNRO, J. E. C., 'The Regulation of Wages by Means of Lists in the Cotton Industry', *Report of the British Association*, 1887, 303–20.

SMILES, S., 'Strikes', *Quarterly Review*, October 1859, 485–522.

—— 'Workmen's Earnings and Savings', *Quarterly Review*, July 1860, 81–120, reprinted with the preceding article as *Workmen's Earnings, Strikes and Savings*, 168 pp., London, Murray, 1861.

SMITH, R., 'A History of the Lancashire Cotton Industry between the Years 1873 and 1896', 752 pp., Ph.D. thesis, University of Birmingham, 1954.

TURNER, H. A., *Trade Union Growth, Structure and Policy. A Comparative Study of the Cotton Unions*, 413 pp., London, Allen, 1962.

WHEATLEY, J., 'Influence of the Cotton Industry on the Health of the Operatives', *Public Health*, April 1896, 218–24.

WOOD, G. H., 'Factory Legislation considered with reference to the Wages, &c. of the Operatives Protected Thereby', *Journal of the Royal Statistical Society*, June 1902, 284–320.

—— 'The Statistics of Wages in the United Kingdom during the Nineteenth Century (Part XV). The Cotton Industry', *Journal of the Royal Statistical Society*, January 1910, 39–58, February, 228–63, March, 283–315, April, 411–34, reprinted as *The History of Wages in the Cotton Trade during the past Hundred Years*, 162 pp., including a bibliography of 57 items on pp. 5–7, Manchester, Sherratt, 1910.

THE GROWTH OF THE WORLD MARKET

CHAPMAN, S. J., *The History of Trade between the United Kingdom and the United States with special reference to the Effect of Tariffs*, 118 pp., London, Swan, 1899.

FEUERWERKER, A., 'Handicraft and Manufactured Cotton Textiles in China, 1871–1910', *Journal of Economic History*, June 1970, 338–78.

FONG, H. D. (Fang Hsien-ting), *Cotton Industry and Trade in China*, 2 vols., Tientsin, Nankai University, 1932.

JAFFÉ, E., 'Die englische Baumwollindustrie und die Organisation des Exporthandels', *Schmollers Jahrbuch für Gesetzgebung*, 1900, 194–217.

KOH, S. J., *Stages of Industrial Development in Asia. A Comparative History of the Cotton Industry in Japan, India, China and Korea*, 461 pp., Philadelphia, University of Pennsylvania Press, 1966.

MARRISON, A. J., 'Great Britain and her rivals in the Latin American cotton piece-goods market, 1880–1914', in B. M. Ratcliffe (ed.), *Great Britain and her world, 1750–1914. Essays in honour of W. O. Henderson*, 309–48, Manchester University Press, 1975.

REDFORD, A., *Manchester Merchants and Foreign Trade 1794–1858*, 252 pp., Manchester University Press, 1934.

REDFORD, A. AND CLAPP, B. W., *Manchester Merchants and Foreign Trade Vol. II, 1850–1939*, 307 pp., Manchester University Press, 1956.

SANDBERG, L. G., *Lancashire in Decline. A Study in Entrepreneurship, Technology and International Trade*, 276 pp., Columbus, Ohio State University Press, 1974.

—— 'Movements in the Quality of British Cotton Textile Exports, 1815–1913', *Journal of Economic History*, March 1968, 1–27.

SAUL, S. B., *Studies in British Overseas Trade, 1870–1914*, Liverpool University Press, 1960.

YEN, Chung-Ping, 'Zur Geschichte der Baumwollenindustrie in China bis zum Ende des Ersten Weltkrieges', *Jahrbuch für Wirtschaftsgeschichte*, 1961, Teil ii, 199–230, reprinted in J. Kuczynski, *Die Geschichte der Lage der Arbeiter unter dem Kapitalismus*, Berlin, Akademie Verlag, 1964, Band 28, Chung-Ping Yen, Jürgen Kuczynski, Wolfgang Jonas, *Die Lage der Arbeiter in der Baumwollindustrie Shanghais inbesondere in den englischen Fabriken*, 13–41.

THE INDIAN MARKET

CLARK, W. A. G., *Cotton Fabrics in British India and the Philippines*, 117 pp., Department of Commerce and Labor, Bureau of Manufactures, Special Agents' Series No. 13, Washington, Government Printing Office, 1907.

DESAI, Meghnad, 'Demand for Cotton Textiles in Nineteenth-Century India', *Indian Economic and Social History Review*, 1971, 337–61.

HARNETTY, P., *Imperialism and Free Trade: Lancashire and India in the*

Mid-Nineteenth Century, 137 pp., University of British Columbia Press, 1972.

Manchester Chamber of Commerce, *Bombay and Lancashire Cotton Spinning Inquiry. Minutes of Evidence and Reports*, 397 pp., Manchester, Ireland, 1888.

MEHTA, S. D., *The Cotton Mills of India 1854 to 1954*, 308 pp., Bombay, Textile Association (India), 1954.

MORRIS, M. D., *The Emergence of an Industrial Labor Force in India. A Study of the Bombay Cotton Mills, 1854–1947*, 263 pp., Berkeley, University of California Press, 1965.

O'GORMAN, D. A., 'Recent Trade Progress and Competition in India', *Journal of the Manchester Geographical Society*, 4 November 1891, 230–63.

PILZ, H., *Die indische Baumwollindustrie. Produktionsgrundlagen, Entwicklung vor und nach dem Weltkriege, soziale Fragen, Zollpolitik*, 188 pp., Berlin, Springer, 1930.

RAI, A., *Die indische Baumwollindustrie*, 198 pp., Delhi, Hindustan Printing Works, 1928.

SLAVEN, A., 'A Glasgow Firm in the Indian Market: John Lean and Sons Muslin Weavers' [1840–70], *Business History Review*, Winter 1969, 496–522.

THE INDIAN COTTON DUTIES

DEY, H. L., *The Indian Tariff Problem in Relation to Industry and Taxation*, 44–50, 91–8, London, Allen, 1933.

DUTT, R. C., *India in the Victorian Age. An Economic History of the People*, 401–16, 537–44, London, Paul, 1904.

HAMILTON, C. J., *The Trade Relations between England and India (1600–1896)*, 231–54, Calcutta, Thacker, 1919.

PARSHAD, I. D., *Some Aspects of Indian Foreign Trade 1757–1893*, 175–204, London, King, 1932.

SHAH, N. J., 'History of Indian Tariff', 158–311, Ph.D. thesis, University of London, 1923.

1875–1879

GUJRAL, L., 'Sir Louis Mallet's Mission to Lord Northbrook on the Question of the Cotton Duties', *Journal of Indian History*, 1961, 473–87.

KNIGHT, R., *Manchester and India. A Protest against Sir John Strachey's Financial Statement in the Legislative Council of India, Dated 15th March, 1877*, 88 pp., Calcutta, Thacker, 1877.

JACKSON, R. R., 'India and Lancashire', *Fortnightly Review*, June 1876, 877–96.

—— *India and Lancashire. An Answer to Recent Arguments Advanced against the Proposed Repeal of the Indian Import Duties on Cotton Goods and Yarn*, 20 pp., Blackburn, Toulmin, 1877.

—— *Lecture delivered by Colonel Jackson, to the Members of the Managers' Mutual Association in the Church Institute*, 23 pp., Blackburn, Thornber, 1878.

1894–1896

ENTHOVEN, R. E., *The Cotton Fabrics of the Bombay Presidency*, 51 pp., Bombay, Government Press (?), 1897.

FOWLER, E. H., *The Life of Henry Hartley Fowler, First Viscount Wolverhampton, G.C.S.I.*, 318–36, 'Cotton Duties, 1895', London, Hutchinson, 1912.

HALLETT, H. S., *Lancashire's Case against the Indian Import Duties*, 44 pp., Blackburn Chamber of Commerce, 1895.

HARNETTY, P., 'The Indian Cotton Duties Controversy, 1894–1896', *English Historical Review*, October 1962, 684–702.

HELM, E., 'The Indian Duties on Cotton Goods', *Economic Journal*, March 1896, 110–14.

KANNANGARA, A. P., 'Indian Millowners and Indian Nationalism before 1914', *Past and Present*, July 1968, 147–64.

PADSHAH, B. J., *The Cotton Industry and the Cotton Duties*, 43 pp., Bombay, Commercial Press, 1902.

TATTERSALL, W., 'Lancashire and the Cotton Duties', *Fortnightly Review*, 1 February 1896, 291–303.

WHITTAKER, J., *The Re-Imposition of the Indian Import Duties on Cotton Goods and Yarn. A Plain Statement of its Effects on the Cotton Trade of Great Britain*, 32 pp., Blackburn, North-East Lancashire Press, 1895.

THE COTTON FAMINE, 1861–1865

GENERAL HISTORY

ADAMS, C. F., *Trans-Atlantic Historical Solidarity. Lectures delivered before the University of Oxford in Easter and Trinity Terms 1913*, 184 pp., Oxford, Clarendon Press, 1913.

ANDREWS, A., 'Cotton Possibilities', *New Monthly Magazine*, September 1864, 70–8, October, 175–85, November, 356–62, December, 449–61.

ARNOLD, R. A., 'The Cotton Famine', *Transactions of the National Association for the Promotion of Social Science*, 1864, 612–17.

—— 'The Economy of Public Works', *Transactions of the National Association for the Promotion of Social Science*, 1866, 708–14.

—— *The History of the Cotton Famine from the Fall of Sumter to the Passing of the Public Works Act*, 570 pp., London, Saunders, 1864, reviewed in the *London Quarterly Review*, January 1865, 313–56, and in the *British Quarterly Review*, 1 April 1865, 358–80. The second edition of 1865 included a ten-page postscript, largely on the operation of the Public Works Act: it was reviewed in *The Times*, 19 August 1865, 8i–v and reprinted by Cass, 1966.

—— 'On the Employment of Workmen in Casual Distress', *Transactions of the National Association for the Promotion of Social Science*, 1868, 619–21.

—— 'Temporary Employment in Casual Distress', *Social Politics*, 265–84, London, Paul, 1878.

BAILLIE, J., *What I Saw in Lancashire: a Plea for the Distressed Operatives*, 30 pp., London, Nisbet, 1862.

BARLEE, E., *A Visit to Lancashire in December 1862*, 156 pp., London, Seeley, 1863.

'Die Baumwollenhungersnoth in Lancashire', *Nauticus*, 1900, 226–36, reprinted in *Die Grenzboten*, 26 April 1900, 182–9, 'Die Baumwollhungersnot von Lancashire'.

BAZLEY, T., 'A Glance at the Cotton Trade', *Report of the British Association*, 1861, 206–8.

—— 'The Difficulties and Dangers of the Cotton Trade', *The Exchange*, January 1863, 201–12.

[BAZLEY, T.], 'The Past, Present, and Future of the Cotton Trade', *New Quarterly Review*, January 1862, 181–90.

BOWRING, J., 'Cotton', *The Exchange*, April 1862, 41–9.

BRADY, E. A., 'A Reconsideration of the Lancashire "Cotton Famine"', *Agricultural History*, July 1963, 156–62.

BROOK, M., 'Confederate Sympathies in North-East Lancashire 1862–1864', *Transactions of the Lancashire and Cheshire Antiquarian Society*, 1965–6, 211–17.

CHADWICK, D., 'On the Cotton Famine, and the Substitutes for Cotton', *Report of the British Association*, 1862, Transactions of the Sections, 150–3.

CHADWICK, E., 'The Cotton Manufacture and Cotton Operatives', *Blackburn Standard*, 5 October 1864, 2vi–vii.

CHEETHAM, J., 'On the Present Position and Future Prospects of the Supply of Cotton', *Journal of the Society of Arts*, 27 February 1863, 255–68.

CODDINGTON, E. B., 'The Civil War Blockade Reconsidered', in D. E. Lee and G. E. McReynolds (eds.), *Essays in History and International Relations in Honor of George Hubbard Blakeslee*, 284–305, Worcester, Clark University Press, 1949.

EARLE, E. M., 'Egyptian Cotton and the American Civil War', *Political Science Quarterly*, December 1926, 520–45.

ELLINGER, B., 'The Cotton Famine of 1861–4', *Economic History*, January 1934, 152–67.

ELLISON, T., *The Cotton Trade of Great Britain*, 91–6, London, Wilson, 1886; Cass, 1968.

—— 'The Critical Position of the Cotton Trade', *The Exchange*, July 1862, 253–6.

—— 'Distress in Lancashire: Prospects of the Cotton Trade', *The Exchange*, June 1862, 152–8.

—— *Gleanings and Reminiscences*, 319–27, Liverpool, Young, 1905.

FAY, C. R., 'Manchester and the Lancashire Cotton Famine', in *Round About Industrial Britain 1830–1860*, 101–14, University of Toronto Press, 1952.

FORCADE, E., 'La Semaine de Noël 1862 dans le Lancashire', *Revue des deux mondes*, 1 Février 1862, 674–704.

FORWOOD, W. B., 'On the Influence of Price upon the Cultivation and Consumption of Cotton during the Past Ten Years, embracing the period of the American War and Cotton Famine', *Report of the British Association*, 1870, Transactions of the Sections, 191–2, printed in full in *Journal of the Statistical Society*, September 1870, 366–83.

GIBBS, H. S., *Autobiography of a Manchester Cotton Manufacturer; or, Thirty Years Experience of Manchester*, 160–94, Manchester, Heywood, 1887.

GRANT, C. W., 'Notes on a Cotton-Chart, showing the Effect on Cotton of the Civil War in America', *Report of the British Association*, 1864, Transactions of the Sections, 166–7.

GREG, W. R., 'The Cotton Famine and Lancashire Distress', *North British Review*, August 1863, 235–49.

HALLE, ERNST VON, *Baumwollproduktion und Pflanzungswirtschaft in den Nordamerikanischen Südstaaten. Zweiter Teil, Sezessionskrieg und Rekonstruktion. Grundzüge einer Wirtschaftsgeschichte der Baumwollstaaten von 1861–1880*, 669 pp., Leipzig, Duncker, 1906.

HARLAND, J., *Lancashire Lyrics: Modern Songs and Ballads of the County Palatine*, 281–308, 'Lays of the Cotton Famine', London, Whittaker, 1866; 3rd edn., 1882, entitled *Ballads and Songs of Lancashire*, reprinted by E. P. Publishing, Wakefield, 1976.

HARNETTY, P., 'Cotton Exports and Indian Agriculture, 1861–1870', *Economic History Review*, August 1971, 414–29.

—— 'The Cotton Improvement Program in India, 1865–1875', *Agricultural History*, October 1970, 379–92.

—— 'The Imperialism of Free Trade: Lancashire and the Indian Cotton Duties, 1859–1862', *Economic History Review*, August 1965, 177–86.

—— 'The Imperialism of Free Trade: Lancashire, India, and the Cotton Supply Question, 1861–1865', *Journal of British Studies*, November 1966, 70–96.

—— 'Indian and British Commercial Enterprise: The Case of the Manchester Cotton Company', *Indian Economic and Social History Review*, 1966.

HARRISON, FREDERIC, 'Lancashire', *Westminster Review*, July 1863, 191–219.

HARRISON, ROYDEN, 'British Labour and the Confederacy. A Note on the Southern Sympathies of some British Working Class Journals and Leaders during the American Civil War', *International Review of Social History*, 1957, 78–105.

—— 'British Labour and American Slavery', *Science and Society*, December 1961, 291–319, reprinted in *Before the Socialists. Studies in Labour and Politics 1861–1881*, 40–77, London, Routledge, 1965.

HARRISON, WILLIAM, 'The Distress in Lancashire, and Present Modes of Relief', *Macmillan's Magazine*, December 1862, 153–60.

HELM, E., 'A Review of the Cotton Trade of the United Kingdom, during the Seven Years, 1862–1868', *Transactions of the Manchester Statistical Society*, 14 April 1869, 67–94, reprinted in *Journal of the Statistical Society*, December 1869, 428–37.

—— 'Cotton Famine (1861–65)' in R.H.I. Palgrave (ed.), *Dictionary of Political Economy*, i. 439–41, London, Macmillan, 1894.

HEMELRYK, P. E. J., *Forty Years' Reminiscences of the Cotton Market: the American War Time and After*, 28 pp., Liverpool, Rockliff, 1916, a lecture given in 1899 to the Liverpool and District Bankers' Institute.

HENDERSON, W. O., 'The Cotton Famine in Lancashire', *Transactions of the Historic Society of Lancashire and Cheshire*, 3 March 1932, 37–62.

—— 'The Cotton Famine in Scotland and the Relief of Distress, 1862–1864', *Scottish Historical Review*, 1951, 154–64.

—— 'The Cotton Famine on the Continent, 1861–1864', *Economic History Review*, April 1933, 195–207.

—— *The Lancashire Cotton Famine 1861–1865*, 180 pp., 2nd edn., 198 pp., Manchester University Press, 1934, 1969. The 38-page bibliography, a monument of scholarship in its own right, is the fullest available on the history of the cotton industry during the nineteenth century as well as on the Cotton Famine. The second edition includes the two above-cited chapters dealing with the Continent and with Scotland.

—— 'The Public Works Act, 1863', *Economic History*, January 1931, 312–21.

HERFORD, B., 'Annals of the Cotton Manufacture: the Cotton Famine', in E. Baines, *History of the County Palatine and Duchy of Lancaster*, J. Harland (ed.), ii. 708–10, London, Routledge, 1870.

JONES, R. H., 'Long Live the King?', *Agricultural History*, July 1963, 166–9.

[LAMB, R.], 'Our Manufacturing Districts and Operative Classes', *Fraser's Magazine*, September 1862, 363–82.

—— 'Our Manufacturing Districts under a Cloud', *Fraser's Magazine*, September 1863, 309–25, reprinted with the preceding article and an epilogue on pp. 349–68, 'The Cloud Dispersing. Postscript—1866', in *Free Thoughts on Many Subjects*, ii. 271-348, London, Longmans, 1866.

LANDES, D. S., *Bankers and Pashas. International Finance and Economic Imperialism in Egypt*, 69–101, 'Klondike on the Nile', London, Heinemann, 1958.

LEACOCK, S., AND MANDELBAUM, D. G., 'A Nineteenth Century Development Project in India: the Cotton Improvement Program', *Economic Development and Cultural Change*, July 1955, 334–51.

LEVERTON, B. J. T., *The Natal Cotton Industry, 1845–1875. A Study in Failure*, 38 pp., Pretoria, Communications of the University of South Africa C41, 1963.

LEVI, L., 'On the Cotton Trade and Manufacture, as affected by the Civil War in America', *Journal of the Statistical Society*, March 1863, 26–48.

MCCREADY, H. W., 'The Cotton Famine in Lancashire, 1863', *Transactions of the Historic Society of Lancashire and Cheshire*, 1954, 127–33.

MCCREADY, H. W., 'Elizabeth Gaskell and the Cotton Famine in Manchester: Some Unpublished Letters', *Transactions of the Historic Society of Lancashire and Cheshire*, 1971, 144–50.

MCHAFFIE, M. J., '*Was it a Cotton Famine?*' *Being Twelve Letters from the 'Times' Money Article*, 24 pp., London, Wilson, 1865.

MCHENRY, G., *The Cotton Trade: its Bearing upon the Prosperity of Great Britain and Commerce of the American Republics*, 292 pp., London, Saunders, 1863.

MARX, K., *Capital, A Critique of Political Economy*, iii. 141–62, Chicago, Kerr, 1909.

MUNRO, A., 'Our Unemployed Females, and what may best be done for them', *Transactions of the Manchester Statistical Society*, 18 March 1863, 25–38.

NINET, J., 'La Culture du coton en Égypte et aux Indes—le travail libre aux États-Unis', *Revue des deux mondes*, 15 Juillet 1866, 350–76.

——'La Question du coton en Angleterre depuis la crise américaine', *Revue des deux mondes*, 1 Mars 1861, 196–222.

NOBLE, D., 'Fluctuations in the Death Rate', *Transactions of the Manchester Statistical Society*, 26 October 1863, 1–18.

Ollerenshaw, J. C., 'Our Export Trade in Cotton Goods to India', *Transactions of the Manchester Statistical Society*, 13 April 1870, 109–24.

Osborne, S. G., *The Letters of S.G.O. . . . published in 'The Times' 1844–1878*, Arnold White (ed.), i. 130–57, 'Lancashire Distress and Relief', 2 May 1862–28 March 1863, London, Griffith, 1890.

Owen, E. R. J., 'Egyptian Cotton and the American Civil War, 1860–1866', in C. Issawi (ed.), *The Economic History of the Middle East 1800–1914. A Book of Readings*, 416–29, University of Chicago Press, 1966.

—— *Cotton and the Egyptian Economy 1820–1914. A Study in Trade and Development*, 89–121, Oxford, Clarendon Press, 1969.

Owsley, F. L., *King Cotton Diplomacy. Foreign Relations of the Confederate States of America*, 614 pp., University of Chicago Press, 1931, 1959.

Penny, K., 'Australian Relief for the Lancashire Victims of the Cotton Famine, 1862–1863', *Transactions of the Historic Society of Lancashire and Cheshire*, 1956, 129–39.

Plummer, J., 'The Distress in Lancashire', *Companion to The British Almanac for 1863*, 25–48.

Potter, E., 'The Position of the Cotton Districts', *Transactions of the National Association for the Promotion of Social Science*, 1863, 649–62, 757–60.

Purdy, F., 'On the Pauperism and Mortality of Lancashire', *Report of the British Association*, 1862, Transactions of the Sections, 165–72.

Rawlinson, R., *Public Works in Lancashire for the Relief of Distress among the Unemployed Factory Hands during the Cotton Famine, 1863–66*, 136 pp., London, King, 1898.

Reclus, E., 'Le Coton et la crise américaine', *Revue des deux mondes*, 1 Janvier 1862, 176–208.

Reybaud, L., 'La Guerre d'Amérique et le marché du coton', *Revue des deux mondes*, 1 Mars 1865, 189–208.

Rothstein, M., 'The International Market for Agricultural Commodities, 1850–1873', in D. T. Gilchrist and W. D. Lewis (eds.), *Economic Change in the Civil War Era. Proceedings of a Conference on American Economic Institutional Change, 1850–1873, and the Impact of the Civil War, held March 12–14, 1964*, 62–82, Greenville, Delaware, Eleutherian Mills-Hagley Foundation, 1965.

Schmidt, L. B., 'The Influence of Wheat and Cotton on Anglo-American Relations during the Civil War', *Iowa Journal of History and Politics*, July 1918, 400–39, reprinted without footnotes in L. B. Schmidt and E. D. Ross (eds.), *Readings in the Economic*

History of American Agriculture, 304–21, New York, Macmillan, 1925.

SLAGG, J., 'The Cotton Trade and Industry', in T. H. Ward (ed.), *The Reign of Queen Victoria. A Survey of Fifty Years of Progress*, ii. 160–6, London, Smith, 1887.

SILVER, A. W., 'Henry Adams' "Diary of a Visit to Manchester"', [8–14 November 1861], *American Historical Review*, October 1945, 74–89.

—— *Manchester Men and Indian Cotton 1847–1872*, 349 pp., Manchester University Press, 1966.

TORRENS, W. T. M., *Lancashire's Lesson; or, the Need of a Settled Policy in Times of Exceptional Distress*, 191 pp., London, Trübner, 1864, reviewed in *Manchester Guardian*, 27 December 1864, 3i–ii.

TUGAN-BARANOWSKY, M. VON, *Studien zur Theorie und Geschichte der Handelskrisen in England*, 353–81, 'Der Baumwollhunger', Jena, Fischer, 1901.

VERDEIL, F., 'La Disette du coton en Angleterre et les comités de prévoyance', *Revue des deux mondes*, 1 Janvier 1863, 211–27.

WATTS, J., *The Facts of the Cotton Famine*, 472 pp., London, Simpkin, 1866; Cass, 1968.

WAUGH, E., *Home-Life of the Lancashire Factory Folk during the Cotton Famine*, 277 pp., Manchester, Heywood, 1867, 1881.

LOCAL HISTORY

ARMSTRONG, W. K., *Memoir of John Ross Coulthart of Ashton-under-Lyne*, 187–98, Edinburgh, M'Farlane, 1876.

ASHMORE, O., 'The Diary of James Garnett of Low Moor, Clitheroe, 1858–65: Part 2 The American Civil War and the Cotton Famine, 1861–65', *Transactions of the Historic Society of Lancashire and Cheshire*, 1971, 105–43.

ASHWORTH, T. E., *A Fragment of Todmorden History*, 8–16, 'Todmorden and the Cotton Famine of 1862–5', Todmorden, Lee, 1911.

ASPIN, C., *Haslingden 1800–1900. A History*, 126–31, Haslingden Printing Works Ld., 1962.

AXON, W. E. A., *The Annals of Manchester*, 286–301, Manchester, Heywood, 1886.

BATESON, H., *A Centenary History of Oldham*, 144–50, Oldham, Borough Council, 1949.

BENNETT, W., *The History of Burnley*, iv. 120–2, Burnley Corporation, 1951.

BOWMAN, W. M., *England in Ashton-under-Lyne*, 447–55, Altrincham, Sherratt, 1960.

BRADLEY, JAMES, *Reminiscences in the Life of Joshua Bradley Donor of Hyde Town Hall Clock and Bells. From Little Piecer to Manager*,

122–9, Oldham, Clegg, 1904; Mottram, Longden Publications, 1974.

The Chronicles of Blackburn, during the Mayoralty of Robert Hopwood Hutchinson, Esq., 1861–2, 60 pp., Blackburn, Haworth, 1863.

FRANCE, R. S., 'A Lancashire Manufacturer and the Cotton Famine', *Lancashire Record Office Report for 1972*, 16–22.

GOURLAY, W., *History of the Distress in Blackburn, 1861–5*, 180 pp., Blackburn, Haworth, 1865.

HEWITSON, A., *History of Preston, 705–1883*, 189–94, Preston Chronicle, 1883.

HILL, S., *Bygone Stalybridge*, 82–100, Stalybridge, Hill, 1907.

KNEESHAW, J. W., *Burnley in the Nineteenth Century*, 31–5, Burnley Express, 1897.

MIDDLETON, T., *The History of Hyde and its Neighbourhood*, 128–31, Hyde, Higham, 1932.

NICHOLLS, S. A., *Darwen and the Cotton Famine. Thirty Years Ago, 1862–1864*, 100 pp., Darwen, Riley, 1893, in Blackburn Library.

REDFORD, A., *A History of Local Government in Manchester*, ii. 242–80, London, Longmans, 1940.

REDFORD, A. AND CLAPP, B. W., *Manchester Merchants and Foreign Trade Vol. II 1850–1939*, 12-20, Manchester University Press, 1956.

THE GREAT DEPRESSION OF 1873–1896

SANDBERG, L. G., *Lancashire in Decline. A Study in Entrepreneurship, Technology and International Trade*, 276 pp., Columbus, Ohio State University Press, 1974.

SAUL, S. B., *Studies in British Overseas Trade, 1870–1914*, Liverpool University Press, 1960.

—— 'The Export Economy 1870–1914', *Yorkshire Bulletin of Economic and Social Research*, 1965, 5–18.

—— *The Myth of the Great Depression 1873–1896*, 63 pp., London, Macmillan, 1969.

SMITH, R., 'A History of the Lancashire Cotton Industry between the Years 1873 and 1896', 752 pp., Ph.D. thesis, University of Birmingham, 1954.

—— 'The Manchester Chamber of Commerce and the Increasing Foreign Competition to Lancashire Cotton Textiles, 1873–1896', *Bulletin of the John Rylands Library*, 38, March 1956, 507–34.

TYSON, R. E., 'The Cotton Industry', in D. H. Aldcroft (ed.), *The Development of British Industry and Foreign Competition 1875–1914. Studies in Industrial Enterprise*, 100-27, London, Allen, 1968.

THE DEPRESSION OF 1877–1879

ARNOLD, R. A., *Free Trade and Reciprocity. An Address delivered in the Town Hall, Pendleton, February 20 1879*, 19 pp., Salford Liberal Association, 1879.

—— 'A Reply to Cassandra', *Social Politics*, 285–321, London, Paul, 1878.

ATKINSON, E., 'An American View of American Competition', *Fortnightly Review*, March 1879, 383–96.

BAGEHOT, W., *Some Articles on the Depreciation of Silver and on Topics Connected with it*, 136 pp., reprinted from *The Economist*, 5 February 1876, 153–4, to 30 December, 1507–8, London, King, 1877.

BEADS, J., *Suggested Remedies for Bad Trade. A Lecture by Councillor Beads, with Strictures on Col. Jackson's Article in the 'Quarterly Review', and his Recent Lecture on 'Foreign Competition'. Reprinted from the Preston Guardian, December 11th, 1878*, 12 pp., Blackburn, 'Times' and 'Guardian' Offices, 1878.

BOURNE, H. R. F., 'Foreign Rivalries—v. Cotton Manufacture', in *Great Industries of Great Britain*, i. 318–22, London, Cassell, 1879.

BOURNE, S., *Trade, Population and Food. A Series of Papers on Economic Statistics*, 348 pp., London, Bell, 1880.

'British and American Textile Industries', *Manchester Examiner and Times*, 19 October 1876, 6i–iii.

CHADWICK, D., 'What are the Causes of the present depressed and stagnant Condition of Industrial Enterprise, and what are the best Remedies?', *Transactions of the National Association for the Promotion of Social Science*, 1878, 570–93, including discussion on pp. 582–93 abridged in reprint, 16 pp., London, Spottiswoode, 1878.

CRUMP, A., *A New Departure in the Domain of Political Economy*, 26–32, London, Longman, 1878.

DANA, W. B., *Cotton from Seed to Loom. A Hand-Book of Facts for the Daily Use of Producer, Merchant and Consumer*, 241–91, New York, Dana, 1878.

DIGGLE, J. W., *The Lancashire Life of Bishop Fraser*, 119–35, 'Commercial Depression', London, Low, 1889.

'Economical Production', *Textile Manufacturer*, February 1878, 40–1.

ELLISON, T., *The Cotton Trade of Great Britain*, 106–16, London, Wilson, 1886; Cass 1968.

Facts Affecting our Cotton Industry, or helps to the Formation of Sound Opinion, 12 pp., Blackburn, Ianson, 1878.

A Few Original Ideas of a Manchester Man respecting our Bad Trade and Government Interference, 31 pp., Manchester, Heywood, 1876.

FIELDEN, J. C., *Lecture on the Government and the State of Trade, delivered at Blackley, October 14th 1879, under the auspices of the National Reform Union*, 16 pp., Manchester, Heywood, 1879.

—— 'On the Employment of Surplus Labour, more especially during Periods of Commercial Depression', *Transactions of the Manchester Statistical Society*, 26 April 1882, 141–58.

—— *Speech on Foreign Competition in the Cotton Trade, &c., delivered by John C. Fielden (in reply to Colonel Jackson, Chairman of the North-East Lancashire Cotton Masters' Association, and Others), at a Meeting held in Manchester, on Saturday, November 30th, 1878*, 32 pp., Blackburn, Tiplady, 1879.

—— 'The Strike and Foreign Competition', *Ashton Reporter*, 17 August 1878, 3i–iii.

GREG, W. R., 'Rocks Ahead; or, the Warnings of Cassandra, Part II', *Contemporary Review*, June 1874, 40–66, reprinted in *Rocks Ahead, or, The Warnings of Cassandra*, 59–114, 'The Approaching Industrial Exhaustion or Decline of Great Britain', London, Trübner, 1874, and reviewed in the *Contemporary Review*, September 1874, 627–62, by R. A. Arnold and Lord Lyttelton.

GUTHRIE, E., *Bad Trade considered in relation to the Present Condition of the Cotton Industry in England*, 24 pp., Manchester, Ireland, 1878.

HELM, E., 'The Depression of Trade', *Transactions of the Manchester Statistical Society*, 11 December 1878, 45–58.

—— 'The Revival of Trade', *Transactions of the Manchester Statistical Society*, 12 November 1879, 9–22.

—— 'The Silver Question', *Transactions of the Manchester Statistical Society*, 13 March 1878, 75–88.

[HIBBERT, F.], *Bad Trade, and How to Avoid It. By a Cotton Spinner*, 31 pp., Manchester, Ireland, 1878.

HOYLE, W., *Crime and Pauperism: a Letter to the Right Honourable William Ewart Gladstone, M.P.*, 16 pp., Manchester, United Kingdom Alliance, 1881.

—— 'The Drink Expenditure and Trade', *Manchester Examiner and Times*, 31 December 1878, 6i–ii.

—— 'Drink Statistics', *Manchester Examiner and Times*, 27 March 1876, 4iii, 4 April, 6v, reprinted as *The Present Depression in Trade*, 24 pp., Manchester, Tubbs, 1876.

—— 'The Economic Conditions of Good Trade', *Transactions of the Manchester Statistical Society*, 12 May 1880, 91–114.

—— 'Over Production and the Present Stagnation in Trade', *Transactions of the National Association for the Promotion of Social Science*, 1877, 659–70, with discussion on pp. 670–7, reprinted in revised form, 16 pp., Manchester, Heywood, 1878.

—— *Problems to Solve: Social, Political, and Economic. An Address*

delivered under the auspices of the Birmingham Liberal Association, 24 pp., London, Simpkin, 1883.
'The Improvement of Our Cotton Textiles', *Textile Manufacturer*, March 1878, 76–7, April, 112–13, May, 146–7, June, 179, July, 215–16.
JACKSON, R. R., 'The Lancashire Cotton-Strike', *Quarterly Review*, October 1878, 485–519.
JONES, LLOYD, 'The Cotton Trade', *Industrial Review*, 7 September 1878, 1–2.
MONTGOMERY, R., 'The Silver Controversy', *Transactions of the Manchester Statistical Society*, 14 January 1880, 43–64.
MORLEY, J., 'Lancashire', *Fortnightly Review*, July 1878, 1–25, 200–13, 547–67.
NEALE, E. V., 'The Strike: its Motives and its Lessons', *Co-operative News*, 8 June 1878, 369, 394.
'Notes from the United States', *Manchester Examiner and Times*, 12 October 1876, 6i–iii.
PARRY, T., *Recent Commercial Crises and their Lessons*, 37 pp., Ashton-under-Lyne Literary and Historical Society, 1878.
SEYD, E., *The Decline of Prosperity: its Insidious Cause and Obvious Remedy*, 104 pp., London, Stanford, 1879.
SHORROCK, E., *Letter to the Working Men of Darwen; Address Delivered in William Street Club, in September, 1878, after the Riots at Darwen and Blackburn, on The Injurious Effects of Strikes upon the Trade of the Country*, 15 pp., Manchester, Ireland, 1879.
SLAGG, J., *Free Trade and Tariffs. A Speech delivered on July 20, 1881, to the Penge and Anerley Liberal Association*, 16 pp., Manchester, National Reform Union, 1881.
SMITH, SAMUEL, *Free Trade* versus *Reciprocity*, 30 pp., Liverpool, Watts, 1881.
SPENCER, J., 'The Growth of the Cotton Trade in Great Britain, America, and the Continent of Europe, during the half century ending with the year 1875', *Transactions of the Manchester Statistical Society*, 15 June 1877, 231–40.
THORNELY, J., *American Competition in the Cotton Trade: The Truth About It*, 71 pp., Manchester, Emmott, 1879, reprinted from *Textile Manufacturer*, October 1879, 339–42, November, 377–9, December, 413–16.
WHITTAKER, THOMAS P., 'Free Trade, Reciprocity and Foreign Competition', *Westminster Review*, July 1879, 1–46, reprinted in revised form, 48 pp., Manchester, Heywood, 1881.
WILLIAMSON, S., 'The Discrediting of Silver', *Contemporary Review*, April 1879, 121–30.
WILSON, ALEXANDER J., *The Resources of Modern Countries. Essays*

Towards an Estimate of the Economic Position of Nations and of British Trade Prospects, 401 pp., 382 pp., London, Longmans, 1878, reprinted from thirteen articles in *Fraser's Magazine*, September 1876, 269–84, to September 1877, 382–98, 'British Trade' with additional chapters on China and Japan, and on Turkey and Egypt.

WINKS, A. F., *Bad Trade, and How to Remedy It. A Letter to a Manchester Merchant*, 16 pp., Manchester, Heywood, 1879.

THE DEPRESSION OF 1884–1885

BROWN, BENJAMIN H., *The Tariff Reform Movement in Great Britain, 1881–1895*, 170 pp., New York, Columbia University Press, 1943.

COLQUHOUN, A. R., *The Opening of China. Six Letters Reprinted from* The Times *on the Present Condition and Future Prospects of China*, 102 pp., London, Field, 1884, reprinted from *The Times*, 7 August 1884, 8, 14, 16, 19, and 20 August.

'The Depression in the Cotton Trade', *Saturday Review*, 4 October 1884, 439–40.

ELLISON, T., *The Cotton Trade of Great Britain*, 297–305, London, Wilson, 1866; Cass 1968.

FIELDEN, J. C., 'A Sketch of the British Cotton Industry—Past, Present, and Prospective', *C.W.S. Annual*, 1887, 313–44.

FOGG, W., 'Objections to Free Trade Answered', *Transactions of the Manchester Statistical Society*, 9 February 1887, 25–56.

GOSCHEN, G. J., *Manchester Chamber of Commerce. Address by the Right Hon. G. J. Goschen, M.P., on the Condition and Prospects of Trade, delivered in the Town Hall, Manchester, Tuesday, June 23rd, 1885*, 39 pp., London, Wilson, 1885, reprinted with introductory note on pp. 185–8 in *Essays and Addresses on Economic Questions*, 189–216, London, Arnold, 1905.

GRANT, W. L., 'The Development of Africa in its Relation to British Commerce', *Transactions of the Burnley Literary and Scientific Club*, 25 November 1884, 86–8.

GREENWOOD, JAMES, 'The Growth of the Cotton Trade', *Journal of the Manchester Geographical Society*, 16 March 1887, 42–52.

GUTHRIE, E., *The Cotton Trade: its Condition and Prospects*, 24 pp., Manchester, Ireland, 1883.

HOYLE, W., 'The Cotton Trade. The Present Position and Future Prospects', *Manchester Guardian*, 10 October 1884, 4vi–vii, 15 October, 4v–vi, 21 October, 4v–vi.

—— *The Depression of Trade: its Cause and Cure*, 32 pp., London, National Temperance Publication Depot, 1885.

—— *Wealth and Social Progress in relation to Thrift, Temperance, and Trade*, 312 pp., Manchester, United Kingdom Alliance, 1887.

JEANS, J. S., *England's Supremacy: its Sources, Economics and Dangers*, 447 pp., especially 189–207, London, Longmans, 1885.

KROPOTKIN, P., 'The Breakdown of Our Industrial System', *Nineteenth Century*, April 1888, 497–516, reprinted in *Fields, Factories and Workshops or Industry Combined with Agriculture and Brain Work with Manual Work*, 1–39, New York, Putnam, 1901.

A Manchester Man (Embejay), *Half-a-Pair of Scissors: or What is Our (So Called) Free Trade? A Criticism of A. Montgredien's* [sic] *'Free Trade and English Commerce'*, 24 pp., Manchester, Heywood, 1885.

Royal Commission on the Depression of Trade and Industry, First Report, C.4621 of 1886, *Second Report*, C.4715 of 1886, *Third Report*, C.4797 of 1886.

SMITH, SAMUEL, 'Gold and Silver and the Depression of Trade', *Manchester Guardian*, 20 July 1885, 8iii–v, reprinted, 13 pp., Liverpool, Turner, 1885, and in *The Bi-Metallic Question*, 85–101, London, Wilson, 1887.

STANLEY, H. M., *Manchester Chamber of Commerce. Address of Mr. H. M. Stanley, on England and the Congo and Manchester Trade, and the Work and Aims of the International Association, Tuesday, October 21st 1884*, 39 pp., Manchester, Ireland, 1884.

WILLOUGHBY, F. S., *The Depression in Trade: True Fair Trade Proposals*, 15 pp., Manchester, Heywood, 1885.

THE DEPRESSION OF 1891–1893

ABRAM, W. A., 'The Prospective Decline of Lancashire', *Blackwood's Edinburgh Magazine*, July 1892, 1–17, reviewed in *Cotton Factory Times*, 8 July 1892, li–ii, and by J. C. Fielden, 'The Position of Lancashire', *Blackwood's Edinburgh Magazine*, August 1892, 284–92; E. Helm, 'The Alleged Decline of the British Cotton Industry', *Economic Journal*, December 1892, 735–44, and March 1893, 121–8; R. Marsden, 'Is the Cotton Trade Leaving the Country?', *Textile Mercury*, 21 January 1893, 42–6.

BAINES, T., 'The Lancashire Cotton Trade', *The Times*, 23 October 1897, 5iii–vi, reprinted in *The Industrial North in the Last Decade of the Nineteenth Century*, 75–80, Leeds, Jowett, 1928. Talbot Baines (1852–1927) was the grandson of Edward Baines.

'BONAMI', *The Doom of the Cotton Trade and the Fall of the Factory System*, 15 pp., Manchester, Heywood, 1896, in the British Library. The author was C. Allen Clarke and reprinted his pamphlet in *The Effects of the Factory System*, 159–73, 'Decline of the Lancashire Cotton Trade', London, Richards, 1899.

COX, HAROLD, *Are We Ruined by the Germans?*, 62 pp., London, Cassell, 1896.

The Crisis in the Cotton Trade, 28 pp., Liverpool, Howell, 1892.

DANIELL, C. J., *The Industrial Competition of Asia. An Inquiry into the Influence of Currency on the Commerce of the Empire in the East*, 387 pp., London, Paul, 1890, in the British Library.

FOGG, W., 'Strikes and Economic Fallacies', *Transactions of the Manchester Statistical Society*, 13 December 1893, 1–42.

—— 'Workers in Cotton Factories and the Eight Hours' Day', *Transactions of the Manchester Statistical Society*, 16 November 1892, 1–24.

GANNAY, P., *L'Impérialisme économique et la grande industrie anglaise*, 185–213, 'L'industrie du coton', Paris, Pichon, 1905.

GASTRELL, W. S. H., *Our Trade in the World in Relation to Foreign Competition, 1885 to 1895*, 99–107, London, Chapman, 1897.

GREENWOOD, J., 'How Far is it Advisable to Interfere by Legislation with the Hours of Labour?', *Transactions of the Burnley Literary and Scientific Club*, 18 October 1892, 40–3.

GUNDRY, R. S., *English Industries and Eastern Competition: the Danger to English Industry from the Competition of Silver-Using Countries*, 32 pp., London, Wilson, 1895, abridged in the *Fortnightly Review*, 1 October 1895, 609–20, 'English Industry and Eastern Competition'.

HALLETT, H. S., 'The Development of Our Eastern Markets for British Cotton Manufactures', *C.W.S. Annual*, 1890, 308–70.

—— 'Foreign Competition in the East', *C.W.S. Annual*, 1893, 371–426.

—— 'The Remedy for Lancashire. A Burma–China Railway', *Blackwood's Edinburgh Magazine*, September 1892, 348–63.

—— 'Sweating in Indian Factories and Workshops', *C.W.S. Annual*, 1890, 199–268.

HELM, E., 'An International Survey of the Cotton Industry', *Quarterly Journal of Economics*, May 1903, 417–37.

—— 'Protection and the Cotton Industry', *Independent Review*, November 1903, 239–45.

—— 'The Recent Wages Dispute in the Lancashire Cotton-Spinning Industry', *Economic Journal*, June 1893, 342–5.

HESFORD, J., 'The Cotton Trade in China and Japan—Present and Prospective', *Lectures and Papers, Bolton and District Managers' and Overlookers' Association*, 1896, 126–39.

MACARA, C. W., *Recollections*, 17–27, London, Cassell, 1921.

MARSDEN, R., 'Optimistic Views of the Cotton Trade', *Textile Mercury*, 15 April 1893, 275–6.

—— 'The Position of the Lancashire Cotton Trade', *Textile Mercury*, 2 November 1895, 345–6, 9 November, 365–6, 16 November, 385–6.

MERTTENS, F., 'The Hours and the Cost of Labour in the Cotton

Industry at Home and Abroad', *Transactions of the Manchester Statistical Society*, 18 April 1894, 125–90.

MILLS, W. H., *Sir Charles W. Macara, Bart.: a Study of Modern Lancashire*, 85–107, Manchester, Sherratt, 1917.

NASMITH, J., 'Inaugural Address', *Transactions of the Manchester Association of Engineers*, 9 January 1897, 1–28.

PORTER, J. H., 'Industrial Peace in the Cotton Trade, 1875–1913', *Yorkshire Bulletin of Economic and Social Research*, May 1967, 49–61.

PRICE, L. L., 'Conciliation in the Cotton Trade', *Economic Journal*, June 1901, 235–44.

RAE, J., 'The Eight-Hours Day and Foreign Competition', *Contemporary Review*, February 1894, 189–206.

Report of the Tariff Commission, Vol. 2 The Textile Trades, 'Part 1—The Cotton Industry', 1153 paragraphs, London, King, 1905, reviewed by S. J. Chapman in *Manchester Guardian*, 6 June 1905, 7vii–8i, and 13 October 1905, 4iii–vi, in the *Economic Journal*, September 1905, 420–7, and in *A Reply to the Report of the Tariff Commission on the Cotton Industry*, 169 pp., Manchester, Sherratt, 1905.

SCHOENHOF, J., *The Economy of High Wages. An Inquiry into the Cause of High Wages and their Effect on Methods and Cost of Production*, 234–68, 'The Textile Industries', New York, Putnam, 1892.

SIMPSON, A., 'The Present Condition of the Cotton Trade', *Chambers's Journal*, December 1902, 10–13.

WILLIAMS, E. E., *The Case for Protection*, 160–2, London, Richards, 1899.

—— '*Made in Germany*', 175 pp., London, Heinemann, 1896.

THE ORGANIZATION OF THE FIRM

COLLECTIVE HISTORIES OF PRIVATE FIRMS

Amalgamated Cotton Mills Trust Ltd., *Concerning Cotton: a Brief Account of the Aims and Achievements of the Amalgamated Cotton Mills Trust, Limited, and its Component Companies*, 265 pp., London, Wilson, 1921.

BLYTH, H. E., *Through the Eye of a Needle: the Story of the English Sewing Cotton Company, 1897–1947*, 112 pp., Derby, Bemrose, 1948.

Bolton (Illustrated) Up-to-Date with . . . Descriptive Sketches of the Chief Industries and Representative Houses in each Branch of Commercial Enterprise, 102 pp., London, Robinson, 1897.

BURNLEY, J., *Summits of Success. How They Have Been reached with Sketches of the Careers of Some Notable Climbers*, 314–36, London, Richards, 1904.

Calico Printers' Association Ltd., *Fifty Years of Calico Printing. A Jubilee History of the Calico Printers' Association*, 64 pp., Manchester, Calico Printers' Association, 1949.

The Century's Progress: Lancashire, 294 pp., London Printing and Engraving Company, 1892.

Fine Cotton Spinners' Association, *The Fine Cotton Spinners' and Doublers' Association Ltd.*, 80 pp., Manchester, Fine Cotton Spinners' Association, 1909.

Fortunes Made in Business. Series of Original Sketches Biographical and Anecdotic from the Recent History of Industry and Commerce by Various Writers, 3 vols., 456 pp., 450 pp., 546 pp., London, Low, 1884–7.

'The Fieldens of Todmorden' in i. 413–56, is reprinted from *London Society*, November 1883, 481–96.

'The Fortunes of the Bright Family' in ii. 181–230, first appeared in *London Society*, June 1880, 481–97.

'Horrockses, Miller & Co.' in iii. 1–61, is reprinted from *London Society*, July 1885, 1–24.

'The Henrys of Manchester and Bradford' in iii. 201–51, appeared first in *London Society*, November 1880, 446–62.

'The Platts of Oldham' in iii. 421–85 is reprinted from *London Society*, January 1885, 1–24.

This work, the first volume of which was harshly reviewed in the *Spectator*, 26 April 1884, 548, as 'comparatively worthless', has not as yet been superseded. The author is identified as James Burnley in W. S. Sonnenschein, *The Best Books*, 265, London, Sonnenschein, 1887, 1891.

Fox, J. H., 'The Victorian Entrepreneur in Lancashire', in S. P. Bell (ed.), *Victorian Lancashire*, 103–26, Newton Abbot, David and Charles, 1974.

Lancashire. Men of the Period. The Records of a Great County. Portraits and Pen Pictures of Leading Men. Part First, 164 pp., London, Biographical Publishing Company, 1895.

Lancashire, the Premier County of the Kingdom. Cities and Towns. Historical, Statistical, Biographical. Business Men and Mercantile Interests, 2 vols., 320 pp., 224 pp., London, Historical Publishing Company, 1888, 1889.

Part First covers Bolton, Preston, Blackburn, Wigan, Bury, Darwen, Chorley, Ramsbottom, Part Second Accrington, Ashton, Stalybridge, Dukinfield, Bacup, Burnley, Colne, Nelson, Padiham, St. Helens, Middleton, Oldham, Rochdale, Heywood, Littleborough, Warrington, Widnes.

Manchester Faces and Places. An Illustrated Record, 16 vols., Manchester, Hammond, 10 October 1889–December 1905.

Manchester of Today. An Epitome of Results. Business Men and Commercial Interests, 224 pp., London, Historical Publishing Company, 1888.

PUSELEY, D., *The Commercial Companion; a Record of Eminent Commercial Houses and Men of the Day*, 232 pp., London, Hall, 1858.

SHAW, W. A., *Manchester Old and New*, ii. 1–72, 'The Trade of the City', London, Cassell, 1894.

TRACY, W. B. AND PIKE, W. T., *Lancashire at the Opening of the Twentieth Century*, 333–406, 'Commercial', Brighton, Pike, 1903.

—— *Manchester and Salford at the Close of the Nineteenth Century: Contemporary Biographies*, 95–143, 'Bankers and Commercial', Brighton, Pike, 1899.

INDIVIDUAL HISTORIES

'E. Ashworth & Sons, Bolton', *British Trade Journal*, 1 February 1883, 95–6.

'Henry Bannerman & Sons', *Manchester City News*, 22 April 1865, 3i–ii, 29 April, 3i–iii.

BOYSON, R., *The Ashworth Cotton Enterprise. The Rise and Fall of a Family Firm 1818–1880*, 286 pp., Oxford, Clarendon Press, 1970.

BROWN, W. E., *Robert Heywood of Bolton 1786–1868*, 68 pp., Wakefield, S.R. Publishers Ltd., 1970.

'Callender, Sons & Co.', *Manchester City News*, 18 February 1865, 2v–vii.

'The Clarks of Paisley', *London Society*, October 1884, 376–91.

CHRISTIE, G., *Storeys of Lancaster 1848–1964*, 256 pp., London, Collins, 1964.

'William Christy & Sons Ltd.', *British Trade Journal*, 1 August 1879, 465–7.

CRANKSHAW, W. P. AND BLACKBURN, A., *The History of Knowles Ltd. of Bolton: a Century and a Half of Cotton Spinning 1797–1947*, 40 pp., Bolton, Tillotsons, 1947, in Bolton Library.

'Joshua Fielden M.P.', *British Trade Journal*, 1 May 1878, 236–7.

G., H. S. [GIBBS, H. S.], *Autobiography of a Manchester Cotton Manufacturer: or, Thirty Years Experience of Manchester*, 227 pp., Manchester, Heywood, 1887.

The author is identified as Henry Steinhauer Gibbs (1829–94) of Turnbull and Gibbs in *Textile Recorder*, 15 April 1887, 285, and in *Textile Manufacturer*, 15 May 1894, 204.

GREENWOOD, J., *The Story of the Formation of the Hebden Bridge Fustian Manufacturing Society*, 23 pp., Manchester, Central Co-operative Board, 1889.

HARGREAVES, B., 'Messrs. Hargreaves Calico Print Works at Broad Oak, Accrington', *Journal of Design and Manufactures*, 1 March

1850, 5–9, April 1850, 44–7, May 1850, 44–7, reprinted, 90 pp., Accrington, Bowker, 1882.

HEGINBOTTOM, H., *Thomas Heginbottom. A Few Slight Impressions of his Life and Times*, 128 pp., Hyde, Higham, 1913.

HENDERSON, W. O., 'The Firm of Ermen & Engels in Manchester', *Internationale Wissenschaftliche Korrespondenz zur Geschichte der Deutschen Arbeiterbewegung*, April 1971, 1–10.

HURST, J. G., *Edmund Potter and Dinting Vale*, 89 pp., Manchester, Potter, 1948.

'Colonel R. Raynsford Jackson', *British Trade Journal*, 1 June 1878, 290–1.

'Kershaw, Leese, Sidebottom & Co.', *Manchester City News*, 21 January 1865, 2vi-vii, 28 January, 3i-iii.

LEE, C. H., *A Cotton Enterprise 1795-1840. A History of M'Connel & Kennedy, Fine Cotton Spinners*, 188 pp., Manchester University Press, 1972.

'Lee Spinning Company', *British Trade Journal*, 1 June 1887, 387–9.

[Lowe, James], 'A Manchester Warehouse' [Bannerman's], *Household Words*, 6 May 1854, 268–72.

M'CONNELL, J. W., *A Century of Fine Cotton Spinning 1790–1906*, 56 pp., Manchester, Falkner, 1906, 1913.

MILLS, W. H., *Sir Charles W. Macara, Bart.: A Study of Modern Lancashire*, 334 pp., Manchester, Sherratt, 1917.

MORTIMER, J., *Henry Bannerman & Sons Ltd.: its Origin, Rise and Progress*, 17 pp., Diary and Buyers' Guide for 1891, Manchester, Palmer, 1891.

PEDRICK, G., *The Story of Horrockses*, 77 pp., Preston, Horrockses, 1950, in Preston Library.

PIGOTT, S. C., *Hollins. A Study of Industry 1784–1949*, 151 pp., Nottingham, Hollins, 1949.

POPE, W. B., *A Memorial of Richard Haworth, Esq., J.P. of Manchester*, 63 pp., Manchester, Day, printed for private circulation, 1885.

'Potters and Taylor', *Manchester City News*, 4 February 1865, 2v–vii.

RAMSBOTTOM, S., *Forty-Three Years Life in Manchester: by an Ex-Policeman and Ex-Director in a Cotton Spinning Company*, 15 pp., Manchester, Heywood, 1882.

ROBERTSON, A. J., 'Robert Owen, Cotton Spinner: New Lanark, 1800–1825' in S. Pollard and J. Salt (eds.), *Robert Owen Prophet of the Poor. Essays in Honour of the Two Hundredth Anniversary of his Birth*, 145–65, London, Macmillan, 1971.

ROSE, MARY B., 'The Role of the Family in Providing Capital and Managerial Talent in Samuel Greg and Company 1784–1840', *Business History*, January 1977, 37–54.

'Rylands & Sons', *Manchester City News*, 1 April 1865, 2vi–3i, 8 April, 2vi–vii–3i, 15 April, 2v–3i–ii.

'Rylands & Sons', *British Trade Journal*, 1 April 1887, 277–8.

John Rylands Ltd., *In Memoriam: John Rylands. Born February 7, 1801. Died December 11, 1888*, 72 pp., Chilworth, Unwin, printed for private circulation, 1889.

'W.G. & J. Strutt', *British Trade Journal*, 1 December 1882, 759–62.

'Tootal Broadhurst Lee & Co.', *British Trade Journal*, 1 July 1887, 429–31.

'S. & J. Watts & Co.', *Manchester City News*, 4 March 1865, 2v–vi, 11 March, 2vi–vii–3i.

'J.P. & E. Westhead & Co.', *Manchester City News*, 6 May 1865, 2vii–3i, 13 May, 2vii–3i, 20 May, 2vi, 3 June, 2iii–iv.

Weston-Webb, W. F. M., *The Autobiography of a British Yarn Merchant*, 247 pp., London, Richards, 1929.

Whitehead, H., *David Whitehead & Sons Ltd., Rawtenstall. A Short History of the Firm 1815 to 1909*, 40 pp., Manchester, Whitehead, 1945.

THE OLDHAM LIMITEDS

A., J.C. [Ashton, J. C.], *Limited Liability and Cotton Spinning. A Paper Read by J.C.A. before the Blackburn Mule Overlookers' Society August 10th, 1886*, 23 pp., Darwen, Leach, 1886. The author is identified as a cotton spinner of Darwen in the *Cotton Factory Times*, 20 August 1886, 7iv, where the original text is printed.

'Albert Cotton Mill Company Limited, Oldham', *C.W.S. Annual*, 1884, 192–3.

Andrew, S., 'The Oldham Cotton Trade. A Quarter of a Century's Experience as Employers' Secretary', *Oldham Chronicle*, 22 December 1900, 8vi–vii.

Ashton, T. S., 'The Growth of Textile Businesses in the Oldham District, 1884–1924', *Journal of the Royal Statistical Society*, May 1926, 567–83.

Campion, H., 'Pre-War Fluctuations of Profits in the Cotton-Spinning Industry', *Journal of the Royal Statistical Society*, 1934, 626–32.

Chapman, S. J. and Ashton, T. S., 'The Sizes of Businesses, mainly in the Textile Industries', *Journal of the Royal Statistical Society*, April 1914, 469–550.

Ashton's main work within the sphere of the textile industry was inspired by Marshall's idea of the representative firm and formed a valuable preparation for his investigation of the history of the iron and coal industries.

CLAPHAM, J. H., *An Economic History of Modern Britain. Free Trade and Steel 1850–1886*, ii. 140–5, Cambridge University Press, 1932.

'The Companies Acts and Cotton Mills', *The Accountant*, 16 October 1886, 579–80, 23 October, 590–1, 30 October, 605–6, 6 November, 621–3, 13 November, 637–9, 27 November, 671–2, 4 December, 685–7.

'Co-operation in Oldham', *Co-operative News*, 30 September 1871, 41, by 'Enterprise'.

'Co-operative Cotton Spinning in Oldham', *Preston Guardian*, 18 July 1874, 5iv–v, reprinted in *Co-operative News*, 1 August 1874, 57, 8 August, 63.

'The Cost of Building and Working a Limited Company's Mill in Oldham', *Oldham Chronicle*, 3 January 1880, 6iii–iv.

'Cotton Spinning Companies in Oldham and District', *C.W.S. Annual*, 1884, 176–185.

ELLISON, T., *The Cotton Trade of Great Britain*, 133–40, London, Wilson, 1886; Cass, 1968, based on information from Samuel Andrew.

FLETCHER, J. AND ANDREW, S., Evidence of the 'Oldham Master Cotton Spinners' Association', *Royal Commission on the Depression of Trade and Industry, Second Report*, 1886, Appendix—Part I, C., 423–7.

'The Growth of Cotton Spinning and Manufacturing Companies in Oldham and District in the Ten Years 1873 to 1882', *C.W.S. Annual*, 1884, 196–212, reprinted in the *Handbook to the Sixteenth Annual Co-operative Congress, to be held at Oldham, on the 24th, 25th, 26th and 27th May, 1885*, 100–29, Oldham, Worrall, 1885.

The author may have been William Nuttall (1835–1905), who edited the *C.W.S. Annual* for 1883 and 1884.

HARDERN, F., 'The Limited Liability Movement in Oldham', *Co-operative News*, 30 May 1885, 483–6, reprinted in E. V. Neale (ed.), *The Seventeenth Annual Co-operative Congress, 1885: held in the Co-operative Hall, King Street, Oldham, May 25th, 26th and 27th*, 11–14, Manchester, Co-operative Printing Society, 1885, by the president from 1882 to 1894 of the Oldham Industrial Co-operative Society.

—— Evidence given before the *Royal Commission on Labour*, Q.1138–1220, 26 October 1892, C.7063–i of 1893, 71–4, Appendixes XLV–XLI to C.7063–iii A. of 1894.

'Joint-Stock Companies in Lancashire', *Manchester Guardian*, 29 January 1875, 4iii, 5 February, 4iv, 12 February, 4iii.

'Joint-Stock Cotton Mills', *The Times*, 18 August 1875, 9ii–iii, 10i–ii.

'The Joint-Stock Movement in Oldham', *Manchester Examiner and*

Times, 1 February 1875, 3v, 11 February, 5iv, 19 February, 3iii.

JONES, B., 'Short Stories of Co-operative Production. xv-Cotton Factories', *Co-operative News*, 22 November 1890, 1178–9, 29 November, 1202–3, 3 January 1891, 8–9, to 28 February, 202–3, 4 April 1891, 322, to 18 April, 370, reprinted in *Co-operative Production*, i. 252–338, 'Cotton Factories', Oxford, Clarendon Press, 1894, reviewed in *Labour Co-Partnership*, September 1894, 23, in *Economic Review*, January 1895, 19–38, by H. W. Wolff, and in H. D. Lloyd, *Labor Copartnership*, New York, Harper, 1898, 273, and reprinted, New York, Kelley, 1968.

Benjamin Jones (1847–1942) was born in Manchester and served as the manager from 1874 until 1902 of the London branch of the C.W.S. He remained a firm believer, like Beatrice Webb, in the federalized 'store democracy' represented by the C.W.S. and had little faith in the ventures into co-partnership production chronicled in his work, which nevertheless remains an indispensable primary source of information.

JONES, FRED, 'The Cotton Spinning Industry in the Oldham District from 1896 to 1914', 229 pp., including on pp. 98–219 case studies of six mills, M.A. Econ. thesis, University of Manchester, 1959.

KIDGER, J., 'The Working of the Limited Companies in Oldham and District', *Royal Commission on the Depression of Trade and Industry Third Report*, 1886, 308–11, Appendix A.viii with table on ninety companies.

'Limited Liability', *Cotton*, 4 May 1878, 270–1.

'The Limited Liability Movement in Oldham', *Oldham Chronicle*, 6 February 1875, 5iii–iv.

LONGWORTH, J. E., *Oldham Master Cotton Spinners' Association Limited Centenary 1866–1966*, 44 pp., Oldham, Oldham Master Cotton Spinners' Association, 1966.

MARCROFT, W., *The Management of a Company's Cotton Mill*, 16 pp., Oldham, Tetlow, 1878.

—— *The Companies Circular. Part First*, 16 pp., Oldham, Clegg, 1879.

—— 'Sun Mill Company Limited: Its Commercial and Social History from 1858 to 1877', 33 chapters published in 45 weeks in the *Oldham Standard*, 27 January 1877, 8vi to 1 December 1877, 7ii, criticized by a correspondent in *Oldham Standard*, 8 September 1877, 8iii, 'History of Sun Mill and Mr. Marcroft', published under the same title, 191 pp., Oldham, Tetlow, 1877, and reviewed in *Co-operative* News, 9 February 1878, 81–2, E. V. Neale, 'The Sun Mill Company', in Oldham Library, together with the two preceding works.

Moss, W., *Cotton Spinning Companies' Accounts*, 147 pp., London, Gee, 1905.

Neale, E. V., *The Distinction between Joint-Stockism and Co-operation*, 8 pp., Manchester, Central Co-operative Board, 1874, a paper read at Batley on 20 June 1874 and published, with discussion, in *Co-operative News*, 27 June 1874, 339–41.

—— 'Oldham and Co-operation', *Co-operative News*, 22 July 1876, 395.

Noton, J., 'The Oldham Joint-Stock Movement', *Manchester Guardian*, 11 February 1875, 4iv.

Nuttall, W., 'Oldham Joint-Stock Companies', *Co-operative News*, 7 April 1877, 167–8, being two letters dated 27 March to the President of the Congress of Co-operative Societies, Auberon Herbert.

'Oldham and its Cotton Spinning Companies', *Co-operative News*, 21 March 1874, 133–4.

'Oldham Cotton Mill Companies', *Manchester Examiner and Times*, 2 July 1877, 2iii–iv, 7 July, 4v, 14 July, 4v, reprinted in the *Oldham Chronicle*, 7 July 1877, 7vii, 14 July, 7i, 21 July, 7iii.

'The Oldham Cotton Trade', nine weekly articles in *Oldham Chronicle*, 11 August 1877, 8i, 'The Short Time Movement', 18 August, 8iii, 'The Past and Present', 1 September, 8ii, 'The Cost of Production', 8 September, 8ii, 'Insurance', 15 September, 6vi, 'Banking', 22 September, 8i–ii, 'Cotton Broking', 29 September, 8iii, 'Pawning', 6 October, 8i, 'Retrospect of Limited Companies', 20 October, 8i, 'Floating, &c.'

'The Oldham Cotton Trade', *Manchester Examiner and Times*, 11 September, 1877, 4iii.

'The Oldham Joint Stock Movement', *Oldham Chronicle*, 13 February 1875, 8vi.

'The Oldham Share Crisis', *Manchester Guardian*, 22 July 1875, 4iii.

Osborn, E. B., 'Co-operation, Partial (Oldham Cotton-Spinning Companies)', in R. H. I. Palgrave (ed.), *Dictionary of Political Economy*, i. 417–18, London, Macmillan, 1894.

Royton Spinning Company, *The Royton Spinning Company Limited, 1871–1951*, 28 pp., Rochdale Observer, 1951, in Oldham Library.

Schulze-Gaevernitz, G. von, *Zum socialen Frieden*, i. 361, Leipzig, Duncker, 1890.

—— *The Cotton Trade in England and on the Continent*, 193–7, London, Simpkin, 1895.

Shaw, A. D., *The Cotton Goods Trade of Lancashire*, 16–21, Manchester, Ireland, 1883.

Shiloh Mills Ltd., *The Shiloh Story 1874–1949*, 44 pp., London, Harley, 1949.

SIMPSON, A., 'Statement respecting the Cotton Mills of Oldham, and the working of the Limited Liability Act in connection with them', *Royal Commission on the Depression of Trade and Industry, Second Report*, 1886, 379–81, Appendix Part I A. (9). II, 17 February 1886, reprinted in *Royal Commission on Labour, Minutes of Evidence taken before Group 'C' (Textile . . . Trades)*, i, Textile, 78–80, Q.2037, 10 July 1891, C.6708. vi, 1892.

SMITH, R., 'An Oldham Limited Liability Company 1875–1896' [Moorfield Spinning Company Ltd.], *Business History*, December 1961, 34–53.

THOMAS, W. A., *The Provincial Stock Exchanges*, 145–68, 'The Oldham Stock Exchange and the "Limiteds"', London, Cass, 1973.

TYSON, R. E., 'The Sun Mill Company Limited—A Study in Democratic Investment, 1858–1959', 405 pp., M.A. thesis, University of Manchester, 1962, a full history as well as a revision of Marcroft's account.

'United Spinning Company, Oldham', *C.W.S. Annual*, 1884, 189–92.

VOGELSTEIN, T., *Organisationsformen der Eisenindustrie und Textilindustrie in England und Amerika*, 116–22, Leipzig, Duncker, 1910.

WIESER, C. W. VON, *Der finanzielle Aufbau der englischen Industrie*, 393–423, 'Die Aktienspinnereien von Lancashire', Jena, Fischer, 1919.

THE REVOLUTION IN WEAVING

THE TECHNOLOGY OF WEAVING

BAGSHAW, J. H., 'Cotton Factories and Sheds', *Journal of the Federation of Insurance Institutes of Great Britain and Ireland*, 1900, 87–121.

BARLOW, A., 'Weaving', 36 articles in *Engineering*, 2 January 1874, 2, to 25 June 1875, 535–6, reprinted in revised form as *The History and Principles of Weaving by Hand and by Power*, 443 pp., London, Low, 1878.

BOLLÉ, C., 'Bowker's Patent Self-Acting Punching Machine for Repeating Jacquard Cards', *Proceedings of the Manchester Scientific and Mechanical Society*, 12 November 1875, 2–16.

BRIDGES, J. H. AND OSBORN, E. H., *Report on the Effects of Heavy Sizing in Cotton Weaving upon the Health of the Operatives Employed*, 16 pp., C.3861 of 1884.

BROOKS, C. P., *Cotton Manufacturing*, 175 pp., London, Spon, 1888, in Blackburn Library.

BUCHANAN, DR., *Report on Certain Sizing Processes used in the Cotton Manufacture at Todmorden, and on their Influence on Health*, 7 pp., C.203 of 1872.

DAVIS, G. E., DREYFUS, C., AND HOLLAND, P., *Sizing and Mildew in*

Cotton Goods, 306 pp., Manchester, Palmer, 1880, in Blackburn Library.

FOSTER, A. R., *Weaving Mill Management*, 110 pp., Manchester, Heywood, 1908.

FOX, T. W., *The Mechanism of Weaving*, 472 pp., London, Macmillan, 1894.

GILROY, C. G., *The Art of Weaving, by Hand and by Power, with an Introductory Account of its Rise and Progress in Ancient and Modern Times for the Use of Manufacturers and Others*, 574 pp., New York, Baldwin, 1844.

In the introduction the author passed off 'a brilliant piece of satirical fiction as genuine textile history', directed against the contemporary practice of uncovering the ancient origins of modern inventions and of denying modern inventors protection for their discoveries. See the *Textile Mercury*, 27 May 1893, 403, and R. Marsden, *Cotton Weaving* (1895), 11.

HALL, S. S., 'Textile Machinery', *Proceedings of the Manchester Scientific and Mechanical Society*, 24 April 1879, 41–7.

HALSTEAD, R., 'The Stress of Competition from the Workman's Point of View', *Economic Review*, January 1894, 43–58.

HARRISON, W., 'Cotton Weaving and Lancashire Looms', *Macmillan's Magazine*, October 1862, 445–58.

HAYTHORNTHWAITE, W., 'Loom Brakes', *Textile Manufacturer*, June 1886, 201–2.

KOHL, F., *Geschichte der Jacquard-Maschine*, 198 pp., Berlin, Nicholai, 1873.

LANDER, C. H., *Ventilation and Humidity in Textile Mills and Factories*, 175 pp., London, Longmans, 1914.

MARSDEN, R., *Cotton Weaving: its Development, Principles, and Practice*, 533 pp., London, Bell, 1895.

NASMITH, F., 'Weaving Appliances', *Transactions of the Manchester Association of Engineers*, 8 January 1910, 473–516.

ROBERTS, C. W., 'The Lancashire Cotton Weaving Shed', *Journal of the Indian Institute of Architects*, II: 4, April 1936, 129–42.

ROLFFS, G., 'Some Unsolved Problems and Difficulties in Power-Loom Weaving', *Journal of the Society for the Promotion of Scientific Industry*, March 1875, 98–104.

THOMSON, W., *The Sizing of Cotton Goods and the Causes and Prevention of Mildew*, 164 pp., Manchester, Palmer, 1877.

—— 'The Sizing of Cotton Goods', *Journal of the Society of Arts*, 16 March 1877, 360–70.

TOMLINSON, C. (ed.), *Cyclopaedia of Useful Arts and Manufactures, Mechanical and Chemical*, II, ii. 952–77, 'Weaving', London, Virtue, 1854.

WATSON, J., *The Theory and Practice of the Art of Weaving by Hand and Power*, 380 pp., Glasgow, Watson, 1863.

WHITE, G., *A Practical Treatise on Weaving, by Hand and Power Looms*, 362 pp., London, Simpkin, 1851.

WILKINSON, W., 'Power Loom Developments', *Special Issue of the Journal of the Textile Institute*, 1927, 122–48, reprinted in *Textile Manufacturer*, June 1927, 218–20.

THE WEAVING TOWNS

Blackburn, Darwen, and Accrington

ABRAM, W. A., 'Accrington its Growth and Progress', *Preston Guardian*, 20 January 1877, 10v–vi, 27 January, 9v–vi.

—— *A History of Blackburn Town and Parish*, 784 pp., Blackburn, Toulmin, 1877.

CROSSLEY, R. S., *Accrington Captains of Industry*, 233 pp., Accrington, Wardleworth, 1930.

—— *Accrington: Chronological Notes and Men of Mark*, 172 pp., Accrington Observer, 1924.

DURHAM, W., *Chronological Notes of Prominent Historical Events, in the Town and Parish of Blackburn*, 32 pp., Blackburn, Tiplady, 1861.

—— *Chronological Notes on the History of the Town and Parish of Blackburn*, 105 pp., Blackburn, Tiplady, 1866.

MILLER, G. C., *Blackburn: the Evolution of a Cotton Town*, 456 pp., Blackburn Town Council, 1951.

SEABROOK, J., *City Close-Up* [Blackburn], 283 pp., London, Lane, 1971.

SHAW, J. G., *History and Traditions of Darwen and its People*, 198 pp., 142 pp., Blackburn, Toulmin, 1889, a work inspired by Abram's classic history.

—— 'Weavers' Wages during Eighty-Three Years. The Blackburn Standard List and its Successors', *Blackburn Times*, 27 March 1937, 9iv–vi.

SHORROCK, E., *Letter to the Workpeople of North and North-East Lancashire. History of the Formation of the Blackburn Association in 1852 and of the North and North-East Lancashire Association, with the Rise and Fall in the Rates of Wages for Twenty-Eight Years*, 23 pp., Manchester, Heywood, 1880, in Blackburn Library.

WHITTLE, P. A., *Blackburn As It Is: a Topographical, Statistical and Historical Account*, 400 pp., Preston, Oakey, 1852.

WILLIAMS, C., *Accrington: a Sketch of its History and a Review of its Institutions*, 30 pp., Accrington, Bowker, 1872.

Burnley, Nelson, Colne, Skipton, Clitheroe, and Padiham

ABRAM, W. A., 'Growth of Nelson and Brierfield', *Preston Guardian*, 12 February 1881, 10vi–vii.

—— 'Padiham: Past and Present', *Preston Guardian*, 27 November 1880, 10v–vii.

ASHMORE, O., 'The Diary of James Garnett of Low Moor, Clitheroe, 1858–65. Part I: Years of Prosperity, 1858–60', *Transactions of the Historic Society of Lancashire and Cheshire*, 1969, 77–98.

—— 'Low Moor, Clitheroe: a Nineteenth-Century Factory Community', *Transactions of the Lancashire and Cheshire Antiquarian Society*, 1963–64, 124–52 with 18 plates.

BENNETT, W., *The History of Burnley. Part III. 1650–1850*, 392 pp., Burnley Corporation, 1948.

—— *The History of Burnley. Part IV from 1850*, 300 pp., Burnley Corporation, 1951.

—— *The History of Marsden and Nelson*, 237 pp., Nelson Corporation, 1957.

BRIGG, M., 'Life in East Lancashire, 1856–60: a Newly Discovered Diary of John O'Neil (John Ward), Weaver, of Clitheroe', *Transactions of the Historic Society of Lancashire and Cheshire*, 19 September 1968, 87–133.

CLARKE, S., *Clitheroe in its Railway Days*, 312 pp., especially 283–9, 'Our Cotton Manufactories', Clitheroe, Robinson, 1900.

DAWSON, W. H., *History of Skipton*, 408 pp., especially 267–88, 'Commercial History of Skipton', London, Simpkin, 1882.

FRANCE, R. S., 'The Diary of John Ward of Clitheroe, Weaver, 1860–1864', *Transactions of the Historic Society of Lancashire and Cheshire*, 1953, 137–85, covers the periods from April 1860 to June 1862 and from April to December 1864.

KNEESHAW, J. W., *Burnley in the Nineteenth Century, being the 'Burnley Express' Souvenir of Queen Victoria's Diamond Jubilee, 1897*, 141 pp., Burnley Express, 1897.

RAWLINSON, J., 'The Rise and Progress of Burnley', *Transactions of the Burnley Literary and Scientific Club*, 14 March 1876, 61–75.

Preston and Chorley

ANDERSON, M., *Family Structure in Nineteenth Century Lancashire*, 230 pp., Cambridge University Press, 1971, based on Preston.

BANKS, T., *A Short Sketch of the Cotton Trade of Preston for the Last Sixty-Seven Years*, 16 pp., Preston, Banks, 1888, in Preston Library, by the Secretary to the Preston Association of Operative Cotton Spinners from 1854 until 1890.

—— 'The Town and Trade of Preston for the Last Forty Years', *Cotton Factory Times*, 15 May 1885, 8v–vi.

BARRON, J., *A History of the Ribble Navigation from Preston to the Sea*, 505 pp., Preston Corporation, 1938.

BLACKBURN, R. H., *Borough of Chorley 1881–1931. Jubilee Souvenir*, 68 pp., Chorley Corporation, 1931.

HARDWICK, C., *History of the Borough of Preston and its Environs, in the County of Lancaster*, 687 pp., Preston, Worthington, 1857.

HEWITSON, S., *History of Preston, 705–1883*, 577 pp., Preston Chronicle, 1883.

POLLARD, W., *A Hand Book and Guide to Preston*, 233 pp., Preston, Oakey, 1882.

ROBINSON, C., *An Historical qnd Descriptive Account of the Parish of Chorley*, 48 pp., Chorley, Robinson, 1835.

SCOTT, N. K., 'The Architectural Development of Cotton Mills in Preston and District', 121 pp., 172 pp., 151 pp., M.A. thesis, School of Architecture, University of Liverpool, 1952.

SIMPSON, A., 'Statement as to the Condition of the Cotton Industry in Preston', *Royal Commission on the Depression of Trade and Industry, Second Report*, Appendix A (9) I, 378–9, 17 February 1886.

TOWNSON, C., *The History of Farington*, 54 pp., Preston, Platt, 1893.

'Weaving in Preston', *Textile Manufacturer*, February 1881, 41, reprinted in *Preston Guardian*, 12 February 1881, 10v.

Index